Martin Luther and the Shaping of the Catholic Tradition

Martin Luther and the Shaping of the Catholic Tradition:

*Proceedings of the International Conference
Held in Washington, DC
May 30 to June 1, 2017*

Edited by
Nelson H. Minnich and Michael Root

The Catholic University of America Press
Washington, D.C.

Copyright © 2021 The Catholic University of America Press

The paper used in this publication meets the minimum requirements of
American National Standards for Information Science—
Permanence of Paper for Printed Library Materials, ansi z39.48–1984.

∞

Design and typesetting by BocaType

Cataloging-in-Publication Data available from the Library of Congress
ISBN 978-0-8132-3532-5 (cloth)

To His Holiness Pope Francis
Who has labored to restore unity to the Church
especially as it commemorated the beginnings of the divisions
with Martin Luther's Posting of the Ninety-five Theses.
May this volume help to deepen our understanding
of the issues that have divided us
and point the way to a shared faith and mutual love
in Jesus Christ, Our Savior

Table of Contents

Contributors ix

Abbreviations xi

Introduction xiii

Greetings xv
   His Holiness Pope Francis xv
   Cardinal Donald Wuerl, Archbishop of Washington xvi
   John Garvey, President, The Catholic University of America xvii
   Mark Morozowich, Dean, School of Theology and
      Religious Studies, CUA xix

I. **Major Presentations and Responses** 1
   1: *Cardinal Kurt Koch*
      Martin Luther's Reformation and the Unity of the Church:
      A Catholic Perspective in Light of the Lutheran–Catholic
         Dialogue 3
   1a. Response: *Bishop Eero Huovinen* 23
   2: *Wolfgang Thönissen*
      Luther in the Focus of Roman Catholic Theology 33
   2a. Response: *Kenneth Appold* 47

II. **Justification** 55
   3: *Theodor Dieter*
      Later Medieval Teaching on Justification 57
   4: *Timothy Wengert*
      Martin Luther's Proclamation of Justification by Faith Alone . . 75
   5: *Michael Root*
      Luther and the Development of Catholic Teaching on
         Justification 91

III. **Eucharist** 107
   6: *Bruce D. Marshall*
      The Eucharist in Late Medieval Thought 109
   7: *Lee Palmer Wandel*
      Martin Luther and the Medieval Mass 163
   8: *Robert Trent Pomplun*
      Eucharistic Sacrifice: Catholic Response to Martin Luther . . . 179

IV. **The Church** 201

   9: *Nelson M. Minnich*
     Late Medieval Models of the Church 203

  10: *Dorothea Wendebourg*
     Martin Luther's Ecclesiology 223

  11: *Johanna Rahner*
     Catholic Ecclesiology—Evolving and in Response 239

V. **Eastern Christianity** 253

  12: *Yuri P. Avvakumov*
     Ecclesia Orientalis: Heretical or Saintly?
       The Leipzig Debate (1519) and Western Approaches
       to Eastern Christianity in the High and Later
       Medieval Periods 255

  13: *Nicolas Kazarian*
     Luther and the Eastern Orthodox Church: Challenges
     and Opportunities of the Reformation 269

  14: *Will Cohen*
     The (Slight) Sensitivity to Eastern Christianity in Trent's
     Condemnations of Luther on Marriage and
     Clerical Celibacy 279

Contributors

KENNETH APPOLD is James Hastings Nichols Associate Professor of Reformation History at Princeton Theological Seminary.

YURI P. AVVAKUMOV is Associate Professor of the History of Christianity at the University of Notre Dame.

WILL COHEN is Associate Professor of Theology at the University of Scranton.

THEODOR DIETER is Research Professor (retired) at the Institute for Ecumenical Research (Strasbourg, France).

EERO HUOVINEN is Bishop emeritus of Helsinki, Evangelical Lutheran Church of Finland.

NICOLAS KAZARIAN is Professor of Church History at the Saint-Sergius Orthodox Institute (Paris, France).

KURT CARDINAL KOCH is President of the Pontifical Council for Promoting Christian Unity.

BRUCE D. MARSHALL is Lehman Professor of Christian Doctrine at Southern Methodist University.

NELSON H. MINNICH is Ordinary Professor of Church History at The Catholic University of America.

TRENT POMPLUN is Associate Professor of World Religions and World Church at the University of Notre Dame.

JOHANNA RAHNER is Professor of Dogmatics, History of Dogma, and Ecumenical Theology at the Eberhard Karls University Tübingen.

MICHAEL ROOT is Ordinary Professor of Systematic Theology at The Catholic University of America.

WOLFGANG THÖNISSEN is Professor of Ecumenical Theology and Director of the Johann-Adam-Möhler Institute for Ecumenism at the University of Paderborn (Germany).

LEE PALMER WANDEL is WARF: Michael Baxandall Professor of History at the University of Wisconsin Madison.

DOROTHEA WENDEBOURG is Chair for Early Modern and Modern Church History at the Humboldt University Berlin.

TIMOTHY WENGERT is Professor Emeritus of Reformation History at the Lutheran Theological Seminary at Philadelphia.

Abbreviations

AL: *Annotated Luther*, ed. Hans Hillerbrand et al., 6 vols. Minneapolis: Fortress, 2015–17

CA: *Confessio Augustana*

CCCM: *Corpus Christianorum Continuatio Mediaevalis*. Turnhout: Brepols, 1966–

DH: Heinrich Denzinger and Peter Hünermann, eds., *Enchiridion Symbolorum Definitionum et Declarationum de Rebus Fidei et Morum*, 43rd ed. (San Francisco, 2012)

DOW: *Declaration on the Way: Church, Ministry, and Eucharist*. Minneapolis: Augsburg Fortress, 2015

JDDJ: The Lutheran World Federation and the Roman Catholic Church, *Joint Declaration on the Doctrine of Justification*. Grand Rapids, Michigan: William B. Eerdmans, 2000

LW: *Luther's Works (American Edition)*. 82 vols. St. Louis: Concordia; Philadelphia: Muhlenberg; Minneapolis: Fortress, 1955–

PG: *Patrologia cursus completus,* ed. Jacques-Paul Migne, *Series Graeca,* 167 vols. plus 2 vols. of Register. Paris, 1857–66, 1928–36

PL: *Patrologia cursus completus,* ed. Jacques-Paul Migne, *Series Latina*, 1. Series, vols. 1–79, 2. Series, vols. 80–217, Index, 1–4. Paris, 1841–64, *Patrologiae Latinae supplementum,* vols. 1–5. Paris, 1958–70

SA: *Smalcald Articles*

VapS: *Verlautbarungen des Apostolischen Stuhls*

WA: D.   *Martin Luthers Werke: kritische Gesamtausgabe (Weimarer Ausgabe)*. 120 vols. Weimar: Böhlau, 1883–2009

WA Br: *Weimarer Ausgabe Briefwechsel* correspondence) 18 vols. Weimar: Böhlau, 1930–85

WA DB: *Die deutsche Bibel* (The German Bible), 12 vols. Weimar: Hermann Böhlaus Nachfolger, 1906–61

WA TR: *Tischreden* (table talk), 6 vols. Weimar: Verlag Hermann Böhlaus Nachfolger, 1912–21

Introduction

October 31, 1517, has for centuries been marked as the day the Protestant Reformation began as a public movement. On that day, Martin Luther, an Augustinian friar teaching at the University of Wittenberg, distributed his 95 Theses on Indulgences, which, to his surprise, became a lightning rod of controversy, a controversy that led within a few decades to the division of Western Christendom.

October 17, 2017, marked the five-hundredth anniversary of that event. How should Catholics respond to that event? Until recently, the response was clear: the Reformation was heretical and schismatic; the only appropriate response was denunciation. Careful historical work and ecumenical discussion, however, have complicated the picture. The theology that drove the Reformation was, even by Catholic standards, a complicated amalgam. Assertions Catholics cannot accept were mixed with deep insights that Catholic theology too often can lose sight of. Today we recognize that responsibility for the loss of unity must be shared. Neither side had a monopoly on narrow-mindedness; a failure of Christian virtue was too often shared. Something different from past denunciations was called for, a more balanced and self-critical approach, one that would include Protestants and Orthodox in the Catholic conversation.

Discussions on how to carry out such a Catholic reflection on the Reformation were proceeding already in early 2014 at the Catholic University of America (CUA) in Washington, DC, and within the Pontifical Committee of Historical Sciences at the Vatican (PCSS)—with Nelson H. Minnich, a member of both the Pontifical Committee and of the CUA faculty, keeping in touch with both discussions. The two institutions decided to focus on different aspects of the topic. The PCSS held a conference at the Vatican in March 2017. It explored the non-theological factors that led to the rupture, especially political and financial conditions within the Holy Roman Empire that fostered the confiscation of ecclesiastical goods and the suppression of religious orders and how Catholic countries reacted. The papers from that conference were published late in 2019 by the Libreria Editrice Vaticana as *Lutero 500 anni dopo: Una rilettura della Riforma luterana nel suo contesto storico ed ecclesiale. Raccolta di Studi in occasione del V centenario (1517–2017)*, edited by Gert Melville and Josep Ignasi Saranyana Closa.

The US conference, held in May 2017, focused more on theological questions, particularly how the Catholic tradition interacted with Luther, both shaping his outlook and being shaped in its turn by Luther and the movement he led. Sponsorship of the conference was shared by CUA with the PCSS, the Secretariat for Ecumenical and Interreligious Affairs of the United States Conference of Catholic Bishops, and with the Metropolitan Washington Synod of the Evangelical Lutheran Church in America. The conference included an ecumenical prayer service led by Catholic and Lutheran bishops at the Lutheran Church of the Reformation on Capitol Hill. Additional financial support for the conference came from the Gladys Kriebler Delmas Foundation and from the United States Embassy of the Federal Republic of Germany. Without its sponsors' generous support, the conference could not have happened.

The conference sought to bring into conversation voices from different ecclesial traditions and from both America and Europe. After greetings from Pope Francis, Cardinal-Archbishop of Washington Donald Wuerl, CUA President John Garvey, and Dean of CUA's School of Theology and Religious Studies Mark Morozowich, major addresses were given on Catholic-Lutheran dialogue by Cardinal Kurt Koch, president of the Pontifical Commission for Promoting Christian Unity, and on the present state of Catholic studies of Luther by Wolfgang Thönissen of the Möhler Institute of the University of Paderborn, Germany. In each case, a response from a different tradition was given.

The bulk of the conference focused on four topics: justification, Eucharist, Church, and Eastern Christianity. In each case, the same pattern was followed: presentations on the Catholic background of Luther's ideas on the subject, on how Luther engaged that background, and on how the Catholic tradition then reacted to and was shaped by Luther's ideas. Presentations on each topic came from varying traditions.

All participants agreed to the publication of their papers, which are here gathered together. Some papers are precisely as given at the conference; a few were significantly expanded by their authors to give a fuller discussion of the topic. For their assistance in preparing the papers for publication, the editors wish to thank Matthew Gore, Adam Urrutia, and Jonathan Gaworski.

The papers revealed points of convergence and remaining differences between the Catholic and Lutheran communities, the complex role the Eastern Church played in the debates, and the difficulties surrounding the thesis of Joseph Lortz that the Latin Church on the eve of the Reformation was plagued by theological *Unklarheit*, a lack of clarity on key theological issues and by distorted ideas on grace, indulgences, and the Eucharistic sacrifice. While Luther took some controversial ideas in late medieval theology and pushed them to the extreme, Catholic teachings after Luther were a reassertion of its mainline, traditional doctrines.

The Reformation of the sixteenth century reshaped Christianity in the West in ways that still inform the daily lives of Christians. We are still coming to terms with what the Reformation wrought. The controversies of that time touched basic concerns of Christian thought and practice and cannot be lightly relegated to the historical archive. Much work—theological, historical, and ecumenical—is needed to understand what happened and what are the present possibilities of rapprochement and ecumenical cooperation. Those tasks are a challenge for Protestants, Catholics, and Orthodox and need to be addressed in conversation: honest, at times sharp, but respectful of the deep commitments on all sides. We hope that this conference and now the published studies contribute to that endeavor.

Greetings
From His Holiness Pope Francis

APOSTOLIC NUNCIATURE
UNITED STATES OF AMERICA

3339 MASSACHUSETTS AVENUE, N.W.
WASHINGTON, D.C. 20008-3610

Prot. N. 3119/17

May 30, 2017

Your Eminence,

    I am happy to communicate to you, as Chancellor of The Catholic University of America, the following message, dated 11 May 2017, for the opening of the International Conference on "Luther and the Shaping of the Catholic Tradition," which will be held at The Catholic University of America from 30 May – 1 June, 2017:

His Holiness Pope Francis sends cordial greetings to all taking part in the Conference on "Luther and the Shaping of the Catholic Tradition" to be held at The Catholic University of America on 30 May-1 June 2017 to mark the fifth centenary of the Reformation. He trusts that this scholarly examination of Martin Luther's reform in its broader historical and theological context will contribute to a greater understanding of the events leading to the conflicts of the sixteenth century and thus to that purification of memory essential to the deepening of ecumenical dialogue and the growth of Christian unity in our own day. With this encouragement, and with the assurance of his closeness in prayer, the Holy Father willingly invokes upon all present an abundance of joy and peace in Christ our Savior.

Cardinal Pietro Parolin
Secretary of State

I take this opportunity to present to you my sentiments of profound esteem, and remain,

Respectfully yours in Christ,

+ Christophe Pierre
Apostolic Nuncio

His Eminence Donald Card. Wuerl
Chancellor, Catholic University of America
Archbishop of Washington
P.O. Box 29260
Washington, DC 20017

From Cardinal Donald Wuerl, Archbishop of Washington and Chancellor of the Catholic University of America

May 30, 2017

To all who are gathered for the conference, "Martin Luther and the Shaping of Catholic Tradition," I offer a warm welcome to the Archdiocese of Washington. As Chancellor, I join John Garvey, President of The Catholic University of America, in expressing appreciation to all who have come to participate in this significant time of reflection and evaluation of the impact of Martin Luther on Catholic tradition.

In a particular way, I extend a warm welcome to His Eminence Cardinal Kurt Koch, President of the Pontifical Council for Christian Unity and former Bishop of Basel in Switzerland. Both Pope Benedict XVI and Pope Francis have recognized and applauded the diligent efforts of Cardinal Koch in the world of ecumenical relations.

I also want to greet Bishop Richard Graham of the Evangelical Lutheran Church in America, with whom I have had the joy of working these past ten years.

My warmest greetings to all of the participants and my particular recognition of Father Mark Morozowich, the Dean of the School of Theology and Religious Studies, for his important part in guiding the work of this conference.

While my obligations in Rome make it impossible for me to be here for this significant conference, I join you in a spirit of ecumenical solidarity and friendship.

Personally, I recall with great satisfaction the publication of the *Joint Declaration on Justification* signed by the Lutheran World Federation and the Holy See that I consider to be one of the great landmarks of ecumenical progress and growing mutual understanding.

This conference on "Martin Luther and the Shaping of Catholic Tradition" continues in that same spirit and with the same shared vision of coming together in faith, understanding and communion.

May God bless this conference with abundant grace and enduring fruit.

Cardinal Donald Wuerl

From John Garvey,
President of the Catholic University of America

May 30, 2017

It is my pleasure to welcome you here today. We are honored to host this conference—in cooperation with the Pontifical Committee of Historical Sciences, the Secretariat for Ecumenical and Interreligious Affairs of the United States Conference of Catholic Bishops, and the Metropolitan Washington Synod of the Evangelical Lutheran Church in America—to mark the 500th anniversary of Martin Luther's 95 Theses on Indulgences. But how should this anniversary be marked? That is, in a sense, the question of this conference.

For Protestants the anniversary is traditionally a holiday to be celebrated. On Reformation Day, or Reformation Sunday, there is exquisite music orchestrated for liturgy, often a guest preacher or lecture.[1] The liturgical color for Reformation Day is red, the same color we use on Pentecost to celebrate the coming of the Holy Spirit and the birth of the Church. This suggests that the Reformation began a divine renewal of the Church. For Catholics, the anniversary of Martin Luther's theses is often considered something to be mourned. It marks an unhappy event, a division within the body of Christ.

In thinking about this question, I have been reflecting on Blessed John Henry Newman's *Essay on the Development of Christian Doctrine*. Whenever a great idea gets possession of the popular mind, Newman says, "There will be a time of confusion, when conceptions and misconceptions are in conflict, and it is uncertain whether anything is to come of the idea at all."[2] But ultimately a great idea "is elicited and expanded by trial, and battles into perfection and supremacy."[3]

From its earliest days the Church's understanding of God, as he revealed himself in the Scriptures and in the person of Jesus, has been clarified and developed by moments of conflict. The controversy over circumcision and the observance of the Mosaic law in Jerusalem led the apostles to clarify that "we are saved through the grace of the Lord Jesus" (Acts 15:11). The Arian controversy in the 4th century led the Church at Nicaea to specify that the Son is truly God, consubstantial with the Father.

---

1. For example: http://www.immanuelnyc.org/reformation-sunday-festival
2. John Henry Newman, *An Essay on the Development of Christian Doctrine*, chapter 1, section, 1.4
3. John Henry Newman, *An Essay on the Development of Christian Doctrine*, chapter 1, section, 1.7

The Catholic Church has also been shaped by her encounter with Martin Luther and the controversies of the Reformation. Thirty years after Luther published his 95 theses the sixth session of the Council of Trent made clear that God is the final, formal, and efficient cause of man's justification,[4] and that the justified[5] ought to feel themselves the more obliged to walk in the way of justice, for being now freed from sin and made servants of God, they are able, living soberly, justly and godly, to proceed onward through Jesus Christ, by whom they have access unto this grace.

In the last 100 years, Catholic theologians have engaged Luther as never before. Protestant scholars have turned their eyes toward the late medieval setting out of which Luther came. Conversations have become less polemical and more focused on a calm assessment of what happened and why it happened. On Reformation Day 1999, after years of dialogue, the Lutheran World Federation and the Catholic Church were able to offer a Joint Declaration on the Doctrine of Justification. We now together confess that "[b]y grace alone, in faith in Christ's saving work and not because of any merit on our part, we are accepted by God and receive the Holy Spirit, who renews our hearts while equipping and calling us to good works."[6]

It is not my intention in these reflections to minimize the grave harm done to the unity of the Church during the Reformation period. Nor do I mean to suggest that there is an inevitable march of history toward progress. But I do believe that the development of the Church's doctrine and the deepening of our understanding of it through the pressure and struggle of controversy show the hand of Providence at work. We know all things, as St. Paul said, work for good for those who love God (Romans 8:28).

That is the last point I want to make today. The Catholic and Protestant scholars at this conference will take up some of the topics that stood at the center of the Reformation debates—justification and grace, the Eucharist, and the Church—to develop a clearer picture of how Martin Luther has shaped the Catholic tradition. But they undertake this work united by their shared faith in Jesus Christ and motivated by their shared love for the Lord.

John Garvey

---

4. Council of Trent, Session VI, chapter 7 https://www.ewtn.com/library/COUNCILS/TRENT6.HTM

5. Council of Trent, Session VI, chapter 11

6. Joint Declaration on the Doctrine of Justification (October 31, 1999), Nr. 15. http://www.vatican.va/roman_curia/pontifical_councils/chrstuni/documents/rc_pc_chrstuni_doc_31101999_cath-luth-joint-declaration_en.html

From the Very Reverend Mark Morozowich, Dean of the School of Theology and Religious Studies, The Catholic University of America

Welcome to our conference marking the 500th Anniversary of Martin Luther's Posting of the Ninety-five Theses and the Shaping of the Catholic Tradition.

This scholarly gathering addresses the historical, social, and theological issues facing Martin Luther and the Catholic response. We examine this history in light of its current reception and our twenty-first century understanding. International scholars and church leaders are here to engage a new appropriation of this important historical event. Our task does not simply look back as if trying to revisit an old photo or painting; rather. we utilize the best scientific methodologies to deepen our interpretations of what the past means to us today and to deepen our understanding of how Luther came out of a complex Catholic context, developed strains within it, and led the Church to privilege certain ideas and reject others. Our discussion and dialogue attempt to further ecumenical engagement, to stimulate scholarly work, and to build mutual understanding today. While we are mindful of this historic rupture in the Body of Christ, we hope that we can learn from the myriad of past errors in a self-critical manner so that the continuing disruption of the unity of the Body of Christ may be healed in the future. I hope that this encounter, this scholarly gathering will benefit each participant not just on a personal level, but also as a gift to be taken to their own ecclesial communities in order to be a leaven of transformation. Certainly, at *the 400th anniversary* in 1917 people did not expect the great strides that lay ahead. We have much optimism for the future.

I. Major Presentations and Responses

1. Martin Luther's Reformation and the Unity of the Church:
A Catholic Perspective in Light of the Lutheran–Catholic Dialogue

Kurt Cardinal Koch

"While we are profoundly thankful for the spiritual and theological gifts received through the Reformation, we also confess and lament before Christ that Lutherans and Catholics have wounded the visible unity of the Church." With these words in the Joint Declaration that they signed during the ecumenical prayer service on the occasion of the Catholic and Lutheran commemoration of the Reformation in the Lutheran Cathedral in Lund on 31 October 2016,[1] Pope Francis and Bishop Munib Younan, the President of the Lutheran World Federation, gave expression to what we can jointly say today from an ecumenical perspective about the 16th century Reformation. In the foreground, one finds, on the one hand, gratitude for all that the Reformation brought about as regards positive religious and theological insights to which Lutherans and Catholics can jointly testify today; on the other hand, one finds confession of guilt and repentance, in view of the fact that the Reformation did not at that time lead to the renewal of the Church but to schism. The accents can certainly be placed differently here: Lutheran Christians will, in the first instance, connect the Reformation with the rediscovery of the gospel of mankind's justification solely through God's grace and its acceptance in faith. Catholic Christians are accustomed to associate the Reformation particularly with schism and the lost unity of the church. But even if the accents are placed differently, both accents belong indissolubly together in any Reformation commemoration today. This is also expressed in the title of the document drafted by the Lutheran–Roman Catholic Commission on Unity with a view to the joint Reformation commemoration in 2017, bearing the significant title *From Conflict to Communion.*[2] A joint Reformation commemoration must take the conflict as seriously as the communion, and above all make a contribution

---

1. "Joint Statement on the Occasion of the Joint Catholic-Lutheran Commemoration of the Reformation, Lund, October 31, 2016," in: *Information Service, Pontifical Council for Promoting Christian Unity*, no. 148 (2016): 20.

2. Lutheran-Roman Catholic Commission on Unity, *From Conflict to Communion: Lutheran-Catholic Common Commemoration of the Reformation in 2017* (Leipzig: Evangelische Verlagsanstalt, 2013).

towards enabling Lutheran and Catholic Christians to progress along the path from conflict to communion.

1. REDISCOVERED COMMUNITY IN THE FAITH

In the first place, we must express a word of gratitude, especially since in 2017 we commemorate not only 500 years of the Reformation but also 50 years of intensive dialogue between Lutherans and Catholics, in which we have been privileged to discover how much we have in common. This dialogue is not only the first that the Catholic Church commenced immediately after the Second Vatican Council, but also the one that over the past half century has proved very fruitful. It has facilitated on the Catholic side a more positive view of the Reformation, and on the Lutheran side a more nuanced view of the circumstances of western Christianity in the late Middle Ages.

a) Revision of the Catholic Image of Luther

The path from conflict to communion began above all with a critical reappraisal, overcoming the traditional negative image of Martin Luther in the Catholic Church.[3] An extremely polemical image had been presented and propagated already in his lifetime by Johannes Cochläus, who in his *Commentaria de actis et scriptis Martini Lutheri* in 1549—just three years after Luther's death—incriminated Luther as destroyer of the unity of the Church, corrupter of morals and impudent revolutionary "who had through his heresies plunged countless souls into ruin and brought unending misery to Germany and the whole of Christendom."[4] This negative view remained one of the most important references of the Catholic image of Luther for centuries. Its aftereffects were still evident at the beginning of last century in the work of the Dominican Heinrich Suso Denifle, who did in fact locate Luther in a positive perspective in the context of scholastic theology, but still raised the old polemics once more, claiming above all that Luther had invented the doctrine of justification through faith and not through works—which certainly forms the crux of his theological thought—solely for the purpose of "being able to feel all the more carefree and secure while living his dissolute life."[5]

---

3. Cf. Werner Beyna, *Das moderne katholische Lutherbild* (Essen: Ludgerus, 1969); Danilea Blum, *Der katholische Luther. Begegnungen—Prägungen—Rezeptionen* (Paderborn: Ferdinand Schöningh, 2016).

4. See the representation of Johannes Cochläus by Hubert Jedin, "Wandlungen des Lutherbildes in der katholischen Kirchengeschichtsschreibung," in: *Wandlungen des Lutherbildes*, ed. Karl Forster (Würzburg: Echter, 1966), 80.

5. Heinrich Denifle, *Luther und Luthertum in der ersten Entwicklung: Quellenmässig dargestellt*, 2nd ed. (Mainz: F. Kirchheim, 1904–6).

The historic breakthrough to a more positive and at least more nuanced image of Luther within Catholic research on him was achieved by the Church historian Joseph Lortz, who has rendered a great service through his thorough historical research into the Reformation in Germany in particular,[6] which has been well–received in ecumenical discussion.[7] In light of the biblical, liturgical, and ecumenical movements between the two world wars, Lortz described the great religious impulses by which Luther was guided; he characterized Luther as a monk who took his Christian life and his life in orders very seriously. Against the background of the crisis of the Church and theology in the late Middle Ages, he responded with great theological understanding to Luther's critique, and on that basis formulated his now famous thesis that "Luther had in his own person wrestled into submission a Catholicism that was not Catholic."[8] This view can be understood as a decisive turning point in the struggle for an historically adequate and theologically appropriate image of Luther in the Catholic Church. Closely connected with this is the perception of Luther as deeply rooted within Catholic thinking, and thence the rediscovery of the "Catholic Luther,"[9] as it were, and the unlocking of his ecumenical significance.[10] On the occasion of the 500th anniversary of Martin Luther's birth in 1983, in conjunction with an evaluation of the essential concerns of the Reformer, the Roman Catholic / Lutheran Joint Commission, in ecumenical communion, gave expression to this positive view with the conviction: "Christians, whether Lutheran or Catholic, cannot disregard the person and

6. Joseph Lortz, *Die Reformation in Deutschland* (Freiburg i. Br.: Herder, 1962).

7. Cf. Rolf Decot and Rainer Vinke, eds., *Zum Gedenken an Joseph Lortz (1887–1975): Beiträge zur Reformationsgeschichte und Ökumeme*, Veröffentlichungen des Instituts für Europäische Geschichte Mainz, Abteilung Abendländische Religionsgeschichte (Stuttgart: F. Steiner, 1989).

8. Jospeh Lortz, *Die Reformation in Deutschland*, 1:176.

9. Cf. Johannes Brosseder, "Der katholische Luther," in: *Von der Reformation zur Reform. Neue Zugänge zum Konzil von Trient*, ed. Günter Frank, Albert Käuflein, and Tobias Licht (Freiburg i. Br.: Herder, 2015), 65–96; Peter Neuner, "Luther—katholisch gesehen," in: *Heillos gespalten? Segensreich erneuert?: 500 Jahre Reformation in der Vielfalt ökumenischer Perspektiven*, ed. Uwe Swarat and Thomas Söding (Freiburg i. Br., Herder, 2016), 119–135; Peter Neuner, *Martin Luthers Reformation. Eine katholische Würdigung* (Freiburg i. Br.: Herder, 2017); Wolfgang Thönissen, *Gerechtigkeit oder Barmherzigkeit? Das ökumenische Ringen um die Rechtfertigung* (Paderborn: Bonifatius, 2016), esp. 177–200; Wolfgang Thönissen, Josef Freitag, and Augustinus Sander, eds., *Luther: Katholizität und Reform. Wurzeln—Wege—Wirkungen* (Paderborn: Bonifatius, 2016).

10. Cf. Hans Friedrich Geisser, et al., *Weder Ketzer noch Heiliger. Luthers Bedeutung für den ökumenischen Dialog* (Regensburg: Friedrich Pustet, 1982); Udo Hahn and Marlies Mügge, eds., *Martin Luther—Vorbild im Glauben. Die Bedeutung des Reformators im ökumenischen Gespräch* (Neukirchen: Neukirchener Verlag, 1996); Karl Lehmann, ed., *Luthers Sendung für Katholiken und Protestanten* (Zürich: Schnell und Steiner, 1982); Peter Manns and Harding Meyer, eds., *Ökumenische Erschliessung Martin Luthers* (Paderborn: Bonifatius, 1983); Otto Hermann Pesch, ed., *Lehren aus dem Luther-Jahr. Sein Ertrag für die Ökumene* (Zürich: Schnell und Steiner, 1984).

the message of this man." Luther's particular ecumenical significance was honored with the title "Witness to the gospel."[11]

This new view of Martin Luther also received official ecclesial affirmation when the second president of the Secretariat for Promoting Christian Unity, Cardinal Johannes Willebrands, spoke very positively of Martin Luther in his keynote address to the fifth General Assembly of the Lutheran World Federation in Evian-les-Bains in 1970, in the conviction that "a more just assessment of the person and work of Martin Luther" on the Catholic side was a necessary path "towards restoring lost unity." In this basic attitude, Cardinal Willebrands acknowledged the Reformer as a "teacher of the faith": "He may be a shared teacher for us in the fact that God must always be the Lord and that our most important human response has to remain absolute trust and reverence of God."[12]

This positive estimation of Luther has subsequently been taken up by various popes. In his message on the occasion of the 500th anniversary of Luther's birth, Pope John Paul II referred to the scholarly endeavors of Lutheran and Catholic researchers in which "Luther's deep religiosity, driven by a burning passion for the question of eternal salvation" has been convincingly demonstrated.[13] And in the year of the 450th anniversary of the death of the Reformer, Pope John Paul II paid a special tribute to Luther's "attentiveness towards the word of God and the high value of his demand for a scriptural theology and his will for a spiritual renewal of the Church."[14] Pope Benedict XVI went even further during his visit to the former Augustinian Convent in Erfurt where Luther had studied theology and been ordained to the priesthood, in highlighting the passionate search for God in the life and work of Martin Luther: "What constantly exercised him was the question of God, the deep passion and driving force of his whole life's journey."[15] Pope Benedict at the same time stressed that Luther was not simply searching for any God, but believed in the God who has shown us his face in the man Jesus of Nazareth, and that he therefore expressed

---

11. Roman Catholic/Lutheran Joint Commission, "Martin Luther—Witness to Jesus Christ (1983)," in: *Growth in Agreement II: Reports and Agreed Statements of Ecumenical Conversations on a World Level, 1982–1998*, ed. Jeffrey Gros, Harding Meyer, and William G. Rusch (Geneva: WCC Publications, 2000), 438.

12. Jan Willebrands, "Sent Into the World," in: *Sent Into the World: The Proceedings of the Fifth Assembly of the Lutheran World Federation, Evian, France, July 14–24, 1970*, ed. LaVern K. Grosc (Minneapolis: Augsburg, 1971), 62–64.

13. John Paul II, "Letter on the Fifth Centenary of Birth of Martin Luther: 31 October 1983," in: *Information Service, Secretariat for Promoting Christian Unity*, no. 52 (1983), 83.

14. John Paul II, "Address to Ecumenical Leaders," in: *Information Service, Pontifical Council for Promoting Christian Unity*, no. 93 (1996), 154f.

15. Benedict XVI, "To Representatives of the Council of the Evangelical Church at the Former Augustinian Convent in Erfurt, 23 September 2011," *Information Service, Pontifical Council for Promoting Christian Unity*, no. 137 (2011), 56.

his concrete and profound passionate search for God in the Christocentrism of his spirituality and theology. This emphasis on the centrality of the question of God and on Christocentrism as the heart's concern of the Christian, theologian, and Reformer Martin Luther, rounds out the image of Luther in the Catholic Church. We would therefore be happy to endorse Cardinal Walter Kasper's opinion when he calls the decision to celebrate the Reformation commemoration as a "joint celebration of Christ" as the "best ecumenical idea I know of for the year 2017."[16]

b) *The More Nuanced Protestant View of the Late Middle Ages*

The positive endeavors on the Catholic side are matched by welcome developments on the Lutheran side, above all towards a more nuanced evaluation of the late Middle Ages and the situation of the Catholic Church at that time. In the first instance, of course, we must remember that the negative and polemical image of Luther in the tradition of the Catholic Church is also to be understood as a reaction to the mirror–image heroic view of Luther in the Protestant tradition, as it came to light in the Reformation celebrations in particular.[17] That is especially true of the first centennial celebration of the beginning of the Reformation in 1617, which was imbued with a spirit of anti–Catholic polemics and aggressive rhetoric, as Luther was seen above all as the champion against Rome and in particular the papacy, from which he had liberated Christianity. Pietism revered Luther as the great religious genius, and in the age of Enlightenment he was glorified as the liberator from the gloom of the Middle Ages and the founder of the modern period. During the Reformation celebration in 1917, Luther was not only celebrated as the creator of the German language, but also as the personification of the authentic German. Even in the immediate aftermath of the European catastrophe of the First World War, the Protestant theologian Adolf von Harnack was able to claim outright that modernity had begun in Germany and had radiated throughout the world from there: "Modernity began with Luther's Reformation, and indeed it was the hammer blows on the door of the Castle Church in Wittenberg on the 31st of October 1517 which initiated it."[18]

16. Walter Kasper, *Martin Luther. Eine ökumenische Perspektive* (Ostfildern: Patmos, 2016), 56.

17. Cf. Thomas Kaufmann, "Reformationsgedenken in der Frühen Neuzeit," *Zeitschrift für Theologie und Kirche*, 107 (2010): 285–324; P. Neuner, *Martin Luthers Reformation*, 36–49; Dorothea Wendebourg, "Vergangene Reformationsjubiläen. Ein Rückblick im Vorfeld von 2017," in: *Der Reformator Martin Luther 2017. Eine wissenschaftliche und gedenkpolitische Bestandsaufnahme*, ed. Heinz Schilling (Berlin: De Gruyter, 2014), 261–281.

18. Adolf von Harnack, "Die Reformation und ihre Vorstellung," in: *Erforschtes und Erlebtes* (Giessen: Töpelmann, 1923), 110.

Such characterizations of Luther as a heroic figure in the most diverse contexts are no longer possible today even in Protestant history writing. For it has become clear, on the one hand, that Martin Luther himself was far more deeply rooted in the feeling and thinking of the medieval world than has previously been admitted. This location is evident in his life, above all in his predominantly apocalyptic tone, in which he saw himself placed in the midst of the final eschatological battle between Christ and the Antichrist, and therefore not only discovered the Antichrist in the Pope but also saw the devil at work in most of his opponents.[19] Against this background, it has finally become possible, on the other hand, even for Protestant history writing to objectively put a name to the dark sides in the life and work of Martin Luther, such as his demeaning and spiteful utterances about Jews,[20] his vehement attacks against the peasants during the Peasant War, and his advocacy and theological justification of the persecution of the Anabaptists by the Lutheran authorities, with the result that the Free Church traditions see themselves not as subjects of the Lutheran Reformation but as its victims.[21] Additionally, one must not forget his increasingly crude attacks against the Catholic Church and above all against the papacy, such as his invective against the Council of Trent, which sinks to a nadir which can hardly be rivalled: "We should take him—the pope, the cardinals, and whatever riffraff belongs to His Idolatrous and Papal Holiness—and (as blasphemers) tear out their tongues from the back, and nail them on the gallows in the order in which they hang their seals on the bulls. . . . Then one could allow them to hold a council, or as many as they wanted, on the gallows, or in hell among all the devils."[22]

At this point, however, the accent is to be placed on the fact that it has become clear in Protestant history writing that Luther himself was deeply grounded both existentially and theologically in the Middle Ages, and indeed within the mystical and monastic tradition of the late Middle Ages. This is true above all with respect to Bernard of Clairvaux, in whose work Luther's interpretation of Holy Scripture as the encounter between Christ and mankind and even his theology of justification by grace are already prefigured.[23] Together

19. Cf. Heiko A. Oberman, *Luther: Man Between God and the Devil*, trans. Eileen Walliser-Schwarzbart (New Haven: Yale University Press, 1989); Heinz Schilling, *Martin Luther. Rebell in einer Zeit des Umbruchs. Eine Biographie* (Munich: C. H. Beck, 2012).

20. Cf. Heinz Kremers, *Die Juden und Martin Luther—Martin Luther und die Juden. Geschichte—Wirkungsgeschichte—Herausforderung* (Neukirchen: Neukirchener Verlag, 1985).

21. Cf. Volker Spangenberg, ed., *Luther und die Reformation in freikirchlicher Sicht* (Göttingen: Vandenhoeck & Ruprecht, 2013).

22. Martin Luther, *Wider das Papsttum in Rom, vom Teufel gestiftet*, WA 54, 243:11–17 (LW 41:309).

23. Cf. Franz Posset, "Luther und der letzte der Kirchenväter, Bernhard von Clairvaux. Der Bernhardfaktor in Luthers Leben und Werken," in: *Luther: Katholizität und Reform. Wurzeln—Wege—Wirkungen* (Paderborn: Bonifatius, 2016), 29–59.

with the discovery of Luther's profound roots in the late Middle Ages has come the more sensitive perception that the Middle Ages were by no means as dark as they have been painted so willingly and for so long. For, on the one hand, the late Middle Ages developed an authentic theology of piety for the laity, so that the Protestant church historian Bernd Moeller was able to judge that the 15th century could be appraised as one of the most ecclesially pious periods of the Middle Ages.[24] On the other hand, it has been rediscovered that in the late Middle Ages diverse and far–reaching reforms did take place, and that church reform was on the whole one of the great themes of the late Middle Ages. Thus, the internal Church reform movement intended by Luther did not stand in isolation in the landscape of the time, but must be seen within this broader context.

A reminder of the ecclesial situation in Spain at the beginning of the 16th century serves as a striking example of where the real impulses to religious reforms in the Catholic Church originated, above all from a number of reform orders strongly influenced by the spirituality of the *devotio moderna* from the Netherlands. Such reform endeavors were substantially advanced by the promotion of book printing by the then Archbishop of Toledo, Francisco Jiménez de Cisneros, who had already in 1517 enabled the publication of the first polyglot edition of the whole Sacred Scripture. In view of this religious and ecclesial reform potential in Spain, the Berlin historian Hans Schilling judges rightly that in Luther's day the Iberian Peninsula already "achieved precursors to reforms" which were "elsewhere only enforced by the Reformation revolt and the subsequent Tridentine reform." From that he draws the conclusion: "That had like nothing else made Spain impervious to the Lutheran 'heresy.'"[25] Or to formulate it more positively: If a similar ecclesial reform to that in Spain had been able to prevail throughout the whole church, and if Martin Luther's call to reform and repentance had found open ears among the bishops of the time and of the Pope in Rome, the reform intended and initiated by him would not have become the Reformation. For the fact that the original reform of the Church became instead a Church–dividing Reformation, the Catholic Church of the time must bear its share of the blame, as the Catholic ecumenist Wolfgang Thönissen expressed in the concise formula: "Because the reform of the church and the Empire did not succeed, the Reformation was the result."[26]

---

24. Berndt Moeller, "Frömmigkeit in Deutschland um 1500," in: *Die Reformation und das Mittelalter. Kirchenhistorische Aufsätze* (Göttingen: Vandenhoeck & Ruprecht, 1991), 81.

25. Heinz Schilling, "Luther und die Reformation 1517–2017," in: *Heillos gespalten? Segensreich erneuert? 500 Jahre Reformation in der Vielfalt ökumenischer Perspektiven*, eds. Uwe Swarat und Thomas Söding (Freiburg i. Br.: Herder, 2016), 22.

26. Wolfgang Thönissen, *Gerechtigkeit oder Barmherzigkeit?*, 40.

2. CHURCH REFORM AND CHURCH SCHISM

On the other hand, however, we are compelled to conclude that the Catholic Church at that time was not only extremely in need of reform but also capable of reform. The Lutheran Reformation of the 16th century therefore cannot be considered the only response to the need for reform of the Church, and can therefore not stake an exclusive claim to the reform of the Church as a whole. With his original concern for reform, Luther stood in a long and great tradition of Catholic renewal before him, which in crisis situations in the Church had always reiterated that in its life and in its mission the word of God must be accorded primacy. We could recall the two founders of the mendicant orders, Saint Francis and Saint Dominic, who in the first instance did not at all intend to found new orders but to renew the Church from within, and indeed by daring to live the Gospel in the evangelical form of life *sine glossa*, in its literal totality. Or we could think of Saint Carlo Borromeo who, on taking possession of his episcopal seat in the Lombard metropolis of Milan, diagnosed the most wide-spread failings of the clergy in the absence of preaching, and saw his primary mission as bishop to be "a witness, to proclaim the mysteries of Christ, to preach the gospel to every creature."[27] Cardinal Joseph Ratzinger has rightly claimed of the great bishop of Milan that his "last great echo" in our century was the figure of John XXIII, who intended with his Council above all to renew that impulse to renewal "which had lit up in Borromeo."[28] The Second Vatican Council may therefore be acknowledged as a reform Council which was intended to once more restore to the word of God the centrality due to it in the life and mission of the Church.[29] By taking up and fulfilling important demands made by Martin Luther, such as the rediscovery of the common priesthood of all the baptized, the celebration of divine worship in the language of the people, and the option of distribution of the cup to the laity, the Second Vatican Council has even prompted the assessment that in the Council, Martin Luther had in fact "found his Council,"[30] which he had called for in his lifetime and which was convoked in Trent only when the unity of the Church could no longer be saved.

27. Cited by Giuseppe Alberigo, *Karl Borromäus, Geschichtliche Sensibilität und pastorales Engagement* (Münster: Aschendorff, 1995), 39–40.

28. Joseph Ratzinger, *Principles of Catholic Theology: Building Stones for a Fundamental Theology*, trans. Mary Frances McCarthy (San Francisco: Ignatius Press, 1987), 265.

29. Cf. Kurt Koch, "Was bedeutet heute 'Reform' der katholischen Kirche in der Schweiz? Zur Lage der Konzilsrezeption," in: *Karl Borromäus und die katholische Reform. Akten des Freiburger Symposiums zur 400. Wiederkehr der Heiligsprechung des Schutzpatrons der katholischen Schweiz*, eds. Mariano Delgado and Markus Ries (Fribourg: Academic Press, 2010), 365–394.

30. Albert Brandenburg, *Martin Luther gegenwärtig. Katholische Lutherstudien* (Paderborn: Friedrich Schöningh, 1969), 146.

a) The Necessity of the Church's Renewal in the Light of the Gospel

Only against this broader background is it possible to properly acknowledge Martin Luther's actual intention. He in no way intended a breach with the Catholic Church or the founding of a new church; his goal was instead a thoroughgoing renewal of the whole of Christianity in the spirit of the Gospel and not a reformation in the sense of the ultimately shattered unity of the Church, as the Protestant ecumenist Wolfhart Pannenberg has repeatedly pointed out: "Luther intended a reform of the whole of Christendom; his goal was anything but a separate Lutheran Church."[31] The Lutheran Reformation of the 16th century is therefore to be understood and acknowledged as a process of the reform of the Church through the rediscovery of the Gospel as its foundation, or more precisely of the Gospel of the justification of sinful mankind not through works but through faith in Jesus Christ. Accordingly, "justice" no longer means or implies a "doing"—as in the Aristotelian tradition, by which a person becomes righteous through right action—but rather a "being, precisely being through God: a gift of God in faith in Jesus Christ."[32] Martin Luther and his Wittenberg Reformation give clear evidence of the fact that a true reform of the Church can only be realized through the concentration of Christian existence and ecclesial life on the person of Jesus Christ as the living word of God, in whom the Church finds its true identity.[33]

These crucial concerns of Luther can also and especially be grasped in the events of 1517, more precisely on the 31st of October, to which this Reformation commemoration of 2017 refers, in remembrance of the so–called posting of the 95 Theses on indulgences on the door of the Castle Church in Wittenberg by the monk and professor Martin Luther. This date is generally considered as the beginning of the Reformation in Germany. But in 1962 the Catholic Church historian Erwin Iserloh judged this so–called posting of the theses to be a legend;[34] and since then many historians support the conviction that the nailing of Luther's 95 Theses did not take place at all in the manner that has been traditionally handed down, which is by the way substantiated by the fact

---

31. Wolfhart Pannenberg, *Problemgeschichte der neueren evangelischen Theologie in Deutschland* (Göttingen:Vandenhoeck & Ruprecht, 1997), 25.

32. Christian Schad, "Rechtfertigung: Gottes Ja zu uns," in: *Nötig zu wissen. Heidelberger Beiträge zum Heidelberger Katechismus,* eds. Helmut Schwier and Hans-Georg Ulrichs (Heidelberg: Winter, 2012), 105.

33. Cf. Kurt Koch, "Die identitätsstiftende Kraft des Wortes Gottes im Licht des Zweiten Vatikanischen Konzils," in: *Reform oder Reformation? Kirchen in der Pflicht,* eds. Peter Klasvogt and Burkhard Neumann (Paderborn: Bonifatius, 2014), 71–100.

34. Erwin Iserloh, *The Theses Were Not Posted: Luther Between Reform and Reformation*, trans. Jared Wicks (Boston: Beacon Press, 1968).

that Luther himself at no time in his life spoke of posting the theses, although the 31st of October remained in his memory as the day on which he moved against indulgences. In keeping with this, the Protestant church historian Volker Leppin sums up the current state of research with the words: "If one wants to take Luther at his word, one can hardly claim for the date of the 31st of October anything more than: The posting of the theses did not take place."[35] From the historical perspective, therefore, we can most likely assume that Luther sent his theses on indulgences to Archbishop Albrecht and to his local bishop Hieronymus Schulz and, at the same time, understood the publication of his theses as an invitation to an academic disputation. With these theses, as the Protestant church historian Thomas Kaufmann states, he primarily wished to confront "the loss of credibility of his beloved Church," and rescue "the Roman papal Church he loved."[36] With regard to the intent of his action, the publication of his theses is in no way to be understood as the beginning of the Reformation in the sense of the ultimately broken unity of the Church, and even the theses themselves can in no way be considered a revolutionary document; they present a thoroughly Catholic issue and remain within the bounds of acceptability in the Catholic theology of the time.[37] With his theses, Luther did not in any case wish to break with the Catholic Church, but to renew it.

The events of 1517 demonstrate, on the one hand, that the momentous conflict that erupted regarding the practice of indulgences involved not only theological questions in the narrow sense, but also divergent spiritualities and piety–related attitudes. It is surely no coincidence that Luther's conflict with the Catholic Church was sparked by the common indulgence piety practice of the time, which Luther was unable to reconcile with his own spiritual experience centered on the gospel of justification by grace alone accepted in faith. On the other hand, it is equally clear that it did not result in a breach between Luther and the Catholic Church in 1517, that the unity of the Church was at that time not yet destroyed, and that Martin Luther was still living and working in communion with the Catholic Church. Since the 2017 Reformation commem-

---

35. Volker Leppin, "Der „Thesenanschlag"—viel Lärm um nichts?" in: *Iserloh. Der Thesenanschlag fand nicht statt*, ed. Uwe Wolff (Münster: Reinhardt, 2016), 245.

36. Thomas Kaufmann, "Reformation und Reform—Luthers 95 Thesen in ihrem historischen Zusammenhang," in: *Reform oder Reformation? Kirchen in der Pflicht*, eds. Peter Klasvogt and Burkhard Neumann (Paderborn: Bonifatius, 2014), 26. Cf. Thomas Kaufmann, *Der Anfang der Reformation* (Tübingen: Mohr Siebeck, 2012).

37. In the reverse direction, the Protestant church historian Berndt Hamm has established astonishing coherencies between the proclamation of indulgences in the late medieval Church and the message of grace favored by the Reformation, so that he not only speaks of the "gospel of the Reformation," but also of the "gospel of the indulgence." Cf. Berndt Hamm, *Ablass und Reformation. Erstaunliche Kohärenzen* (Tübingen: Mohr Siebeck, 2016), 5.

oration refers back to this time and involves Lutherans and Catholics to the same extent, this must be seen as a further reason why the Reformation commemoration today cannot be celebrated other than in ecumenical communion.

The controversy over Luther's theses on indulgences subsequently focused increasingly on the question of the Church and the question of the ecclesial ministry which can speak and act in the name of the Church. In Luther's Augsburg Disputation with Cajetan in 1518 and in the Leipzig Disputation with Eck in 1519, the understanding of the Church, and more precisely the question of the authority of Councils and the Pope, formed the crux of the disputes.[38] While Luther in his early period shared the Catholic understanding of the Church to a great extent,[39] in the later phase of his life and work he fundamentally called into question the Catholic understanding of church and ministry, above all in his reforming treatise "To the Christian Nobility of the German Nation" of 1520,[40] with its pointed emphasis on the common priesthood of all believers. And in his second treatise, "De captivitate Babylonica ecclesiae,"[41] also in 1520, he also rejected the sacramental order of the Catholic Church, at least in the manner in which he had encountered it at that time. With these and other writings he had, as rightly stated by Cardinal Walter Kasper, initiated "a breach with the Catholic understanding of the Church."[42]

In this sense, the Reformation of the 16th century led to the formation of a different type of church, characterized by the fact that the churches derived from the Reformation want to be church in a different way: "As they themselves insist, it is precisely not the same mode in which the Churches of the great tradition of antiquity are Churches, but is based on a new understanding."[43] That this judgement does not simply represents a Catholic outsider's view but represents the Protestant churches' understanding of themselves is demonstrated, for example, by the basic text of the Evangelical Church in Germany for the Reformation commemoration in 2017, entitled *Justification and Freedom*, in which

---

38. Cf. Erwin Iserloh, "Die protestantische Reformation," in: *Handbuch der Kirchengeschichte*. Vol 4. *Reformation, Katholische Reform und Gegenreformation*, eds. Erwin Iserloh, Josef Glazik, and Hubert Jedin (Freiburg i. Br.: Herder, 1979), 56 ff, 64 ff.

39. Cf. Theodor Dieter, "Die Eucharistische Ekklesiologie Joseph Ratzingers—eine lutherische Perspektive," in: *Kirche—Sakrament und Gemeinschaft. Zu Ekklesiologie und Ökumene bei Joseph Ratzinger*, Ratzinger-Studien 4, ed. Christian Schaller (Regensburg: Pustet, 2011), 276–316, esp. 288–299.

40. WA 6, 381–469 (LW 44:115–217).

41. WA 6, 497-573 (LW 36:3–126).

42. Walter Kasper, *Martin Luther*, 31.

43. Benedict XVI, *Light of the World: The Pope, the Church and the Signs of the Times. A Conversation with Peter Seewald*, trans. Michael J. Miller and Adrian J. Walker (San Francisco: Ignatius, 2010), 95.

it is emphatically stressed that the insights of the Reformers had led to a "complete restructuring of the church's essence." This new polity is further heightened to the extent that pastors, male and female, exist "only for the sake of order," since in principle "every Christian can administer the sacraments, i.e., impart baptism and dispense the Lord's Supper."[44]

In the Reformation period, the disputes between Luther and his Catholic adversaries on the all–important question of the nature of the Church were, unfortunately, unable to lead to a satisfactory conclusion. In view of that, this question must today constitute a key element on the agenda in ecumenical dialogues between the Catholic Church and the churches which emerged from the Reformation. It is therefore to be hoped that, 500 years later, the Reformation commemoration today will lead to further clarification of this ecclesiological question.

b) *The Schism of the Church and Its Fateful Consequences*

The renewal of the whole Church originally intended by Martin Luther, with his rediscovery of the biblical message of justification by grace alone, was not able to attain fulfillment at that time, but instead led in schism. This historical paradox was expressed already in 1950 by the Catholic church historian and ecumenist Joseph Lortz in the memorable words, "The Reformation set out to reform the head and the members of the one Church that belongs to all Christians. That was not achieved, and what has happened instead was the rupture that split the church and Christendom apart."[45] That this schism occurred is also due, at least in part, to political factors. While Luther was originally intent on an internal ecclesial movement of the renewal of Christianity in its entirety in the spirit of divine truth, the splitting of the Church and the resulting establishment of a separate new Lutheran church structure were primarily the result of political decisions, whereby Luther himself to an extent sought refuge and support from political powers and was, over time, increasingly manipulated by certain princes for their own interests.

We must furthermore recall with shame that, in the 16th and 17th centuries, the schism resulted in cruel confessional conflicts, above all the Thirty Years War, which transformed Europe into a Red Sea of blood. In particular, the first centennial celebration of the beginning of the Reformation in 1617 was overshadowed by such warlike conflicts. At the time it was clear that Europe was moving

---

44. *Rechtfertigung und Freiheit. 500 Jahre Reformation 2017. Ein Grundlagentext des Rates der Evangelischen Kirche in Deutschland (EKD)* (Gütersloh: Gütersloher Verlagshaus, 2014), 90–91.

45. Joseph Lortz, *How the Reformation Came*, trans. Otto Knab (New York: Herder and Herder, 1964), 16.

towards a momentous conflict and even a cruel religious war. The first centenary celebration of the Reformation—which was at the same time the origin of the Reformation Day—was characterized by anti–Catholic polemics and aggressive rhetoric, as the Lutheran pastor and former General Secretary of the World Council of Churches, Olav Fykse Tveit, states frankly: "The first celebration in memory of 1517 was the prelude to a series of destructive religious wars, the Thirty Years War, which turned the remembrance of Luther's courageous deed in 1517 into a weapon."[46]

It is impossible to downplay the fatal consequences of the schism in the Western church and the subsequent bloody confessional wars of the 16th and 17th centuries in the life of European society.[47] Because, as a consequence of the confessional wars, Christianity was historically tangible only in the form of various confessions that were fighting against one another to the death, this historical constellation had to have the inevitable consequence that confessional peace could only be bought at the costly price of disregarding confessional differences—and in the long term, Christianity itself—in order to give the social peace a new foundation. Modern secularization—or more precisely, the process of depriving the Christian faith of its mandate for social peace, and as a consequence its privatization—is to be judged as an unwanted and unintended but tragic ramification of the splitting of the Western church and thus to a large extent the fault of Christianity itself, as the Protestant ecumenist Wolfhart Pannenberg above all has rightly diagnosed: "Where the secularization of the modern world has taken the form of an alienation from Christianity, it did not befall the churches as an external fate, but as the consequence of their own sins against unity, as a consequence of the church division of the 16th century and the indecisive religious wars of the 16th and 17th, which left the people in confessionally mixed territories no choice than to restructure their co–existence upon a common foundation untouched by confessional conflicts."[48]

Considered in historical retrospect, we may judge that the Religious Peace of Augsburg in 1555 was indeed able to achieve a certain degree of pacification for a time, but the principle "Cuius regio, eius religio," which was elevated to an Imperial law at that time, led to a political ecclesial system in which the reli-

---

46. Olaf Fyske Tveit, "Das Erbe der Reformation und seine Bedeutung für die ökumenische Bewegung heute," in: *500 Jahre Reformation. Bedeutung und Herausforderungen. Internationaler Kongress der EKD und des SEK auf dem Weg zum Reformationsjubiläum 2017 vom 6. bis 10. Oktober 2013 in Zürich*, eds. Petra Bosse-Huber et al. (Leipzig: Evangelische Verlagsanstalt, 2014), 110.

47. Cf. Kurt Koch, *Christsein in einem neuen Europa. Provokationen und Perspektiven* (Freiburg/Switzerland: Paulusverlag, 1992), esp. 137–166.

48. Wolfhart Pannenberg, "The Unity of the Church: A Reality of our Faith and an Ecumenical Goal," in: *The Church*, trans. Keith Crim (Philadelphia: Westminster, 1983), 24–25. On the question as a whole, see Pannenberg, *Christentum in einer säkularisiierten Welt* (Freiburg i. Br.: Herder, 1988).

gious freedom of the individual Christian was not guaranteed. Rather, it was placed at the disposal of the ruler of the land, insofar as the possibility of choice between the Catholic or the Lutheran community was not given to individual Christians but to their rulers. The development of secular nation-states with strong denominational boundaries must therefore be seen as a consequence of these tragic conflicts and developments, and therefore as a great burden of guilt left from the Reformation era, for which both sides in the conflict must bear great responsibility.

When we call to mind these fateful historical developments and above all recognize the fact that Catholics and Lutherans have wounded the one body of Christ in which they have become members through baptism, and have committed violence against one another in the name of faith, they have every reason for self–recrimination and repentance for the misunderstandings, wrongs, and hurts that they have perpetrated against one another over the past 500 years. A first step in this direction was taken by Pope Hadrian VI, who was open to the renewal of the Catholic Church, but who was not given the opportunity to prevent the schism. With his message to the Diet of Nuremberg in 1522, he regretted the mistakes and sins of the authorities of the Catholic Church. As his successors, the Popes during and after the Second Vatican Council have again and again asked for forgiveness for what Catholics perpetrated against the members of other churches. Here we think of Pope Paul VI, who in his opening address at the beginning of the second session of the Second Vatican Council expressed a plea for forgiveness for all offenses that have occurred through the Roman Catholic Church;[49] of Pope John Paul II, who during the celebration of the Holy Year 2000 on the "Day of Pardon" confessed great historical guilt;[50] and Pope Francis, who on his visit to the Waldensian Church in Turin asked for "forgiveness for unchristian-like and even inhuman attitudes and conduct which, historically, we have had against you."[51]

On the Lutheran side we recall above all the declaration of the Lutheran World Federation at its Fifth General Assembly in Evian in 1970 which declared its readiness to see "how the judgement of the Reformers on the Roman Catholic Church and the theology of the time was not free from polemical distortions which in part remain in effect to this day," and therefore sincerely regretted

---

49. *Acta Synodalia Sacrosancti Concilii Oecumenici Vaticani II* (Vatican City: Typis polyglottis Vaticanis, 1970), II-1, 194.

50. John Paul II, Homily during the Holy Mass on the Day of Pardon in the Holy Year 2000 on 12 March 2000; http://www.vatican.va/content/john-paul-ii/en/homilies/2000/documents/hf_jp-ii_hom_20000312_pardon.html.

51. Francis, Address at the Waldensian Temple on 22 June 2015; http://w2.vatican.va/content/francesco/en/speeches/2015/june/documents/papa-francesco_20150622_torino-chiesa-valdese.html.

"that our Roman Catholic brothers have been offended and misunderstood by such polemical representations."[52]

3. Renewal of the Church and Restoration of Unity

Such a joint public act of repentance must today, too, form a significant component of an honest joint Reformation commemoration, and it must be accompanied by the purification of historical memory, as Pope Francis has admonished: "We cannot erase what is past, nor do we wish to allow the weight of past transgressions to continue to pollute our relationships. The mercy of God will renew our relationships."[53] It follows that mercy and reconciliation must be an important guiding perspective on the ecumenical course of the future, to which we will turn our attention in conclusion.

a) Distinction and Connection between Reform and Reformation

As a result of our reflections thus far, we must distinguish between the reform of the Church in the sense of her always necessary renewal, and the Reformation in the sense of the ultimately shattered unity of the Church; but at the same time, the two must be seen in connection with one another. History documents the fact that the concept and the reality of reform have a home within the Catholic Church, too, which understands itself as an *Ecclesia semper reformanda,* and, consequently, the Reformation does not represent the only response to the necessity for reform in the Catholic Church. Since reform therefore demonstrates a greater radius than Reformation, the question arises even more pertinently of precisely how the constantly necessary reform of the Church and the historical process of the Reformation relate to one another. The historical fact that Martin Luther's reforming work led to the Reformation and subsequently to church schism and the development of new ecclesial communities prompts us to name the difference between reform and Reformation.

This difference can be defined with the church historian Cardinal Walter Brandmüller, that reform "can never have the result that that which has been reformed is no longer identical with that which was previously to be reformed."[54] Reform involves the concrete appearance and realization but not

---

52. LaVern K. Grosc, ed., *Sent Into the World: The Proceedings of the Fifth Assembly of the Lutheran World Federation, Evian, France, July 14–24, 1970* (Minneapolis: Augsburg, 1971), 156.

53. Francis, Homily at the Vespers for the Feast of the Conversion of St. Paul held in the Basilica of St. Paul Outside the Walls on 25 January 2016; http://w2.vatican.va/content/francesco/en/homilies/2016/documents/papa-francesco_20160125_vespri-conversione-san-paolo.html.

54. Walter Brandmüller, "Die Reformation Martin Luthers in katholischer Sicht," in: *Licht und Schatten. Kirchengeschichte zwischen Glaube, Fakten und Legenden* (Augsburg: Sankt Ulrich, 2007), 108.

the essence of that which is to be reformed. Otherwise, it would not represent a reform but a transformation of essence, which would make that which is to be reformed into something else with respect to what was before. The word "reform," however, indicates that the Church in the original sense has by means of historical developments lost its form and reveals a deformation, and must be restored to its original and authentic form. True reform of the Church has to be "re–form" in its original meaning, that is, restoration and restitution of the true form of the one Church, or with the apt formula of the Catholic biblical theologian Thomas Söding, "restoration of the original, the essential and authentic—or at least the earnest endeavour to that end."[55] In the light of this definition arises the fundamental question from the perspective of ecumenism: whether the 16th century Reformation understood itself as a reform of the Church, or whether it did not in a much more radical sense lead to a transformation of the essence.

In order to approach an answer to this question, it seems appropriate to call to mind the undoubtedly most radical reformer in the history of the Church, namely Saint Francis of Assisi. Historical memory of him brings to light that it was not the mighty Pope Innocent III who, in those troubled times, preserved the Church from collapse and renewed it, but the humble and insignificant monk; but also brought to light is the fact that Francis of Assisi reformed the Church not in any way that induced schism, and without or against the Pope, but only in communion with him. Saint Francis of Assisi is the successful example of a radical church reform in unity with the whole Church and with the ecclesial hierarchy, and he shows that "reform" is a positive word also in the Catholic Church, but that the Catholic principle of a permanent need for reform seeks to avoid any breach with the ecclesial community and the Pope as guarantee of unity. By contrast, the church reforms of the Reformers all led to schism, which, in addition, continued to lead to further divisions and fragmentations within Protestantism,—indeed, already in Luther's lifetime. It seems therefore that church reform and maintaining unity represented an insurmountable contradiction in the Reformation of the 16th century.

b) Church Reform and the Endeavor for Unity

A significant counter–testimony is provided by the Diet of Augsburg in 1530 and the Augsburg Confession prepared for this important event, with which the reformers wanted to testify that they stood in agreement with the faith of the Catholic Church. The Confessio Augustana is essentially due to the

---

55. Thomas Söding, *Umkehr der Kirche. Wegweiser im Neuen Testament* (Freiburg i. Br.: Herder, 2014).

tireless efforts of the great reformer Philipp Melanchthon[56] who, even in the moment when he perceived that his efforts at the Diet of Augsburg were failing and that unity could no longer be maintained, held fast to the unity of the Church right up to the limits of what was possible, in the conviction that the renewal of the Church and maintaining its unity were indissolubly linked. Melanchthon proved to be "the great ecumenist of his age," who—under the existing historical conditions—sought to "plumb the ultimate possibilities for maintaining the unity of the Church."[57] The Augsburg Confession drafted by him is not a document of schism, but of the determined intent for reconciliation and maintaining unity, as the Joint Roman Catholic–Evangelical Lutheran Commission claimed in its statement on the Augsburg Confession on the occasion of the 450th anniversary of its publication in 1980: "The express purpose of the Augsburg Confession is to confess the faith of the one, holy, catholic, and apostolic Church. Its concern is not with peculiar doctrines nor indeed with the establishment of a new Church (CA 7,1), but with the preservation and renewal of the Christian faith in its purity—in harmony with the Ancient Church, and 'the Church of Rome,' and in agreement with the witness of Holy Scripture."[58]

If one takes the self–understanding of the Confessio Augustana seriously, one must—with the Protestant ecumenist Wolfhart Pannenberg—consider the historical fact that Martin Luther's reform concerns could not be fulfilled at that time, but instead gave rise to separate evangelical churches which split from the Catholic Church, not as the "success" of the Reformation but its "failure" or at least an emergency measure.[59] The real success of the Reformation will by contrast only be fulfilled when the inherited divisions between Christians are overcome, in the restoration of the unity of the renewed Church in the spirit of the Gospel. To that extent, the ecumenical search for the restoration of Christian unity signifies the—even though terribly belated—fulfillment of the Reformation itself.

This envisaged goal was not achieved at the Diet of Augsburg with the Confessio Augustana. It is, as Pope John Paul II emphasized in his address on the occasion of the 450th anniversary of the Confessio Augustana, the "last

56. Cf. Günter Frank, ed., *Der Theologe Melanchthon* (Stuttgart: frommann-holzboog, 2000); Jörg Haustein, ed., *Philipp Melanchthon. Ein Wegbereiter für die Ökumene* (Göttingen: Vandenhoeck & Ruprecht, 1997); Stefan Rein and Johannes Weiss, eds., *Melanchthon—neu entdeckt* (Stuttgart: Quell, 1997).

57. Wolfgang Thönissen, *Gerechtigkeit oder Barmherzigkeit?*, 138.

58. Lutheran-Roman Catholic International Commission, "All Under One Christ," in: *Growth in Agreement: Reports and Agreed Statements of Ecumenical Conversations on a World Level*, ed. Harding Meyer and Lukas Vischer (New York: Paulist Press, 1984), paragraph 10.

59. Wolfhart Pannenberg, "The Reformation and the Unity of the Church," in: *The Church*, trans. Keith Crim (Philadelphia: Westminster, 1983), 85.

powerful attempt at reconciliation," which by its failure brought about the visible schism.[60] For John Paul II, however, the Confessio Augustana is explicit testimony to the fact that the constant renewal of the Church in the power of the Gospel and the preservation—or where necessary, restoration—of its unity are indissolubly intertwined.

This constituted the fundamental concern, too, of the Second Vatican Council, for there were above all two main concerns that moved Saint Pope John XXIII to convene the Council—namely, the renewal of the Catholic Church and the restoration of Christian unity. The same fundamental conviction also motivated Pope Paul VI, for whom the ecumenical question was also, and indeed especially, a leitmotif of the renewal of the Catholic Church, so that one must speak of the essential reciprocity between the ecumenical opening of the Catholic Church and the renewal of its ecclesiology.[61] This reciprocity forms also the foundation for the way the Second Vatican Council identified the ecumenical movement as a conversion movement and viewed conversion as the elixir of life of true ecumenism:[62] "There can be no ecumenism worthy of the name without a change of heart. For it is from newness of attitudes, from self-denial and unstinted love that yearnings for unity take their rise and grow towards maturity."[63]

In this light, the Confessio Augustana represents in retrospect the determined effort of the Wittenberg Reformation to renew the Church and thereby to rescue its endangered unity. This confession can therefore not be underestimated in its ecumenical significance,[64] as the Ecumenical Working Group of

---

60. John Paul II, Address on the occasion of the 450th anniversary of the Confessio Augustana, 25 June 1980. http://www.vatican.va/content/john-paul-ii/de/speeches/1980/june/documents/hf_jp-ii_spe_19800625_confessio-augustana.html.

61. Cf. Hermann J. Pottmeyer, "Die Öffnung der römisch-katholischen Kirche und die ekklesiologische Reform des 2. Vaticanums. Ein wechselseitiger Einfluss," in: *Paolo VI e l'Ecumenismo. Colloquio Internazionale di Studio Brescia 1998* (Brescia: Instituto Paolo VI, 2001), 98–117.

62. Cf. Kurt Koch, "Innere Reform und Umkehr als Voraussetzung von Ökumene," in: *Blick zurück nach vorn. Das Zweite Vaticanum aus der Perspektive der multilateralen Ökumene*, eds. Elisabeth Dieckmann and Karl Lehmann (Würzburg: Echter, 2016), 161–186.

63. Unitatis redintegratio, 7.

64. Cf. George W. Forell and James F. McCue, eds., *Confessing One Faith: A Joint Commentary on the Augsburg Confession by Lutheran and Catholic Theologians* (Minneapolis: Augsburg Pub. House, 1982); Heinrich Fries et al., *Confessio Augustana. Hindernis oder Hilfe?* (Regensburg: Pustet, 1979); Bernhard Lohse and Otto Hermann Pesch, eds., *Das Augsburger Bekenntnis von 1530 damals und heute* (Munich: Kaiser, 1980); Harding Meyer, Heinz Schütte and Hans–Jocachim Mund, eds., *Katholische Anerkennung des Augsburgischen Bekenntnisses. Ein Vorstoss zur Einheit zwischen katholischer und lutherischer Kirche* (Frankfurt a. M.: Lembck, 1977). Cf. also Kurt Koch, "Die Confessio Augustana—Ein katholisches Bekenntnis?" in: *Gelähmte Ökumene. Was jetzt noch zu tun ist* (Freiburg i. Br.: Herder, 1991), 65–106.

Lutheran and Catholic Theologians rightly judges: "It is possible that the churches of Western Christendom were indeed at the Diet of Augsburg in 1530 as close to one another as they have ever been since."[65] On that basis, it would be appropriate to celebrate in 2030 the 500th anniversary of the Diet of Augsburg and the Confessio Augustana proclaimed there in at least as intensive ecumenical community as the Reformation commemoration in 2017.

4. ON THE WAY TO BINDING ECCLESIAL COMMUNITY

There is an additional reason for the Confessio Augustana retaining its prime significance: for ecumenical dialogues that are to prepare ecclesial decisions, it is ultimately not sufficient for the position of one individual theologian—even if that theologian is the great Reformer Martin Luther—to serve as their foundation; that must instead be perceived in the ecclesial confessional writings. In the same way, for binding statements of ecumenical consensus, documents by ecumenical commissions do not suffice, no matter how deserving they may be. Only those texts can lead us forward into the future that have actually been received by their respective churches and authoritatively accepted by their leaders. Therein we can and must see the particular significance of the *Joint Declaration on the Doctrine of Justification*, which was agreed between the Lutheran World Federation and the Pontifical Council for Promoting Christian Unity on 31 October 1999 in Augsburg, which represents a milestone in the ecumenical encounter between the Catholic Church and Lutheranism.[66] With this document, a wide–ranging consensus was reached on what was surely the most central question leading to the Reformation and the subsequent schism in the 16th century.

The formula "consensus in fundamental truths of the doctrine of justification" used in the Joint Declaration, of course, expresses the fact that unity was nevertheless not achieved thereby, since no full consensus has yet been reached above all on the consequences of this doctrine for the understanding of the Church and the question of ministry.[67] Since the still-remaining questions con-

65. Volker Leppin and Dorothea Sattler, eds., *Reformation 1517–2017: Ökumenische Perspektiven* (Göttingen: Vandenhoeck & Ruprecht, 2014), 67, 107.

66. The Lutheran World Federation and The Roman Catholic Church, *Joint Declaration on the Doctrine of Justification* (Grand Rapids, MI: Eerdmans, 2000). Cf. also Lutheran World Federation and the Pontifical Council for Promoting Christian Unity, eds., *10 Jahre Gemeinsame Erklärung zur Rechtfertigungslehre* (Paderborn: Bonifatius, 2011); *The Biblical Foundations of the Doctrine of Justification: An Ecumenical Follow-Up to the Joint Declaration on the Doctrine of Justification* (New York: Paulist Press, 2012).

67. Cf. Bernd Jochen Hilberath and Wolfhart Pannenberg, eds., *Zur Zukunft der Ökumene. Die „Gemeinsame Erklärung zur Rechtfertigungslehre"* (Regensburg: Pustet, 1999); Ernst Pulsfort and Rolf Hanusch, eds., *Von der „Gemeinsamen Erklärung" zum „Gemeinsamen Herrenmahl"? Perspektiven der Ökumene im 21. Jahrhundert* (Regensburg: Pustet, 2002).

verge on the precise understanding of what the Church is, the ecclesiological implications of the consensus that has been reached must be placed on the agenda of ecumenical conversations. Work on this question will form a further important step on the path towards ecumenical agreement between Lutherans and Catholics, which could ultimately result in the drafting of a future Joint Declaration, analogous to the Joint Declaration on the Doctrine of Justification, on Church, Eucharist and Ministry.[68] I note with gratitude that the national dialogue in Finland is dealing with this subject, and the Lutheran–Catholic dialogue in the USA has drafted a *Declaration on the Way: Church, Ministry, and Eucharist* has already been drafted on this issue.[69] Such a joint declaration would undoubtedly be a decisive step towards visible church communion, which is the goal of all ecumenical endeavors, and to raise awareness of this goal is an important task of the common commemoration of the Reformation.

It is indeed no coincidence that my reflections have merged into the question of the essential nature of the Church, for this question was also the crux of the 16th century Reformation. Deepening the discussion on this ecumenically urgent issue must be an obligation of the Reformation commemoration. To celebrate it and then to simply accept the status quo, or even abandon the goal of unity entirely and rest content with the existing plurality of churches, would not do justice either to the intentions of the Reformers or the expectations of the Reformation commemoration. After 500 years of division, of prolonged opposition and juxtaposition, we must strive for a binding communion and put it into effect already today. In this common endeavor, Catholics will affirm what the Reformation means to them and what they can learn from it, and Protestant Christians will testify to what they can learn from the Catholic Church today and what enrichment they can receive from it.

A common Reformation commemoration will only represent an ecumenical opportunity if the year 2017 is not the conclusion but a new beginning in the ecumenical struggle for full communion between Lutherans and Catholics, celebrated in the triad chord of gratitude, repentance, and hope—from which no component can be omitted if the Reformation commemoration is to be perceived as a symphony.

---

68. Cf. Kurt Koch, "Auf dem Weg zur Kirchengemeinschaft. Welche Chance hat eine gemeinsame Erklärung zu Kirche, Eucharistie und Amt?" *Catholica* 69 (2015): 77–94.

69. *Declaration on the Way: Church, Ministry, and Eucharist* (Minneapolis: Augsburg Fortress, 2015).

1a. Towards a Common Understanding on Eucharist, Church and Ministry:
Response to Cardinal Kurt Koch

Eero Huovinen

The *Joint Declaration on the Doctrine of Justification*[1] states in paragraph 43 that there are still questions of varying importance which need further clarification between the churches. Among other topics, the Declaration mentions, for example, ecclesiology, ecclesial authority, church unity, ministry, and the sacraments.

Much was achieved on these topics prior to the JDDJ and during fifty years of dialogues. In the last years, some eminent ecumenists have proposed that there is a need to proceed towards a common or joint Declaration on Church, Eucharist and Ministry. I have in my mind suggestions from Harding Meyer, Walter Kasper and, last but not least, our dear Cardinal Kurt Koch.

DECLARATION ON THE WAY

In the United States, Catholics and Lutherans prepared a new ecumenical document, *Declaration on the Way (DOW)*, which sought to express the consensus achieved on the topics of church, ministry, and the Eucharist as the result of the ecumenical dialogues between the two communions since 1965.[2]

I am not sufficiently competent to judge what kind of methodological character this document has. On the one hand, it speaks about a consensus; on the other hand, the consensus is "on the way" (*in via*), because the dialogue has not yet resolved all the differences dividing the churches on these topics. In the United States, William G. Rusch has raised important questions concerning the status of the document in the journal *Ecumenical Trends*.[3]

---

1. The Lutheran World Federation and The Roman Catholic Church, *Joint Declaration on the Doctrine of Justification* (Grand Rapids, MI: Eerdmans, 2000).

2. *Declaration on the Way: Church, Ministry, and Eucharist* (Minneapolis: Augsburg Fortress, 2015).

3. William G. Rusch, "*Declaration On The Way: Church, Ministry, and Eucharist*: Quo Vadis?" *Ecumenical Trends* 45 (2016): 65–69.

Nevertheless, the document seeks to enumerate the many points of agreement which have been achieved. The writers of the document hope that both communities, Lutheran and Catholic, could affirm the agreements they have reached together, although in what manner seems to me a little bit unclear.

In order to look forward to a growing and deeper communion between Lutherans and Catholics, I would like to emphasize the agreements we have already reached, while taking up some questions on which we still have work to carry out together. We are still '*in via*,' but a fundamental consensus is not far away. My intention is—with help of the *DOW*—to ask how we can proceed together "Towards a common understanding on Eucharist, Church, and Ministry."

TRINITARIAN AND CHRISTOLOGICAL BASIS FOR COMMON UNDERSTANDING

Before speaking about the three main topics, I would like to express my satisfaction with the clear Trinitarian and Christological basis of the *DOW*. Already the first agreement assures us that we, as members of church, are God's own people, assembled by the Triune God, who grants us a share in the Triune divine life. We are the body of the risen Christ and the temple of the Holy Spirit (*DOW*, p. 9).

The Trinitarian and Christological emphasis is present also when the document speaks about the ordained ministry. This ministry is "of divine origin" and "instituted by Jesus Christ." At the same time, the ministry is "subordinated to Christ, who in the Holy Spirit is acting in the preaching of the Word of God, in the administration of the sacraments and in pastoral service" (*DOW*, p. 11).

The agreements on the Eucharist are also structured in a Trinitarian and Christological way. The section begins by saying: "Lutherans and Catholics agree in esteeming highly the spiritual benefits of union with the risen Christ given to them as they receive his body and blood in Holy Communion. . . . In Eucharistic worship the church participates in a unique way in the life of the Trinity" (*DOW*, p. 14).

In its strong Trinitarian and Christological emphasis, the *DOW* is along the same lines as the *Joint Declaration on the Doctrine of Justification*. I would like to point to the central paragraph in JDDJ, number 15:

> In faith we together hold the conviction that justification is the work of the triune God. The Father sent his Son into the world to save sinners. The foundation and presupposition of justification is the incarnation, death, and resurrection of Christ. Justification thus means that Christ himself is our righteousness, in which we share through the Holy Spirit in accord with the will of the Father. Together we confess: By grace alone, in faith in Christ's saving work and not because of any merit on our part, we are accepted by

God and receive the Holy Spirit, who renews our hearts while equipping and calling us to good works.

I am convinced that all ecumenical attempts to create a deeper common understanding between the churches on the topics of ecclesiology depend on a sound and solid basis in the Trinitarian and Christological character of our faith. If the foundation is firm, it is easier to build the house.

Agreements and Differences on the Church

First, I have some thoughts about the agreements and differences on the Church. The *DOW* says many spiritually deep things about the theological character of the church. Ecumenically, perhaps the most important agreement is: "Lutherans and Catholics recognize in both their ecclesial communities the attribute of apostolicity grounded in their ongoing continuity in apostolic faith, teaching, and practices" (*DOW*, p. 10).

Later this recognition is broadened: "Catholics and Lutherans affirm the ecclesial character of one another's communities. This affirmation is an essential first step toward a mutual recognition of ordained ministry, for mutual recognition of one another's ecclesial character is intertwined with the mutual recognition of one another's ministry" (*DOW*, p. 11).

The *DOW* refers to the Study Document of the Lutheran-Roman Catholic Commission on Unity, *The Apostolicity of the Church* (2006). "The Catholic Church and the churches and ecclesial communities of the Reformation both participate in the attribute of apostolicity because they are built up and live by many of the same 'elements and endowments' pertaining to the one and multiple apostolic tradition."[4]

If I understand correctly, the arguments of the *DOW* are stated in the terminology of the Second Vatican Council, which in a positive manner speaks about the shared "elements of sanctification and truth" in ecclesial communities outside the Catholic Church.

Yet, the *DOW* prefers to use the wording "ecclesial communities" about the churches of the Reformation. The text of the *DOW* is diplomatic or a little bit vague. Sometimes it speaks about both churches as "ecclesial communities," sometimes it speaks about "The Catholic Church," sometimes about "the churches and ecclesial communities of the Reformation."

We all are aware that behind this terminological flexibility is what is for Catholics a difficult question—whether the churches of the Reformation can

---

4. Lutheran-Roman Catholic Commission on Unity, *The Apostolicity of the Church: Study Document of the Lutheran-Roman Catholic Commission on Unity* (Minneapolis: Lutheran University Press, 2006), para. 121.

be honored with the word "church." We surely remember the complicated and highly sophisticated discussions on what it means that the Church of Christ *"subsistit"* in the Roman Catholic Church and that the churches of Reformation are not churches "in the proper sense."

I have a certain understanding of the Catholic opinion about the possible theological defects in Lutheran ecclesiology and for the desire for a deeper awareness of the theological character of ecclesiology in the churches of the Reformation. But at the same time, I ask whether the Catholic wording of church "in the proper sense" may be unfruitful, and also an obstacle in the relations between the churches.

I can imagine that my Catholic colleagues would not be very happy if I were to say that the Catholic Church is not a church "in the proper sense," namely in the Lutheran sense. If Catholics say that we Lutherans have too few elements of the church in our churches, we Lutherans can ask whether the Catholic Church has too many elements of the church.

I can also imagine that behind the Catholic terminology there is a long tradition and many important arguments, and I really do not want to undermine them. But instead of using the word "church" only in two opposite meanings, only in on- or off-positions, it perhaps might be more fruitful to ask whether we could approach the question from a more nuanced perspective. Perhaps we could ask to what degree those things which belong to the essence of the church are present in our churches.

So, I do hope that you allow me the question of whether, with a slight terminological change, we could create a more open and positive atmosphere between the churches. If we follow the agreements of the *DOW* and if we take seriously the "mutual recognition of one another's ecclesial character," could it not be implemented also in the way in which we speak about our sisters and brothers?

AGREEMENTS AND DIFFERENCES ON THE EUCHARIST

Secondly, I want to bring in some thoughts about the agreements and differences on the Eucharist. On the character of the Eucharist, Lutherans and Catholics have found much in common within the last decades. Particularly, we have reached a fundamental consensus on two old controversial topics: on the understanding of the real presence of Christ in the Eucharist and on the sacrificial character of the Eucharist.

The *DOW* describes the presence of Christ in the Eucharist as follows: "Lutherans and Catholics agree that in the sacrament of the Lord's Supper, Jesus Christ himself is present: He is present truly, substantially, as a person, and he is present in his entirety, as Son of God and a human being" (*DOW*, p. 15).

These words describing the presence of Christ are close to those of the Encyclical of John Paul II, *Ecclesia de Eucharistia*, in which the Holy Father says that the presence "is a presence in the fullest sense: a substantial presence whereby Christ, the God-Man, is wholly and entirely present."[5]

The sacrificial character of the Eucharist is also described in the *DOW* in a good spirit of mutual understanding: "Catholics and Lutherans agree that Eucharistic worship is the memorial (*anamnesis*) of Jesus Christ, present as the one crucified for us and risen, that is, in his sacrificial self-giving for us in his death and in his resurrection (Romans 4:25), to which the church responds with its sacrifice of praise and thanksgiving" (*DOW*, p. 15).

In a well-balanced manner, the *DOW* looks at the old controversial issue of whether or not the Eucharist can in some way be seen as a sacrifice. "The traditional contrast is between the Catholic emphasis on the movement *ad Patrem* (to the Father) and the Lutheran emphasis on the movement *ad populum* (to the people)" (*DOW*, p. 62).

The sacrificial interpretation of the Eucharist offended Martin Luther and it was to him "the greatest and most terrible abomination" (*Smalcald Articles*).[6] For him the uniqueness of Christ's sacrifice on the cross was a once-and-for-all event which cannot be repeated.

In the late Middle Ages, Luther was faced with interpretations in which the Eucharist was not only a memory and representation of Christ's unique sacrifice but in which the priest was seen as the primary subject of the sacrifice: the priest was sacrificing Christ to the Father also for the benefit of the absent. The most difficult obstacle for Luther was the teaching that the fruits of the sacrifice of the Eucharist were to benefit also absent parishioners and those in purgatory.

The *DOW* attempts—by quoting the Swedish-Finnish Lutheran-Catholic dialogue statement from 2010[7]—to explain what was at stake during the Reformation. When Luther and the Reformers criticized the medieval teaching about the Sacrifice of the Eucharist, "they were afraid . . . that the view of the sacrament as God's free gift would be dissolved and the Mass would be perceived as a human work, performed in order to satisfy God" (*DOW*, pp. 64–65). Simply put, Luther was afraid that the doctrine of the sacrifice of the Mass would distort the doctrine of justification.

---

5. John Paul II, "Ecclesia de eucharistia" (2003), para. 15, Http://w2.vatican.va/content/john-paul-ii/en/encyclicals/documents/hf_jp-ii_enc_20030417_eccl-de-euch.html.

6. Part II, Art. 2, para. 1. In Robert Kolb and Timothy J. Wengert, eds., *The Book of Concord: The Confessions of the Evangelical Lutheran Church* (Minneapolis: Fortress Press, 2000), 301.

7. Roman Catholic-Lutheran Dialogue Group for Sweden and Finland, *Justification in the Life of the Church* (Uppsala: Church of Sweden, 2010), paras. 222–31.

During the last 50 to 60 years, in the dialogues between the churches it has become possible to overcome the old controversy and break the deadlock between the churches. The term 'sacrifice' has now been interpreted in a more diverse and versatile way. Today, both churches agree on two aspects.

We Lutherans can rejoice over the convergence when we read: "According to the Catholic doctrine the sacrifice of the Mass is the making present of the sacrifice of the cross. It is not a repetition of this sacrifice and adds nothing to its saving significance. When thus understood, the sacrifice of the mass is an affirmation and not a questioning of the uniqueness and full value of Christ's sacrifice on the cross" (*DOW*, pp. 112–13).

Catholics can rejoice over the common agreement with Lutherans: "Our two traditions agree in understanding the Eucharist as a *sacrifice of praise*. This is neither simple verbal praise of God, nor is it a supplement or a complement which the people from their own power add to the offering of praise and thanksgiving which Christ has made to the Father. The Eucharistic sacrifice of praise has only become possible through the sacrifice of Christ on the cross: therefore this remains the main content of the church's sacrifice of praise" (*DOW*, pp. 63–64).

★ ★ ★ ★ ★

Although there is this joyful agreement on the sacrificial character of the Eucharist, the *DOW* points to some different emphases between the churches. The first question on the remaining differences is "the Eucharist as sacrifice." On this topic the *DOW* mentions hesitations on the Lutheran side. "Some Lutherans continue to regard the language of 'sacrifice' found in Catholic theology and the Catholic Eucharistic rite to be a potential stumbling block to unity" (*DOW*, p. 111).

The *DOW* is aware that *lex credendi* is always related to *lex orandi*. What we theologians can agree on, that should also be incorporated into the liturgical life. I know well that when speaking about worship life, I am treading upon holy ground. I will try to be careful and tentative.

The *DOW* mentions one example from the Roman Missal, where the priest says: "Pray, brothers and sisters, that my sacrifice and yours may be acceptable to God, the almighty Father." The people respond: "May the Lord accept the sacrifice of your hands for the praise and glory of his name, for our good and the good of his holy church" (*DOW*, p. 111).

The *DOW* also refers to the General Instruction of the Roman Missal, where it is stated that the people of God may both "give thanks to God" and "offer the unblemished sacrificial Victim not only by means of the hands of the Priest but also together with him and so that they may learn to offer their very selves" (*DOW*, p. 111).

★ ★ ★ ★ ★

Six weeks ago, during the Easter Vigil Service, I had the opportunity to participate in the Paschal Mass in St. Peter's in Rome, celebrated by the Bishop of Rome. It was really an impressive and positive experience. The joy of the resurrection of our Lord Jesus was present.

In the beginning of the offertory prayer, the Holy Father said the classical words of the Roman Missal, the same words mentioned also in the *DOW*: "Pray, brethren, that my sacrifice and yours may be acceptable to God, the almighty Father" (*Orate, fratres, ut meum ac vestrum sacrificium acceptabile fiat apud Deum Patrem omnipotentem*).

★ ★ ★ ★ ★

On the one hand, it seems that the Missal speaks about the sacrifice of praise and love; on the other hand, the offering by the faithful touches also the unblemished sacrificial Victim.

Naturally, I am well aware that the Roman Canon Prayer or *canon missae* is a traditional and important part of the Roman Catholic rite. Today the Roman Missal also includes at least three other Eucharistic Prayers. Thus, I would like to raise these questions: What does the *canon missae* mean when it refers to the "sacrifice" in different parts and with different words in the text, also after the words of Institution? Who is offering, what is offered, to whom is it offered, and whom does it benefit? Can we read the text of the *canon missae*—or other Eucharistic Prayers—in a manner that does not call into question the uniqueness of the sacrifice of the Christ on the cross?

These questions are not easy, because the prayers of the liturgy are always open to different interpretations, and the Roman Canon uses different expressions, such as *hostia, sacrificium,* and *oblatum*.

If the text means that, in the Eucharist, the priest is sacrificing Christ to the Father for the benefit of the dead, then that is problematic, not only for Lutherans but also for the other ecumenical partners of the Catholic Church. If, however, the text means that we are celebrating the Eucharist, in which we, together as priest and congregation, remember Christ's unique sacrifice with joy (*memoria*), worship the real presence of this sacrifice in the consecrated bread and wine (*repraesentatio*) with adoration, and distribute the fruits of this sacrifice to the people (*applicatio*), then the *canon missae* is not an ecumenical obstacle.

Today many Lutheran Churches, for example the Evangelical Lutheran Church of America and the Evangelical-Lutheran Church of Finland, have restored and rehabilitated the classical Eucharistic Prayers in their rites. However, the pattern of the modern prayers follows more closely the Eastern or Byzantine rites than the pattern of the *canon missae*: The Prayers place emphasis on the salvific actions of the Triune God by telling the same story as the Nicene Creed:

From the Father to the Son in the Holy Spirit. This pattern is also used in the fourth Eucharistic Prayer of the Roman Missal. The "theocentric" emphasis of the Eastern rites seems to fit better with the Lutheran understanding of the doctrine of justification.

★ ★ ★ ★ ★

I hope the *DOW* is aware of these difficulties when it states: "Thus we encourage increased attention to the instruction and formation of clergy, as well increased catechesis of the laity, regarding the teachings of their own traditions, and greater knowledge and sympathetic understanding of one another's traditions" (*DOW*, p. 113).

Such instruction is needed, at least on the Lutheran side. I have a lot of sympathetic understanding for my Catholic sisters and brothers when they ask me whether we Lutherans really take seriously in our worship life the real presence of the body and blood of Jesus Christ in the bread and wine of the Lord's Supper.

AGREEMENTS AND DIFFERENCES ON THE MINISTRY

Thirdly, let me introduce some thoughts about the agreements and differences on the Ministry. It has often been said that the topic of the Ministry is the greatest hindrance to the visible unity between the churches. That is why we can rejoice when the *DOW* so clearly says: "Lutherans and Catholics affirm together that ordained ministry is of divine origin and that it is necessary for the being of the church" (*DOW*, p. 12).

The *DOW* seems to address especially Lutherans when it states: "Ministry is not simply a delegation 'from below,' but is instituted by Jesus Christ" (*DOW*, p. 12). It further states, "Catholics and Lutherans agree that entry into this apostolic and God-given ministry is not by baptism but by ordination. They agree that ministers cannot ordain themselves or claim this office as a matter of right but are called by God and designated in and through the churches" (*DOW*, p. 13).

★ ★ ★ ★ ★

In our Lutheran tradition, there has been much discussion and many different interpretations about the character of the ministry, about the *Predigtamt*, about *ministerium ecclesiasticum*. I am not going into the details of these disputes. I only want to point to a newly published, profound, and highly learned book about Martin Luther's understanding of the ministry, Jonathan Mumme's *Die Präsenz Christi im Amt*.[8]

---

8. Jonathan Mumme, *Die Präsenz Christi im Amt: Am Beispiel ausgewählter Predigten Martin Luthers, 1535–1546* (Göttingen: Vandenhoeck & Ruprecht, 2015).

Mumme, who is a professor of theology in the United States, analyzes carefully and critically the different theories about the origin of ministry, especially in the twentieth century. The debate surrounding Luther's understanding of ministry has gone in two different directions.

On the one hand, there is a Protestant interpretation of the Christian faith, in which an immediacy to God exists as an *a priori* fact, leading to a functionalist and pragmatic view of the ministry. Influenced by Friedrich Schleiermacher and some other theologians from the nineteenth century (Johann W. F. Höfling, Albrecht Ritschl, later also Harald Goertz[9]), this line sees the ministry only as a matter of good order or, in the spirit of a theory, of the delegation of functions by the believers (*Übertragungstheorie*).

On the other hand—and this is what Jonathan Mumme is arguing in a convincing way—the ministry is, according to Martin Luther, something more. On the basis of his research on the sermons of the mature Luther after 1529, Mumme states:

> If Christ is understood as one who continually comes to people, speaking to and dealing with them through external, physical, and institutional entities that are in accord with his own incarnation, this results in a different understanding of the ecclesial office. In this case it is appropriate to speak of the presence of Christ in the office of the ministry and in those who bear this office—to speak of their theophoric instrumentality, and of ordination as something carried out by Christ himself.[10]

In a very interesting way, Mumme reminds us in his book that this interpretation of Luther has similarities with the results of recent ecumenical dialogues. He hopes that this view of Luther could "be of some use in ecumenical discussion between the Roman Catholic Church and the Lutheran churches." Mumme points to the Constitution on the Sacred Liturgy of the Second Vatican Council, *Sacrosanctum Concilium,* where the presence of Christ in the spiritual life of the church has a central and strong role.

According to the Council, "Christ is always present in His Church."[11] Important for the topic on ministry is that Christ is present also "in the person of His minister" (*in ministri persona*).[12] Mumme argues that "perhaps this facet of *Sacrosanctum Concilium,* which coincides with the central motif of the later

---

9. Harald Goertz, *Allgemeines Priestertum und ordiniertes Amt bei Luther,* Marburger Theologische Studien (Marburg: N. G. Elwert Verlag, 1997).

10. Jonathan Mumme, "The Presence of Jesus Christ in the Office of the Ministry: Rethinking Luther from his Pulpit out." *Pro Ecclesia,* 29.3 (2020), 352–380.

11. *Sacrosanctum Concilium,* para. 7.

12. *Sacrosanctum Concilium,* para. 7.

Luther's homiletically communicated understanding of the ministry, might in some small way contribute to the healing of schism under which the church still labours."

Allow me to share in the intention of Jonathan Mumme.

2. Luther in the Focus of Roman Catholic Theology

Wolfgang Thönissen

Catholics began to concentrate on the life and work of Martin Luther at the end of the nineteenth century with new energy. This Catholic research became one of the driving forces of the international ecumenical movement. Initially confined to Germany and the German linguistic area, a specific methodological approach emerged in this sphere which determines the ecumenical methodology within the international Lutheran–Catholic dialogue. The methodology of a differentiating consensus, applied in the Lutheran-Catholic dialogue, paves the way for a common understanding of the Gospel of Jesus Christ regarding justification. It becomes obvious that neither the theology of Martin Luther nor the decrees of the Council of Trent are insurmountable obstacles for the dialogue. It is surprising to note that the results of this research did not remain restricted to theology and ecumenical dialogue, but become gradually appreciated in the teaching of the Catholic Church, and by the popes after the Second Vatican Council.

For centuries, Catholics considered Martin Luther a heretic and schismatic. At no time after the conflict of 1521 was he said to be a Catholic. Catholic theologians first began a careful approach to the person of Martin Luther at the end of the nineteenth century. Catholic research managed to free itself from the one-sided approach to the person and work of Martin Luther practiced for centuries. The emerging Catholic research on Luther during the twentieth century is the product of renewed interest in Reformation history on the part of Catholic theologians since the second half of the nineteenth century.[1] Two famous Roman Catholic theologians, Johann Adam Möhler with his work *Symbolik*

---

1. Cp. Hubert Jedin, *Die Erforschung der kirchlichen Reformationsgeschichte seit 1876,* (Münster: Aschendorff, 1931); Hubert Jedin, *Joseph Greving (1868–1919). Zur Erinnerung an die Begründung der "reformationsgeschichtlichen Studien und Texte" im Jahre 1905* (Münster: Aschendorff, 1954); Joseph Vercruysse, "Katholische Lutherforschung im 20. Jahrhundert," in: *Lutherforschung im 20. Jahrhundert. Rückblick—Bilanz—Ausblick,* ed. Rainer Vinke (Mainz: Philipp von Zabern, 2004), 191–212; Rolf Decot, "Katholische Lutherforschung," in: *Die Entdeckung der Ökumene,* eds. Jorg Ernesti and Wolfgang Thönissen (Paderborn: Bonifatius, 2008), 17–34; Peter Walter, *"Reformationsgeschichtliche Studien und Texte." Vergangenheit und Zukunft einer wissenschaftlichen Reihe* (Münster: Aschendorff, 2008); Theo Bell, "Roman Catholic Luther Research in the Twentieth Century: From Rejection to Rehabilitation," in: *Oxford Handbook of Martin Luther's Theology* (Oxford: Oxford University Press, 2014), 584–597; Wolfgang Thönissen, "Katholische Lutherforschung," in: *Das Luther-Lexikon,* eds. Volker Leppin and Gury Schneider-Ludorff (Regensburg: Bückle & Böhm, 2014), 338–341.

(1832) and Ignaz Franz Döllinger with *Die Reformation* (1846-48), sparked this interest. Both church historians paved the way for an objective examination (somewhere between polemics and irenicism) of the theological arguments of the Reformers. Interest in the history of the German people and nation became more relevant in the sphere of German Catholicism in the nineteenth century. After the collapse of the old Holy Roman Empire in 1806, this debate followed the desire of the Catholic population in the now Protestant-dominated German empire to release research into pre- and post-Reformation history from the burden of a one-sided anti-Roman historiography, by founding historical institutes and by taking up historical work. The person and work of Martin Luther was evaluated anew, due to the exceptional achievement of some Catholic theologians who shaped the research of the twentieth century on Luther by their initial studies.

1. Beginning with a Catholic Luther: An Independent Catholic Research

Prior to the relevant works of Catholic researchers, the Catholic theologian Joseph Greving (1868-1919) initiated an intra-Catholic dispute about the term "Reformation."[2] Contrary to the well-established views of Catholic colleagues, Greving turned away from the term "*Glaubensspaltung*" (a schism of faith). As the works of Heinrich Denifle[3] and Hartmann Grisar[4] contributed again to a distinctive characterization of Martin Luther, Greving expressed his regret that the conflict about confessional opposites intensified in this dispute. By standing up for the term "Reformation," Greving pursued a pre-ecumenical interest.

However, the breakthrough in Catholic research on Luther came through the works of Joseph Lortz. No other author shaped the Catholic view on Luther as did Lortz in his multiple-editions book *Die Reformation in Deutschland*.[5] He faced intra-Catholic opposition because he elaborated the thesis of a Catholic Luther. Catholicism, as Luther understood it, became the negative foil of the upcoming Reformation; the focus of opposition was a distorted, not-truly-Catholic Catholicism. The concentration on the person of Luther led to a consideration of him as an earnest religious person, a conscientious man of prayer. Luther was no politician and no jurist; what remains is Luther as a proclaimer and confessor of the Gospel. The late Peter Manns tried to understand Luther as a father in faith. Luther found formulations for the truth of the faith which

---

2. Walter, "Reformationsgeschichtliche Studien und Texte," 9-11 (note 1).
3. *Luther und Luthertum in der ersten Entwickelung*, 2 vols (Mainz: F. Kirchheim, 1904/1909).
4. *Luther*, 3 vols. (Freiburg i. Br.: Herder, 1911/12).
5. Freiburg i. Br.: Herder, 1939/40.

seemed to be unacceptable to the Church.[6] For the sake of the truth, Luther became a heretic. This concentration on the person of Luther had a further result: The more Luther comes into focus as an earnest and religious person, as a conscientious man of prayer, the more visible is the Reformer who has risked the unity of the Church. Does the unconventional Reformer Luther really disturb the unity of the Church? The recent Catholic research on Luther has good reasons to expect an ecumenical reception.

The German church historian Adolf Herte, to whom greater notoriety was denied, showed through a painstaking attention to detail in his historic work that the Catholic literature on Luther for four centuries—up until the modern age—was shaped by the comments of Johannes Cochläus, a contemporary opponent of Luther and counsellor of Duke George of Saxony. Cochläus characterized Luther as an apostate monk, the destroyer of the unity of the Church, a corruptor of morals, and a heretic.[7] These judgements are reflected in the 1520 papal bull of Leo X *Exsurge Domini* and the 1521 bull *Decet Romanum Pontificem,* threatening and then enacting Luther's excommunication. It is the achievement of a critical, yet favorable approach to the person of Luther in the early years of the Reformation that Catholic research on Luther has been freed from the spell of one-sided comments and biographies. Erwin Iserloh completed this approach with his historic analysis and proved that the division of the Church was not due to the Reformers' core concern, i.e., the doctrine of justification, but that it was caused by the resultant criticisms of Luther regarding the situation of the Church in his times.[8]

2. LUTHER AND THOMAS AQUINAS. TYPOLOGICAL-HERMENEUTICAL RESEARCH ON LUTHER

Since the sixties of the twentieth century, younger Catholic theologians argued about the basic orientation of Catholic research on Luther. As a result of his engagement with earlier Catholic research, Otto Hermann Pesch dissociated himself from the former biographical-psychological approach and pleaded for a theological-systematic approach. Unfolding the complementarity of different theologies, Pesch presented a careful comparison of the theological approaches of Thomas Aquinas and Martin Luther.[9] So this discussion, which is not to be viewed in historical perspective, confronted the different ways of thinking (exis-

---

6. *Vater im Glauben. Studien zur Theologie Martin Luthers* (Stuttgart: Franz Steiner, 1988).

7. *Das katholische Lutherbild im Bann der Lutherkommentare des Cochläus* (Münster: Aschendorff, 1943).

8. *Geschichte und Theologie der Reformation im Grundriß* (Paderborn: Verlag Bonifacius, 1980).

9. *Theologie der Rechtfertigung bei Martin Luther und Thomas von Aquin. Versuch eines systematisch-theologischen Dialogs* (Mainz: Matthias-Grünewald Verlag, 1967).

tential vs. sapiential) which initially remained concealed. This results in a research on Luther which could now take open-minded steps to approach the typological peculiarities of Luther´s theology.

This new historical, theological perspective—here applied for the first time—compares Luther's understanding of Catholicism with the not-truly-Catholic views of Ockham. The intent is not a comparison of epochs, but the juxtaposition of different confessional ways of thinking. Unlike Thomas Aquinas, the distinctive and specific shape of Luther´s theology becomes important in its new and original view of the Gospel. In this perspective, Luther appears as a "great theologian of Christianity."[10] Luther is our common teacher. Luther´s reforming theology is more existential and based on experience than traditional medieval theology could ever have expressed.

This typological-hermeneutical method of systematic theological research on Luther has another consequence. The Catholic church historian Vinzenz Pfnür widened the frame to include the question of the importance of the doctrine of justification of the Augsburg Confession (*Confessio Augustana* or CA). Facing the accusation that the concerns of the reformers were expressed without restrictions and impartiality, the CA should now be evaluated in the context of the development of the Lutheran confessions.[11] The question becomes how the reforming concern of Luther is located in the comprehensive perspective of Lutheran confessionalization. In addition, the methodologically important question must be taken up of how to assess the interrelation between the way an opponent's position has been understood and the perspective from which that position it is opposed. It is one of the most difficult tasks in the history of Reformation research to detect and to document as precisely as possible the standpoint from which the opponent's position is rejected. The result of this new hermeneutical method leads to far-reaching insights and consequences: Now, apart from the rejected positions, justified concerns worthy of appreciation are brought out particularly well. Furthermore, the limited point of view of each side on factual issues has to be considered. Thus, the exclusive focusing on the opposing position as the key to understanding is overcome, and the horizon opens for different ways of thinking concerning methodology, hermeneutics, and factual argumentation. These different ways of thinking initially appear to be mutually exclusive, but a complementary perspective becomes accessible. The frontlines give way to a methodological-hermeneutical method to clarify each factual issue.

---

10. *Hinführung zu Luther* (Mainz: Matthias-Grünewald, 1982; 2nd ed. 2004).

11. *Einig in der Rechtfertigungslehre? Die Rechtfertigungslehre der Confessio Augustana (1530) und die Stellungnahme der katholischen Kontroverstheologie zwischen 1530 und 1535* (Wiesbaden: F. Steiner, 1970).

3. ECUMENICAL CONCLUSIONS.
OVERCOMING THE DOCTRINAL CONDEMNATIONS

The conclusions which developed from this differentiated methodological point of view became visible for the first time in the study project of an ecumenical examination of the CA. The study was carried out by Lutheran and Catholic theologians in 1980, and the results led directly to the ecumenical project of an acknowledgement of the Catholic character of the CA which Lutheran and Catholic theologians had undertaken on the occasion of the 450th commemoration of the CA in 1980. The result was the recognition that the CA not only has the intention of confessing and keeping the Catholic faith, but that it is also an expression of the Catholic faith. The question which must be asked is whether this doctrinal document could be approved for this purpose and in this shape from the Catholic side. The CA is not a divisive document; it is expression of catholicity and unity in faith. Exegetical and patristic studies, historical and dogmatic research, carried out jointly by Lutheran and Catholic theologians, indicate a common understanding of fundamental questions of the Christian faith. A fundamental consensus between Lutherans and Catholics when reflecting on the Augsburg Confession's teaching on justification seems to be possible.[12]

Catholic dealings with Martin Luther had ecumenical intentions from the beginning. Soon after the announcement of the Second Vatican Council, the German church historian Hubert Jedin asked whether the Council of Trent is an obstacle to the reunification of the Christians.[13] Although the Council of Trent did not cause the division of the church, it confirmed the existing division. The Tridentine Council did not condemn the persons pushing forward the Reformation, but only their doctrines, because it did not want to bar the way of the Reformers to Trent. The Council rather focused on the condemnation of errors, and thus on the differentiation between Catholic doctrine and the doctrine of the Reformers. For this reason, the condemnatory canons of the decrees were basic. The doctrinal chapters prefacing the canons did not seek to alter this differentiating character. The aim of this realignment was to overcome the uncertainty in the development of doctrine. Indeed, the effect of this Council was the confessionalization of the Catholic doctrine. The post-Tridentine Church became a Counter-Reforming institution which rejected error.

---

12. Harding Meyer and Heinz Schütte, eds., *Confessio Augustana. Bekenntnis des einen Glaubens. Gemeinsame Untersuchung lutherischer und katholischer Theologen* (Paderborn: Verlag Bonifacius, 1980).

13. Hubert Jedin, "Ist das Konzil von Trient ein Hindernis der Wiedervereinigung?," in: *Kirche des Glaubens, Kirche der Geschichte. Ausgewählte Aufsätze und Vorträge*. Bd. II: *Konzil und Kirchenreform* (Freiburg i. Br.: Herder, 1966), 540–552, here 541.

As a direct consequence of these historic investigations, the German Ecumenical Working Group of Protestant and Catholic theologians conducted extensive research into the respective theological condemnations of the sixteenth century. Catholic and Lutheran researchers came together to author the study *Doctrinal Condemnations—Church-dividing?*[14] and worked hand in hand toward overcoming the mutual condemnations. They wanted to ascertain whether the condemnations of the past still apply to the partner in today's dialogue. These condemnations, however, are based on still existing doctrinal teachings and so are still binding for the churches with their own confession. Thus, the churches cannot simply ignore the previously expressed condemnations. Nevertheless, in spite of their doctrinal validity, there is now a broad agreement on many controversial matters of faith and doctrine. To overcome the tension between the former doctrinal judgments and today's ecumenical understanding, the differences within the Catholic-Lutheran relation must be revealed in a historical-critical questioning of the past. The conclusions of this research have effects on the relationship between the confessions. If the former misinterpretations lose their church-dividing effects, the conditions for the full communion of the Church will not yet be fulfilled, but negotiations will be enabled under facilitated conditions. The historical-critical studies led to a differentiated overall judgement. As far as justification is concerned, previous contradictions can be overcome and give way to a differentiated consensus, a consensus that accepts differences.

The *Joint Declaration on the Doctrine of Justification* between the Lutheran World Federation and the Roman Catholic Church, signed in 1999 in Augsburg, refers to these preliminary studies and shows that the consensus on the basic truths of the doctrine of justification is justified.[15] This consensus is expressed in the following basic statement: "By grace alone, in faith in Christ's saving work and not because of any merit on our part, we are accepted by God and receive the Holy Spirit, who renews our hearts while equipping and calling us to good works."[16] On the basis of this consensus it is possible to link together the respective confessional differentiations and theological prioritizations in a common statement. Both the Lutheran World Federation and the Roman Catholic Church agreed to this consensus, as have the World Methodist Council and the World Communion of Reformed Churches. The research of Catholic theologians of the twentieth century and the studies of Lutheran theologians about basic issues of Martin Luther's theology and the Lutheran Confessions

---

14. Karl Lehmann and Wolfhart Pannenberg, eds., *The Condemnations of the Reformation Era: Do They Still Divide?* trans. Margaret Kohl (Minneapolis: Fortress, 1989).

15. The Lutheran World Federation and The Roman Catholic Church, *Joint Declaration on the Doctrine of Justification* (Grand Rapids, MI: Eerdmans, 2000).

16. *Joint Declaration*, Nr. 15.

has thus led to important ecumenical consensus documents. *The Joint Declaration on the Doctrine of Justification* can today be understood as an outstanding document of our time.

In association with the commemoration of the Reformation in 2017, the report of the Lutheran-Roman Catholic Commission on Unity titled *From Conflict to Communion*[17] focuses on Luther, and initially draws attention to two new fields: a historic outlining of the Lutheran Reformation and the corresponding Catholic answer, as well as the main issues of the theology of Martin Luther. Themes which have been analyzed from opposed perspectives and presented as foci of controversy are now presented jointly and treated as shared theological concerns. So, in this quite exciting synthesis, a special comprehensiveness becomes apparent, which recognizes the commonalities in faith in Jesus Christ, without hiding or denying the differing theological accentuations or prioritizations. The differences between Lutherans and Catholics are not suppressed; the emerging consensus is acknowledged, but not in an exaggerated manner. In order to describe this type of consensus, ecumenical theology created the term "differentiated consensus." This means that the consensus in question can withstand differences concerning main issues of the Christian faith and Church doctrine, which are now released from their contradictory framework. Furthermore, confessional differences and accentuations are still allowed.

4. YOUNGER CATHOLIC RESEARCHERS

During the last decades, a number of younger Catholic scholars have dealt with different questions and issues. The discussion has evolved in quite different directions. Jared Wicks, for example, studied the conflict between Luther and Cajetan,[18] Theo Bell discovered Luther´s Bernardine roots,[19] and Franz Posset dealt with the Augustinian-Bernardine tradition in Luther´s works.[20] Augustinus Sander investigated the question of whether the ordination theology of Luther can be placed within Catholic thought and practice.[21] Three main new aspects can be highlighted.

17. Lutheran-Roman Catholic Commission on Unity, *From Conflict to Communion: Lutheran-Catholic Common Commemoration of the Reformation in 2017* (Leipzig: Evangelische Verlagsanstalt, 2013).

18. Jared Wicks, *Cajetan und die Anfänge der Reformation* (Münster: Aschendorff, 1983).

19. Theo Bell, *Divus Bernhardus. Bernhard von Clairvaux in Martin Luthers Schriften* (Mainz: Philipp von Zabern, 1993).

20. Franz Posset, *The Real Luther. A Friar at Erfurt and Wittenberg* (Saint Louis: Concordia Publishing House, 2011).

21. Augustinus Sander, *Ordinatio Apostolica. Studien zur Ordinationstheologie im Luthertum des 16. Jahrhunderts*. Bd. I: *Georg III. von Anhalt (1507–1553)* (Innsbruck: Tyrolia, 2004).

On the basis of previous research, it is possible to analyze more closely the "Bernard factor" within the theology of Luther. The documents of Luther not only contain a huge number of citations of St. Bernard, but while citing Bernard, Luther deals with these citations in a way that adopts the monastic theology shaped by Bernard of Clairvaux himself, and which Luther thus highlights in his own theology. Specifically, Bernard draws Luther's attention to the interpretation of the Pauline dictum of justifying faith. In the opinion of Philipp Melanchthon, Bernard is not the mystic who refers to the inwardness of the religious life, but the theologian who draws the attention of the Reformers to the correct interpretation of the apostles. "Luther did not invent a new theology, but discovered the old Bernardine theology of justification by grace alone through faith alone. This was the matrix of Luther's later theology and reforms efforts of popular piety."[22]

The Wittenberg Renewal Movement of the sixteenth century and its theology of ordination can be recontextualized more closely. It can be shown that its reform impulses stem from a "confessional catholicity" and are Catholic in principle. According to Augustinus Sander, in 1530 the CA was not a confession of members of a Lutheran Church divided from Rome, but of Catholics of the AC who confessed their faith in God, Emperor, and Empire.[23] Finally, the more accurate analysis of the reform impulses and their reception through Catholic theologians, especially in relation to doctrine, shows that the reforming proposals of Luther were not rejected by the Magisterium, as should have been the logical consequence of the canons of the Tridentine decrees. Rather, they have been taken into consideration over time in a specific way, even if only implicitly. This is what the Lutheran–Catholic text *From Conflict to Communion* pointed out. On a broad range of issues—especially justification, the Eucharist, ministry, and Scripture—this analysis helps to determine more accurately how the Council of Trent and the Second Vatican Council dealt with Luther's critical reform impulses, but without having confronted Luther directly. On these issues, the Councils did not react in general, but attended to a differentiation of church doctrines and traditions. It can be assumed that "confessional catholicity" has been taken into consideration not only in the later decisions of the Council of Trent and the Second Vatican Council, but even at the Augsburg Diet of 1530. Thus, the Magisterium implicitly received the theological insights of Martin Luther.

---

22. Posset, *The Real Luther*, 116.

23. Augustinus Sander, "Erstrittene Ordination. Georg III. von Anhalt (1507–1553): ein Beispiel für die Ordinationstheologie im Luthertum des 16. Jahrhunderts," *Catholica* 60 (2006): 23–52.

5. A New View on Luther. Implicit Reception

These scholarly investigations, which lasted more than a century, have been fruitful in two respects. Although the texts of the Second Vatican Council did not mention Luther´s name or give an explicit analysis of his theology, it cannot be ignored that this Council adopted some of his core insights. The high estimation and the veneration of Sacred Scripture in the life of the Church is the core concern of the Constitution on Divine Revelation, *Dei Verbum*. The Constitution on the Church, *Lumen gentium,* highlights the common priesthood of the faithful as the fundamental vocation of all Christians. The ecumenical concern links the Decree on Ecumenism, *Unitatis redintegratio*, with a call to the renewal of the Church. The Pastoral Constitution, *Gaudium et spes*, and the Declaration on Religious Freedom, *Dignitatis humanae*, emphasize the importance of freedom and the responsibility of the human person before God and the world, including the recognition of religious freedom. Overall, these important achievements gained from the theology of Martin Luther lead to a theology oriented towards the Word of God. A detailed theology as declared by the Second Vatican Council considers the sovereignty of both the reality and truth of the Word of God in Jesus Christ. From here, this theology develops the individual issues of theology.

This implicit understanding of Luther led to a re-evaluation of his catholicity in the context of a recognition of his desire for reform, as especially Cardinal Johannes Willebrands and Pope John Paul II expressed. After the Second Vatican Council, Cardinal Willebrands emphasized particularly the tendency (which is the result of the Catholic research on Luther) "to re-discover a real Catholic heritage in Luther´s theological positions and either to consider his obvious errors as heretical or to transform them, so that the whole Luther can be integrated into the continuity and catholicity of the Roman Catholic Church."[24] From the Catholic side, "the deep religiousness of Luther and his burning passion for the question of eternal salvation"[25] and an understanding of the justification of the sinner as not being a church-dividing matter can be detected. On the occasion of his visit to the Augustinian Monastery in Erfurt in September 2011, Pope Benedict XVI referred to the deep religiousness of Luther: "What constantly exercised him was the question of God, the deep passion and driving force of his whole life´s journey. 'How do I receive the grace of God?': this question struck him in the heart and lay at the foundation of all his theological searching and inner struggle. For Luther, theology was no mere academic pursuit, but the strug-

24. Johannes Willebrands, "Martin Luther und die Reformation aus heutiger Sicht," in: *Mandatum Unitatis. Beiträge zur Ökumene* (Paderborn: Bonifatius, 1989), 262–268.

25. Willebrands, "Martin Luther," 266.

gle for oneself, which in turn was a struggle for and with God."[26] The discovery of these two central characteristics of his person and of his theology within Catholic theology leads to a new ecumenical understanding of Luther´s "witness to the gospel," as the Lutheran-Catholic Commission stated in its joint document.[27] Thus, the person Martin Luther and his theology are today a spiritual as well as a theological challenge for Catholic theology.

It is due to the great achievement of the twentieth century's Catholic research on Luther that the defensive attitude toward him handed down through the centuries has been overcome. This research enabled a new encounter with the Catholic and Reformer Martin Luther, and thus contributed to freeing Luther from the one-sided burden of being the divider of the Western Church. This Catholic research on Luther, arising out of disputes over Catholic understandings of the Reformation, its preconditions and effects, prepared the way for the ecumenical contribution of Catholic theology after an inner struggle over methods. This Catholic theology later resulted in an ecumenical theology. Since the Second Vatican Council, the Popes confirmed the central statements of the results of the Catholic research on Luther.

6. EXPLICIT RECEPTION.
EFFECTS OF CATHOLIC LUTHERAN STUDIES

The twentieth century's new understanding of Martin Luther and Reformation theology gave Catholic theology the opportunity to re-evaluate Martin Luther. For Catholic theology, there was an opportunity for a common ecumenical reflection on the presuppositions, course, and effects of the Reformation, centered on Martin Luther. This extensive historical research into Luther's person and his theology led to new systematic insights that challenge Catholic theology. They can be interpreted as an explicit reception of the theological reform impulses of Martin Luther.

(1) "Luther's call for a reform of the Church was, in its original intention, a call to repentance and renewal, which must begin in the life of every individual."[28] That the life of every Christian had to do with daily repentance was the

---

26. Benedict XVI, "To Representatives of the Council of the Evangelical Church at the Former Augustinian Convent in Erfurt: 23 September 2011," *Information Service*, Pontifical Council for Promoting Christian Unity 137, no. 2–3 (2011): 56.

27. Roman Catholic/Lutheran Joint Commission, "Martin Luther—Witness to Jesus Christ (1983)," in: *Growth in Agreement II: Reports and Agreed Statements of Ecumenical Conversations on a World Level, 1982–1998*, ed. Jeffrey Gros, Harding Meyer, and William G. Rusch (Geneva: WCC Publications, 2000), 438–442.

28. John Paul II, "Address During Ecumenical Service," *Information Service*, Pontifical Council for Promoting Christian Unity 93, no. 4 (1996): 157.

content of Luther's first thesis on indulgence. Luther emphasized the pastoral challenge of all Christian life. To strive to reach the Gospel, to follow Jesus Christ, to pursue his will is a basic Christian requirement which Jesus himself has asked of his own followers. In this basic focus on penance and renewal, Luther's spiritual and theological reforms are apparent from the very beginning. This focus finally finds expression in Luther's doctrine of justification. In this context, the Catholic theology of the twentieth century also comes to a renewal of the understanding of penance. In its exploration of the reconciliation of the sinner with the Church, the Second Vatican Council sought a renewal of the sacrament of Penance. In this connection, indulgences can be seen as a moment in the reintegration of the person into fellowship with God, the intent of the sacrament of Penance. This goal remains the perspective for a right understanding. Pope Francis, therefore, has given the traditional ecclesiastical indulgence a new point. He describes the mercy of God as an indulgence, which God gives to the sinner. The indulgence in this form is not a pious work, but is an expression of the mercy of God. As a result, the renewal of life needs to be expressed in a more appropriate manner. This view has already been explicitly adopted into Catholic theology in the 1999 *Declaration on the Doctrine of Justification.*

(2) During the Reformation, Luther's concerns over the nature of repentance and its renewal were not properly heard by the Church and theological authorities in Germany and Rome. "Not Luther's understanding of the gospel and his spiritual concern for reform as such have led to separation, but the ecclesiastical and political effects of his fundamental concern in the understanding of church, ministry, and magisterium have done so."[29] As the renewal of the whole Church from its biblical origin was the core concern of the Reformation, it is important today to appreciate this concern in the context of a theological investigation of dogmatic divisions, on the way to a recovery of ecclesial communion. This investigation includes a "cleansing of memory," in which past events which influence and determine our present action are remembered and re-appropriated. "What has happened in the past cannot be changed, but what is remembered of the past and how it is remembered can, with the passage of the time, indeed change."[30] Christians today have a duty to recount the past together. In this way, it is possible to rethink the effects resulting from past actions and to subject them to revision. This process of renewal in dealing with the past has been developed in the report of the Lutheran–Catholic International Dialogue Commission *From Conflict to Communion.* Pope Francis confirmed the fruits of more than fifty years of joint work on the issues of conflict in the six-

---

29. "Wort zum 450. Todesjahr Martin Luthers aus der evangelischen und katholischen Kirche in Thüringen und Sachsen-Anhalt," *Ökumenische Rundschau* 45 (1996): 218.

30. *From Conflict to Communion,* Nr. 16.

teenth century when he spoke at the Lutheran World Federation's service to commemorate the Reformation on 31 October 2016 in Lund, Sweden. The Reformation, according to the Pope, has contributed to placing Sacred Scripture at the center of the life of the Church. Luther's search for a merciful God raised the question of the right relationship with God. The doctrine of justification expresses the essence of human existence before God. The credibility of Christians in the world is finally growing with their witness of mercy. Man is always in need of the grace and mercy of God. To defend the dignity of each individual is the central service of Christians in the world. Here too, Luther's legacy emerges explicitly in the proclamation of the Pope.

(3) In understanding the Reformation, it is not sufficient to attend only to the events at the end of the late Middle Ages. Undoubtedly, the Church was in need of reform. However, the Church was also capable of reform. Luther's plans for reform can be included in this situation in light of the state of the Church at that time. Luther maintained the fundamental reformability of the Church. Thus, the manifold late medieval and early modern reform efforts can be included in the assessment of the Reformation. Reformation is no longer connected with the division of the Western Church, but with the recognition that the Church is always dependent on renewal and reform. The Second Vatican Council emphasized the necessity of the reform of the Church: the Church is called on its earthly path to a lasting reform. Catholicity, as fidelity to the vocation of the Church, includes the reform of the Church. The reform of the Church has always been a legitimate concern of the Church and has continued into our time. The essence of the reform is described by the Second Vatican Council, which gives new space to this matter, with the need for purification, repentance, and renewal. It has added a new meaning to the confession of the *Ecclesia semper reformanda*, which emerged from the later reform movement, insofar as it was recognized that it came from an old Catholic tradition. *Reformatio* as restoration and *renovatio* as a renewal of the life of the Church from the spirit of the Gospel characterize the attitudes of the Council as fidelity to one's own vocation and as a dynamism of the historical path of the Church.[31]

(4) Luther's reform approach referred to a renewal of all theology in the spirit of the Sacred Scriptures. Luther shared this approach with humanists such as Erasmus. His ideas of reform were based on the religious struggle for a proper understanding of God at that time. They came from a renewed understanding of the Gospel as a message of God's mercy. Staupitz had begun the teaching; Luther expressed his agreement with the basic stance of the Augustinian tradition. As we now better understand, the monastic theology of Bernard of Clairvaux stands behind this. "While Luther had a predominantly critical attitude toward scholastic

---

31. *Unitatis redintegratio*, Nr. 6.

theologians, as an Augustinian hermit for twenty years, he lived, thought, and did theology in the tradition of monastic theology. One of the most influential monastic theologians was Bernard of Clairvaux, whom Luther highly appreciated. Luther's way of interpreting Scripture as the place of encounter between God and human beings shows clear parallels with Bernard's interpretation of Scripture."[32] Monastic theology as bible-oriented theology is a discourse proceeding from Bernard and Luther, which still needs to be fully implemented.

(5) Luther always appealed to a future council, and renewed the call for it. When the Council of Trent was finally convened, it was too late for a solution of the contentious questions within the one ecclesial communion. The Council of Trent largely remained a compromise. The decisions of the Council, however, formed the basis for the formation of a Catholic identity in the age of confessionalism. Catholic life was standardized from its center, because the inner-church reform efforts were determined by the anti-evangelical orientation. This was shown by the fact that theological thought and ecclesiastical action were determined not by positive doctrine, but by the canons of the decrees condemning false doctrine. The condemnations dominated action and thought in such a way that action and thought were marked by antithesis to the Reformation. Thus, the Catholic Church was largely determined by the Reformation, albeit with a definite intention. It was only in the Second Vatican Council that the attempts to reform the confessional point of view, and to open the Catholic Church to Luther's theological reform efforts, came to fruition. On the questions raised by the Council of Trent, the Second Vatican Council sought to give a more balanced response to the whole apostolic legacy of the Church.

(6) The Reformation aimed at a renewal of the whole Church from its biblical origins. The splitting of the Western Church in the sixteenth century cannot be regarded as a result of the Reformation initiated by Wittenberg, especially since the Confession of Augsburg expressly declared its intention to bear witness to the faith of the one, holy, Catholic, and apostolic Church and to hold fast to the unity of the Church. This Confession does not concern the foundation of a new church, but the renewal of the Christian faith in harmony with the Old Church and in accordance with the Sacred Scripture in the unity of the Church. Today it can be jointly stated that the ecclesiastical grievances mentioned in the Augsburg Confession have largely become irrelevant because of the changes that have taken place in the life and judgment of the churches. The churches are now on their way to ecclesial communion. Although Catholic-Lutheran agreement on the Eucharist and Eucharistic communion has not yet been achieved, today's church-to-church relations are not just the expression of a loose community, but of a growing communion.

32. *From Conflict to Communion*, Nr. 99.

These insights and reflections even describe a reform program of Catholic theology, which emerged from a retrospective discussion with Martin Luther and his theology. To this extent, Catholic theology can no longer be described without rethinking the conditions, the course, and the effects of the Reformation of the sixteenth century. The division of the Western Church is the effect of the Wittenberg reform movement. The presuppositions and the course of the disputes since 1517 show, however, that the split cannot be traced back to the Reformers' intentions. The chance exists to regain unity and fellowship in faith. This result cannot, of course, be attained by separating the effects from the course of the events. The ecumenical understanding, the real challenge, must also include the causes of and reasons for the division. This is the program of catholicity in reform.[33] It represents the challenge for the ecumenical process of communion insofar as catholicity includes the reform of the Church.

7. CONCLUSION

Catholic work on the life and work of Martin Luther at the end of the nineteenth century contained an ecumenical question from the outset. The emerging Catholic research on Lutheranism in the twentieth century is the driving force of the international ecumenical movement. The results of this research are, surprisingly, not limited to theology and ecumenical dialogue, but are successively absorbed by the magisterium of the Catholic Church and the popes after the Second Vatican Council, at least implicitly. Catholic doctrine can today speak of Martin Luther as a witness to Jesus Christ and theological teacher, as a Catholic reformer, without having yet revised the condemnations in the sixteenth century. The reopening of Martin Luther by Catholic theology documents its ability to reform and leads to an overcoming of the controversialist aspects of Catholic theology as a whole. To this extent, Catholic theology is determined by the Reformation of Martin Luther.

---

33. Wolfgang Thönissen, Josef Freitag, and Augustinus Sander, eds., *Luther: Katholizität und Reform. Wurzeln-Wege-Wirkungen* (Paderborn: Bonifatius, 2016).

2a. Lutheran Views on Catholic Views on Luther:

A Response to Wolfgang Thönissen

Kenneth G. Appold

Wolfgang Thönissen's account of modern Roman Catholic scholarship on Martin Luther is notable for several reasons. Perhaps most importantly, it reminds us of how vital and interesting that scholarship has been over the past century. In fact, speaking as a Lutheran, I am tempted to claim that it has been more dynamic and more varied than the in-house efforts of my own confession. Catholic scholars have traveled a much longer road and overcome more obvious obstacles to arrive at their appreciation of Luther, and this is evident in the variety of approaches, assumptions and viewpoints represented in Thönissen's survey. Secondly, much of the scholarship Thönissen treats appears motivated by a genuine ecumenical spirit, an eagerness to find a Luther free from confessional stereotypes or church-political presuppositions. For anyone unfamiliar with that literature, it may come as a surprise to see a Roman Catholic scholar claim Luther as a "Father in the Faith," as Peter Manns does in the title to both a book and an article.[1] And yet Manns' appreciation is hardly an outlier; it is simply one of the stronger of the many endorsements one encounters in the literature.

If all of this seems almost too good to be true, then perhaps it is. Thönissen's survey is also notable for its selection of works. It is heavily weighted toward German-language studies, and tends to focus on the Catholic scholars who fit the ecumenical pattern. Those of us who pay attention to studies of the Reformation in English, for example, will likely find more diversity and quite a lot that does not lend itself to ecumenical edification. The survey appears a bit streamlined at times, speeding ahead to its *terminus ad quem*, the admittedly remarkable document *From Conflict to Communion*.[2] Many of the surveyed works therefore focus on reclaiming Luther from past misconceptions, or take pains to point out that his positions were misunderstood in his own day but could, with suitable effort and good will, be claimed by Catholics today. Largely missing

---

1. Peter Manns, *Vater im Glauben: Studien zur Theologie Martin Luthers* (Stuttgart: Franz Steiner, 1988).

2. Lutheran-Roman Catholic Commission on Unity, *From Conflict to Communion: Lutheran-Catholic Common Commemoration of the Reformation in 2017* (Leipzig: Evangelische Verlagsanstalt, 2013).

from the lineup are works which either continue or find new ways to blame Luther for dividing the church, or which otherwise find it hard to appreciate the Reformer. Nonetheless, Thönissen's selection can be justified for a number of historical and theological reasons, and it retains its considerable value even as one keeps in mind some of these formal limitations.

German scholars often hear criticism from non-Germans for restricting their focus to works written in German. Of course, German reading skills in the US and UK are generally so poor that, for many, this remains one of the few means of encountering German scholarship at all, and perhaps Anglophone scholars should be grateful for the service. But even if there is often merit to such criticisms, there are also a number of factors that make the German ecumenical context unique, and Thönissen's survey reminds us of a few of those.

Because Germany was the principal site of the Lutheran Reformation, and because of the unique terms of the Peace of Augsburg, it was one of the few regions which saw Lutherans and Catholics coexist as neighbors or near-neighbors over an extended period. That occasioned a hardening of confessional boundaries, but also numerous efforts to cross or break through such lines of demarcation. Germans learned early on to think ecumenically, even if their expressions were often more polemical than irenic. An important additional impetus came especially for Catholics after the collapse of the Holy Roman Empire in 1806, and the subsequent decades of Germany's gradual political unification. This thrust Catholics into a minority position within a Protestant-dominated political and cultural landscape, and created significant incentives for better understanding the confessional other. Catholics not only needed to get to know Lutherans and Reformed more seriously, they also had to find ways to interact with them in situations whose terms they rarely set themselves. It is therefore unsurprising that, as Thönissen reminds us, groundbreaking Catholic ecumenical works such as those of Johan Adam Möhler and Ignaz Franz Döllinger appeared during the first half of the 19th century; they set the stage for traditions and perspectives that reach into the present. These and other factors make the German example an interesting ecumenical laboratory, and a useful case study for contemporary reflection.

Many of the works Thönissen describes have wrestled with a durable charge that has hounded Luther since the days of the Reformation itself: that it was he who divided the church. That had long been a staple of Catholic polemic—and indeed surfaces even today in some literature. Most of the authors surveyed by Thönissen take pains to address that charge. A characteristic strategy for counteracting these views takes a line espoused by Joseph Lortz, among others. It begins with the important observation that Luther did not intend to start a new church at all. Instead, his reform efforts sought to cleanse Catholicism of non-Catholic elements. For Lortz, the evil was Okhamism, but other authors pointed to other factors. In such a light, Luther aimed to restore Catholicism to a purer version of itself. Most historians would agree that there is considerable truth to such observations, and the correction they introduce is significant and salutary. There is, however, a problem with these strategies. They tend to overlook an awkward remaining fact: regardless of the Reformer's intentions, the Luther affair did indeed divide the church.

If one concedes that Luther did not intend such an outcome, then one needs to advance some account of why it happened nonetheless. Some authors have observed that pre-Reformation Catholicism was not nearly as unified as Luther's traditional critics appear to assume. It contained unmistakable fault lines, most obviously around a set of insufficiently resolved issues concerning church authority, church-state relations, and proper church governance. Memories of the Western Schism and of the consequent conciliar movement had not receded by 1517. The rise of quasi-national churches in France and Spain, as well as of newer intellectual currents such as humanism, and independent lay spiritual movements all contained potential threats to Catholic unity, particularly as it was envisioned by Rome. In addition to these structural fissures, pre-Reformation—or more precisely: pre-Tridentine—Catholicism contained a considerable diversity of views on many of the central doctrinal issues Luther raised. This went beyond the more obvious differences between schools and orders; it applied to topics such as justification and grace, eucharistic doctrine, and of course penance. Early commentaries on the Council of Trent (e.g., Sarpi)[3] made the point, taken up again in ecumenical settings today, that Luther's theological positions had not been defined "out" of Catholicism until Trent and, had some of the conversations at the Council proceeded only slightly more expansively, those positions, particularly on justification, may have remained "in."

That observation signals another approach to reassessing Luther. Many authors argue that Luther was simply misunderstood. Such views typically focus on Luther's theology, above all on his doctrine of justification. Building on studies which have reassessed Luther's thought and its place within the larger Catholic tradition, they point out that many of Luther's teachings can in fact be reconciled with Catholic doctrine when both are properly understood. One thinks, for example, of the work of Otto Hermann Pesch, Vincenz Pfnür, and Hubert Jedin, as well as the studies emanating from the German *Ökumenischer Arbeitskreis*, including the landmark achievement, *Lehrverurteilungen—kirchentrennend?* of the 1980s.[4] Such efforts reached a preliminary climax in the *Joint Dec-*

---

3. Paolo Sarpi, *Istoria del Concilio tridentino* (Florence: Sansoni, 1982).

4. Karl Lehmann and Wolfhart Pannenberg, eds., *Lehrverurteilungen - kirchentrennend? I. Rechfertigung, Sakramente und Amt in Zeitalter der Reformation und heute*, Dialog der Kirchen, 4 (Freiburg i.B.: Herder, 1986); ET Karl Lehmann and Wolfhart Pannenberg, eds., *The Condemnations of the Reformation Era: Do They Still Divide?* trans. Margaret Kohl (Minneapolis: Fortress, 1989).

laration on the Doctrine of Justification, adopted by Roman Catholic and Lutheran churches in 1999. As all of these texts make clear, no one wishes to suggest that Luther's thought can be reconciled fully with Catholic doctrine, but, more modestly, that the remaining differences are not church-dividing and that the condemnations of Trent do not apply to Luther's teachings once these have been understood properly. Such an approach, commonly called "differentiated consensus," has important ecumenical implications: if Trent does not exclude Luther's thought as both Catholics and Lutherans understand it today, then the table is clear for deeper reconciliation between the churches.

Even these highly nuanced approaches miss an important point, however. If Luther was misunderstood, then one needs to ask why. What went wrong so disastrously in the 16th century? This question has proven more difficult to answer. Part of the problem no doubt stems from the fact that most of the authors who analyze Luther's thought and who engage in this kind of ecumenical dialogue are systematic theologians; they are accustomed to viewing doctrine on its own terms and are less interested in examining the contexts within which such teachings were formulated, understood, and misunderstood. Recent Lutheran-Catholic ecumenical dialogue has tended to be content with identifying congruities between respective thought models, arguing that these now allow the confessional cultures which produced those thoughts to reconcile. Missing, however, is a plausible account of how the misunderstandings arose in the first place. If we can recognize the Catholic orthodoxy of Luther's teachings on justification today, then why couldn't his contemporaries do so?

Several authors in Thönissen's survey do attempt explanations of this kind. Both Joseph Lortz and Peter Manns direct their attention to aspects of Luther's personality, such as his unique religious subjectivity, which made his language hard to integrate into existing systems of thought at the time. This is often coupled with a respect for the personal integrity that drove much of Luther's thinking and writing. Otto Hermann Pesch, for example, writes of the "existential" and "richly experiential" nature of Luther's thought;[5] others speak of a "prophetic" or "confessional" element. Pope Benedict XVI echoed such sentiments in his own comments on Luther during a visit to the Augustinian monastery in Erfurt in 2011: "For Luther, theology was less an academic pursuit than a struggle with himself, and that in turn was a struggle for God and with God."[6] Because

---

5. Otto Hermann Pesch, "Existential and Sapiential Theology—The Theological Confrontation Between Luther and Thomas Aquinas," in: *Catholic Scholars Dialogue with Luther,* ed. Jared Wicks (Chicago: Loyola University Press, 1970), 61–81.

6. Apostolische Reise Seiner Heiligkeit Papst Benedikt XVI. nach Berlin, Erfurt und Freiburg, 22.–25. September 2011. Predigten, Ansprachen und Grußworte, hg. v. Sekretariat der Deutschen Bischofskonferenz, Bonn 2011 (VApS 189), 71. [My translation].

Luther was driven by deeply existential questions in his own faith-life, his language had an immediacy and originality that went beyond existing forms of expression and exploded conventional terminologies. In that respect, one may speak of an "avant-garde" character to some of Luther's early writing. Only in retrospect does its compatibility with his context become evident.

One can see this fairly easily in the first two of the 95 Theses. Luther begins by asserting that when Christ called us to repent, "he willed the entire life of the believers to be one of repentance"[7] [Th. 1]. In Luther's telling, the specific action of repenting dissolves into a comprehensive existential attitude or way of being. The notion is grounded in his own religious experience, specifically in his discovery of himself as someone defined primarily by his relatedness to God. Equally important, though, is Luther's observation in Th. 2: "This word [repentance] cannot be understood as referring to the sacrament of penance, that is, confession and satisfaction, as administered by the clergy."[8] Luther recognizes that his own experientially-derived understanding of the term "repentance" goes beyond available ecclesial language and norms. In fact, he declares that language inadequate. In doing so, he shows both the extraordinary originality of his thought—and its alarming revolutionary potential. Luther's formulations are not only "new," they are new in a way that appears to discredit the old. This dual quality makes them problematic and even threatening to an institution invested in the "old" language and practices. The institution's protective reflexes close ranks and take aim at the intruder.

Much ecumenical energy of recent decades has sought to open those ranks and offer a more sober and less reflexive assessment of Luther's language. As Thönissen's presentation makes wonderfully clear, those efforts have seen considerable success. The recent publication, *From Conflict to Communion*, both summarizes the highpoints of those successes and goes beyond them by crafting a common Lutheran-Catholic narrative that retells the story of the Reformation in a way that is more charitable to Luther's historical reform initiatives and shows how doctrinal consensus may today be possible. Issues that seemed church-dividing in the 16th century no longer need be church-dividing today.

As encouraging as those ecumenical efforts are, they continue to miss the point raised earlier: while they argue that the misunderstandings of the 16th century were unfortunate and ultimately unnecessary, they provide no account of how those misunderstandings arose. That is unfortunate and may suggest a deficit in contemporary ecumenical method. If we do not know what caused the historical misunderstandings, we cannot be sure that they will not happen again. That is troubling. If the object of contemporary ecumenism, as manifested in *From Con-*

7. WA 1:233; LW 31, 25.
8. Ibid.

flict to Communion, lies not only in mutual recognition of Luther's orthodoxy, but also in a reception, as Thönissen nicely puts it, of some of Luther's driving concerns, then we need to be able to have some confidence that the mechanisms which suppressed Luther originally are no longer operative. Stated more simply: if Luther reminds us that the church is in constant need of reform, and we wish to adopt that insight into the life of our church, then we should be sure that reform as Luther understood it has a better chance of success today than it did back then. Stated a bit more bluntly: if we wish to persuade Lutherans that the time for reconciliation with Rome has come, then we need to be able to assure them that the mechanisms which caused their exclusion and sought to suppress their thought no longer exist. That will not be possible without a deeper account of the 16th-century breakdown in communication and in particular of the Roman institutional dynamics which at the very least abetted that breakdown.

Indeed, if we retrace the historical path of the *causa Lutheri* through the back chambers of 16th-century Rome, we could conclude that at least one of the causes for its inadequate reception lay in the nature of the institution itself. Clearly, Luther's formulations posed challenges to traditional ways of thinking and speaking. But a healthy institution should be able to cope with such challenges more effectively than this one did. The undesirable outcome—a hardened and durable division of Western European Christianity—should have been avoidable. That seems particularly clear in the case of the "95 Theses," whose critique of the indulgence trade was at least partly absorbed a year later by Leo X's bull *Cum postquam.* Had Rome's reaction been different, had, for example, Luther been invited to participate in a broader conversation on the issues rather than been threatened with prosecution, the ecclesial outcome might also have been different.

Rome's failure to resolve the Luther crisis in 1517–1518 suggests a deeper, institutional inadequacy: either the church did not have effective instruments for such conflict resolution, or it did not possess the proper personnel to make effective use of such instruments. To be clear, the problem I am describing is not confined to the small circle of curial officials, such as Silvester Prierias, surrounding Leo X. The depressing track record of failed negotiations, diets and religious colloquies that marks the middle decades of the 16th century underscores the point. Even Trent's outcome raises questions about whether this particular instrument proved adequate.

To the extent that such questions are raised today, they tend to focus on the office of the papacy. Even Pope Paul VI described the papal office as the "greatest obstacle on the path to Christian unity."[9] Such statements strike me as

---

9. Thomas F. Stransky and John B. Sheerin, eds., *Doing the Truth in Charity: Statements of Pope Paul VI, Popes John Paul I, John Paul II, and the Secretariat for Promoting Christian Unity, 1964–1980* (New York: Paulist Press, 1982), 273.

short-sighted. It was not the fact of the pope's existence that short-circuited Reformation-era theological discourse, but much broader deficits in hermeneutical culture, doctrinal conflict-resolution, and the practical use of teaching authority. Luther's views were not given adequate "space" to unfold in a way that could be beneficial to the church as a whole; they were not engaged charitably or even deeply by those whose positions in the institution gave them authority over such matters. Whether a more open and flexible institution, an institution which grants more space to such conversations and is less concerned about patrolling its borders, could include a pope at its head strikes me as a secondary question.

The Reformers themselves tended to believe that Rome had an institutional problem, and many of their most conspicuous reform measures sought to correct this. This is why Lutherans, Calvinists, Anabaptists, and even Anglicans all devised and implemented polity changes to their churches. The initial debates over theology soon transitioned into debates over how best to create and maintain a context within which theological discourse could take place freely. The wide range of resulting ecclesiological models reminds us that there is likely no golden formula for getting this right. However, though they may have disagreed on much else, all the Reformers were convinced that Rome was incapable of providing such a context: an environment conducive to free theological thinking. Lutherans put stock in their universities, Calvinists focused more heavily on changing ecclesial structures and making them more participatory, and Anabaptists went even further in flattening hierarchies and fostering local communities of mutual support and discipline.

Since this presentation is simply a brief response to the paper of a colleague, it cannot provide a full historical study of the institutional factors involved in the breakdown of communication during the Reformation. But it is important that we recognize the issue. The fact that such analyses have not figured prominently in ecumenical dialogue should be cause for concern. Is it enough to establish consensus on a list of previously problematic theological doctrines? Or is it not equally important to determine whether, once such consensus has been achieved, our church institutions are properly equipped to resolve theological conflict today? Doesn't our failure to ask—and address—these questions make it more likely that, even if our churches did reconcile completely, future reformers would precipitate crises similar to the Luther affair? Are we inviting history to repeat itself?

One can frame the issue more theologically. As Prof. Thönissen observes, the Second Vatican Council affirmed the sovereignty of the Word of God as the appropriate starting point of all theology. We may hope that Lutherans would agree. But it is one thing to acknowledge the sovereignty of the Word of God, and another thing entirely to create an institutional context within which the

Word of God is actually allowed to be sovereign. Is today's Roman Catholic Church such an institution? Is it fundamentally better in this respect than it was during the 16th century? Is Rome—and, to be fair, are the Reformation churches, as well—capable of integrating and providing space for conceptually disruptive experiences or for thinkers such as Luther, whose language explodes existing conventions? If we cannot determine what, if any, structural factors contributed to the misunderstandings of the Reformation, we cannot be certain that those structural or ecclesial deficits have been corrected and overcome. And without such clarity, ecumenical dialogue remains a bit "un-grounded."

These comments should not be misconstrued as a criticism of the Catholic church. If anything, one could pose similar questions of today's Lutheran church: do they provide a space for free and meaningful theological discourse? There are good reasons to be skeptical. But those are questions for another day. I simply wish to point to a problem of ecumenical method—a problem which emerges from the literature in Thönissen's survey, but which remains largely ignored and therefore unresolved.

II. Justification

3. Later Medieval Teaching on Justification

Theodor Dieter

Later medieval teaching on justification is anything but uniform. Instead of giving an overview of the many different teachings, it seems to be more interesting to focus on two positions which Martin Luther explicitly referred to: one that he criticized and rejected sharply, and one that he praised very warmly. The first one comes from Gabriel Biel, the Tübingen theologian who lived from about 1415 to 1495. Luther's later so-called *Disputation against Scholastic Theology* has at its core a short text of Gabriel Biel; nearly two-thirds of the 97 theses of this early disputation deal directly or indirectly with this text.[1] It may seem to be unfair and one-sided to look at medieval positions from Luther's perspective, but in the context of a conference with the topic "Luther and the Shaping of the Catholic Tradition," this can hardly be avoided. The task will be to define the critical points of encounter as clearly as possible. The second medieval position to be presented here is that of an unknown author from the late 14th century whose text was first published in 1516 by Martin Luther without a title.[2] Luther introduced it with the words: "A spiritual, noble booklet concerning the right distinction and understanding of the old and new man, who Adam's and God's children are, and how Adam should die in us while Christ should rise."[3] Some time later, Luther obviously got to know another manuscript that contained the whole treatise; he published the complete text in 1518 with the title "Eyn deutsch Theologia" or "A German Theology."[4] In a later print, this title was changed to "Theologia deutsch," and with this title the short booklet became widespread and influential over centuries. In his preface to the second edition, Luther declared that, besides the Bible and St. Augustine, he had not read a book from which he had learned

---

1. See fn. 24 below and Theodor Dieter, "Martin Luthers kritische Wahrnehmung 'der' Scholastik in seiner so genannten *Disputatio contra scholasticam theologiam,*" in: *Die Reformation und ihr Mittelalter*, Günter Frank and Volker Leppin, eds. (Stuttgart-Bad Cannstatt: frommann-holzboog Verlag, 2016), 153–188.

2. Luther's "Preface": WA 1: 153. Luther does not know who the author is, but he identifies the content as being "of the kind of the enlightened doctor Tauler," the mystic.

3. WA 1, 153 (my translation).

4. Luther's "Preface": WA 1: 378,1–379,14; LW 31, 75f. See also Luther's praise of Tauler's sermons in his letter to Georg Spalatin as of December 14, 1516 (WA Br 1: 79,58–64; LW 48, 32–36). Luther added a copy of the newly published "German Theology," stating that he had not seen "a more salvific theology that is more in line with the gospel" (lines 62f.).

more about God, Christ, and the human being than this one. And he added that this book was proof against the accusation that was already expressed in 1518, that the Wittenberg theologians taught new things. By reading this book, Luther thought, the readers could convince themselves that this was not the case.

Now to begin. In medieval times, human life was seen as a pilgrimage whose final point was either eternal life in heaven or eternal damnation in hell. The starting point was the disastrous situation of every human being, born into a state of original sin, separated from God and thus a candidate for eternal damnation. The basic issue was how one might receive grace in order to overcome the state of separation from God and be able to live in hope of eternal life. The first turning point in this pilgrimage was the transition from the state of sin to the state of grace; the transition from being a sinner to being a righteous person. Receiving grace, being justified, happened basically in the sacrament of baptism. However, the grace received in baptism was lost through any mortal sin committed by the baptized after baptism. Thus the sacrament of penance became the main turning point from sin to grace again and again during the course of one's life. The *Sitz im Leben* of justification, the places where justification happened, were the sacraments of baptism and especially penance. So baptism and penance were the turning points from sin to grace. But there was a second turning point: the transition from a life in grace on earth to eternal life after death. Both turning points—from sin to grace, and from a life in grace to eternal life— were inwardly connected with justification. In both cases, the concept of merit played a role, such that the relationship between human activity and divine activity had to be clearly defined.

Concerning the turn from sin to grace, medieval theologian Gabriel Biel stated that sinners must detest their sins and decide to obey God and his commands in everything. But Biel also emphasized the otherness and freedom of God: "nothing that is created can be the reason for a divine act [of acceptation],"[5] Biel wrote, not even the greatest human act of love for God. Even if a supernatural form, namely infused grace, is given by God to a person, and this person's acts are done as a result of this grace, God is still not *forced* to accept them and in exchange grant eternal life—the second turning point mentioned earlier. The relationship between a human act, even a God-granted human act, on the one side and the divine activity of accepting that act on the other side could only be established by the free and eternal self-determination of God. This self-determination has the structure of "If A, then B." "A" denotes a reality on the human side, "B" denotes the divine reaction. Only based on such a divine ordination, also called *pactum* could one expect with certainty that human acts would be

    5. Gabriel Biel, Sent. I, lib. 1, dist. 17, qu. 3, art. 3, dub. 2, G 5; *Collectorium circa quattuor libros Sententiarum*, vol. 1, ed. Wilfried Werbeck and Udo Hofmann (Tübingen: Mohr Siebeck, 1973), 433.

accepted by God for justification or beatification (that is, the granting of eternal life).[6] To make such an ordination is an act of grace. Thus it is by grace, Biel concluded, that sinners are justified and beatified. Biel was convinced that with this explanation he rejected the Pelagian heresy condemned by the church.[7] He described this heresy as the conviction that God is *forced* to give eternal life to those who have done morally God acts, and this does not happen by grace; for God would be unjust if he did not do so. Biel even goes beyond the debate with Pelagius in denying that God could be forced to respond positively to the gift of grace given by himself, since such a gift is a created entity, too.[8]

God in his freedom has established the rule "If A, then B." To get back to the first human turning point, from sin to grace, this means: "If a human being does what is in his or her power, God gives his grace to that person," that is: God justifies the person. For this law, Biel refers to biblical texts as Zechariah 1:3 ("Return to me, says the Lord of hosts, and I will return to you, says the Lord of hosts") and James 4:8 ("Draw near to God, and he will draw near to you.").[9] If the required condition is fulfilled, grace is received by necessity. This necessity does not destroy God's freedom; rather, it is the necessity of divine immutability (*necessitas immutabilitatis*).[10] In his freedom, God himself has established the rule or the law "If A, then B." Therefore, he would be changing his mind if he did not follow his own law as soon as the human requirement is fulfilled, and this is impossible.

But what *is* the human activity that is required by the law "If A, then B" and that lies within human power? Biel answers: "The most perfect way of doing what is in one's power, to seek God, to draw near to God, to convert to God is an act of friendship-love for God"—that is, an act of love for God for God's own sake. "There is no act by which we can draw closer to God than by loving God above all. For this act is the most perfect act of all with respect to God that is possible for the pilgrim by his natural power."[11] Thus with respect to that ordination or pactum ("If A, then B"), justification happens by grace alone, but with

---

6. Gabriel Biel, Sent. II, dist. 27, qu. un., art. 3, dub. 4, O 7–10, *Collectorium circa quattuor libros Sententiarum*, vol. 2, ed. Wilfried Werbeck and Udo Hofmann (Tübingen: Mohr Siebeck, 1984), 523; and Sent. II, dist. 27, qu. un., art. 1, not. 3, C 1–D 6 (op. cit., 510–512).

7. Wilhelm Ernst, *Gott und Mensch am Vorabend der Reformation* (Leipzig: St. Benno Verlag, 1972), 394–409, especially 408.

8. Biel, Sent. I, dist. 17, qu. 1, art. 2, concl. 3, E 1–5 (op. cit., 416).

9. Biel, Sent. II, dist. 27, qu. un., art. 2, concl. 4, K 11–16 (op. cit., 517). Luther sharply criticizes Biel's reference to these biblical authorities as Pelagianism in thesis 28 of the *Disputation against Scholastic Theology* (WA 1; 225,22–26; LW 31, 11). Thomas Aquinas thinks quite differently than Biel: STh I-II, qu. 109, art 6, ad 1.

10. Biel, Sent. II, dist. 27, qu. un., art. 3, dub. 4, O 1–10 (op. cit., 523).

11. Biel, Sent. III, dist. 27, qu. un., art. 3, dub. 2, prop. 2, Q 70–75 (op. cit., 505f.).

respect to A, the human activity that is required in order that B comes into being, justification happens by works alone. This is the Janus face of justification in Biel.

Biel knows, of course, that Jesus declared the commandment to love God with all one's being as the highest commandment and the summary of all the commandments, along with the commandment to love one's neighbor. In Mark 12:30, Jesus explains love for God as follows: "You shall love the Lord your God with all your heart, and with all your soul, and with all your mind and with all your strength." Biel relates these four qualifications to the will, the intellect, the sensual power, and finally to the power that moves the members of the body. After he has explained in detail that God is to be loved with all the members and aspects of the person just mentioned, Biel summarizes and concludes: "Thus the commandment is fulfilled by loving God above all."[12] This is highly surprising since "to love" here simply means an act of the will. We should keep this in mind, since Luther understood this love commandment quite differently, namely as comprising the whole person and not only her will. This difference in how they understand love for God has far-reaching consequences.

As an act of the will, love for God is *the highest possible act* of the will, since it is directed to the highest object, God, the *summum bonum*. Thus the question of love for God is to be discussed as a question of the freedom of the will, and vice versa. Biel claims that the law, as summarized in the commandment to love God, can be fulfilled with a person's natural power, with one's will.[13] These aspects belong together when Biel addresses the human contribution to justification, the transition from the state of being a sinner to a state of grace. As soon as an act of the will, an act of love for God above all, is performed, Biel asserts, then God gives his grace to that person. There is a sequence in order, but not in time. "An act of friendship-love for God above all cannot stand in the pilgrim without grace and infused love (*caritas*)—this is true according to the ordained power of God."[14] In this way, forgiveness of sins, receiving grace, or justification happens while the pilgrim is living on earth.

But there is still the other transition, also belonging to justification: the person living in grace and acting out of grace will receive eternal life. Biel uses a twofold distinction in order to answer the question which is the major principle of the meritorious act: the will or infused grace. He distinguishes between *the substance of the act*, namely its content with the intention to love God—in which the act is elicited by the will according to the right reason, on the one hand, and the *cause for the merit* (on the other hand): the divine acceptation of the act according to the divinely given order and with reference to infused grace

12. Biel, Sent. III, dist. 27, qu. un., art. 1, not. 5, H 1–36 (op. cit., 490f.).
13. Biel, Sent. III, dist. 27, qu. un., art. 3, dub. 2, Q 1–R 65 (op. cit., 503–507).
14. Biel, Sent. III, dist. 27, qu. un., art. 3, dub. 2, prop. 2, Q 59f. (op. cit., 505).

in the person. The content of the meritorious act stems from the human will, which is an active principle or power, while divine grace as a quality of the soul is not active but provides the inclination to act. It is the will that is responsible for the content of the act, but grace or *caritas* is the condition for the meritorious character of the act. The will is basically the same before and after it has received grace, for if human beings exist at all, they have a will, and if they have a will, they also have freedom of the will.[15] Freedom means: having the ability to start anew. Even people who have sinned to the maximal degree nevertheless have at every moment the possibility to make a new beginning, to create an act of their will that loves God above all and for God's sake.[16] So says Biel.

One may allow me here a first sidelong glance at Luther. What I just described is the background that helps us understand better Luther's phrase *maledictum vocabulum illud formatum* ("That damned word 'formed,'" namely "formed by *caritas*") which has often been misunderstood by Catholics and Protestants alike. People mistakenly assume that Luther was not interested in the change that *caritas* brings with it when he criticized the concept of the *fides caritate formata* (faith formed by the God-given love of God). But Luther says just the opposite: "That damned word 'formatum' forces us to think that the soul remains *the same* before and after having received the *caritas* ... even though it must be totally brought to death and become a different one."[17] Luther's point here is not that the *caritas* is not important, but rather that its significance has actually been *underestimated* when it is said that *caritas* only makes acts of the will meritorious while the human capacities are sufficient on their own as far as the substance of the acts is concerned. For Biel, *caritas* simply makes the fulfilment of the law a little bit easier, but in principle *caritas* is not needed for the fulfilment of the law with respect to the substance of the act.

Biel's distinction between the aspect of the substance of the act attributed to the will, and the aspect of the meritorious character attributed to *caritas*, is closely connected with another distinction that Biel used in order to answer the question whether the precepts of the Decalogue require fulfilment out of *caritas*. Biel denies this, arguing that if *caritas* were required for the fulfilment of those precepts, a person would sin if she took care for her parents or refused to kill *without having caritas* but for the sake of another, still honorable aim. In short, these would be morally good acts but not motivated by love for God. Thus Biel declares that the precepts do not need to be obeyed simply (*simpliciter*) out of love, but only conditionally.[18] The condition is taken from the conversation between Jesus and the

15. Biel, Sent. I, dist. 17, qu. 1, art. 2, concl. 1, C 8f. (op. cit., 415).
16. Biel, Sent. II, dist. 28, qu. un., art. 3, dub. 3, O 1–P 14 (op. cit., 543–545).
17. WA 56; 337,18–21 (my translation; italics added); LW 25,325.
18. Biel, Sent. III, dist. 37, qu. un., art. 3, dub. 1, P 18–23 (op. cit., 639f.).

rich man (Matthew 19:17). Jesus said: "If you wish to enter into life, keep the commandments." Biel explains this as follows: "If someone will enter into eternal life, it is necessary that he keeps the precepts out of *caritas*, because it is necessary that he keeps the precepts in a meritorious way, and this requires that he keeps them out of *caritas*. If the condition is given that one wished to gain eternal life, it is necessary that he observes the precepts out of *caritas*. If he observes them, but not out of *caritas*, he does not sin, but in this case he will not merit to enter into eternal life."[19] The distinction concerning the two types of fulfilment of the Decalogue speaks on the one hand of a fulfilment according to the substance of the law (with a morally good intention) and the fulfilment according to the intention of the lawgiver, namely that the person wishes to gain access to eternal life.

In passing, it may be mentioned that this understanding creates an aporia in motivation. Let us imagine this situation: I have committed a mortal sin and therefore lost infused grace, the condition for meriting eternal life. But I wish to gain eternal life, thus I want something that is good *for me*, but in order to do so, I have to love God *only for God's sake*, not for my own sake. It is difficult to overcome this aporia if one is in it. Mystics took this problem very seriously when they discussed and spiritually experienced the idea of loving God in hell, that is; loving God without expecting any reward.

In his *Disputation against Scholastic Theology*, Luther offers two objections against Biel's position. First, he denies that Biel's consequence is correct: If the precepts of the Decalogue had to be fulfilled out of *caritas*, one would sin by not killing, not stealing, not committing adultery. Instead, Luther argues that the right consequence would be: If one fulfils the precepts without *caritas*, he sins because he does not fulfil the law in a spiritual way. This would mean to be without anger and without covetousness, which is not possible without grace, and even with grace it does not happen perfectly.[20] The second objection is: If one understands the role of *caritas* or grace as Biel does, grace is not helping to fulfil the law; rather, it is an additional requirement beyond the fulfilment of the law in terms of the substance of the act. As an additional requirement, grace may be hated more than the law itself is hated.[21]

Luther reversed Biel's dictum, "If one does what is in his power, God will give his grace," by saying: An act of friendship-love for God is not prior to receiving grace, rather it is the consequence of conversion, following grace in order and time. Luther's order of the relation between divine and human activity is the exact reversal of Biel's order.[22] Luther is exclusively focused on the sub-

19. Biel, Sent. III, dist. 37, qu. un., art. 3, dub. 1, P 36–41 (op. cit., 640).
20. WA 1; 227,12–20; LW 31, 13f.
21. WA 1; 227,6–11; LW 31, 13.
22. WA 1; 225,17–21; LW 31, 10f.

stance of the act and whether or not grace is needed for it. If this is not the case, grace is not needed at all. Luther cannot see the role of grace as mainly enabling the possibility of meriting. Otherwise, Luther would be following Ockham's statement: "God can accept a human being without justifying grace." Quite the contrary, Luther explicitly rejects Ockham's famous opinion in his *Disputation against Scholastic Theology*.[23] This clearly demonstrates that Luther does not think along the lines of a "Nominalist" theory of acceptation (if it makes sense at all to call such a theory "Nominalist"). One should actually reject the idea that Luther's thinking is to be understood in the line of a Nominalist theory of *acceptatio Dei*. This idea is often linked with a very negative evaluation of what some people think "Nominalism" to be, understanding it as the destruction of sound scholastic theology, while Luther only drew the consequences of that decline.

The basic difference that prompts Luther's further development is his different understanding of the love for God and the fulfilment of God's law. Luther does not focus his concept of the love for God on acts of the will; rather, he understands love for God as the complete dedication of the whole person to God with all aspects of her being. This full dedication to God is not in the power of any human person—no scholastic theologian had claimed this—thus the rule of "do what is in your power, and God will bestow his grace on you" does not make sense; it must be reversed. This also changes the understanding of acceptation by God, since the question is no longer whether a created entity on the human side is accepted by God; rather the divine activity is prior to human activities by granting *caritas*.

The difference in understanding love for God also touches the understanding of the freedom of the will. Luther takes his opponents seriously with their claim that human beings are able to fulfil the law of God with their own powers, but Luther introduces *his own understanding* of the law and its fulfilment, which comprises the whole person. He is convinced that his understanding is the biblical one, and because his opponents claim to follow the biblical commandment, he sees himself entitled to attribute his understanding to his opponents' understanding. Since scholastic theologians like Biel attribute the capacity to fulfil the law of God to the freedom of the will, Luther argues that this freedom of the will does not exist, because it is only grace that allows for the fulfilling the law according to its substance. This is a tricky argument to make. Luther has a *theological or spiritual understanding* of the fulfilment of God's law that is different from a *moral understanding* of the fulfilment of the law. As we have seen, Biel also distinguished between a theological understanding of fulfilling the law (according to the intention of the lawgiver) and a moral understanding of the fulfilment of the law (according to the substance of the law). In Biel's case, the difference lies

23. WA 1: 227,4f.; LW 31, 13.

in the aim that the will intends in both cases, either love for God for God's sake or aiming at an honorable aim. In Luther's case, on the contrary, the difference lies in the fact that in the theological understanding the whole person is challenged to fulfil the law, while the moral understanding focuses on the will (including, of course, the external dimensions of the respective actions).

Since this is Luther's distinction, he should not draw the following conclusion: Because the theological statement says that a human person without grace does not have the ability to fulfil the law (*in a theological sense*), therefore also the freedom of the will *in a moral sense* has to be denied. Even if one assumes that the freedom of the will exists (in a moral sense, as philosophers claim it), one has (following Luther) to declare that good acts of the will alone are not the true fulfilment of the law in a theological sense. *It does not simply follow from Luther's theological argument that the freedom of the will in the way in which moral philosophers understand it does not exist.* But taking these different distinctions into account, Lutherans should reconsider the question of the freedom of the will in the philosophical sense in relation to grace, love for God, fulfilling the law, being well aware that Biel's understanding of the freedom of the will comes very close to that of Immanuel Kant.

Justification of the sinner in Biel follows the rule "To the one who does what is in his power, God will give his grace." The famous saying "How can I find a gracious God?," very often attributed to Luther, is related to this understanding. How can I find a gracious God? Biel's scholastic answer is: If I as a sinner do what is in my power, then God will bestow his grace on me. This is the question of the Pre-Reformation Luther, even though he did not like the answer. What his Reformation question is, we will hear later. Luther's *Disputation against Scholastic Theology* has at its core a short text of Gabriel Biel, a question, the *dubium*: "Whether the human will of the pilgrim is able to love God above all with his natural power and so fulfil the commandment of love of God?"[24] Luther addresses Biel's arguments one after the other.[25] He does not omit one of them. Obviously, this question is crucial for him.

Having this in mind, and also with a glance at the topic of the conference "Luther and the Shaping of the Catholic Tradition," I will take a leap now and come to the *Joint Declaration on the Doctrine of Justification* that in § 19 addresses precisely this problem:

> We confess together that all persons depend completely on the saving grace of God for their salvation. The freedom they possess in relation to persons and the things of this world is no freedom in relation to salvation. [... They] are

24. Biel, Sent. III, dist. 27, qu. un., art. 3, dub. 2, Q 1f. (op. cit., 503).
25. WA 1: 224,13–225,6; LW 31, 9f.

incapable of turning by themselves to God to seek deliverance, of meriting their justification before God, or of attaining salvation by their own abilities. Justification takes place solely by God's grace.

And when in § 20 Catholics speak of "consenting to God's justifying action, they see such personal consent as itself an effect of grace, not as an action arising from innate human abilities."[26] Compared with Biel's position and being aware of the significance Luther attributed to this problem, JDDJ makes decisive progress here. It is not possible to marginalize Biel as an extreme position. Thirteen years before the JDDJ, in the German study, "The Condemnations of the Reformation Era–Do They Still Divide?," we find quite similar sentences on this topic.[27] In a statement on the "Condemnations" study, Peter Hünermann, an expert on the history of doctrine, was very reluctant to say whether the Catholic Magisterium could agree with these sentences. He explained: "Gabriel Biel is a theologian who especially in this topic holds a position that from Scotus on to the 20th century was held to a very wide extent in Catholic theology [...] Up to the present day, this theology has formed the frame for the interpretation of the Council of Trent."[28] All the more important are those paragraphs of the JDDJ and the agreement achieved in this matter.

The *Theologia Deutsch* is quite different in style and genre, content and method. Before a first manuscript was discovered in the mid-nineteenth century, the treatise was only known from Martin Luther's two publications of the text, from the second edition as *Eyn deutsch Theologia*. The title of that manuscript is *Der Franckforter*. Since its discovery, this title has been used beside *Theologia Deutsch*.[29] The author is still unknown. The Prologue calls him a "friend of God"

26. The Lutheran World Federation and the Roman Catholic Church, *Joint Declaration on the Doctrine of Justification* (Grand Rapids, Michigan: William B. Eerdmans, 2000)/ Hereafter, JDDJ.

27. Karl Lehmann and Wolfhart Pannenberg, eds., *The Condemnations of the Reformation Era—Do They Still Divide?* (Minneapolis: Augsburg Fortress, 1990), 42f.

28. Peter Hünermann, "Theologische Kriterien und Perspektiven der Untersuchung zu den gegenseitigen Lehrverwerfungen des 16. Jahrhunderts", in: *Ein Schritt zur Einheit der Kirchen? Können gegenseitige Lehrverurteilungen aufgehoben werden?*, ed. Wolf-Dieter Hauschild et al. (Regensburg: Pustet, 1986), 58.

29. In the 19th and 20th centuries several manuscripts of the text were discovered, but the two editions by Luther should be regarded as two manuscripts, too, since their manuscripts have not yet been identified. The manuscripts have slightly different divisions of the text, different numbering of the chapters, and they partly differ in content. The authoritative critical edition is Wolfgang von Hinten, ed., *"Der Franckforter" ("Theologia Deutsch")*. *Kritische Textausgabe* (Zürich: Artemis, 1982; following the so-called Dessau manuscript; quoted as „Hinten"); von Hinten's edition in modern German: Alois Haas, ed., *"Der Franckforter." Theologia Deutsch* (Einsiedeln: Johannes, 1980; quoted as „Haas"). English translations: *Theologia Germanica. Modern English Edition*, trans. Susanna

"of the Teutonic order, a Priest and a Warden in the house of the Teutonic order in Frankfort"[30] aiming at discerning "God's righteous friends and the unrighteous, false, disorderly spirits who harm the holy church."[31] Nevertheless, in his 1516 edition, Luther chose the title "A spiritual, noble booklet concerning the right distinction and understanding of the old and new man, who Adam's and God's children are, and how Adam should die in us while Christ should rise."[32] The author was focused on Christ and a Christ-like life, but all the same he used philosophical motifs from the neo-platonic tradition in order to develop his understanding. Many questions arise from what he says, but according to his own purpose of offering practical guidance, he does not answer them. So. in interpreting the text, we should focus on his intentions. They were the reason that the text was so popular for so many centuries.[33] The text does not show a logical line of thought, rather it is a collection of reflections and meditations on "one and the same topic: the deification of the human being by grace in the light of the mediating exemplarity of the 'Christ-life.'"[34]

The *Theologia Deutsch* starts by distinguishing between God and creatures by calling God "the perfect" while the creatures are understood as "that which is in part," referring to a sentence of the Apostle Paul in 1 Cor 13:10: "When that which is perfect is come, then that which is in part shall be done away with." God relates to created things like the sun relates to the light. Thus the many things, the "this and that" have their substance or essence in God, the perfect being which comprises all creatures.[35] Without or outside of the perfect

---

Winkworth (Mesa, Arizona: Scriptoria Books, 2010; following the so-called Bronnbach manuscript; quoted as "Winkworth"); *The Theologia Germanica of Martin Luther*, trans. and ed. Bengt Hoffman (Mahwah, NJ: Paulist Press, 1980; following Luther's edition of 1518; quoted as "Hoffman"). For an overview see: Christian Peters, "Theologia deutsch," in *Theologische Realenzyklopädie* 33, ed. Gerhard Müller (Berlin: Walter de Gruyter, 2002), 258–262. For an excellent interpretation see: Andreas Zecherle, "Die *Theologia Deutsch*. Ein spätmittelalterlicher mystischer Traktat," in: *Gottes Nähe unmittelbar erfahren. Mystik im Mittelalter und bei Martin Luther*, ed. Berndt Hamm and Volker Leppin (Tübingen: Mohr Siebeck, 2007), 1–95. See also Arno Mentzel-Reuters, "Reformatoren drucken das Mittelalter. Luthers 'Theologia deutsch' und Melanchthons Lampert von Hersfeld," in: *Die Reformation und ihr Mittelalter*, ed. Günter Frank and Volker Leppin (Stuttgart: frommann-holzboog Verlag, 2016), 79–112.

30. Hinten, 67,3f., 6; tr. Winkworth, XLIV.

31. Hinten 67,5–7; tr. Hoffman, 55. See Hoffman, 6–14.20–24.

32. See fn. 3 above.

33. Until 1961, 190 editions were identified, 124 of them in German, the others were translations in many languages (Hinten, 4; see also Hoffman, 24–34). Alois M. Haas speaks of a "breite Ruhmesgeschichte und schier unübersehbare Nachwirkung der 'Theologia Deutsch'" ("wide history of praise and almost immeasurable influence of the *Theologia Deutsch*": Haas, 14).

34. Haas, 17.

35. Hinten, 71 (ch. 1,1–12); tr. Winkworth, 1.

there is nothing. In a certain way, the perfect is all things, but at the same time, it is above all things. It is the one, while the created things are the many, but they exist insofar the one shines in them. It is the good, and all the created things are good insofar as the one good that is the perfect is present in them. The *Theologia Deutsch* says: "Now that creature in which the Eternal Good most manifests itself, shines forth, works, is most known and loved, is the best, and that wherein the Eternal Good is least manifested is the least good of all creatures."[36] Creatures are dependent on a constant communication of being (*Sein*) from the perfect.

The one, perfect and good, is present in all created things. Nevertheless, the author, referring to Paul, asserts that the perfect is still to come. Obviously, there are two different forms of presence of the perfect: one is the presence in an ontological sense, the other is the presence as being recognized by the human creature. How is the knowledge of the perfect possible for the creature, "that which is in part?" This question leads the author to discuss the problem of sin and salvation.

He offers the traditional definition of sin as turning away from God—who is *the perfect*—and turning instead to creatures—who are *the many* (*aversio a Deo* and *conversio ad creaturas*), but the author immediately interprets this definition in his own way: "Now mark: when the creature claims for its own anything good, such as Substance, Life, Knowledge, Power, and in short whatever we should call good, as if it were that, or possessed that, or that were itself, or that proceeded from it,—as often as this comes to pass, the creature goes astray."[37] Sin is a contradiction to the ontological condition of the creature. This is what the author is emphasizing again and again:

> [...] praise and honor and glory belong to none but to God only. But now, if I call any good thing my own, as if I were it, or of myself had power or did or knew anything, or as if anything were mine or of me, or belonged to me, or were due to me or the like, I take unto myself somewhat of honor and glory [...] I touch God in His honor and take unto myself what belongs to God only.[38]

Turning away from God and turning instead to the creatures is the presumption to be something, the presumption (in early modern German: *annemen*) that something belongs to oneself, the presumption of the "I," "My," and "Me." The fall of Adam did not happen, as the author explains, because he ate an apple, but because of his presumption, claiming his "I," "My," "Me," claiming anything for his own.[39]

36. Hinten, 77 (ch. 6,10–12); tr. Winkworth, 8.
37. Hinten, 73 (ch. 2,5–8); tr. Winkworth, 3.
38. Hinten, 74f. (ch. 4,1–5.7f.); tr. Winkworth, 5f.
39. Hinten, 73 (ch. 3,1–6); tr. Winkworth, 4.

But how can this situation of sin be overcome? The author declares:

> [...] man could not without God, and God should not without man. Therefore God took human nature or manhood upon Himself and was made man, and man was made divine. Thus the healing was brought to pass. So also must my fall be healed. I cannot do the work without God, and God may not or will not without me; for if it shall be accomplished, in me, too, God must be made man; in such sort that God must take to Himself all that is in me, within and without, so that there may be nothing in me which strives against God or hinders His work.[40]

The author applies the principle of Athanasius: "God was made man that we might be made God,"[41] describing the healing process of Adam's fall. He does so from the perspective of the neo-Platonic interpretation of the relation between the creator and the creatures. This comprises the following aspects: (1) The healing is something that rests on God's initiative, since God is "that which is perfect." Thus: "man could not [be healed] without God." (2) In sin, human creatures arrogate being and goodness to themselves; thus overcoming sin means that they recognize God as the one in whom they have their being, and love Him as the one who is the good. Healing happens *within* the sinful creature. (3) In Jesus Christ, God took human nature upon Himself, "was made man, and man was made divine." Jesus Christ is the one human creature in whom this is the case by nature: that both, his intellect and his will, completely originate in and are in line with God's knowledge and will. "And he who lives in the true Light and true Love, has the best, noblest, and worthiest life that ever was or will be [...] This life was and is in Christ to perfection, else He were not the Christ."[42] (4) What is the case in Jesus Christ, is the example of what should happen with every human being: They also should become divinized by offering themselves as the space for God's presence and work in them. The "nothingness" of the creatures, compared with the one "which is perfect," corresponds to the aim of "being made God" in the sense that nothing hinders God's presence and working in them. (5) Since Jesus Christ is the normative example for every human being, the unknown author does not attribute to Christ vicarious suffering and atonement for human sins. The incarnation is the central salvific event, not Christ's death and resurrection.[43] What was the case in Jesus Christ with respect to Adam's fall, can and must happen in us—in an analogous way.

---

40. Hinten, 74 (ch.3,12–19); tr. Winkworth, 4f.

41. Athanasius, *De incarnatione verbi* 54,3 (http://www.newadvent.org/fathers/2802.htm; seen April 2, 2018).

42. Hinten, 136 (ch. 43,52–56); tr. Winkworth, 80.

43. See Zecherle, Die ‚Theologia Deutsch', 46, with reference to Hinten, ch. 3.

(On 1) God is the agent in that healing process: "And in this bringing back and healing, I can, or may, or shall contribute nothing, except a mere, pure suffering, so that God alone may do all things in me and work, and I may suffer Him and all His work and His divine will."[44]

God is both the object and the subject of blessedness: "For blessedness lies not in much and many, but in One and oneness. In one word, blessedness lies not in any creature, or work of the creatures, but it lies alone in God and in His works."[45] This refers to the object of blessedness, but at the same time, for this very reason, God is the subject of blessedness. The author of the *Theologia Deutsch* continues: "Therefore I must wait only on God and His work, and leave on one side all creatures with their works, and first of all myself."[46] In addition to this argument that one could call "ontological," one should be aware that the way to salvation or blessedness does not start from a neutral position, but from sin. True self-awareness reveals that "a man, of himself and his own power, is nothing, has nothing, can do and is capable of nothing but infirmity and evil."[47] Focusing on "I," "My," "Mine," human beings are still looking for their own interest in everything, even in spiritual matters. They cannot do anything good in this respect because they would be claiming an act as their own act, and thus in attempting to overcome sin, they would in fact affirm sin. For an act to be good in the theological sense, it is not sufficient to be in line with the will of God in terms of its content; it is also required that such an act originates from the divine will: "'But all that is done from your own will is contrary to the Eternal Will.' [This is said by God to Adam.] It is not that every work which is thus done is in itself contrary to the Eternal Will, but in so far as it is done from a different will, or otherwise than from the Eternal and Divine Will."[48] God loves all works that are done under the guidance of the true light and out of true love.[49] While God and His light are without selfishness and self-seeking, "the I, the Me, the Mine, and the like, belong to the natural and false light; for in all things it seeks itself and its own ends, rather than Goodness for the sake of Goodness. This is . . . the property of nature or the carnal man in each of us."[50]

Nevertheless, as the author states, the "I" can hinder God's acting: "And because I will not suffer [God's acting], rather I count myself to be my own, and say 'I,' 'Mine,' 'Me' and the like, God is hindered, so that He cannot do His

44. Hinten, 74 (ch. 3,23–26); tr. Winkworth, 5 (translation altered).

45. Hinten, 82 (ch. 9,21–23); tr. Winkworth, 14.

46. Hinten, 82 (ch. 9,23–25); tr. Winkworth, 14.

47. Hinten, 105 (ch. 26,2–4), tr. Winkworth, 41.

48. Hinten, 143 (ch. 50,17–20), tr. Winkworth, 90.

49. See Hinten, 141 (ch. 47,14–22), tr. Winkworth, 88.

50. Hinten, 126 (ch. 40,17–19); tr. Winkworth, 67.

work in me alone and without hindrance; for this cause my fall and my going astray remain unhealed. Behold! this all comes of my claiming somewhat for my own."[51] Thus if the perfect will not come, it is my hindrance that causes the problem, but when the perfect comes, it is God's grace that is doing it. In line with his practical intention, the author does not address the tension between these two sentences further.

(On 2) As much as the author emphasizes that God is the subject of that healing process, he also insists that this process must happen *in us*: "Now if God took to Himself all human beings that are in the world, or ever were, and were made a human being in them, and they were made divine in Him, and this work were not fulfilled in me, my fall and my wandering would never be amended except it were fulfilled in me also."[52]

This is the emphasis of many mystics: it is not enough to believe that God in Christ has been made man; it is also important that this happens *in me*.

The author describes two opposite experiences in this process. What first happened with Christ, should also happen with the human being becoming righteous: Christ had to go to hell first, and then he ascended into heaven.[53] The author writes:

> When a man truly perceives and considers himself, and finds himself utterly vile and wicked, and unworthy of all the comfort and kindness that he may ever receive from God, or from the creatures. [. . .] And it seems to him that he shall be eternally lost and damned [...] And therefore also he will not and dare not desire any consolation or release, either from God or from any creature that is in heaven or on earth; but he is willing to be unconsoled and unreleased, and he does not grieve over his condemnation and sufferings; for they are right and just, and not contrary to God, but according to the will of God. Therefore they are right in his eyes, and he has nothing to say against them. Nothing grieves him but his own guilt and wickedness; for that is not right and is contrary to God, and for that cause he is grieved and troubled in spirit. This is what is meant by true repentance for sin.[54]

But this spiritual experience of hell—feeling to be eternally lost and damned—is not the final experience of a person to be justified since God does not forsake this person in hell. Rather, in the midst of this *resignatio ad infernum* (willingness to be damned), he creates in the human being a pure desire for the eternal good alone, and this desire leads the person to bliss, peace, joy, rest, and

51. Hinten, 74 (ch. 3,26–29); tr. Winkworth, 5 (translation altered).
52. Hinten, 74 (ch. 3,19–22); tr. Winkworth, 5.
53. Hinten, 84 (ch. 11,1f.); tr. Winkworth, 16.
54. Hinten, 84 (ch. 11,2–17); tr. Winkworth, 17 (translation altered).

satisfaction. God has turned the turning-away-from-him of this person into her turning-to-him. The *aversio a Deo* is overcome in the hell of repentance, and the *conversio ad Deum* leads to partaking in the eternal good. The author emphasizes that both, hell and heaven, come about "a man in such sort, that he knows not from where they come; and whether they come to him, or depart from him, he can of himself do nothing towards it."[55]

(On 3) "No man comes to the Father, except through Me"

The author explains this saying of Jesus (John 14:6) together with the other: "No man can come to Me, unless the Father, which has sent Me, draws him" (John 6:44). The first saying calls for becoming a disciple of Christ. Christ is with the Father, and His disciple is with Him. In this way—according to John 17:24—the disciple comes to the Father through Christ. Coming to the Father through Christ means: coming to Him through a Christ-like life. Repentance is not only mourning and suffering one's wrongdoings; even more, it means returning to obedience to God. "For disobedience is itself sin. But when a man enters into the obedience of the faith, all is healed, and blotted out and forgiven, and not else."[56] This life requires a very critical self-awareness of internal or external desires, loves, ideas, thoughts, and lusts ("war nemen seyn selbs"): "And whenever he becomes aware of any thought or intent rising up within him that does not belong to God and were not suitable for Him, he must resist it and root it out as thoroughly and as speedily as he may [...] in whom it should be thus, whatever he had inwardly, or did outwardly, would be all of God [...]."[57]

That a person becomes a disciple is the result of the Father's "drawing." The Father is the one, perfect good. If something of this good is revealed to human beings, a desire for this good arises in them, a desire of coming closer to and uniting with this good. This makes people aware that there is no true good and no true being outside the perfect, and that they cannot claim any being, power, or knowledge for themselves. In a process of increasingly knowing and loving the one perfect, the person does not wish anything else than realizing completely the will of the one perfect, the Father, and this is the Christ-like life.[58] Thus the two sayings of Jesus explain each other.

(On 4 & 5) Christ-like Life

Since, in the view of the author, God wants to become a human being in every righteous person, they must orient themselves by the life, works, and words of Jesus. The life of these persons is a life of discipleship of Jesus, a Christ-life. Thus, willing obedience to God, spiritual poverty, and deep humility are

---

55. Hinten, 85 (ch. 11,43–45); tr. Winkworth, 19.
56. Hinten, 91f. (ch. 16,31–33); tr. Winkworth, 26.
57. Hinten, 148 (ch. 52,[2–5]7–9.17f.; tr. Winkworth, 98; translation altered.
58. See ch. 53 (Hinten, 149–154; Winkworth, 99–103).

its marks, and also 'Gelassenheit,' being prepared to suffer and do what God decides. As Christ did the will of his Father, such Christians wish to grow in the unity of their will with God. Willing differently from God (that is: having one's own will: Eigenwille) is sin. The enlightened person could say: "I would gladly be to the Eternal Goodness, what his own hand is to man."[59] Taking up Paul's word in Gal 3 ("No longer I, but Christ who lives in me"), one could say with the Theologia Deutsch: No longer I, but God who wills in me. This Christ-life is good and fulfilling in itself. Those who wish to achieve anything with it have already failed. Thus the concept of merit is excluded from this understanding of justification, the author rather speaks of deification of the human person. "It is a great folly when a man, or any creature, dreams that he knows or can accomplish anything of himself, and above all when he dreams that he knows or can fulfil any good thing whereby he may merit much at God's hands, and gain from Him."[60]

"Moreover, these men are in a state of freedom, because they have lost the fear of pain or hell, and the hope of reward or heaven, but are living in pure submission to the Eternal Goodness, in the perfect freedom of fervent love."[61]

Several aspects of the Theologia Deutsch seem to be quite foreign to Luther: the foundational role of neo-platonic ontological reflections, for example, or the infrequent use of biblical arguments even though the biblical tradition is strongly in the background but not so often made explicit. What about this book made such an impression on Luther? It confirmed a number of basic aspects of Luther's theology at that time and also later: the understanding of the human being as originally self-centered, seeking his own interest in everything (in omnibus suum quaerere)[62] and thus being unable to love God purely and with one's whole self; therefore the complete dependence on the divine activity for salvation, emphasizing that the whole life is a life of suffering from sin and thus a life of repentance; Luther's often-quoted sentence from the prayer of Hannah, the mother of the prophet Samuel: "The Lord kills and makes alive, the Lord brings to hell, and brings up" (1 Sam 2:6)—this sentence resonates with the author's description of the hell of repentance and the bliss of loving God. In 1518, the time of the edition of the complete "Eyn deutsch Theologia," Luther described in his theology of the cross, as presented at the "Heidelberg Disputation" in the same year, how grace is present under its opposite form, under the accusation of sin. Human beings seek their own interest in everything, thus they do it also

---

59. Hinten, 82 (ch. 10,9f.); tr. Winkworth, 15.
60. Hinten, 138 (ch. 44,31–33); tr. Winkworth, 84; translation altered.
61. Hinten, 83 (ch. 10,16–19); tr. Winkworth, 15.
62. See Theodor Dieter, Der junge Luther und Aristoteles: Eine historisch-systematische Untersuchung zum Verhältnis von Theologie und Philosophie (Berlin: de Gruyter, 2001), 80–107.

in relation to God. They even use God, the highest good, the *summum bonum*. Therefore God cannot present himself to them as the highest good, but must do so in the crucified Christ. The *summum bonum* at the cross! This is God's way of breaking and overcoming human beings' self-seeking tendency. If the righteousness of Christ appeared to the sinners simply as a positive reality, they would appropriate it as their own; thus the salvific presence of Christ's righteousness needs to be hidden under the accusation of the sinner. Even though Luther's theology had different sources and a different logic in its development from the *Theologia Deutsch*, Luther could see in it an ally for his contested theology.

In his "Explanations of the 95 Theses," Luther states:

> When God begins to justify a man, he first of all condemns him; him whom he wishes to raise up, he destroys; him whom he wishes to heal, he smites; and the one to whom he wishes to give life, he kills, as he says in I Kings 2 [I Sam. 2:6], and Deut. 32[:39], "I kill and I make alive, etc." He does this, however, when he destroys man and when he humbles and terrifies him into the knowledge of himself and of his sins [...] Actually man knows so little about his justification that he believes he is very near condemnation, and he looks upon this, not as infusion of grace but as a diffusion of the wrath of God upon him. [...] However, as long as he remains in this wretched, perplexed state of conscience, he has neither peace nor consolation, unless he flees to the power of the church and seeks solace and relief from his sins and wretchedness which he has uncovered through confession. For neither by his own counsel or his strength will he be able to find peace; in fact, his sadness will finally be turned into despair. When the priest sees such humility and anguish, he shall, with complete confidence in the power given him to show compassion, loose the penitent and declare him loosed, and thereby give peace to his conscience.[63]

Here we can see that, and why, Luther could find support in the *Theologia Deutsch* for his developing understanding of justification; nevertheless, we can also recognize that he experienced this understanding as a perplexity to be overcome. Indeed, in his "Explanations," Luther was on the way to discover the performative character of the priest's word of absolution, which Luther—in agreement with an opinion widespread among theologians in medieval times—so far had understood as being only declarative, that is, affirming that, due to true repentance, God had already forgiven the penitent when he or she came to the priest in the sacrament of penance. The explanation on thesis 7, quoted previously, assumes that the word of the priest is effective, but it only effects the peace of the conscience. The forgiveness of the sins is still thought to have occurred earlier through divine activity, including the accusation of the sinner.

---

63. WA 1: 540,8–41; LW 31, 99f.

Later, in his explanation on thesis 38, however, Luther also attributes the effect of forgiving sins to the word of the priest, in which the penitent should trust without any hesitation. Luther also here retracts the declarative understanding of forgiveness in confession found in thesis 38.[64]

In reflecting on the arguments for his 95 Theses, Luther gained the insight that shaped his further theology: The basic event in justification is neither the love for God by means of a person's natural capacities, as in Biel, nor the repentance created by God (as in Luther's own early theology). Rather, it is the divine activity in the promise of forgiveness and justification, a performative event by the word or in the sacraments, that calls for trusting in it, which in this way effects salvation in us. Now, law and gospel can and must be distinguished. Repentance and good works following justification have to be coordinated to this event. Thus, the Reformation question is no longer: *How* can I find a gracious God? Rather it is: *Where* can I find a gracious God? And the answer is: in the gospel that communicates Christ's promise to me.

Luther's understanding of justification as just indicated was sharply criticized by Cardinal Cajetan in 1518 as being the equivalent of "building a new church."[65] But 481 years later, the Roman Catholic Magisterium could say, in agreeing with the *Joint Declaration on the Doctrine of Justification*: "Catholics can share the concern of the Reformers to ground faith in the objective reality of Christ's promise, to look away from one's own experience, and to trust in Christ's forgiving word alone (cf. Mt 16,19; 18,18)."[66] These words are precisely related to the Luther-Cajetan-debate. We find here another highly remarkable movement in Catholic attitude toward the Lutheran doctrine.

We have seen two medieval traditions, one that Luther rejected and one which he agreed with. In both cases, he was debating these traditions in order to find his own theological way. It is astonishing and exhilarating that the solutions he found for the challenges can no longer be seen as church-dividing, but are open to a common understanding among Catholics and Lutherans.

---

64. WA 1: 596,38f. (LW 31, 196: "So, as it stands, I do not maintain this thesis in its entirety, but deny a large part of it"). See the whole explanation 38 (WA 1: 593,39–596,39; LW 31, 191–196) together with the Disputation "On exploring the truth and comforting the terrified consciences" (WA 1: 630–633). See also theses 6-7 (WA 1: 233,20–24; LW 31, 26) and 37-38 (WA 1: 235,9–13; LW 31, 29). Oswald Bayer offers a careful analysis of Luther's discovery of the performative character of Christ's promise through the priest: *Promissio: Geschichte der reformatorischen Wende in Luthers Theologie*, 2nd ed. (Darmstadt: Wissenschaftliche Buchgesellschaft, 1989), 164–202.

65. Cajetan, "De fide ad fructuosam absolutionem sacramentalem necessaria;" English translation: *Cajetan Responds. A Reader in Reformation Controversy*, ed. and trans. Jared Wicks (Eugene, Oregon: Wipf & Stock, 2011), 49-55 ("Faith in the Sacrament as Certainty of Forgiveness"). See Theodor Dieter, "Misslungene Kommunikation und Kirchenspaltung: Augsburg 1518," in *Kommunikation ist möglich*, ed. Christine Büchner et al. (Ostfildern: Matthias Grünewald, 2013), 227–242.

66. JDDJ, § 36.

4. Martin Luther's Proclamation of Justification by Faith Alone

TIMOTHY WENGERT

The original invitation to this august gathering noted that "one session will be devoted to the *doctrine* of justification." In English, "doctrine" is a rather peculiar word, the significance of which differs slightly from the Latin *doctrina* or the German *Lehre*. In the sixteenth century, while the word *sophismata* (sophistries) was completely negative and the word *dogmata* could be used either positively or negatively (the latter especially by humanists like Erasmus of Rotterdam or Philip Melanchthon), *doctrina* and *Lehre* were quite positive and should thus always be translated "teaching," and only rarely "doctrine." One could perhaps blame nineteenth-century Frenchmen for any negative connotations of the word "doctrine" in English, since "doctrinaire" was initially their invention as a label for a political group favoring a constitutional monarchy. Only because ultra-royalists and revolutionists derided the group as totally impractical, did the term become completely negative.[1] Now "doctrinaire" carries only a negative meaning: "dogmatic, authoritarian, impractical or merely theoretical." That negativity has over the centuries rubbed off on the word "doctrine."

This etymology lesson is not designed to insult the reader's intelligence, but to emphasize that Martin Luther and his colleagues in Wittenberg had a very different understanding of how one did theology from many their contemporaries—let alone from people today. One must, therefor, take into account that justification for them was less "doctrine," which denotes the careful analysis of a teaching (as used, for example, among seventeenth-century orthodox Lutheran theologians or in the dogmatic-historical approach of nineteenth- and twentieth-century scholars like Friedrich Loofs and Reinhold Seeberg), and more teaching, what Peter Fraenkel labeled "verbal nouns."[2] When Philip Melanchthon constructed a commonplace (*locus communis*) for justification, he maintained that "teaching moment" by naming it not *iustificatio* but *de iustificatione et fide*: "concerning justification and faith."[3] When Luther set out to compose a tract

---

1. Merriam-Webster online: accessed 16 August 2016 at: http://www.merriam-webster.com/dictionary/doctrinaire.

2. Peter Fraenkel, "Revelation and Tradition: Notes on Some Aspects of Doctrinal Continuity in the Theology of Philip Melanchthon," *Studia Theologica* (Lund) 13 (1959): 97-133.

3. Philip Melanchthon, *Loci communes rerum theologicarum seu Hypotyposes theologicae* (1521), in: *Melanchthons Werke*, vol. 2/1: *Loci communes von 1521 Loci praecipui theologici von 1559 (1. Teil)*, ed. Hans Engelland and Robert Stupperich (Gütersloh: Gerd Mohn, 1978), 106.

on justification, he or his scribe called his never-completed attempt a "rhapsody" on justification.[4]

Indeed, to understand what the Wittenbergers were attempting in theology, one must underscore at the outset that, in their teaching especially, Luther and Melanchthon always combined two aspects of a topic: what a thing is with what its effects are.[5] These questions (derived in Melanchthon's case from two questions in Aristotle's *Analytics*) offered a solution to a Renaissance dilemma that often pitted rhetoric against dialectics, especially in the humanists' criticisms of scholastic theology. Melanchthon built upon the work of the Renaissance thinker, Rudolf Agricola, whose dialectics Melanchthon had devoured as a young Master of Arts in Tübingen, and combined it with Luther's dynamic understanding of how a person is justified before God. The modern dilemma, which divides intellect from emotions, had no place in the pre-Enlightened world of the Reformation—despite later scholars' attempts to remove all vestiges of affect from descriptions of Luther's theology.

With these preliminaries out of the way or, rather, with this foundation to Wittenberg's theology firmly in place, one can, save for one final caveat, begin to examine Luther's understanding of justification. Not only is Luther's understanding of justification not so much doctrine as teaching, but also it is best analyzed *not* so much on the basis of what Luther may have said in the lecture hall before 1518 but on the basis of the actual tracts that he penned once the Reformation was underway. Now, it is true that in 1515, after having lectured for two years on the Psalms, Luther in short order lectured on Romans, Galatians, and Hebrews before returning in late 1518 to the Psalms.[6] In all of these early sources, he discusses various aspects of justification. But, historically speaking, these early lectures were unknown to Luther's contemporaries and remained a-moldering in German archives and libraries until printed in the nineteenth and twentieth centuries. Luther's contemporaries encountered Luther's early understanding of justification in his published tracts (the *Explanation of the 95 Theses*, *Sermon on the Two-Fold Righteousness, Freedom of a Christian*), in his published commentaries (on *Galatians, Psalms 1-22*, and his *Christmas Postil* on the Sunday

---

4. See *Luthers Werke* [*Schriften*], 73 vols. (Weimar: Böhlau, 1883–2009), 30/2: 652–76. The title likely stems from Veit Dietrich: *Rhapsodia seu Concepta in Librum de loco Iustificationis 1530*. Henceforth: *WA*.

5. Timothy J. Wengert, *Philip Melanchthon's 'Annotationes in Johannem' of 1523 in Relation to Its Predecessors and Contemporaries* (Geneva: Librairie Droz, 1987), 203–12.

6. See *WA* 3–4 & *WA* 55/1–2 (*Dictata super Psalterium*); *WA* 56 (lectures on Romans, Galatians and Hebrews). For English translations see *Luther's Works*, ed. J. Pelikan et al. 55+ vols. (Philadelphia: Fortress & St. Louis: Concordia, 1956–), vol. 10–11, 25, 29. Henceforth: *LW*.

lectionary) and in his preface to Romans written with Melanchthon for the 1522 translation of the New Testament.[7]

Of course, other published materials from the time also contain important aspects of this teaching (especially his occasional sermons, such as *The Sermon of Martin Luther Delivered in Erfurt on Quasimodogeniti* [7 April 1521, 2nd Sunday of Easter], or the sermons delivered in Borna and Weimar in 1522).[8] For the later Luther, his second published commentary on Galatians dominates any discussion of his explication of justification, although one may also glean insights from the *Smalcald Articles* (published in 1538) and from his 1528 *Great Confession on the Lord's Supper*, which includes a more general confession of faith at the end.[9] In short, these documents give a far more accurate reading of—to use social psychologist Erving Goffmann's phrase—Luther's presentation of his self, or at least of his theology, in everyday life, that is, to the commoners and scholars of his day.[10] They will comprise the bulk of the sources used here as well.

BREAKING LATE-MEDIEVAL NOTIONS OF GIFT-GIVING

In recent years, Lutheran systematic theologians have dabbled in explaining Luther's teaching of justification in terms of gift giving. As Berndt Hamm has shown, however, this fruitful approach sometimes ignores the commercial aspects of late-medieval understanding of the practice, and imposes on Luther the very notions to which he was most adamantly opposed.[11] In late-medieval piety and practice, the slogan, "*Do ut des*," dominated thinking. "I give so that you may give." Under this rubric, God's grace became a kind of celestial bribe, which demanded some sort of response from the recipient. Moreover, when turned on its head, human giving then obligated God to reciprocate. For example, by taking a phrase long used in pastoral theology, namely, *facientibus quod in se est, Deus non denegat gratiam*, Gabriel Biel made this the centerpiece of his approach to justification. To be sure, justifying grace was earned through a *meritum de con-*

---

7. *WA* 1: 522–628 (*LW* 31: 77–252); *WA* 2: 145–52 (*LW* 31:293–06); *WA* 7: 39–73 (*LW* 31:327–77); *WA* 2: 436–618 (*LW* 27:151–410); *WA* 5: 1–673; *WA* 10/1/1 (*LW* 52); *Luthers Werke: Bibel*, 12 vols. (Weimar: Böhlau, 1906–1961), 7: 2–27 (*LW* 35:365–80). Henceforth: *WA* Bi.

8. *WA* 7: 801–13; *WA* 10/3: CLXII–CLXIV, 352–61.

9. *WA* 40/1:33–688; *WA* 40/2: 1–184 (LW 26–27:1–149); *Smalcald Articles*, trans. William Russell, in: *The Book of Concord*, ed. Robert Kolb & Timothy J. Wengert (Minneapolis: Fortress, 2000), 295–328; *WA* 26:241–509 (LW 37: 151–372). Henceforth: *SA* and *BC*, respectively.

10. Erving Goffman, *The Presentation of Self in Everyday Life* (New York: Doubleday, 1959).

11. Berndt Hamm, "Martin Luther's Revolutionary Theology of Pure Gift without Reciprocation," *Lutheran Quarterly* 29 (2015): 125–61, translation of: "Pure Gabe ohne Gegengabe," *Jahrbuch für biblische Theologie* 27 (2012): 241–76.

gruo, where one gave God a leaden coin to receive gold in return; nevertheless, the obligatory nature of gift exchange, the "*Do ut des*," remained intact. Thus, when we examine the work of the Erfurt Augustinian Johann von Paltz, whose time in the cloister there briefly overlapped with Luther's, we find that his robust defense of the sale of indulgences—as suffused with references to grace as it was—relied upon the merciful action of the pope who, for a mere pittance, allowed an unheard of grace that could release the contrite sinner from all penalty for sin and could free the soul being purified in purgatory from its flames.

Luther, on the contrary, insists that with God there is only and always "Gabe ohne Gegengabe," to use Hamm's apt phrase, "gift without a reciprocal gift." Thus, the *95 Theses* lack any reference to a *quid pro quo* in the Christian life. God empowers priest, bishop and pope to declare the forgiveness of sin [thesis 6]. The penalties for sin remain in God's hands alone as a means of driving the sinner to cry out for God's grace. These penalties, especially in the form of the fear of death, may even surpass all suffering in purgatory. The unconditional, gracious nature of the justifying God, then, forms the bedrock of Luther's understanding. Upon this foundation, Luther makes several other crucial steps in developing his approach to justification focused on: 1) The function of the Word of God and faith; 2) redefining grace; 3) the nature of faith; 4) the role of good works as the fruit of faith; and, finally, 5) the foolishness of it all.

THE WORK OF THE WORD OF GOD

Here, despite recent criticism by some, the historical investigation by Gerhard Ebeling helps unlock the crucial role of the Word in Luther's view of justification[12] (Leif Grane, in a different way, came to similar conclusions).[13] Beginning with his *Evangelische Evangeliumauslegung* of 1942, continuing with his work on Luther's *Dictata* in the 1950s and culminating in his *Introduction to Luther's Thought*, Ebeling realized that Luther's teaching on justification was more experience than theory and thus was intimately connected to his insight into how God's Word functions to put to death the old creature and bring to life the new.[14] As Ebeling described it, Luther reassessed the proof text for allegorization from 2 Cor. 3:6 ("The letter kills and the Spirit gives life") and returned to an

---

12. See especially *Luther: An Introduction to His Thought*, transl. R. A. Wilson (Philadelphia: Fortress, 1972), 93–124.

13. Leif Grane, *Modus loquendi theologicus: Luthers Kampf um die Erneuerung der Theologie (1515–1518)* (Leiden: Brill, 1975).

14. Gerhard Ebeling, *Evangelische Evangelienauslegung: Eine Untersuchung zu Luthers Hermeneutik* (Munich: Kaiser, 1942); *idem*, "Die Anfänge von Luthers Hermeneutik," *Zeitschrift für Theologie und Kirche* 48 (1961): 172–230; *idem*, *Luther: An Introduction to His Thought*, trans. R. A. Wilson (Philadelphia: Fortress, 1972).

Augustinian position that distinguished commands from promises, eventually moving to the classic Lutheran distinction between law and gospel. Only when later theologians divorced justification from this distinction did Lutheran insistence on forensic justification lose its true meaning. What Luther admits in 1545 to having discovered in his early lectures was that the letter truly kills its reader so that the Holy Spirit may give life and faith.[15] Justification, then, is the ongoing event in the life of the baptized, where the law terrifies, drowns and puts to death and the gospel comforts, raises and creates the life of faith. Thus, faith's definition is intimately connected to what it does.

THE CENTRALITY OF FAITH NOT WORKS

In addition to what would come to be called the distinction between law and gospel, Oswald Bayer has shown that, first in 1518, Luther permanently associated the Word that works on the hearer with justification by faith, specifically in Luther's *Explanations of the 95 Theses*.[16] Up until that time, Luther tried to blend Augustine's central concepts of humility and pride into his newfound respect for law and gospel. To be sure, in the early part of the *Explanations* he writes (about thesis 7) in this way: "So it seems to me, and I declare: When God begins to justify individual human beings, he first of all condemns them; those whom he wishes to raise up, he destroys; those whom he wishes to heal, he smites; and the ones to whom he wishes to give life, he kills."[17] Yet at this stage, God's work still implied for Luther a concomitant work of the human recipient: not doubting God's promise. In explaining thesis 62, however, Luther offers a definition of the gospel that finally eliminates all works, even humility, from his understanding of faith.

> The gospel of God is something that is not very well known to a large part of the church. Therefore I must speak of it at greater length. Christ has left nothing to the world except the gospel. . . . Moreover, according to the Apostle in Romans 1, the gospel is a preaching of the incarnate Son of God, given to us without any merit on our part for salvation and peace. It is a word of salvation, a word of grace, a word of comfort, a word of joy, a voice of the bridegroom and the bride, a good word, a word of peace. . . . But the law is a word of destruction, a word of wrath, a word of sadness, a word of grief, a voice of the

15. *WA* 54: 176–87 (*LW* 34:323–38).

16. Oswald Bayer, *Promissio: Geschichte der reformatorischen Wende in Luthers Theologie* (Göttingen: Vandenhoeck & Ruprecht, 1971).

17. *LW* 31: 99 (*WA* 1: 540). Cf. *LW* 31: 100 (*WA* 1: 540f.): "To be sure, the person who is to be absolved must guard himself very carefully from any doubt that God has remitted his sins, in order that he may find peace of heart."

judge and the defendant, a word of restlessness, a word of curse. . . . Through the law we have nothing except an evil conscience, a restless heart, a troubled breast because of our sins, which the law points out but does not take away. And we ourselves cannot take it away. Therefore for those of us who are held captive, who are overwhelmed by sadness and in dire despair, the light of the gospel comes and says, "Fear not," "comfort, comfort my people," "encourage the fainthearted," "behold your God," "behold the Lamb of God, who takes away the sin of the world." Behold that one who alone fulfils the law for you, whom God has made to be your righteousness, sanctification, wisdom, and redemption, for all those who believe in him. When the sinful conscience hears this sweetest messenger, it comes to life again, shouts for joy while leaping about full of confidence, and no longer fears death, the types of punishment associated with death, or hell. . . . Therefore the true glory of God springs from this gospel.[18]

This distinction between the work of the law and gospel on the hearer to create and sustain faith and, thus, to justify the believer stays with Luther throughout his life. Nowhere does he explain it and its connection to justification more clearly than in *Freedom of a Christian*. In the Latin version of that central tract, Luther begins by criticizing the scholastic definition of faith that placed it among the virtues and ties it instead directly to experience, which he narrowed in the following paragraphs to the work of God's word on the believer. Hence he could conclude: "The soul can lack everything except the word of God. . . . For the word of God cannot be received or honored by any works but by faith alone. Therefore, it is clear that the soul needs the word alone for life and righteousness, because if the soul could be justified by anything else, it would not need the word and, consequently, would not need faith."[19]

The other important source for Luther's early exposition of justification is his preface to the book of Romans, written in 1522 for his German translation of the New Testament. As I have shown elsewhere, this piece was actually written in conjunction with Philip Melanchthon, whose nearly contemporaneous lectures on Romans contain many of the aspects of Luther's exposition.[20] This preface, perhaps more than any other writing by Luther, had the most lasting impact on later generations of Lutherans and, from what John Wesley says of his strangely warmed heart, other Christians as well.

18. *LW* 31: 230–31 (*WA* 1: 616–17).

19. Translation by the author from the *Annotated Luther*, ed. Hans Hillerbrand et al., 6 vols. (Minneapolis: Fortress, 2015–2017), 1: 491–92 (*WA* 7: 50). Henceforth AL.

20. Timothy J. Wengert, "Philip Melanchthon's 1522 Annotations on Romans and the Lutheran Origins of Rhetorical Criticism," in: *Biblical Interpretation in the Era of the Reformation*, ed. Richard A. Muller and John L. Thompson (Grand Rapids: Eerdmans, 1996), 118–140.

Luther, borrowing from Melanchthon then, insisted that the book of Romans functioned as the *argumentum* for Scripture—Paul's summary of the Bible's central points.[21] Often reduced to sin, law, gospel, grace and faith, Melanchthon in his *Loci communes* of 1521, also included other topics from Romans: "signs" (i.e., sacraments; cf. Rom. 6), political authority (Rom. 13), and Christian freedom (Rom. 14–15). On the specific terms of faith and righteousness, Luther begins by once again criticizing his scholastic opponents. "Faith is not the human notion and dream that some people call faith. . . . Faith, however, is a divine work in us which changes us and makes us to be born anew of God (John 1[:12–13]). It kills the old Adam and makes us altogether different people in heart and spirit and mind and powers; and it bring with it the Holy Spirit."[22] To underscore the divine origin of faith, Luther continues: "And this is the work which the Holy Spirit performs in faith. . . . Pray God that he may work faith in you."[23] Turning to righteousness, Luther finds a way to use the Ciceronian definition (*iustitia* is giving to each his [or her] own) without reducing the centrality of God's action.

> Righteousness, then, is such a faith. It is called "the righteousness of God" because God gives it, and counts it as righteousness for the sake of Christ our Mediator, and makes a person fulfill his [or her] obligation to everybody. For through faith a person becomes free from sin and comes to take pleasure in God's commandments, thereby giving God the honor due him and paying him what that person owes him.[24]

REDEFINING GRACE

Another aspect of Luther's approach to justification revolves around the meaning of grace. Medieval theologians had already developed several different definitions of the term, many derived from Augustine and his varied use of the word *gratia* in his writings. Two stand out as most important.[25] The word *gratia* could mean *gratia gratis data*, grace given freely. Theologians like St. Bonaventure had argued that this grace occurred, among other places, in preaching, where the hearers—especially those in a state of sin—heard the preacher's gracious call to take part in the sacrament of penance so that they could move from their present state into a state of grace. Others, like Gabriel Biel, associated this grace

---

21. *LW* 35: 365 (*WA* Bi 7: 2).

22. *LW* 35: 370 (*WA* Bi 7: 8 & 10).

23. *LW* 35: 371 (*WA* Bi 7: 10).

24. *LW* 35: 371, alt. (*WA* Bi 7: 10). This same Ciceronian definition appears in *Freedom of a Christian* in Luther's description of the second power of faith (AL 1: 497–99 [*WA* 7: 53]).

25. Heiko Augustinus Oberman, *The Harvest of Medieval Theology: Gabriel Biel and Late Medieval Nominalism*, 2d ed. (Durham, NC: Labyrinth Press, 1983), 470.

given freely with the gifts of creation, part of the *potentia Dei ordinata*, the ordained power of God, God's gracious bestowal on sinners of the law and free choice (*liberum arbitrium*).[26] This allowed sinners to do what is in them and to merit *de congruo* (in accord with God's gracious intention) the second and most important form of grace, the *gratia gratum faciens*, the grace that makes acceptable. This grace was infused into the penitent's soul and moved them from a state of sin into a state of grace. It was, in medieval terms, an infused *habitus charitatis*, a disposition of love that perfected the inchoate faith of the believer through love.

In his early lectures, and later in criticizing his Roman opponents, Luther could occasionally employ these terms.[27] From Erasmus's *Annotations on the New Testament*, however, Luther discovered a very different rendering of the Greek *charis*, which the Dutch humanist rendered not as *gratia* but as *favor Dei* (God's favor). In his 1519 commentary on Galatians, Luther was still skeptical of Erasmus's rendering and preferred to understand Paul's use of *charis* to mean both "God's favor" and "the grace that makes acceptable."[28] Two years later, however, in the attack on Latomus, Luther specifically rejected understanding grace as an infused power and insisted instead that it meant God's favor or mercy.[29] Rolf Schäfer argues that this change took place under the influence of Philip Melanchthon, who started to use Erasmus's understanding in 1520 and convinced Luther to do the same. Thus, in the Preface to Romans (1522), Luther speaks of the difference between grace and gift (Rom. 5:15) this way. "Grace actually means God's favor, or the good will which in himself he bears toward us, by which he is disposed to give us Christ and to pour into us the Holy Spirit with his gifts."[30]

For Luther, such a shift eliminated an ontological construal of justification and left the sinner dependent upon God's mercy alone. Here is what he responded to Latomus. In Rom. 3:21, "as ought to be done, I take grace in the proper sense of the favor of God—not a quality of the soul, as is taught by our more recent writers. This grace truly produces peace of heart until finally a person is healed from corruption and feels he [or she] has a gracious God."[31]

26. Ibid., 175–78.

27. See, for *gratia gratis data*, WA 3: 111, 25; WA Br 9: 461, 47–55 (letter of Bugenhagen and Luther rejecting the Regensburg Colloquy's proposal on justification from 29 June 1541). For *gratia gratum faciens*, see WA 4: 262, 4–7; WA 55/1: 590.

28. WA 2: 511, 12 (cf. LW 27: 252).

29. See Rolf Schäfer, "Melanchthon's Interpretation of Romans 5:15: His Departure from the Augustinian Concept of Grace Compared to Luther's," in: *Philip Melanchthon (1497–1560) and the Commentary*, ed. Timothy J. Wengert & M. Patrick Graham (Sheffield: Sheffield Academic Press, 1997), 79–104.

30. LW 35: 369 (WA Bi 7: 8).

31. LW 32: 227 (WA 8: 106). For an interpretation of Luther's postscript to Melanchthon's letter to Johannes Brenz from 1531, which some use to demonstrate the ontological nature of

CHRIST ALONE

Jesus Christ is the embodiment of God's grace, and thus Luther also posits a connection between grace alone and Christ alone. For him, if human works get mixed in with God's righteousness given in Christ, then Christ is no longer truly humanity's savior. This conviction permeated early Lutheran thought and became ensconced in the Augsburg Confession, article 20, which Philip Melanchthon drafted.

> In the first place, our works cannot reconcile us with God or obtain grace. Instead, this happens through faith alone when a person believes that our sins are forgiven for Christ's sake, who alone is the mediator to reconcile the Father. Now all who imagine they can accomplish this by works and can merit grace, despise Christ and seek their own way to God contrary to the gospel.[32]

Positing a meriting of grace, for these early Lutherans, meant rejecting both Christ and the gospel and led in their view to a version of Christianity centered on the self and its ultimate control of the process of salvation. "Christ alone" prevented despising Christ. Indeed, as we have seen, this is the equivalent of both faith alone and grace alone for Lutherans.

In his Latin works, Luther uses the phrase *"solus Christus"* hundreds of times. As early as 1515, in a sermon on St. Stephen's Day, Luther wrote, "Because we are carnal, it is impossible for us to fulfill the law, but Christ alone came to fulfill it."[33] In his sermons on the Ten Commandments from the following year (published by Johann Agricola in 1518), he writes, "Faith and hope have no other basis except the God Jesus Christ, its rock, and absolutely no created thing."[34] Then, in 1519, in the *Argumentum* of his commentary on Galatians (that Renaissance introduction to the main points in the epistle), Luther announces in the very first sentence, "The Galatians were taught first by the Apostle [Paul] a sound faith, that is, to trust in Jesus Christ alone and not in their own righteousness or the righteousness of the law."[35]

Luther's view of justification, see Timothy J. Wengert, "Face-to-Face Meetings between Philip Melanchthon and Johannes Brenz: Differentiated Consensus in the Reformation," in: *Collaboration, Conflict, and Continuity in the Reformation: Essays in Honour of James M. Estes on His Eightieth Birthday,* Konrad Eisenbichler, ed. (Toronto: Centre for Reformation and Renaissance Studies, 2014), 83–106.

32. Augsburg Confession, XX.9–10, trans. Eric Gritsch, in: *BC,* 54. Henceforth: *CA.*
33. *WA* 1: 35, 26–27.
34. *WA* 1: 428.
35. *LW* 27: 161 (*WA* 2: 451).

This emphasis combining justification and Christ alone continues through-out Luther's career, but takes on a particularly interesting turn in the *Smalcald Articles*, written in 1536 and published by Luther in 1538. After describing in part one of the *Articles* the basic creedal agreement between Lutherans and Catholics on the Trinity, Luther writes, "The second part is about the articles that pertain to the office and work of Jesus Christ, or to our redemption." Here he outlines what he sees as the greatest differences between Wittenberg's theology and its Roman opponents.

> Here is the first and chief article: That Jesus Christ, our God and Lord, "was handed over to death for our trespasses and was raised for our justification" (Rom. 4[:25]); and he alone is "the Lamb of God, who takes away the sin of the world" (John 1[:29]); and "the Lord has laid upon him the iniquity of us all" (Isa. 53[:6]); furthermore, [3] "All have sinned," and "they are now justified" without merit "by his grace, through the redemption which is in Christ Jesus . . . by his blood" (Rom. 3[:23-25]). Now because this must be believed and may not be obtained or grasped otherwise with any work, law, or merit, it is clear and certain that this faith alone justifies us, as St. Paul says in Romans 3[:28, 26]: "For we hold that a person is justified by faith apart from works prescribed by the law"; and also, "that God alone is righteous and justifies the one who has faith in Jesus." Nothing in this article can be conceded or given up, even if heaven and earth or whatever is transitory passed away. As St. Peter says in Acts 4[:12]: "There is no other name given among mortals by which we must be saved." "And with his bruises we are healed" (Isa. 53[:5]). On this article stands all that we teach and practice against the pope, the devil, and the world. Therefore we must be quite certain and have no doubt about it. Otherwise everything is lost, and the pope and the devil and whatever opposes us will gain victory and be proved right.[36]

Here Luther demonstrates how seamlessly he can move from Christ alone to justification by faith alone and back again. By quoting a variety of Scriptural sources, he also demonstrates that he views this teaching as arising from all of Scripture, not just Paul. Attributing salvation to Christ implies that he alone is the Lamb. Thus, the *solus Christus* arises out of redemption itself and provides the only basis for the *sola fide* ("Now because this must be believed and may not be obtained or grasped otherwise with any work, law, or merit, it is clear and certain that this faith alone justifies us"). At this juncture, Luther's manner of citing Romans 3 is also interesting, in that, while omitting the "*sola*" from faith he places it instead with God ("God alone is righteous and justifies"). This "alone" also appears in Luther's translation of Romans 3:26 but, unlike his

---

36. *SA* II.i.1–5, in *BC*, 301.

addition of "alone" to the word "faith" in v. 28, raised no criticism from opponents, in part, perhaps, because the original Greek includes the word "*auton*" which could be construed reflexively: "God himself" and, thus, "God alone." Yet for Luther, redemption, justification, Christ, and faith are all baked into a single cake. This explains how he can easily move back to his emphasis on Christ alone, quoting Acts: "As St. Peter says in Acts 4[:12]: 'There is no other name given among mortals by which we must be saved.'" For Luther, then, the "no other name" excludes not only the saviors of other religions but also, and more importantly, the claim to be—at any level at all—one's own savior by one's own efforts, works and merits.

Luther concludes this first and primary article with an attack on the pope, precisely because he was penning these articles for presentation at a future council. While we may find his words particularly un-ecumenical, they actually underscore his deep commitment to honest conversation: "On this article stands all that we teach and practice against the pope, the devil, and the world. Therefore we must be quite certain and have no doubt about it. Otherwise everything is lost, and the pope and the devil and whatever opposes us will gain victory and be proved right." First, by placing the pope next to the devil and world, he demonstrates that this was not simply a vendetta against a single person but against a churchly institution, one that he thought had lost its way.

Second, by reducing the dispute to this single issue, he made (perhaps inadvertently) ecumenical conversations far easier. For, if it could be proven that the papacy held a view of justification in common with Luther, suddenly the door is open to far deeper discussion of other articles as well. Moreover, Luther does not begin this part of the *Smalcald Articles* by addressing the question of papal or episcopal authority—that occurs in article four of this part of the document. Thus, by concentrating on coming to a joint declaration on justification, current ecumenical conversations between Lutherans and Roman Catholics have taken Luther's ranking of doctrinal divisions seriously. Moreover, it helps put the *Smalcald Articles*' later discussion of the papacy in context and under the aegis of this "first and chief" article, so that Luther's harsh rejection of the papacy must be interpreted in the light of its understanding of justification, not the other way around.

THE FRUIT OF FAITH

From nearly the beginning, one of the most serious objections to Wittenberg's understanding of justification revolved around the role of good works. Article XX of the Augsburg Confession begins with the sharpest rebuke of the entire document: "Our people are falsely accused of prohibiting good works."[37]

---

37. *CA* XX.1 in: *BC*, 52.

But already ten years earlier, in the second half of the *Freedom of a Christian*, Luther took up the same charge. His comments there have sometimes been misconstrued, especially when readers ignore the rhetorical shape of the document. As Birgit Stolt has shown, the Latin version evinces all of the rules of Ciceronian rhetoric that Luther would have been taught in Eisenach and Erfurt.[38] The second half of the tract forms a lengthy rebuttal or *confutatio*, to use the technical term, for opponents' objections to the arguments in the first half of the text. Thus, Luther begins, "Let us now turn to the second part, which concerns the outer person. Here we will respond to all those people who are offended by the word of faith and what has been said about it."[39]

These opponents express their offense by using derision, taunting Luther with a *reductio ad absurdum*: "If faith does all things and alone suffices for righteousness, why then are good works commanded? We will therefore be content with faith, take our ease and do no works."[40] This objection does *not* come from the mouth of what Luther and others will later label "gross antinomians," but rather from those who insist that at some level works must directly play a role in justification. To such people Luther replies, "Not so, you wicked people, not so!" Their wickedness for Luther consists *not* in licentiousness but rather in their legalism and their resistance to the notion that the human being is *simul iustus et peccator* (at the same time a righteous person and a sinner), so that he adds: "To be sure, this would be true if we were completely and perfectly inner, spiritual persons, which will not happen until the resurrection of the dead on the last day."[41] In the meantime, the inner person, "fully and completely justified through faith," lives on earth to rule the flesh and its desires and to serve others. Throughout the second part of this tract, then, Luther never talks of works except in the context of faith's freedom. Good works are for him and later Lutherans *never* a separate subject but always directly connected to justification by faith alone. The person *coram Deo*, in God's sight—what Luther here calls the inner person— "conformed to God and created in the image of God through faith—is joyful and glad on account of Christ. . . ."[42] That very person of faith then disciplines the body. Faith for Luther puts a person back in Paradise where works were not done to become righteous but in order not to be idle.

At the heart of all good works for Luther (whether disciplining the body or benefitting the neighbor) is the notion that good trees bear good fruit. Faith

---

38. Birgit Stolt, *Studien zu Luthers Freiheitstraktat mit besonderer Rücksicht auf das Verhältnis der lateinischen und der deutschen Fassung zu einander und die Stilmittel der Rhetorik* (Stockholm: Almqvist & Wiksell, 1969).

39. *AL* 1: 510 (*WA* 7: 59).

40. *AL* 1: 510 (*WA* 7: 59).

41. *AL* 1: 510 (*WA* 7: 59).

42. *AL* 1: 511 (*WA* 7: 60).

alone justifies and makes a good tree; that good tree then bears good fruit. Whatever positive views Luther had of Aristotle at this time, he completely rejected
the notion that people become good by doing good. "For just as works do not
make someone a believer, so also they do not make a person righteous. On the
contrary, just as faith makes someone a believer and righteous, so also it produces
good works."[43] But this approach to the relation of faith and works also drives
Luther to insist that good works are not coerced but spontaneous. "These things
are absolutely clear: that faith alone—because of the sheer mercy of God
through Christ [given] in his word—properly and completely justifies and saves
a person; and that no law is necessary for a Christian's salvation, since through
faith one is free from every law and does everything that is done spontaneously,
out of sheer freedom."[44] For him, works not done in the freedom of faith
"become completely compulsory and extinguish freedom along with faith. By
this kind of linkage, such works are no longer good but instead truly damnable.
For they are not free, and they blaspheme against the grace of God. . . ."[45] To
underscore this freedom, Luther also insists that faith is not a human work but
rather the result of hearing "the law and the word of grace," the former of which
terrifies and the latter of which is preached "to awaken faith."[46]

The *Smalcald Articles*, which after Luther's death became especially important
in the disputes that arose between his Gnesio-Lutheran followers and the so-
called Philippists, had a convoluted history. In the midst of writing them, Luther
was stricken with a heart attack and, confined to bed, had to dictate the final
articles to two scribes hovering around him. As a result, the final articles are somewhat shorter and, despite the exposition of justification in the first article of the
second part already explained above, include one entitled: "How a Person Is Justified and concerning Good Works." This article, often neglected by Lutheran
theologians and historians, contains some interesting "ecumenical" characteristics,
in that some things, which became the fodder for later disputes, are completely
lacking here. We find no direct reference to "faith alone" or to the *simul iustus et
peccator*, both of which received harsh judgment from Trent. Instead, we discover
a very mild account of justification and its relation to good works.

> I cannot change at all what I have consistently taught about this until now,
> namely, that "through faith" (as St. Peter says [Acts 15:9]) we receive a different,
> new, clean heart and that, for the sake of Christ our mediator, God will and
> does regard us as completely righteous and holy. Although sin in the flesh is
> still not completely gone or dead, God will nevertheless not count it or con-

43. *AL* 1:515 (*WA* 7:62).
44. *AL* 1:515 (*WA* 7:62).
45. *AL* 1:517 (*WA* 7:63).
46. *AL* 1:519.

sider it. Good works follow such faith, renewal, and forgiveness of sin, and whatever in these works is still sinful or imperfect should not be even counted as sin or imperfection, precisely for the sake of this same Christ. Instead, the human creature should be called and should be completely righteous and holy—according to both the person and his or her works—by the pure grace and mercy that have been poured and spread over us in Christ. Therefore we cannot boast about the great merit of our works, where they are viewed apart from grace and mercy. Rather, as it is written, "Let the one who boasts, boast in the Lord" [1 Cor. 1:31; 2 Cor. 10:17]. That is, if one has a gracious God, then everything is good. Furthermore, we also say that if good works do not follow, then faith is false and not true.[47]

In this rendition, we once again see that for Luther the central issue is *not* faith but Christ and God's mercy. In part, Luther's mildness arises from the very different audience that he imagines for the third part of the Articles: "We could discuss the following matters or articles with learned, reasonable people or among ourselves."[48] Thus, Luther's position on justification, shorn of polemic, quickly becomes an invitation for true ecumenical discussion. Even more, the very fact that he in this article, and Melanchthon in CA XX, explicitly explain the role of good works in justification shows how their opponents' criticisms impacted the way in which they discussed this issue.

THE FOOLISHNESS OF IT ALL

Without this final aspect of Luther's approach to justification, his entire proposal to the church catholic comes a cropper. The reason, finally, that I am so critical of the Finnish school of Luther research and its insistence on an implied ontology as central to Luther's doctrine of justification and related to *theosis* comes precisely from his development of the *theologia crucis*: that is, the revelation of God under the appearance of the opposite.[49] Ontology offers precisely the kind of reasonable solution to theological problems that the theology of the cross rejects. "Greeks seek wisdom . . . we preach foolishness." This paradox is hardwired into Luther's proclamation of God's righteousness in Christ for humanity. Although the Heidelberg Disputation, which contains the most extensive working out of this theology, remained to a large extent unpublished and

---

47. *SA* III.xiii.1–4 in: *BC*, 325.

48. *SA* III, introduction, in: *BC*, 310. He continues: "The pope and his kingdom do not value these things very much, because the conscience means nothing to them; money, honor, and power mean everything." This, too, has an ecumenical side, since, if his charge of avarice proves false, then the attack falls on its own.

49. See Carl E. Braaten and Robert W. Jenson, eds., *Union with Christ: The New Finnish Interpretation of Luther* (Grand Rapids: Eerdmans, 1998).

unknown to his contemporaries, the *Explanations of the 95 Theses* contains an important exposition of the same themes, where for the former's "theology of glory" Luther uses the term *theologia illusoria* to criticize late-medieval theology.[50] Luther seeks not an irrational theology but rather an anti-rational one—and specifically in this sense is he anti-ontological when it comes to the doctrine of justification.

For him, medieval approaches to justification that included the infusion of a *habitus charitatis* into the soul obscure the believer's own experience of sin and lead to despair. God could well be infusing all kinds of things into believers and even transforming us into God's children, but because we do not experience them as such but continue to see only our sin and weakness, an ontological approach to justification leaves the very uncertainty that God's promise is out to destroy: "Have I done enough?" Or, in this specific case, "Have I been transformed enough?" Moreover, such appeals to essential change finally undermine the centrality of God's promise, which always and only remains a word. This very weakness is its strength. For example, in baptism, when the pastor or priest says, "I baptize you...," that is what really happens. That person over whom the water is poured and the words spoken is truly justified before God. Similarly, in the Lord's Supper the priest or pastor offers the elements with the word: "This is the body of Christ given for you; the blood of Christ shed for you." Again, the very thing promised (Christ's presence for participants) is what the communicant receives. Even more poignant are the words of absolution: "Absolvo te!" or, as in the liturgy of confession in Luther's *Small Catechism*: "And I by the command of our Lord Jesus Christ forgive you your sin in the name of the Father and of the Son and of the Holy Spirit. Amen. Go in peace."[51] Here what is loosed on earth is loosed in heaven through the very promise communicated in words. How foolish! To claim, as Paul does in the midst of a discussion of predestination (Rom. 10), that "faith comes by hearing and hearing by the preaching of Christ," puts the lie to all attempts to explain or "ontologize" that very Word of God.

This theology of the cross explains why, throughout his career, Luther becomes more and more adamant about the efficacy of external means of grace and rails against what he calls *Schwärmerei* (raving) or *Enthusiasmus*, that ancient heresy that insisted one could trust some internal assurance shorn of all external means. Nowhere does he attack this notion more forcefully than in an addition to the *Smalcald Articles* from 1538.

---

50. *LW* 31: 225 (*WA* 1: 613). See Timothy J. Wengert, "'Peace, Peace . . . Cross, Cross': Reflections on How Martin Luther Relates the Theology of the Cross to Suffering," *Theology Today* 59 (2002): 190–205.

51. Small Catechism, Confession, 28, trans. Timothy J. Wengert, in: *BC* 361–62.

In these matters, which concern the spoken, external Word, it must be firmly maintained that God gives no one his Spirit or grace apart from the external Word which goes before. We say this to protect ourselves from the *Enthusiasten*, that is, the "spirits," who boast that they have the Spirit apart from and before contact with the Word. On this basis, they judge, interpret, and twist the Scripture or oral Word according to their pleasure. . . . This is all the old devil and old snake, who also turned Adam and Eve into *Enthusiasten* and led them from the external Word of God to "spirituality" and their own presumption. . . . In short: *Enthusiasmus* clings to Adam and his children from the beginning to the end of the world—fed and spread among them as poison by the old dragon.[52]

This, then, is the heart of Luther teaching justification by faith. God's righteousness comes foolishly from the outside as sheer gift, proclaimed to the sinner in the Word, oral and visible, and received by faith in Christ alone, which faith that very Word, working as terrifying law and comforting gospel, creates in the sinner's heart, and from which pour forth spontaneous, free works of obedience, discipline, and love of neighbor.

52. *SA* III.viii.3, 5, 9, in: *BC*, 322–23.

5. Luther and the Development of Catholic Teaching on Justification

Michael Root[*]

Martin Luther's understanding of justification presented a challenge to the Catholic Church, to Catholic piety, and to Catholic theology. While the roots of Luther's understanding of justification in the writings St. Paul and in the theology of Augustine are obvious, the precise content and form of Luther's understanding of justification, of the acquittal of the Christian before the judgment of God, was innovative. Luther did not simply take up a new position within an established context of argument; he framed the discussion in a new way: new, again, in both form and content. How a theologian who adhered to the Catholic side of what quickly became a polarized debate was to respond to Luther was not clear. Doctrine, i.e., normative magisterial teaching, on justification was thin. Little had been said by councils and popes on precisely the questions raised by Luther on justification. Yet, not only did theologians need to respond; the Church needed to respond. And respond it did, in the Decree on Justification of the Council of Trent, completed in early 1547. The Decree was intensely debated within the Council, radically re-written more than once, but in the end adopted unanimously.[1] The Decree set the framework and much of the content for all later Catholic doctrine and theology of justification. The *de auxiliis* and Jansenist controversies of the following decades and centuries would focus on particular aspects and implications of what Trent taught, but they did not alter or significantly expand that teaching.

In this presentation, I will ask how Martin Luther shaped that teaching on justification of the Council of Trent and thus shaped Catholic doctrine and theology. My interest, I will admit, is more theological and ecumenical than strictly historical. My hope is that a clearer picture of Luther's impact on the shape of Catholic teaching on justification will help provide a clearer picture of where Catholic and Lutherans (and Protestants more generally) stand on justification today, especially in the wake of the *Joint Declaration on the Doctrine of Justification*.

[*] Ordinary Professor of Systematic Theology, The Catholic University of America. I received helpful comments during the conference especially from Bruce Marshall, Nelson H. Minnich, and Dorothea Wendebourg.

1. The most detailed history of the writing of the decree remains Hubert Jedin, *A History of the Council of Trent*, Vol. 2: *The First Sessions at Trent 1545–1547*, trans. Ernest Graf (London: Thomas Nelson and Sons, 1961), 166–316.

I. The Existence of a Catholic Doctrine on Justification

Let me begin with the obvious: were it not for Luther, there would be no comprehensive, normative Catholic doctrine of justification. The topic of grace had been the subject of intense medieval debates, but justification was but one aspect of the theology of grace, and the scholastic debates on grace for the most part did not produce the sort of disputes that required magisterial intervention. There were no grounds for a decree on justification prior to Luther.[2]

Luther's challenge called for more than the typical form of conciliar action. Generally, councils responded to theological challenges in the form of canons, rules that specified what cannot be rightly said. For example, one cannot rightly say that the Word is a creature or that the Virgin Mary is not the Mother of God. Canons state theological limits, but they do not elaborate a theology in any detailed sense. (The negative form of canons thus leaves more freedom to the theologian than a more positive teaching.)

The bishops at Trent definitely wished to exclude certain teachings they identified with Martin Luther. They wanted to draw a clear line between certain ideas they ascribed to Luther and what they understood to be Catholic truth.[3] In this sense, the Council's concern was not ecumenical understanding or finding common ground with Luther. Most bishops at the Council thought that if there had ever been a time for theological reconciliation, it was well past.

The bishops also recognized, however, that on the topic of justification they needed to do more than specify errors. They had to offer an alternative. If Luther's understanding of justification is incorrect, what is the correct understanding?

Thus, at an early stage in the drafting of the Decree on Justification, a new sort of form was introduced. Instead of consisting of a collection of canons, each with an explanatory paragraph or two attached (as did the Council's immediately previous decree, on Original Sin), the Decree would preface the canons with a comprehensive account of Catholic teaching on justification. This section of the decree eventually reached sixteen chapters and constitutes the most thorough analysis of any theological subject at the Council of Trent. As historical commentators regularly note, the Council's intent in the expository chapters of the Decree was pastoral.[4] Catholic teachers and preachers needed a clear picture of justification that could guide their work. If the decree was to offer an alter-

---

2. A reliable history of these discussions remains Henri Rondet, *The Grace of Christ: A Brief History of the Theology of Grace*, trans. Tad W. Guzie (Westminster, MD: Newman Press, 1967).

3. Jedin, *History*, Vol. 2, 179, 243, 309.

4. Jedin, *History*, Vol. 2, 310.

native to Luther and his associates, its biblical grounding needed to be evident (and thus the decree is awash in biblical citations). The decree needed to address the issues, and thus needed technical precision at some points, but it should avoid the technical terms of the schools. To provide general guidance, the decree needed to be generically Catholic, i.e., it needed to avoid taking sides in the debates over the details of grace and justification that had divided Scotists, Thomists, and Nominalists of various stripes. A Franciscan text that Thomists might ignore would not do the job. The drafting task for the Council was daunting.

The historical and ecumenical importance of this decision about the form of the Decree is difficult to exaggerate. The expository chapters sought not only to differentiate Catholic teaching from that of Luther, but also to expound the essential elements and the logic of Christian teaching on how the sinner comes to be accepted by the all-righteous God. In the process, the Council was more ecumenical, in the modern sense, than it either knew or intended. As Hubert Jedin says about the decree on justification: "if the decree delimitates and, as a consequence, separates, it also lays bare foundations that unite."[5] Like Luther, the council fathers sought to be true to the gospel and, in the process, they exposed a greater commonality than they thought existed.

II. Luther's Influence on the Decree on Justification

Did Luther's influence shape the content of Trent's decree on justification, either negatively, as the contrast case that sets off the contours of that with which it is contrasted, or positively, by pushing the Council to emphasize certain aspects of justification or providing ideas that the Council adopted, knowingly or unknowingly?

There are good grounds for answering 'no,' that Luther did not in any significant way shape the content of the Council's teaching, even if he was the occasion for it. At least two sorts of arguments can be made to justify such a 'no.'

First, it has become a cliché of modern scholarship on the Council's treatment of justification that the majority of Council fathers and even of the technical theologians present had inaccurate views of Luther.[6] The bishops present during the Sixth Session, which dealt with justification, were almost all Spanish and Italian. (Only a few French representatives were present; no German residential bishop was in attendance; remember, the Smalcald War between the Emperor and the Lutheran estates was going on in Germany at precisely this time.[7]) Most bishops had read little more than snippets extracted from Luther's

---

5. Jedin, *History,* Vol. 2, 310.

6. See, e.g., Karl Lehmann and Wolfhart Pannenberg, eds., *The Condemnations of the Reformation Era: Do They Still Divide?* trans. Margaret Kohl (Minneapolis: Fortress, 1989), 21.

7. Jedin, *History,* Vol. 2, 232.

works (a practice that especially with Luther leads to misunderstanding). Luther's influence was inevitably limited because his views were not well known and understood at the Council.

This point can be overdrawn, however. Some influential bishops at the council had been significantly influenced by Luther, most notably Cardinal Girolamo Seripando, the Superior General of the Augustinians and drafter of an early version of the decree. (It was Seripando who introduced the separation of the expository chapters of the decree from the canons.[8]) As I will argue below, Luther's most important influence on the Decree came through Cardinal Seripando and those associated with him.

I would note here briefly a problem that Catholic theologians at the Council had in understanding Luther, a problem that limited his influence. The theologians at the Council were almost all trained in the scholastic theology of the day. As I have noted, within that scholastic theology, justification was one topic within a more comprehensive and quite detailed discussion of grace. The goal was objective, analytic precision. Pastoral concerns were not absent, but they were thought to be served by clear thought. Teaching on justification was shaped by the anthropological object, the human self as it moves from sin to righteousness in God. Teaching on justification sought to describe that movement objectively and accurately.

Luther was self-consciously *not* a scholastic theologian. Recent scholarship has stressed his background in what has been called 'piety theology' (*Frömmigkeitstheologie*), with roots in a monastic theology focused more on the expression and edification of piety than the objective elaboration of the biographical movement of the self.[9] If scholastic theologies of grace were shaped by the anthropological object, Luther's theology was shaped by the anthropological *subject*, the self which turns away from itself and toward God's free offer of grace. Theological discourse is shaped by the first-person language of the self *coram deo*, facing God, and by the second-person language of proclamation addressing that self, not by the third-person language of scholasticism. Misunderstanding was not simply a function of an ignorance of Luther's theology; it was also function of a clash of discourses.[10]

A second argument that indicates Luther's limited influence on the Council's deliberations looks to the internal dynamics of the Council. Analyses of the *acta*

8. Jedin, *History,* Vol. 2, 240.

9. See, e.g., Berndt Hamm, *The Early Luther: Stages in a Reformation Reorientation*, trans. Martin J. Lohrmann (Eerdmans: Grand Rapids, MI, 2014).

10. This observation is a further development of the argument made in Otto Hermann Pesch, "Existential and Sapiential Theology—The Theological Confrontation Between Luther and Thomas Aquinas," in: *Catholic Scholars Dialogue with Luther,* ed. Jared Wicks (Chicago: Loyola University Press, 1970), 61–81.

of the Council, of the speeches and drafts of the Council, show that debate over Luther's theology in fact played little role. The most intense debate over justification in the Council was occasioned by a difficult condition of the Council's work. As noted, grace was a topic on the details of which the Catholic theological schools of the time disagreed. Distinct Thomist, Scotist, Nominalist and other views had become markers of theological identity. An agreed, if implicit, rule of procedure at the Council was to avoid conciliar decisions that would imply the condemnation of any of the recognized and established schools of Catholic theology.[11] This procedure was probably necessary. If it appeared that, say, established Franciscan or Thomist assertions about grace and justification were condemned in the canons on justification, then a "war of the schools" might break out in the Council and the project of a decree on justification would be put at risk.

This condition affected both the canons and the expository decree. The canons had to be written in such a way that what was perceived as erroneous in Luther's theology was excluded, but no accepted Catholic position was condemned. This task was not simple. Significant time was absorbed in the Council, for example, by the difficulty of condemning what Luther said on occasion about the justified person being certain of his or her salvation without condemning Scotist views on the possibility of a kind of moral certainty that one was in a state of grace.[12] This careful drawing of distinctions forced the Council to think carefully both about what it found objectionable in Luther's assertions and about the range of acceptable options in Catholic theology.

In the expository chapters laying out the Catholic understanding of justification, the task was to describe the heart of Catholic theology without committing the Church to any particular intra-Catholic option. The general wish to avoid the technical terminology of scholastic theology in some ways helped in this regard. The goal of transcending the differences among the schools did have the effect of directing the Council toward what was truly fundamental. One can say that a quasi-ecumenical feature of Trent was the pursuit of that which could be said in common by the various stands of Catholic theology.

The drafting of the chapters involved more, however, than just mediating school differences. Two aspects of the process did provide openings for the influence of Luther. First, a strategy visible in the decree is the attempt to portray the Catholic understanding as a *via media* between the extremes of an overestimation of the value of human activity by the Pelagians and an underestimation of the value of human activity by Luther. But how was such a middle way to be described? Some Scotists presented their own approach as a middle way between the Thomists and the Pelagians, not an approach likely to win over the Dom-

11. Jedin, *History,* Vol. 2, 309.
12. Jedin, *History,* Vol. 2, 250–53.

inicans. And how were Pelagius and Luther to be understood as two ends of the same spectrum? However the middle way was described, it did allow a kind of influence on the picture presented to be exercised by the posited extremes.[13]

Second, and more significantly, debate on justification did not just involve the traditional Catholic schools. Especially in the drafting of the expository chapters, new trends in Catholic thinking that had arisen out of an engagement with Luther's thought were involved. Most notable was the idea that the righteousness of the Christian which is the foundation of justification was twofold, a double righteousness, constituted both by an inherent righteousness given by sanctifying grace and by the imputation of Christ's merits which make up for any defects in the Christian's regeneration by sanctifying grace.[14] This idea had been developed by Catholics in discussions with Lutherans around 1540, most importantly by Johann Gropper and Gasparo Contarini, and was represented at the Council most forcefully by Girolamo Seripando.[15] The debate over twofold righteousness was as close as the Council came to a true debate over Luther's theology and was one of the primary ways Luther's theology entered into the conciliar discussions, if only obliquely. I will come back this topic later in the presentation.

Another trend from outside the scholastic schools, but one whose influence at the Council was minimal, was the anti-scholastic trend in Italian spiritual life that has recently been labeled *evangelismo*,[16] embodied especially in the circle of *spirituali* associated with Cardinal Reginald Pole.[17] Although Pole is sometimes

13. Heiko A. Oberman, "Duns Scotus, Nominalism, and the Council of Trent," in his: *The Dawn of the Reformation: Essays in Late Medieval and Early Reformation Thought* (Grand Rapids: Eerdmans, 1986), 218–20.

14. On the concept of a twofold righteousness, see Anthony N. S. Lane, "Twofold Righteousness: A Key to the Doctrine of Justification?" in: *Justification: What's at Stake in the Current Debates*, ed. Mark Husbands and Daniel J. Treier (Downers Grove: InterVarsity Press, 2004), 205–24; Edward Yarnold, "*Duplex Iustitia*: The Sixteenth Century and the Twentieth," in: *Christian Authority: Essays in Honour of Henry Chadwick*, ed. Gillian R. Evans (Oxford: Oxford University Press, 1988), 204–23.

15. During the conference, the question was asked whether a defender of Luther at the Council might be Bartolomé Carranza de Medina, OP, who was not a bishop, but present among the 'minor theologians.' Whatever Carranza may have advocated on other occasions (and he was later accused by the Spanish Inquisition of harboring Protestant views on justification), in presentations on September 27 and October 18, 1546, he supported variations of the double justice theory, the second very close in its logic, though not its language, to the final decree (Görres-Gesellschaft, ed., *Concilium Tridentinum: Diariorum actorum epistularum tractatuum,* 13 tomes [Freiburg i. B.: Herder, 1901–2001], tome 5, pp. 432 and 549–51). Jedin also lists Carranza as a defender of twofold righteousness (Jedin, *History,* Vol. 2, 245).

16. On this group and this label, see Elisabeth G. Gleason, *Gasparo Contarini: Venice, Rome, and Reform* (Berkeley: University of California Press, 1993), 190–201.

17. On Pole's circle and its interrelation with others of similar tendencies, see Thomas F. Mayer, *Reginald Pole: Prince and Prophet* (Cambridge, UK: Cambridge University Press, 2000), 103–42.

associated with the twofold justification understanding,[18] such a reading misunderstands the distinctive character of his outlook. It has been asserted with some frequency that Pole presented views on justification at the Council that were either Lutheran or 'indistinguishable' from Luther's, a view that I think misreads Pole, Luther, or both.[19] In addition, Pole was absent from Trent for almost all of the discussions on justification, and thus his views played little role in shaping the text.

In summary, Luther's influence in shaping the Council was in one sense decisive—Luther's theology of justification was the reason the topic was taken up—but in another sense indirect. No one sought to defend Luther's ideas at the Council and debate mostly centered on intra-Catholic issues raised by the need to respond to Luther both in the canons with their anathemas and in the larger decree, with its comprehensive outline of a Catholic understanding of justification.

III. Two Aspects of Luther's Influence

To say that Luther's influence was indirect is not to say that it was insignificant. I will look at two aspects of the Council's discussions and their final text which in particular show the impact of Luther. In both aspects, the Council was moved to affirm the decisive importance of God's grace in ways that were true to the Catholic tradition and also responsive to the concerns of the Reformation.

A. Preparations for Justification

First, what is the relation between justification and that which precedes justification in the life of the Christian? Justification, it was agreed, is instantaneous. Justification has to be instantaneous, since it is an all-or-nothing reality. One is either justified or one is not; one cannot be half justified.[20] The Council took as its paradigm of justification the adult convert to Christianity and identified justification with baptism. Baptism is the moment of the communication of sanctifying, that is, justifying grace. (Whether it was a good idea to take the adult

18. See, e.g., David C. Steinmetz, *Reformers in the Wings* (Philadelphia: Fortress Press, 1971), 44. Dermot Fenlon is particularly clear on the difference between the understandings of Pole and Seripando (Dermot Fenlon, *Heresy and Obedience in Tridentine Italy: Cardinal Pole and the Counter Reformation* [Cambridge: Cambridge University Press, 1972], 130).

19. Particularly influential in propagating this view has been Fenlon, *Heresy and Obedience*, see especially pp. 179, 189. While Fenlon is very helpful for understanding many aspects of Pole, I believe he fails to perceive the difference between the humility piety of Pole and Luther's mature understanding of justification. I hope to elaborate that difference in another essay in the near future.

20. See, e.g., Thomas Aquinas, *Summa theologiae*, I-II, q. 113, a. 7.

convert, of which there were very few in sixteenth-century Europe, as the paradigm of justification is debatable.)

Nevertheless, justification does not fall from sky, unrelated to the biography of the justified. There are events that lead up to justification: a growing understanding of the gospel, an awareness of and remorse for one's sinfulness, a desire for communion with God. These prior events do not require God to respond with the grace of justification, but they are preparations for justification in creating the disposition for justification. They are an aspect of the self's opening to sanctifying grace. Some such biographical preparation for justification is a normally necessary part of coming to justification.

That justification occurs in the context of a person's biography and is the culmination of events leading up to the acceptance of grace in baptism should be uncontroversial. Think of Luther's description in the 1545 Preface to his Latin writings, where he describes the process leading up to his insight into the active righteousness of God (granted, not perhaps the moment of justification, but for Luther, something much like it).[21] The controversy comes in trying to understand just how these events that prepare for justification relate to justification itself. As I noted, medieval theologies of grace focused on the anthropological object; they sought to delineate the human realities and movements as they were acted upon and cooperated with God's action in moving the justified to salvation. A complicated question was the interrelation of divine grace and human merit. On the one hand, grace and merit seem mutually exclusive; something cannot be a gift of grace if I have merited it and thus it is owed to me. On the other hand, the New Testament abounds in both the language of grace and divine gift and the language of God rewarding the faithful and responding to their turning to him. How does justification relate to grace and to merit? In particular, do the preparations for justification in any way merit justification?

Medieval theology was uniformly Augustinian in insisting that nothing prior to justification, no preparation or disposition, in the proper sense merits sanctifying grace. Sanctifying grace is always an unmerited gift. It is never owed; nothing we can do obliges God to give us sanctifying grace. To say that sanctifying grace was truly merited was rejected by all as the very essence of Pelagianism.[22] But if preparations for justification were not meritorious in the strict sense, how does one describe the relation between these preparations and jus-

21. Martin Luther, "Preface to the Complete Edition of Luther's Latin Writings," *LW*, 35, 336–337.

22. See Heiko Oberman, *Forerunners of the Reformation: The Shape of Late Medieval Thought Illustrated from Key Documents*, 2nd. ed. (Philadelphia: Fortress Press, 1981), 125–27. Even Ockham is clear on this point. See Rega Wood, "Ockham's Repudiation of Pelagianism," in: *The Cambridge Companion to Ockham*, ed. Paul Vincent Spade (Cambridge: Cambridge University Press, 1999), 350–73.

tification itself, the relation that makes them in fact preparations for justification? Could one say that while remorse for past sin and a desire for communion with God do not obligate God to grant grace, it is nevertheless fitting that the all-merciful God in fact does respond to such preparations with the gift of sanctifying grace? Thus, while not meritorious in the strict sense, such preparations might be seen as meritorious in an analogous sense; it is fitting or congruous for God in his mercy to respond to such preparations and so they might be called congruous merits.[23] The precise nature of such congruous merits was a matter of debate.

Unfortunately, however the concept of congruous merits might seem in the abstract, it was open to abuse. It was all too pastorally plausible that, with such a theology in the background, one might say to persons anxious about their justification that, while you can do nothing to merit justification in the proper sense, you can dispose yourself to receive it, and God will always respond to that disposition mercifully. As a medieval slogan put it: "God does not deny grace to those who do what is in them." The pastoral impulse here should not be missed, however misguided we judge it. The same impulse can be found in American Protestants of a more Arminian sort who say "do your best, and let God do the rest." The danger in such an application of the idea of congruous merit is clear. Instead of trusting in and focusing on God, one focuses and trusts in one's preparations, which God infallibly rewards with justification.

What was Trent to say about the relation between the preparations or disposition for justification and justification itself? Two important chapters of the Decree are dedicated to these preparations. These paragraphs assert the necessity of such preparations. Their status, however, is clear. "We are therefore said to be justified freely, since none of those things which precede justification—whether faith or works—merit the grace itself of justification. For, if it be by grace, it is not by works, otherwise, as the same Apostle says, grace is no longer grace" (Ch 8).[24]

There has been some debate over the last fifty years whether the verb translated as 'merit' in this quotation excludes only merit in a strict sense and leaves room for some sense of congruous merit.[25] I am convinced that while reading the passage as open to congruous merit was and is possible, it is not the most natural reading of the passage, either now or at the time of the Council. As

23. See Oberman, *Forerunners of the Reformation*, 129–32.

24. The text of the decrees of the Council of Trent can be found in Norman P. Tanner, ed., *Decrees of the Ecumenical Councils* (London: Sheed & Ward, 1990). I have often modified the translation.

25. See especially Oberman, "Scotus, Nominalism, and Trent" and Hanns Rückert, "Promereri: eine Studie zum tridentinischen Rechtfertigungsdekret als Antwort an H A Oberman," *Zeitschrift für Theologie und Kirche* 68 (1971): 162–94.

noted, the Council generally sought to avoid condemning positions that had become established as at least permissible options. The idea of congruous merit is not condemned by the Council, even if it is not mentioned. It is certainly pushed to the margins. As the Lutheran historian Hanns Rückert said in one of the best treatments of this question, the idea of a congruous meriting of justification received "a grievous blow" (*eine empfindliche Schlappe*) at the Council.[26]

Ecumenically even more decisive, the Council made clear in its discussion of the preparations for justification that any such preparations are not the works of unaided human nature. "[I]n adults, justification takes its beginning or origin [*exordium*] from the prevenient grace of God through Jesus Christ, that is to say, from his call [*vocatione*], whereby, without any merits existing on their parts, they are called" (Ch 5). In the description of this preparation for justification, passive voice verbs dominate. "People are disposed" for justification when "they are moved freely towards God and believe to be true what has been divinely revealed and promised." The needed disposition comes about "by God's grace inciting and helping them." The Council is clear that the initiative is always on God's side. The biographical events leading to justification do play a role, but they are themselves gifts of grace. The justified have nothing to boast of; all is gift.

Trent's Decree on Justification is a clear reaffirmation of the gracious character of justification. While it is true to say that Trent sought to avoid condemning established options, it did close off certain tendencies within such options, most notably, the idea that in some sense there is a human initiative not itself moved by grace which stands at the beginning of the preparation for justification. Justification is grace from beginning to end.

Was this affirmation a function of Luther shaping the Catholic tradition? Yes and no. No, in the sense that the sovereignty of grace had always been the dominant motif in Western understandings of salvation and justification. Trent called on traditional resources of the Catholic tradition to makes its point. Yes, however, in the sense that this particular affirmation was a response to Luther's attack on established understandings as an unevangelical abandonment of grace. Luther goaded the Catholic Church to declare in a much clearer and more comprehensive sense the inner logic of the insistence on the gracious character of justification.

B. Twofold Righteousness and Inherent Justice

But to say that justification is a function of grace does not settle all questions. How does grace function in the Christian's life? How does grace relate the justified person to Christ? Does grace function as a mere efficient cause, making

26. Rückert, "Promereri," 187.

us righteous in ourselves without an ongoing dependence on Christ, the way a
large inheritance from my parents might make me rich, but subsequently no
longer dependent on my parents? Does grace function as a legal fiction, treating
me as righteous when in fact—*in re*—I am not? Such questions are complex
and much in the basic attitudes of the Christian life is determined by how we
answer them.

As the canons on justification make clear, the Council heard Luther as
implying justification as a kind of legal fiction, as a strictly extrinsic imputation of Christ's righteousness to a person who remains untransformed by
grace (canons 11 and 12). I think that was not what Luther meant to say or
said at most times, though there are occasional remarks of Luther which can
give rise to such a reading. Over against what they understood to be Luther's
position, the Council insisted that grace brings with it an inherent righteousness, such that God's judgment on the justified as justified is a true judgment,
not a legal fiction. As First John says: "See what love the Father has given us;
that we should be called children of God; and that is what we are" (1 John
3:1). Citing that passage, the Council states: we "are not merely considered
to be just but we are truly named and are just" (Ch 7). Herein lies a basic
issue of how Christ works salvation in his own, an issue that all sides in the
Reformation saw as crucial.

Trent's question was not whether to assert such an inherent righteousness;
few if any disagreed on this point. The question was the nature of such an inherent righteousness and how it related to the righteousness of Christ. As I have
mentioned, this issue arose most pointedly at the Council in the debate on twofold righteousness. The idea of the Christian's twofold righteousness was complex and not perhaps held in the same way by all of its proponents, but the
outline is clear.[27] The Christian's righteousness is said to be twofold in that two
factors are involved in God' judgment that someone is justified, especially in
what was called final justification, the acquittal that will take place in God's
eschatological final judgment. On the one hand, the created grace that inheres
in man is a righteousness that is truly his. The righteousness of Christ is not
simply imputed to the Christian, but truly is made the Christian's own. The
possession of this inherent righteousness is a necessary condition of justification.
It is the wedding garment without which one is not permitted to enter the
marriage feast of the lamb (Matt 22:11–14). On the other hand, however, that
inherent righteousness as it concretely exists in the fallible, fragile Christian,

27. A useful description can be found in James F. McCue, "Double Justification at the Council
of Trent: Piety and Theology in Sixteenth Century Roman Catholicism," in: *Piety, Politics, and Ethics:
Reformation Studies in Honor of George Wolfgang Forell*, ed. Carter Lindberg (Kirksville, MO: Sixteenth
Century Journal Publishers, 1984), 39–56.

who inevitably falls into at least venial sin, is not sufficient to meet the demands of divine justice. It must be supplemented, especially at the Last Judgment, by an application of the merits of Christ.[28]

The idea of a twofold righteousness was an attempt to take some aspects of Luther's theology of justification into a Catholic understanding in two closely related ways. In terms of content, it affirmed a righteousness that truly belongs to the justified, while also accepting some idea of imputation, right up to God's final judgment. In terms of method, the advocates of a twofold righteousness were seeking to bring into a Catholic theology framed by the scholastic analysis of the anthropological object Luther's way of allowing the anthropological subject and its first-person discourse to shape theology. If we are exhorted to look to Christ and not to our own merits, an exhortation realized in the lives of the greatest saints, then shouldn't that appeal to Christ find a place in the formal doctrine of justification?

The concept of the Christian's twofold righteousness was intensely debated at Trent. To varying degrees, it found a place in preliminary drafts of the text. In the end, however, it was eliminated.[29] It was not rejected in the sense of "condemned," but it finds no place in the text and seems at a crucial point to be implicitly excluded. In perhaps its most technical section, the Decree outlines the various causes of justification, utilizing Aristotelian categories. It insists that justification has "one formal cause," which is "the justice [or righteousness] of God: not that by which he himself is just, but that by which he makes us just and endowed with which we are renewed in the spirit of our mind" (Ch. 7). Two phrases are crucial here. First, justification has "one formal cause," not two; and second, that cause is not the justice or righteousness by which God is himself just, but the justice or righteousness by which we are made just, i.e., a righteousness that inheres in the justified.

The Council's rejection of the concept of twofold righteousness has sometimes been seen by Protestants as a decisive rejection of Protestant concerns by the Council. The voices at the Council most friendly to the Lutheran outlook were sidelined; a potential compromise position suppressed. Careful commentators have noted, however, that the situation was more complicated. The various scholastic Catholic options and what was being put forward by Luther were not commensurable positions of some agreed upon thing called 'theology.' As I have stressed, they were framed in different ways, with different goals and answering to different standards. A compromise of the sort put forward in the concept of

---

28. Carl E. Maxcey, "Double Justice, Diego Laynez, and the Council of Trent," *Church History* 48 (1979): 271–72.

29. The most important arguments against double righteousness put forward in the Council debates are described in Maxcey, "Double Justice," 272–78.

twofold righteousness risked being an unworkable hybrid, problematic for both sides, rather than a *via media*.

Such was the judgment of the Council. It is important, however, to see precisely why they reached this conclusion. The Council was not motivated by a disinterest in the Christian's constant dependence on Christ or by a dogged commitment to works-righteousness. The strongest argument against the concept of twofold righteousness was that it undercut the concept of sanctifying grace and the justification it communicates. To say that, in addition to sanctifying grace, the Christian now and before God's final judgment will require an additional application and communication of the merits of Christ is to say that sanctifying grace is not itself sufficient. The grounds for that insufficiency can only be that sanctifying grace is then not itself the adequate application and communication of the saving merits of Christ. As Otto Hermann Pesch asks: "What sort of concept of justification through grace would it be to which must be added the Christological reference?"[30]

Decisive for Trent's understanding of justification is that the Christian's righteousness is a participation in the righteousness of Christ. As Jedin puts it: "In the Catholic conception, sanctifying grace, identified . . . with *iustita inhaerens*, precisely brings about that ontological union with Christ—that communion between Head and members—which makes it possible for us to be acknowledged as God's children and renders works done in a state of grace meritorious, in spite of their imperfection."[31] That participation in Christ's righteousness is real; it is genuine reality in the life of the justified and thus a righteousness that inheres in them, not a matter of the mere extrinsic imputation the Council thought Luther was asserting. The "righteousness of God," the *iustitia dei*, by which the justified are just is not to be identified with the righteousness by which God is righteous, but it is still called "the righteousness of God," even while it is said to inhere in the justified. Faith without hope and love is said not to justify because without hope and love faith does not unite the justified "perfectly with Christ nor makes him a living member of his body" (Ch 7). In its final chapter on merit, a stumbling block for many Protestant readers, the participatory quality of the justice or righteousness of the justified is clearly stated: "Our own personal righteousness is not established as something coming from us, nor is the righteousness of God disregarded or rejected; what is called our righteousness, because we are justified by its abiding in us, is that same righteousness of God, in that it is imparted to us by God through the merit of Christ" (Ch 16).

---

30. Otto Hermann Pesch and Albrecht Peters, *Einführung in die Lehre von Gnade und Rechtfertigung* (Darmstadt: Wissenschaftliche Buchgesellschaft, 1981), 185.

31. Jedin, *History*, Vol. 2, 255f.

In an odd way, the rejection of those who explicitly favored a certain move in a Lutheran direction was in the name of an understanding of grace as participation that bears certain similarities with Luther, at least with Luther read in a certain way. The similarity should not be exaggerated, but it is real.

I have emphasized that the understanding of justification put forward by Trent was focused on grace and Christ.[32] Was that a matter of Luther "shaping the Catholic tradition"? Luther's polemic certainly forced the council not only to take up the topic but to answer the charge that grace and Christ were being inadequately stressed in Catholic thought and practice. But the Council did not appropriate aspects of Luther's thought in formulating its decree; the atmosphere was far too poisoned for that to occur. The few Council fathers who did so were not successful in their attempt. The Council framed its discussion in terms drawn out of the pre-Reformation Catholic tradition. It framed its answer, however, in a way that, in the long run, had important ecumenical potential. If the Council's understanding of justification is read in the participatory way I have indicated (and in which I think it must be read if one is to be true either to the text or to the historical data behind the text) and if Luther's understanding of justification is also read in a similar participatory manner (as I think it is most accurately read, but that is a more controversial matter), then the door is opened for the sort of agreement found in the *Joint Declaration on the Doctrine of Justification*. Luther and Trent are not, as some try to argue, saying the same thing, just in different words or conceptualities. Even when the difference in theological form is taken into account, there are significant differences between what they say on justification, differences which echo across various other differences. But in themselves, as the *Joint Declaration* affirms, the differences on justification need not be church-dividing.

IV. CONCLUSION

In this presentation, I have focused only on Luther's shaping of the Catholic tradition in the form of its doctrinal response on the topic of justification at the Council of Trent. What was Luther's influence on Catholic teaching on justification in the decades and centuries following Trent? That is the subject for a large monograph, not a conference presentation, and would require what is for the most part missing in post-Vatican II theology, a careful engagement with Baroque Catholic theology.

My narrow focus, inevitable in this context, has a drawback. If Luther and the Catholic tradition on justification and grace are to be rightly understood in

---

32. For a useful summary stressing the centrality of grace, see John W. O'Malley, *Trent: What Happened at the Council* (Cambridge, MA: Harvard University Press, 2013), 113–15.

their interrelation, they must be seen as strands within the complex and internally diversified discussion of these topics flowing from St. Paul and Augustine and still going on today. The Catholic and Lutheran or Protestant threads in the conversation quickly became unattached from one another. Already by the mid-1540s, the conversation on each side was becoming preoccupied with internal debates: I have noted the way the debate at Trent focused on internal Catholic questions; on the Lutheran side great energy would be absorbed by the series of internal disputes that arose in the wake of Luther' death in early 1546, disputes that threatened to divide the Lutheran movement. The ecumenical historical task is to see these isolated threads as still part of a single larger history, dealing in diverse ways with a similar set of problems and utilizing a common set of resources; the ecumenical theological task is to bring these strands back into conversation, not pretending that differences don't exist in form and content—the differences are part of what can make the conversation fruitful—but seeking at the very least a deepening of the evangelical commitment of each strand. These tasks are the ones that I believe ecumenical scholarship needs to take up in the coming decades.

III. Eucharist

6. The Eucharist in Late Medieval Theology

Bruce D. Marshall

Two matters pertaining to the Eucharist were deeply contested in the sixteenth century: first, whether and how Christ is present in the Eucharist, and second, whether and how the Eucharist (or the Mass) should be thought of as a sacrifice.

Of these the first, Christ's Eucharistic presence, had already generated intense controversy in the Western tradition long before the sixteenth century, and had correspondingly been made the topic of significant doctrinal decisions. As a result of controversy and doctrine, this aspect of Christian faith in the Eucharist had been the subject of very extensive theological reflection, and the basic alternatives for understanding the nature of Christ's Eucharistic presence searched out and assessed in fine-grained detail, by the time Luther turned his hand to the issue.

By contrast the second matter, the sacrificial character of the Mass, had never been a subject of widespread and lasting controversy in the West, and at the dawn of the sixteenth century there was virtually no established doctrine concerning it. That in the Mass we genuinely offer a sacrifice pleasing to God was taken for granted by all. A dossier of patristic texts, especially from Augustine, vouched for the reality of the Eucharistic sacrifice and gave some indications as to its nature or content. From these, medieval theology drew a few crucial axioms, and offered some commentary of a more or less piecemeal variety on the sacrificial aspect of the Eucharist, much of that in the form of observations on the text and practice of the Mass itself. This is unsurprising, since intellectual effort tends to be drawn by doubt and controversy, and there was little of either regarding the sacrifice of the Mass in the Middle Ages.

In the early fourteenth century, a focused discussion did arise about the fruits or benefits of the Mass and how they are "applied"—that is, how they reach those in this world or the next for whom they are intended. By the end of the fifteenth century, there was visible disagreement about this nest of issues. The late medieval discussion about the fruits or merits of the Mass touched on what everyone recognized to be a basic issue, the relationship between the cross and the Mass. Still, when Protestants began to reject the Eucharistic sacrifice in the early sixteenth century, they did not confront a developed body of doctrine, as they did when they rejected medieval teaching on Christ's Eucharistic presence, and they confronted a relatively modest and in part unsettled body of theological argument. Instead, they rejected something even more basic than either doctrine or theology, but less explicit—what had been recognized in the West until then as immemorial Christian tradition about a sacrificial act that takes place in the Eucharist.

PRESENCE

By the end of the eleventh century, there was general agreement, in the wake of the heated controversy over the Eucharistic teaching of Berengar of Tours, not only about the reality of Christ's presence in the sacrament of the altar but about the way that presence should, in the most basic sense, be understood. This theological agreement, fortified by papal teaching against Berengar, had both a positive and a negative aspect.[1]

Positively, the very body and blood of Christ are on the altar, precisely where the consecrated elements are—the very body born of the Virgin, the blood poured out on the cross, the human body now ascended into heaven and glorified at the Father's right hand. This could be put in various ways, but the most common formulation was that the body and blood of Christ are there "in truth" (*in veritate* or *secundum veritatem*), or, equivalently, that the "true" body and blood of Christ are on the altar. In Peter Lombard's formulation, "His [Christ's] truth, that is, his true body, is on every altar wherever [the Eucharist] is celebrated."[2] Negatively, the body and blood of Christ are not present in the sacrament merely as what is signified is present—indicated or brought to mind—by way of the signifying sign. The consecrated elements are signs, to be sure, but the reality they signify is not absent from where they are and present elsewhere; it is present exactly where they are.

Writing in the 1150s, the Lombard already takes agreement on both the negative and the positive aspects of the matter for granted in Bk. IV of his *Sententiae*: the true body and blood of Christ are on the altar, and not merely the signs of them. The followers of Berengar make the most grievous of all errors concerning the Eucharist when they assert that "the body of Christ or his blood is not on the

---

1. Berengar was twice induced to subscribe to repudiations of his own Eucharistic teaching, first by Pope Nicholas II in 1059 (see DH 690), and later by Pope Gregory VII in 1079 (see DH 700) (DH=Heinrich Denzinger, *Enchiridion Symbolorum: A Compendium of Creeds, Definitions, and Declarations of the Catholic Church* [Latin-English], 43rd ed., ed. Peter Hünermann [San Francisco: Ignatius Press, 2012]).

2. *Magistri Petri Lombardi Sententiae in IV libris distinctae*, 3rd ed., ed. Ignatius C. Brady, O.F.M., 2 vols., [Spicilegium Bonaventurianum, 4-5] (Grottaferrata: Editiones Collegii S. Bonaventurae Ad Claras Aquas, 1971-81), Bk. IV, distinction 10, ch. 1 [5]), 292.9-10. For an English version, see Peter Lombard, *The Sentences*, Book 4: *On the Doctrine of Signs*, trans. Giulio Silano (Toronto: Pontifical Institute of Mediaeval Studies, 2010), here 51. All translations, however, are my own.

altar." They say that Christ's words, "This is my body," should be taken in the same figurative way as Paul's words, "The rock was Christ." And they cap off their mistakes by holding that "the body of Christ is there only [as] in a sacrament, that is, [as] in a sign." In other words, what is on the altar is not the true body and blood of Christ, but only signs of them. The normally cautious Lombard is confident enough about agreement on the reality and basic shape of Christ's Eucharistic presence that he can dismiss this teaching as "dangerous insanity."[3]

This contrast between the (vitally important) teaching that the true body and blood of Christ are present in the Eucharist, contained under their visible sacramental signs, and the (erroneous, indeed grossly heretical) teaching that only the signs are truly present, instead of Christ's own body and blood, remained basic to Latin theology up to the end of the Middle Ages. The Fourth Lateran Council of 1215, in its important statement of faith *Firmiter credimus*, spelled out Catholic doctrine on the matter in the positive terms already familiar since the time of Peter Lombard: Christ's "body and blood are truly contained in the sacrament of the altar under the species of bread and wine."[4] Writing in the late 1240s, William of Militona similarly accentuates the positive, in his extensive and influential *quaestiones* on the sacraments. "In his completeness and his whole truth Christ is everywhere in the sacrament of the altar" (that is, wherever the sacrament of the altar is celebrated); he is present "in his truth, that is, in the truth of his twofold nature."[5]

Typically, however, theologians clarify this teaching on the truth or reality of Christ's Eucharistic presence by explicit contrast to the error that is, above all, to be avoided. Christ is on the altar "in truth (*secundum veritatem*)," Bonaventure argues, and "the opinion of some that Christ was not on the altar, except merely as in a sign (*nisi tantum sicut in signo*), and he is said to be eaten because a sign of him is received and eaten, is the worst possible error." Those who hold this view "might seem to be moved by piety, as though no one were worthy to touch, let alone to eat, the true flesh of God (*veram carnem Dei*)." On the contrary: "This is the worst possible error and against the faith's devotion, which simply recognizes and gives thanks for the benefit given to it by God—that he is with us, in his own flesh and his own nature."[6] Bonaventure's younger contemporary

3. All from *Sententiae* IV, d. 10, ch. 1 [1] (Brady, 290.13-20); Silano, 49: "Dangerous insanity": "alii praecedentium insaniam transcendentes . . . periculosius veritati contradicunt" (Brady, 290.13, 15).

4. DH 802.

5. *Guillelmi de Militona Quaestiones de sacramentis*, vol. 2, ed. Gedeon Gal, O.F.M., [Bibliotheca Franciscana Scholastica Medii Aevi, 23] (Quaracchi: Ex Typographia Collegii S. Bonaventurae, 1961), Tractatus IV, pars vi, q. 31, 7.b (Gal, 643.30-31; 16-17).

6. *In IV Sent.* d. 10, pt. 1, a. 1, q. 1, resp. [*S. Bonaventurae Opera Omnia*, 4] (Quaracchi: Ex Typographia Collegii S. Bonaventurae, 1889), 217b; for "secundum veritatem," see 216a). There is now a Latin/English version: *Bonaventure on the Eucharist (Commentary on the* Sentences, *Book IV,*

Thomas Aquinas writes in much the same vein. "That the true body and blood of Christ are in this sacrament cannot be grasped by the senses, but by faith alone (*sola fide*), which relies on divine authority." Failing to grasp this elemental point, "some proposed that the body and blood of Christ are not in this sacrament, except as in a sign (*nisi sicut in signo*). This is to be abjured as heretical, since it is contrary to the words of Christ. Hence Berengar, who was the first to invent this error, was later compelled to retract his error and to confess this truth of faith."[7]

In the Middle Ages, the Eucharist and the questions it poses were discussed not only in scholastic treatises but in other genres of literature, including the *expositio missae*, or "explanation of the Mass." This was a type of treatise designed to help priests, and those giving instruction to priests, understand what they were doing when they celebrated the Mass. Of these there were a great many, going back to the Carolingian period. Among the most formative, though controversial in its own time, was the *Liber officialis* of Amalar of Metz (†850). Another, which retained its impact into modern times, was the *Rationale divinorum officiorum* of William Durand of Mende (†1296).[8] In the late fifteenth century, Gabriel Biel turned his hand to this well-established genre in a long series of lectures at Tübingen, first published in 1488 as his *Canonis missae expositio*.[9] Biel combines the traditional line-by-line explanation of the words and actions of the Mass with an extensive scholastic analysis of questions concerning the Eucharist, including, characteristically, a detailed summary and assessment of numerous scholastic forebears on each question he treats.

Biel sums up his own extensive presentation of the Church's authoritative teaching on Christ's Eucharistic presence in the same twofold way already plain

---

dist. 8-13), ed. and trans. Junius Johnson. [Dallas Medieval Texts and Translations, 23] (Leuven: Peeters, 2017), here 155, 153.

7. *Summa theologiae* III, 75, 1, c. The sacrifices of the "Old Law," Aquinas here observes, already served as genuine figures or signs of Christ's saving passion; it belongs to "the perfection of the New Law" to make Christ himself present in a yet better way, "not only in a sign or figure, but in truth (*in rei veritate*)."

8. For a Latin/English edition of the *Liber officialis*, see Amalar of Metz, *On the Liturgy*, 2 vols., ed. & trans. Eric Knibbs (Cambridge, MA: Harvard University Press, 2014). The critical edition of Durand of Mende's *Rationale* is *Guillelmi Duranti Rationale divinorum officiorum*, 3 vols., eds. Anselme Davril, Timothy M. Thibodeau, and Bertrand G. Guyot, [Corpus Christianorum Continuatio Mediaevalis—hereafter CCCM], (Turnhout: Brepols, 1995-2000), 140, 140A, 140B. Book IV deals with the Mass, and is available in an English translation: William Durand, *Rationale Book Four: On the Mass and Each Action Pertaining to It*, trans. Timothy M. Thibodeau (Turnhout: Brepols, 2013).

9. *Gabrielis Biel Canonis missae expositio*, 5 vols. (Wiesbaden: Franz Steiner Verlag, 1963-1976), vols. 1-4 (text) ed. Heiko A. Oberman and William J. Courtenay, vol. 5 (detailed conspectus and index), ed. Wilfrid Werbeck.

in Peter Lombard. "[U]nder the species of bread and wine after the consecration has been rightly carried out the true body of Christ and his true blood are really contained in themselves, and not as in a sign, against the condemned heresy of those who deny this truth."[10] Biel here identifies the position he attributes to Berengar in the same way as had generations of scholastic theologians before him, by using the formulation (perhaps puzzling to us) that Christ's body and blood are present "as in a sign" (*sicut in signo*) but not present "really" (*realiter*) or in truth. He goes on, however, to formulate the contrast in a way that brings out more clearly what he and his predecessors took to be at stake in the controversy over Berengar centuries before, and why they saw in this position the "worst error" on the Eucharist. According to Berengar, as Biel puts it, "after the consecration of the bread and wine on the altar the true body and blood of Christ *are not there*, but only a sacrament is there, that is, a sign signifying the body of Christ."[11] To say that Christ is present in the Eucharist "really" or "in truth" is to say just the opposite. His body and blood *are* there on the altar, exactly where their signs are.

Later medieval Eucharistic theology thus took as basic the conviction that the body and blood of Christ are in truth present on the altar wherever the Mass is celebrated, and was correspondingly emphatic in its repudiation of the views it attributed to Berengar. Nonetheless papal teaching against Berengar, specifically the first "confession" to which he was compelled to subscribe in 1059, included a formulation soon seen as posing a difficulty in its own right, one that needed precise explanation. "The true body and blood of our Lord Jesus Christ," according to the confession of 1059, "are not only in the sacrament, but in truth, handled and broken by the hands of the priests, and rent by the teeth of the faithful."[12] For many theologians, this came to seem like a straightforward, and thereby misleading, identification of the reality (*res*) present in the sacrament with the sign (*signum* or *sacramentum*) that marks its presence.

In the first half of the twelfth century, caution on this score was already evident in Gratian's *Decretum*.[13] Similarly, Peter Lombard observes that "it is cus-

---

10. Biel, *Canonis missae expositio*, L(ectio) 39 O (Oberman and Courtenay, II, 97).

11. Biel, *Canonis missae expositio*, L. 80 N (Oberman and Courtenay, IV, 17; my emphasis): *non est ibi verum corpus et sanguis christi, sed tantum est ibi sacramentum, id est signum corporis christi significativum.*

12. DH 690: [*V*]*erum corpus et sanguinem Domini nostri Iesu Christi esse . . . non solum sacramento, sed in veritate, manibus sacerdotum tractari et frangi et fidelium dentibus atteri.* On the interpretation of the "confession of Berengar" in the late eleventh and twelfth century, see Ludwig Hödl, "Die confessio Berengarii von 1059: Eine Arbeit zum frühscholastischen Eucharistietraktat," *Scholastik* 37 (1962): 370-394.

13. Gratian gives Berengar's confession of 1059 in distinction 2, chapter 42 of his *De consecratione* (the third part of the *Decretum*); the cautions come in chs. 44, 70, and 75. See Emil Ludwig Richter and Emil Albert Friedberg, eds., *Corpus Iuris Canonici* (2nd edn, Leipzig, 1879; reprint Graz: Academische Druck- u. Verlagsanstalt, 1955), I, cols. 1328-30, 1341, 1345.

tomary to ask" what is really broken in the Eucharist, when the host is divided into pieces before the communion, or "in what thing" the breaking takes place (*in qua re fiat*). "Since no other substance is there than that of Christ himself," it seems as though we have to say that the Eucharistic fraction is a breaking of Christ's very body. On the other hand, "since that body is incorruptible, because it is immortal and impassible" following Christ's resurrection and ascension into heaven, it seems that the fraction "cannot take place in that body." For just this reason, Christ warned his apostles (Jn. 6:62-4) against taking their Eucharistic eating of his body in a "carnal" way.[14] Those who say that Christ's very body is broken when the species or form of bread is broken in the Mass appeal, under-standably, to the confession Berengar made before Nicholas II.[15] But we do better to focus on the incorruptibility of Christ's risen body. Because of that, "it can reasonably be said that the breaking and division take place not in the sub-stance of [Christ's] body, but in the sacramental form of bread itself, so that a true breaking and division takes place there, but not in the substance, rather in the sacrament, that is, in the species."[16] The authoritative teaching of the *confessio Berengarii* should be interpreted accordingly. "It is certainly true that the body of Christ 'is broken and rent by the teeth,' but only in the sacrament . . . in each of the parts [of the divided species] the whole Christ remains."[17]

This teaching was controversial in the Lombard's own time, but eventually it became standard.[18] The whole Christ is present under any part of the con-secrated bread and wine (or more precisely, of the consecrated species or forms of bread and wine), no matter how these are broken or divided up. Accordingly many things that are true to say of the body and blood of Christ are not true to say of the species by means of which they become present, and conversely. Jesus plainly teaches that we are to eat his body and drink his blood (Jn. 6:53-7), and we do so just by eating and drinking the consecrated bread and wine. As Aquinas and many others observe, however, we do not eat Christ's body "in its own species"—we do not take a bite out of his hand—rather we eat his body in, or by means of, "the sacramental species." Christ's body can be said to be "broken" or "ground with the teeth" in the same sense in which it can be said to be "eaten"—in its sacramental form or shape, not in its own natural form or shape.

14. *Sententiae* IV, d. 12, ch. 2 [1] (Brady, 304.13-20; Silano, 61).
15. See *Sententiae* IV, d. 12, ch. 3 [1] (Brady, 305.16-21; Silano, 61-2).
16. *Sententiae* IV, d. 12, ch. 3 [2] (Brady, 304.22-25; Silano, 62).
17. *Sententiae* IV, d. 12, ch. 3 [4] (Brady, 306.21-307.3; Silano, 63).
18. In the late 1170s Walter of St. Victor objected that the Lombard "proves himself to be another Berengar," in that "by his customary kinds of argument he makes a distinction"—between reality and sign, *res* and *signum*, in the Eucharist—"where Catholic faith sees no need at all for any distinction." From Walter's *Contra quattuor labyrinthos Franciae*, ch. 11; cited in *Lombardi Sententiae* (Brady, II, 306, note to IV, d. 12, ch. 3 [4]).

"Thus," Thomas concludes, "we should understand the confession of Berengar: the breaking and grinding with teeth should be said of the sacramental species, under which the body of Christ truly is."[19]

At first glance it might seem as though the Lombard and Aquinas alike are simply siding with Berengar, and rejecting what had been proposed, in 1059, as an essential Catholic truth. They appear to suppose that Christ's body is handled, broken, and eaten (or rent by the teeth) only "in the sacrament" and not "in truth"—just the position Berengar was induced to repudiate. In fact, however, Aquinas and the many scholastic theologians who take basically the same view already offered by the Lombard are not saying that we break and eat the sacramental forms *instead of* the body of Christ, as they held Berengar to have believed. We break and eat the body of Christ, in truth, *by* breaking and eating the sacramental forms. This requires not only a bond of unity between the sacramental forms and Christ's body, but also a distinction between them.

The Eucharist, to be sure, is one thing, not two. It is the body of Christ sacramentally present; equally, it is the blood of Christ sacramentally present. In particular, the Eucharist is not made up of a self-contained or already available sign (bread or wine) joined from the outside, as it were, to Christ's previously existing body and blood. The sacrament, that is, the *consecrated* bread and wine, the visible signs or species, continue to exist with their natural properties only insofar as they mark the presence of Christ's true body and blood. Within the one reality of the Eucharist, though, we must nonetheless distinguish between the sacrament, or sign, and what the sacrament signifies or makes present.

A distinction between the *sacramentum* and the *res* of the Eucharist was already current by the time of the *Summa sententiarum* and Peter Lombard. "The reality (*res*) contained and signified is the flesh of Christ, which he drew from the Virgin, and the blood that he poured out for us." There is in fact "a double realty" in this sacrament, "a twofold flesh of Christ" given in the Eucharist: the personal flesh, unique to him, that he took from the Virgin, and the "flesh" of his mystical body, the unity of all those who belong to him and make up that body. This, as the Lombard puts it, is the reality "signified but not contained" in the Eucharist.[20]

These aspects of the Eucharist form a trio that will be part of the basic conceptual equipment of later scholastic sacramental theology. Within the one reality of the Eucharist there should be recognized, first of all, the visible forms or

---

19. *Summa theologiae* III, 77, 7, ad 3: "Corpus autem Christi non manducatur in sua specie, sed in specie sacramentali . . . ideo ipsum corpus Christi non frangitur, nisi secundum speciem sacramentalem. Et hoc modo intelligenda est confessio Berengarii: ut fractio et contritio dentium referatur ad speciem sacramentalem, sub qua vere est corpus Christi."

20. All from *Sententiae* IV, d. 8, ch. 7 [1] (Brady, 284.15-285.1; Silano, 44).

species of bread and wine, whose purpose is simply to be a sign, indicating the presence of something not simply identical with themselves. They are "only a sign," the *sacramentum tantum*. The reality they signify is the true body and blood of Christ, fully present wherever they are. But Christ's own body and blood present in the Eucharist are themselves also a sign. They are at once the reality signified by the visible species and the sign of something not identical with themselves, *res et sacramentum*. What they signify is the unity of Christ's mystical body, the ultimate or final reality signaled and brought about by the Eucharist, the *res tantum*. Peter Lombard influentially spells out the grammar of the terms: "Here three matters must be distinguished: one which is only a sign (*tantum est sacramentum*), another which is a sign and a reality (*sacramentum et res*), and a third which is a reality and not a sign (*res et non sacramentum*). The sign which [signifies but] is not a reality [signified] is the visible species of bread and wine; the sign which is also a reality is Christ's own flesh and blood, the reality which is not a sign is his mystical flesh."[21] Spelling out the precise relationship among these three became a major interest of later medieval sacramental theology, not only in the Eucharist but in the other sacraments as well.

Christ's real presence in the Eucharist, Aquinas argues, is in a sense the most apt of all the truths Christian faith embraces. It belongs to faith's perfection or completeness (*competit perfectioni fidei*) to apprehend precisely this mystery above all. Faith concerns matters invisible, and here Christ does not just use his visible humanity to exhibit his invisible divinity, as he did before his resurrection and ascension; he uses the humble forms of bread and wine to exhibit both his divinity and his humanity, alike invisible to us and accessible by faith alone.[22] Distinguishing between sign and *res* in the Eucharist locates a conceptual space in which some of faith's deepest commitments regarding Christ's presence in the sacrament can, so far as the matter allows, be understood.

Since nothing less than Christ's true body is present wherever its divinely appointed signs are, the body on the altar must retain its natural properties, even if they are invisible to us. It must be the very body he received from the

---

21. *Sententiae* IV, d. 8, ch. 7 [2] (Brady, 285.8–12; Silano, 45). As in many other places, the Lombard here closely follows the *Summa sententiarum*, an influential twelfth century treatise of uncertain authorship. See Patrologia Latina—hereafter cited as PL 176 (Paris: Migne, 1854), 140A–B.

22. "That the true body and blood of Christ are in this sacrament . . . is suitable to the perfection of faith, which concerns both his divinity and his humanity. . . . Because faith concerns matters invisible, just as Christ shows us his divinity invisibly, so also, in this sacrament, he shows us his flesh in an invisible way." *Summa theologiae* III, 75, 1, c. Aquinas here develops a standard topos of medieval Eucharistic theology. "For three reasons Christ handed over his body and blood under other species, and commanded that they henceforth be consumed: [first], so that there might be merit to faith, which has to do with things that are not seen." Peter Lombard, *Sententiae* IV, d. 11, ch. 3 [1] (Brady, 299.14–16; Silano, 57).

Virgin, the body that bore the cross, the body in which he now reigns in heaven. At least in its present state, as the Lombard and many others pointed out, that body, risen and ascended to the Father's right hand, is immortal and incorruptible.[23] As a result Christ's body cannot now be broken in its natural mode of existence, or "in its own species," yet it remains essential to believe that it is broken, as it is eaten, "sacramentally." We must put the matter this way not because Christ's true body is absent from the species, but precisely because it is present there, requiring us to affirm some things of the species that we cannot affirm of his body. Moreover, Christ's body is present, whole and entire, not just wherever the consecrated host is present, but wherever any piece of it is present, no matter how small. This requires that the body of Christ, in the mysterious manner in which it is present just where the signs of it are, cannot, as Biel notes, be coextensive with the species or any part of them, even though it is just where they are.[24]

Medieval theology thus saw the need for a fine-grained explanation of identity and distinction in the Eucharist—a way of vigorously upholding the reality of Christ's presence without flatly identifying the present Christ with his visible sacramental signs. In order to get this right, the idea of "being contained" will consistently prove to be another useful, indeed quite basic, conceptual tool. We have already encountered it several times.[25] Christ's body and blood, in all their reality, are present on the altar just where the sacramental signs are. Yet they are not simply the same as the signs. Rather, they are "contained under" the visible forms of bread and wine. These are signs that, in a manner indeed unique to the sacrament of the Eucharist, fully contain the reality they signify. Characteristically, Thomas Aquinas takes this truth about the Eucharist to instruct us concerning the general relation of substance, accident, and place in a way we would not otherwise have suspected. Christian doctrine, that is, requires us to revise our metaphysics. The first relation of substance to accidents is not, as Aristotle held, to be their subject, that which they identify, to which they belong, and in virtue of which they exist. The first relation of substance to accidents is to be contained under them, as in the Eucharist. In every case but the Eucharist, as it

---

23. See above, n. 14.

24. "That which is not coextensive with the sacrament [that is, with the sign, the *sacramentum*] is not divided when the sacrament is divided. But the body of Christ is not coextensive with the sacrament, because one part of Christ's body is not under [one] part of the sacrament, and another under another. . . . Therefore, because the parts of Christ's body are not commensurate with the parts of the sacrament, or host, it does not follow that the body of Christ is broken with the breaking of the host, just as the soul of a human being is not divided with the division of the body, because it is not coextensive with the body." *Canonis Missae expositio*, L. 80 M (Oberman and Courtenay, IV, 16).

25. In the Lombard (n. 20), in *Firmiter* (n. 4), and in Biel (n. 10).

happens, what is contained under a collection of accidents is also their subject, but first contained, then subject—the Eucharist teaches that.[26]

In his turn, Luther would warmly embrace Berengar's confession of 1059, regarding it, at least when he was writing against Swiss and South German Protestantism in the late 1520s, as an admirably clear and forceful statement of correct Christian teaching on the reality of Christ's Eucharistic presence. Led by Zwingli, the Swiss (or "the fanatics," as Luther called them) saw in the confession of 1059 an especially loathsome error of the traditional religion. "The fanatics are wrong," Luther replies, "as well as the gloss in canon law, when they criticize Pope Nicholas [II] for having compelled Berengar to make such a confession that he said he 'pressed and ground the true body of Christ with his teeth.'Would to God that all popes had acted in such a Christian manner in all matters, as this pope acted with Berengar in this confession."[27]

The gloss to which Luther here disapprovingly refers is probably one of those discussed by Biel in his own more detailed treatment of the confession of 1059.[28] Biel's explicit source for Berengar's confession is, naturally enough, Gratian's *Decretum*, and when it comes to the language of "breaking" and "grinding," he accepts the interpretation of several glosses on the confession long since included in editions of the *Decretum*.[29] When Berengar's confession says that the

26. *Summa theologiae* III, 76, 5, c: "The body of Christ is not in this sacrament as in a place, but in a substantial mode, in the manner, that is, in which a substance is contained by dimensions. For in this sacrament the substance of Christ's body follows (*succedit*) the substance of bread. Hence, just as the substance of bread was not under its dimensions in a local manner, but in the manner of a substance, neither is the substance of the body of Christ. However, the substance of Christ's body is not the subject of these dimensions, as the substance of bread was."

27. Vom Abendmahl Christi. Bekenntnis (1528);WA 26: 442.39–443.3 (LW 37: 300–301).

28. Luther seems to have made a close study of Biel's *Canonis Missae expositio* around 1506–8, in preparation for his ordination to the priesthood, and at one time thought it "the best book." See Martin Luther, *Erfurter Annotationen 1509–1510/11* [Archiv zur Weimarer Ausgabe der Werke Martin Luthers, 9], ed. Jun Matsuura (Cologne: Böhlau Verlag, 2009), xlix, cxxvii (esp. n. 576). Luther also made a very small number of marginal notations in the copy of the 1514 Lyon edition of Biel's *Canonis Missae expositio* that belonged to the Wittenberg Augustinians. These do not, however, touch on any of the glosses to Gratian's *Decretum* discussed by Biel, and so offer no help in identifying the gloss to which Luther might have been referring in his later polemic against the Swiss. Cf. Hermann Degering, ed., *Luthers Randbemerkungen zu Gabriel Biels Collectorium in quattuor libros sententiarum und zu dessen Sacri canonis missae expositio Lyon 1514* (Weimar: Hermann Böhlaus Nachfolger, 1933), 19–20.

29. See above, n. 13, for the location of Berengar's confession in Gratian. Richter and Friedberg print only the text of Gratian's collection of canons, but within a decade of its appearance the collection was already being accompanied by glosses, soon quite extensive, which became a standard part of its interpretation. For the glosses cited by Biel in something like the context in which he would have known them, see, e.g., *Decretum Gratiani emendatum et notationibus illustratum una cum glossis, Gregorii XIII Pont. Max. iussu editum* (Venice: Apud Iuntas, 1595), 1796.

body of Christ is "broken and ground with the teeth" we should take this to mean, as the gloss rightly says, that "the body of Christ is truly contained under the particles of the sacrament that are broken and ground, and under them is really and most truly eaten."[30] In standard late medieval fashion, Biel insists that we should not simply identify the sacramental signs with the reality they truly and fully contain. Against this, the gloss offers a salutary warning: "Unless the words of Berengar are rightly understood, you will fall into a greater heresy than Berengar himself held. Therefore everything"—everything, Biel adds, that speaks of breaking and grinding—"you should refer to the species themselves."[31]

Luther evidently takes this standard late medieval warning as a repudiation of the Eucharistic teaching required by Nicholas II, akin to the later rejection of the real presence by Luther's own Swiss Protestant opponents. It is, at any rate, hard to imagine what other gloss on Berengar's confession, as it appears in medieval canon law, Luther could have in mind at this point. While he gestures critically at the warning, he omits the gloss's (and Biel's) corresponding affirmation that, in the Eucharist, Christ's body "is really and most truly eaten," a point with which he vigorously agrees: "Whoever eats and chews this bread, eats and chews what is quite truly the body of Christ and not simply mere bread."[32] Like the gloss, moreover, he too insists on a distinction within the one reality of the Eucharist between the bread and the body of Christ, if not exactly the same distinction (since he thinks the full reality of the bread remains present). "Nonetheless it remains entirely true that no one sees, handles, eats, or chews the body of Christ as one sees or chews other flesh. For what one does to the bread is rightly and correctly ascribed to the body of Christ, on account of the sacramental unity" (between the Eucharistic bread and Christ's body).[33] Here, perhaps not untypically, Luther reflexively puts more distance between himself and medieval Eucharistic theology than his position itself seems to require.

Later medieval theology was, in sum, consistently aware of the need to avoid two extremes, two opposed errors, on the basic matter of Christ's Eucharistic presence. On the one hand, it is wrong to say or imply that the only substances or realities (res) present on the altar are bread and wine. Christ's true body and blood are present there in substance and in their total reality. On the other hand, it is wrong simply to identify the reality of Christ's body and blood present in the Eucharist with the visible signs of their presence. In the sacrament of the altar, as in the other sacraments, res and signum must be distinguished in order to be properly related. Christ's presence, we could say, cannot be reduced to the

30. Biel, *Canonis Missae expositio*, L. 80 N (Oberman and Courtenay, IV, 17-18).
31. Ibid. (Oberman and Courtenay, IV, 18).
32. WA 26: 443. 3-5 (LW 37: 301).
33. WA 26: 442. 35-8 (LW 37: 300).

presence of the signs, as Berengar was supposed to have taught. Nor, conversely, can the signs be reduced to the present Christ, as an incautious reading of the confession of 1059 might lead us to suppose.

CONVERSION AND IMPANATION

By the beginning of the twelfth century, there was general agreement on Christ's real presence in the Eucharist, as opposed to the presence of mere signs or symbols of Christ's body and blood. With agreement on the reality of Christ's presence clarity did not immediately emerge regarding how that presence comes about.

Peter Lombard considers several opinions on this score. The more common view, of which there were several types, was that Christ comes to be present on the altar by the conversion of the bread and wine into his true body and blood. The Master of the *Sentences* clearly embraces this idea, especially on the authority of some well-known texts from Ambrose that speak forcefully of Christ's true presence on the altar coming to be by some kind of conversion.[34] But he hesitates to go further. "If you ask what kind of conversion that is, whether it is formal, substantial, or of some other sort, I am not able to determine."[35]

Hugh of St. Victor and the *Summa sententiarum*, two of the Lombard's chief sources, argue that the Eucharistic conversion should be understood as substantial. "They say that substance is converted into substance, in such a way that this essentially becomes that."[36] The Lombard himself leans toward this view, saying that it "seems to agree with the sense" of the patristic authorities that speak strongly of conversion, and offering replies to various objections to substantial conversion.[37] The idea that what takes place in the Eucharist is a total conversion of substance will gradually receive doctrinal approbation, and the term "tran-

---

34. E.g., Ambrose's *De sacramentis* IV.iv.15-19, presented by the Lombard compressed and arranged in *Sententiae* IV, d. 10, ch. 2 [6]. "In the Lord's utterance" there is enough power to bring into being the things that were not; so much the more can that same utterance change what was one thing into another. "What was bread before the consecration is now the body of Christ after the consecration, because the utterance of Christ (*sermo Christi*) changes the creature" (Brady, 295.18-20; Silano, 53-54). By such authoritative texts as these, the Lombard comments may be refuted the views of those "who follow the law of nature when it comes to a divine mystery" (IV, d. 10, ch. 2 [1]; Brady, 294.13-14; Silano, 52).

35. *Sententiae* IV, d. 11, ch. 1 [1] (Brady, 296.9-10; Silano, 54).

36. *Sententiae* IV, d. 11, ch. 1 [1] (Brady, 296.12-14; Silano, 54). See especially Hugh, *De sacramentis* II.viii.9: "By the words of sanctification the true substance of bread and wine is converted into the true body and blood of Christ, only the species of bread and wine remaining, substance changing (*transeunte*—"going over") into substance," PL 176 (Paris: Migne, 1854), 468A.

37. *Sententiae* IV, d. 11, ch. 1 [1] (Brady, 296.14; Silano, 54). For the replies, see d. 11, ch. 2 [1-4].

substantiation" will be used to designate this conversion. The term itself, however, is absent from many twelfth century defenses of substantial conversion, including Peter Lombard's own, and only gradually does it come to label the view that this conversion is how Christ's Eucharistic presence comes about.[38] A century after the Lombard, Thomas Aquinas offers a lucid summary of what was, by his time, a theological and lexical consensus on how Christ comes to be truly present in the Eucharist. "By divine power, in this sacrament the whole substance of the bread is converted into the whole substance of the body of Christ, and the whole substance of the wine into the whole substance of the blood of Christ. This conversion is not formal, but substantial. It is not included among the kinds of motion that occur in nature, but can be called by a name of its own: transubstantiation."[39]

The Lombard also briefly considers two alternative views, both of which had some currency in the twelfth century. One of these, motivated by doubts about whether one substance can be wholly converted into another while its species or sensible properties remain, held that the substances of bread and wine are not converted into Christ's body and blood, but annihilated, and replaced by the substances of body and blood under species that enable us to locate them (or alternatively, reduced to their most basic material elements, then replaced).[40] Long after anyone actually held it, this "annihilationist" view of how the real presence of Christ comes about remained a standard topic in scholastic treatments of the Eucharist, as one of the "three opinions" considered by the Lombard. Since it did not figure in the sixteenth century debates, however, we can leave this view aside for our purposes.

The third view taken up by Peter Lombard wants to account for the real presence without requiring any change, whether by way of conversion or annihilation, in the elements of bread and wine themselves. This account holds that Christ's presence on the altar comes about in such a way that "the substance of bread and wine remains there, and the body and blood of Christ are in the very same place; that substance is said to become this [substance], in the sense that

---

38. On the idea, the term, and their history, see Ludwig Hödl, "Der Transsubstantiationsbegriff in der scholastischen Theologie des 12. Jahrhunderts," *Recherches de théologie ancienne et médiévale,* 31 (1964): 230-259; Joseph Goering, "The Invention of Transubstantiation," *Traditio,* 46 (1991): 147-170.

39. *Summa theologiae* III, 75, 4, c. Cf. 75, 8, c: "In this sacrament the whole substance of the bread changes (*transit*) into the whole body of Christ."

40. Upon the consecration, this position's advocates hold, "where there was bread, now there is the body of Christ." So far they agree with the Lombard's own preference for substantial conversion. But in response to the question, "'If this is so, what then becomes of the substance of bread and wine?' they say that it is either resolved into its preexisting matter, or reduced to nothing (*in nihilum redigi*)." *Sententiae* IV, d. 11, ch. 2 [5] (Brady, 298.5-7; Silano, 56).

where this is, that is also." As the Lombard sees it, this makes for "a wonder," presumably by proposing that two things really distinct are in just the same place at the same time.[41] He firmly rejects this opinion. An argument from authority, rather than a metaphysical or other explanatory argument against the content of the position, supplies his reason. All of the weighty patristic texts on the Eucharist, Ambrose in particular, clearly state or imply that the bread and wine are changed by divine power, and that Christ's body and blood come to be on the altar by the conversion of the bread and wine, in whatever way that conversion should further be understood. "That no other substance is there except the body and blood of Christ is manifestly shown by the authorities."[42] So, the Lombard concludes, "after the consecration the substance of the bread and wine is not there, although the species remain."[43]

In the eleventh century, Guitmund of Aversa and others had already polemicized vigorously against the idea that the substances of bread and wine are present, or co-present, on the altar along with Christ's body and blood, seeing it as the last subtle refuge of Berengarian error.[44] Guitmund called its advocates *impanatores*, or "bread-minglers," a term he seems to have coined, and the position itself was sometimes called "impanation," the "embreading" of the body of Christ or the "mingling" of his body with the bread.[45] The term itself seems largely to have been forgotten in the later Middle Ages, and scholastic theologians typically discuss the position without giving it any label at all. They simply speak, as the Lombard had done, of the view that the substances of bread and wine "remain" in the Eucharist after the consecration. This has led some scholars to call the position "remanescence," though unlike "impanation" the term is not medieval. Basi-

---

41. *Sententiae* IV, d. 11, ch. 2 [6] (Brady, 298.8-10; Silano, 56).

42. Ibid. (Brady, 298.11-13).

43. *Sententiae* IV, d. 11, ch. 2 [10] (Brady, 299.10-11; Silano, 57).

44. "They are unable to deny that the substance of Christ's body is present in the Lord's food, yet not at all believing that the bread and wine are changed (*verti*) by the words of the Savior into his flesh and blood, instead they mix Christ with the bread and wine, and thus have created another heresy by a more subtle reasoning." Guitmund, *De corporis et sanguinis Christi veritate in eucharistia*, III.27—in *Sanctorum Patrum Opuscula Selecta*, vol. 38, ed. Hugo Hurter, SJ (Innsbruck: Libraria Academica Wagneriana, 1879), 148-149; PL 149 (Paris, Migne, 1853), 1480D-1481A. In English as Guitmund of Aversa, *On the Truth of the Body and Blood of Christ in the Eucharist*, trans. Mark G. Vaillancourt (Washington, DC: Catholic University of America Press, 2009), here 193.

45. According to Guitmund, "All of the Berengarians agree that the bread and wine are essentially not changed (*essentialiter non mutantur*)." Among these, some say that the bread and wine are "merely shadows and figures," in which the body and blood of Christ are not present at all, while others "say that the body and blood of Christ are truly there, but contained in a hidden way, and so that they may be eaten are somehow, if I may put it this way, embreaded (*impanari*)." *De corporis veritate* I.8 (Hurter, *Opuscula,* 12-13 [PL 149 (Paris: Migne, 1853), 1430C-D]; Vaillancourt, *On the Truth*, 97). Cf. *De corporis veritate* III. 1.

cally the same position on how the real presence comes about would, in the six-teenth century and after, be called "consubstantiation," in deliberate contrast with "transubstantiation." Where a label is useful, I will speak of "impanation," since the term is medieval, while recognizing that the application of any label to the view is a scholarly convenience rather than a reflection of medieval usage.

Impanation had never been widely held in the Latin Middle Ages. In 1215, the Fourth Lateran Council characterized the bread and wine as "having been transubstantiated by divine power" into the body and blood of Christ.[46] This passage is sometimes said to have "defined" transubstantiation, and *a fortiori* real presence by conversion, as binding doctrines about the Eucharist, but that would be an overstatement. It was, however, a clear indication of where things were going.[47] After Lateran IV, impanation became not a position to defend but an error to avoid, although this was as much because of the continuing force of patristic authority affirming Eucharistic conversion as because of the influence of Lateran IV and *Firmiter* itself.

It was not forgotten, however. Impanation continued to be debated throughout the Middle Ages in commentaries on Bk. IV of the *Sentences* and in scholastic treatises on the Eucharist. At issue was not whether Christ's bodily presence actually comes about in this way—everyone agreed that it does not—but whether it would be possible, counterfactually, for God to bring it about in this way (or so to have brought it about). The issue was not trivial. Depending on how the counterfactual question gets answered, either substantial conversion (transubstantiation) will be necessary for coherent belief in Christ's Eucharistic

---

46. DH 802: *transsubstantiatis pane in corpus, et vino in sanguinem potestate divina*, so that the body and blood of Christ are now "truly contained under the species of bread and wine" (cf. above, n. 4). In 1202, Innocent III had already said in a letter to the Archbishop of Lyon that at the Last Supper, Christ "transubstantiated (*transsubstantiavit*) bread and wine into his body and blood" when he first spoke the words the Church now uses for consecration in the canon of the Mass (DH 782). This passage was included in the *Decretals* of Gregory IX (1234), the most important medieval collection of canon law after Gratian, which added to its influence in the later Middle Ages. See Richter-Friedberg, *Corpus Iuris Canonici*, II, 637. Innocent III would later preside over the Fourth Lateran Council, and himself composed a substantial and influential treatise on the Mass shortly before he became pope (*De sacro altare mysterii libri sex* [PL 217 (Paris: Migne, 1855)], 763–916, under a different title). On his Eucharistic theology, especially in Bk. IV of this treatise, see Marcia L. Colish, "The Eucharist in Early Franciscan Tradition" (forthcoming).

47. See the affirmations of transubstantiation at the Second Council of Lyon (1274; DH 860) and at the Council of Florence (1442; DH 1352). While not much elaborated, these are clear doctrinal indications that Christ's Eucharistic presence should be believed to come about by substantial conversion. The Council of Florence underlines this point: "By the power of these words [of Christ, spoken by the priest] the substance of the bread is converted into the body of Christ, and the substance of the wine into [his] blood" (DH 1321, from *Exsultate Deo*, the decree of union with the Armenians, 1439).

presence, or it will not be. The answer to this question has obvious significance for later arguments between Catholics and Protestants.

On various grounds, metaphysical, semantic, devotional, and liturgical, Thomas Aquinas argues that it is impossible for the substance of the bread and wine to remain after the consecration. To suppose that they do "takes away the truth of this sacrament," namely that "the true body of Christ exists in this sacrament," and so "this position is to be avoided as a heresy."[48] For Aquinas, the only possible way that Christ can become truly present in the Eucharist is by substantial conversion of the bread and wine into his body and blood. Denying transubstantiation therefore requires denying the real presence altogether. To affirm the real presence while rejecting transubstantiation is simply inconsistent.

Beginning in the sixteenth century and after, as the *Summa theologiae* became the primary textual basis for university theology in much of the Catholic world, Aquinas's view came to seem like the normal position on this counterfactual question. It was not seen that way in the late Middle Ages, however. John Duns Scotus argues in detail that Aquinas is wrong about this. While the Church knows with certainty that Christ's true body and blood come to be present on the altar by substantial conversion, the scriptural data about Christ's Eucharistic presence could also be saved by the view that the substances of bread and wine remain along with Christ's body and blood, or for that matter by Peter Lombard's other alternative, according to which the substances of the bread and wine are not converted, but annihilated, and replaced by the substances of body and blood. "Each of these [opinions] wanted to save the common teaching that 'the substance of Christ's body is truly there,' since to deny that is manifestly against the faith."[49] Without doubt a rationally satisfying explanation of transubstantiation is available to us, an account, that is, "of how what is believed is possible."[50] Scotus offers his own explanation, *in extenso*. But good arguments can also be made for impanation and annihilation, not least their relative simplicity in contrast with transubstantiation. "In matters of faith we should not posit more than the truth of what we believe can convince us of, but," so the opponents of transubstantiation reasonably argued, "the truth of the Eucharist can be saved without" it.[51] We cannot decide how Christ comes to be present in the Eucharist

48. *Summa theologiae* III, 75, 2, c.

49. *Ordinatio* IV, d. 11, p. 1, a. 2, q. 1 [no. 99]. *B. Ioannis Duns Scoti Opera Omnia*, vol. 12, ed. Barnabas Hechich, OFM (Vatican City: Typis Vaticanis, 2010), 208.587-89.

50. *Ordinatio* IV, d. 10, p. 1, q. 1 [no. 14] (Hechich, 58.79). Cf. *Ordinatio* IV, d. 11, p. 1, a. 2, q. 1 [no. 97] (Hechich, 207.577-78).

51. *Ordinatio* IV, d. 11, p. 1, a. 2, q. 1 [no. 100] (Hechich, 209.597-9). Cf. idem [no. 108] (Hechich, 212).

simply by applying the tools of reason, metaphysical, logical, or otherwise, to his words over the bread and wine at the Last Supper. Reason leaves us with several alternatives, and cannot further narrow the field.

In supposing otherwise, Scotus argues, Aquinas carelessly conflates actuality with necessity, hastily concluding, in a manner all too common among theologians of the generation or two that came before him, that God could not bring about a theologically significant state of affairs—in this case, Christ's Eucharistic presence—except in the way that he actually has brought it about.[52] Since transubstantiation is only one among several different ways of accounting reasonably for how Christ's words, "This is my body," come to be true when spoken in the Mass, Scotus naturally relies on Church tradition, including recent tradition (especially Lateran IV's *Firmiter*), when it comes to deciding among the rationally available alternatives. As Scotus sees it, this is simply part and parcel of the Holy Spirit's guidance of the Church over time into all truth, fulfilling the promise of Christ (Jn. 16:13).[53]

Outside of the Dominican Order, Scotus's position was often accepted in the late Middle Ages. In fact, William of Ockham at times goes considerably further, depending on his mood. That the substances of bread and wine remain after the consecration is not only conceptually possible as an alternative to transubstantiation, it is highly reasonable (*multum rationabilis*). Or rather, "this opinion would be highly reasonable were it not for the determination of the Church to

52. Scotus presents Aquinas's arguments against impanation and annihilation in *Ordinatio* IV, d. 11, p. 1, a. 2, q. 1 [nos. 109–115] (Hechich, 212–214), followed by a detailed refutation [nos. 116–132] (Hechich, 214–218): "Whatever may be the case with these opinions, [Thomas's] arguments do not seem effective at disproving them" [no. 116] (Hechich, 214.729–730). For more on this disagreement between Scotus and Aquinas, see my essays, "The Eucharistic Presence of Christ," in: *What Does it Mean to "Do This"?* ed. James J. Buckley and Michael Root (Eugene, OR: Cascade Books, 2014), 47–73, and "Identity, Being, and Eucharist," *The Saint Anselm Journal,* 9/2 (2014): 1–22 (online: https://www.anselm.edu/sites/default/files/Documents/Institute%20of%20SA%20 Studies/Identity,%20Being,%20and%20Eucharist.pdf).

53. "The Catholic Church . . . chose this understanding [viz., transubstantiation as the way Christ comes to be present in the Eucharist] because it is true. For it was not in the power of the Church to make it true or not true, but of God when he instituted [the Eucharist]. But the Church has made explicit (*explicavit*) the understanding handed on to it by God, directed in this—so we believe—by the Spirit of truth." *Ordinatio* IV, d. 11, p. 1, a. 2, q. 1 [no. 141] (Hechich, 221). For the appeals to *Firmiter* (by way of Gregory IX's *Decretales*), see nos. [135, 140] (Hechich, 219, 221). Aquinas, thinking he has knock-down arguments for the view that transubstantiation is necessary given the truth of Christ's words, sees no need to appeal to Lateran IV. He was certainly familiar with *Firmiter*, having written a commentary on it in the early 1260s (the *Expositio super primam Decretalem*), but even after having written the commentary, he passes over *Firmiter* in silence when offering his own theological defense of transubstantiation (e.g., in *Summa theologiae* III, 75, 2). For Thomas's exposition of the lines on the Eucharist in *Firmiter*, see Leonine ed., vol. 40E, 38.696–746.

the contrary."[54] In fact, taken simply as a metaphysical proposal, impanation (to recall our label for the position) is more reasonable than transubstantiation, since it does not pose the considerable difficulty (to which Ockham devotes extended attention) of accounting for how accidents can exist without inhering in a subject.[55] At other times, to be sure, Ockham's position is much milder.[56] In any case, Ockham does not remotely think that Christ's Eucharistic presence actually comes about by impanation. The Church knows by revelation that it has pleased God to bring about Christ's real presence in the Eucharist by a far greater miracle than impanation, and so she sets the theologian the considerable task of understanding transubstantiation.[57]

In his *Canonis Missae expositio*, well known to Luther, Biel rehearses the foregoing argument in detail, and sides firmly with Scotus over against St. Thomas.[58] Led by the Spirit of truth, the Church chose this difficult way of understanding Christ's Eucharistic presence because it is the true one, not because it is the only possible one.[59] "Faith," he concludes, "leads us to salvation when we rely upon

---

54. *Quodlibet* IV, q. 30. *Guillelmi de Ockham Opera Theologica* (St. Bonaventure, NY: St. Bonaventure University, 1967–1986), vol. 9 (1980): *Quodlibeta Septem*, ed. Joseph C. Wey, 450.30-1. Cf. William of Ockham, *Quodlibetal Questions*, trans. Alfred J. Freddoso and Francis E. Kelley (New Haven: Yale University Press, 1991), 370.

55. The supposition that the substances of bread and wine remain "avoids all the difficulties that follow from the separation of accidents from a subject" (*Quodlibet* IV, q. 30; Wey, 450.31-2; Freddoso and Kelley, 370). Cf. *Quaestiones in IV Sententiarum*, q. 8: This opinion "is not opposed to reason, nor to any biblical authority, and it is more reasonable and easier to hold than the other ways [of understanding the true presence of Christ] . . . because among all the difficulties (*inconvenientia*) which are held to follow from this sacrament, the greatest is that an accident is without a subject. But by positing [impanation] it is not necessary to hold this." *Opera Theologica*, vol. 7, eds. Rega Wood and Gedeon Gál (St. Bonaventure, NY: Franciscan Institute, 1984), 138.22-139.6.

56. See *Tractatus de corpore Christi*, ch. 6. After noting the disagreement between Aquinas and Scotus as to whether impanation "involves a contradiction," Ockham simply observes that Scotus's opinion "seems more probable to me, without prejudice to the other." *Opera Theologica*, vol. 10, ed. Carolus A. Grassi (St. Bonaventure, NY: Franciscan Institute, 1986), 101.45-46.

57. Embracing transubstantiation because it is taught by the Church, while denying, with Scotus, its necessity to account for Christ's Eucharistic presence, "is more consonant with theology, because it more greatly exalts the omnipotence of God, taking away nothing from him except what evidently and expressly implies a contradiction" (*De corpore Christi*, ch. 6; (Grassi, 101.46-8). Cf. *Quodlibet* IV, q. 30: "I hold [transubstantiation] because of the determination of the Church, and not because of any argument (*rationem*)" (*Opera Theologica*, 9; Wey, 450.1-2; Freddoso and Kelley, 370).

58. See *Canonis Missae Expositio* L. 40 M (Oberman and Courtenay II, 108–09) for Biel's statement of the impanationist position and the arguments for it, and L. 41 G-N (Oberman and Courtenay, II, 120–126) for his resolution of the question.

59. *Canonis Missae Expositio* L. 41 I (Oberman and Courtenay, II, 122). Biel closely follows Scotus's formulation of the point (above, n. 53): "[E]cclesia catholica . . . ideo intellectum hunc difficilem [viz., transubstantiation] elegit, quia verus est." "Difficult" is Biel's addition. He continues:

the truth founded in Christ, not upon the vanity and infirmity of natural knowledge."[60] Impanation is more amenable to reason, but faith, undeterred, embraces
the hard truth of transubstantiation. In the late 1480s, then, the tradition that saw
impanation as a quite plausible, though nonetheless incorrect, way of understanding how Christ comes to be present in the Eucharist remained very much alive.

It was vital enough, in fact, to draw Luther's attention. In 1520, he appeals
to this tradition, by way of Pierre d'Ailly's questions on Book IV of the *Sentences*, to back up his own now settled conviction that Christ's presence in the
Eucharist actually does come about by impanation (though he does not here
use the term) rather than by conversion. "When I was drinking in school theology," he recalls, "the Cardinal Doctor of Cambrai [viz., d'Ailly] gave me occasion to reflect when he argued quite acutely that it is much more probable,
and posits fewer unnecessary miracles, if the true bread and true wine are present on the altar and not the accidents alone, except that the Church had determined to the contrary."[61] Having come to the conclusion that the decisions of
the Church (of pope or council, as he puts it) carry no weight in matters of

---

"[D]irected by the Spirit of truth, [the Church] cannot err in what belongs to faith" (Oberman
and Courtenay, 122-123).

60. *Canonis Missae Expositio* L. 41 N (Oberman and Courtenay, II, 126).

61. *De captivitate Babylonica ecclesiae*, WA 6: 508.7-11 (LW 36: 28-29). D'Ailly's *Sentences* commentary dates from the late 1370s, and was available in several printed editions by the time Luther
was a student (on the date, manuscripts, and editions of d'Ailly's questions on the *Sentences*, see
Monica Brinzei's "Introduction" to her critical edition of the text, currently in progress; CCCM
258, especially x-xxxviii). In *IV Sent.*, q. 6, a. 2, d'Ailly notes that "there is a question as to whether
the body of Christ could coexist with the substance of bread by way of union," and argues that
"this mode [of Christ's presence] is obviously possible, and is opposed neither to reason nor to the
authority of the bible (*ille modus est possibilis nec repugnat rationi nec auctoritati bibliae*)." *Questiones
magistri Petri de Alliaco super primum tertium et quartum sententiarum* (Paris: Petit, 1508), fol. 265va.
Luther, however, misrepresents d'Ailly's understanding of Church authority in this matter, since
"the Cardinal Doctor of Cambrai" does not regard it as certain that the Church has decided to
reject impanation. Nonetheless, he himself follows "the more common opinion" that impanation,
while possible, is not the way the real presence comes about, and accepts a version of transubstantiation. "While it does not follow in an evident way from scripture that this [transubstantiation] is
the case, nor even, it seems to me, from the determination of the Church, nevertheless I hold it,
because the common opinion of the saints and doctors is more favorable to it" (*Et licet ita esse non
sequatur evidenter ex scriptura nec etiam videre meo ex determinatione ecclesiae, quia tamen magis favet ei et
communi opinioni sanctorum et doctorum ideo teneo eam*). Fol. 265vb. On d'Ailly's Eucharistic theology
in its late medieval context (though not specifically on the matter that interests Luther), see Paulus
J. J. M. Bakker, *La raison et le miracle: Les doctrines eucharistiques (c. 1250–c. 1400)* (Nijmegen: Selbstver-
lag, 1999), I, 149-153. On Luther's knowledge and use of d'Ailly, see Pekka Kärkkäinen, "Martin
Luther," in: Philipp Rosemann, ed., *Mediaeval Commentaries on the Sentences of Peter Lombard*, vol.
2 (Leiden: Brill, 2010), 471-494.

faith, Luther now finds himself free to embrace the position that, as he sees it, d'Ailly would have accepted if his undue regard for the decisions of the Church had not prevented him from doing so. The opinion that Christ's true body and blood come to be present on the altar by substantial conversion lacks the backing not only of scripture, but of reason, while the view that "true bread and true wine" remain fully accords with both. "Since it is not necessary to posit a transubstantiation that comes to pass by divine power, this ought to be regarded as a figment of human opinion, because it has the support of neither scripture nor reason."[62]

When Luther says that transubstantiation lacks the support not only of reason, but of scripture, he means, at least in the *Babylonian Captivity*, that it fails to agree with Christ's words at the Last Supper. When Jesus (and the Eucharistic celebrant after him) says, "Take, eat, this is my body," the demonstrative "this" plainly refers to "this *bread*, which he had taken and broken," so that when he has finished speaking, what is on the altar is both bread and his body.[63] Luther takes this to be quite obvious, though he gestures at some semantic principles that he thinks apply here, and reinforce the point. The words of scripture "are as far as possible to be preserved in the simplest signification, and unless the manifest context compels it, they are not to be taken outside their grammatical and proper [signification]."[64] To deny that "hoc" in the words of Christ, "Hoc est corpus meum" refers straightforwardly to bread is thoroughly unreasonable, a "novel and absurd way of taking the words."[65] There is no bright line here

62. WA 6: 509.19-21 (LW 36: 31). "Transsubstantiatio" is "a hideous word and a fantasy" (*portentoso . . . vocabulo et somnio*), unknown for the first 1200 years of the Church's life (509.28-9). "This opinion of Thomas [that is, transubstantiation] floats free of the scriptures and reason (*sine scripturis et ratione fluctuat*) to such an extent that [Thomas] seems to me to have known neither his philosophy nor his logic. For Aristotle speaks far otherwise concerning accidents and subject than St. Thomas does" (WA 6: 508.20-3 [LW 36: 29]). Insistence on the *fact* of transubstantiation Luther here associates with Aquinas, though his comment on d'Ailly suggests that he is at least implicitly aware that the theologians who found impanation more accessible to reason nonetheless also insisted on this fact.

63. WA 6: 511.22-3 (my emphasis; LW 31: 34).

64. WA 6: 509.10-12 (LW 31: 30).

65. WA 6: 509.22: *Absurda est ergo et nova verborum impositio* (LW 36: 31). "Impositio" is a technical term in late medieval semantics and logic, denoting the meaning assigned to a term. How to fix correctly the referent of "hoc" in the consecration formula had been extensively mooted in the Middle Ages. If Christ's Eucharistic presence in fact comes about by substantial conversion (whether or not it could have come about otherwise), then "the context manifestly compels" us (in Luther's phrase) to take "hoc" not as referring straightforwardly to bread, or "this bread," but to something else (e.g., "this substance"). For one influential account, see Aquinas, *Summa theologiae* III, 78, 5. On the wider medieval debate over the question and the semantic theories that informed it, see Irène Rosier-Catach, *La parole efficace: Signe, ritual, sacré* (Paris: Éditions du Seuil, 2004).

between arguments from scripture and arguments from reason, since Luther's main argument from scripture rests on some claims about how the text is reasonably to be interpreted.

Luther's own position on the role of reason in this matter is, however, a bit difficult to pin down. Unlike impanation, transubstantiation has no rational basis, according to Luther, and this clearly counts against accepting it as a way of understanding theologically how the true presence of Christ's body and blood in the Eucharist actually comes about. At the same time, he says that a person can accept either opinion. How the real presence of Christ comes about is simply not a matter of faith, as long as one believes that it actually does come about.[66] Luther thus offers a manifold reversal of Ockham and d'Ailly: like many late medieval theologians they thought impanation was reasonable but false, and so should not be believed, whereas Luther thinks transubstantiation is unreasonable and false, yet may be believed.

Luther, moreover, evidently introduces two different ideas of impanation in the Babylonian Captivity. The weaker of the two is the one that had been standard in the counterfactual discussions of the late Middle Ages, according to which Christ's body and blood could be present precisely where the bread and wine remain present. This is the idea of impanation that he draws from d'Ailly, and expresses by way of the ancient image of the red hot iron, which completely mingles, without identifying, two different substances.[67] The stronger and more radical of the two positions holds that the consecrated bread is not simply co-present with the body of Christ, it is the body of Christ. When Jesus says "This is my body," the meaning is, "Bread (or this bread) is my body." The "simplest signification" of the words evidently requires this. "Cleaving simply to his words, I firmly believe not merely that the body of Christ is in the bread, but that the bread is the body of Christ."[68]

This latter position was uniformly rejected in the Middle Ages as simply impossible, since it involves a contradiction. What is bread cannot be what is

66. "Here there is no necessity of faith." WA 6: 508.31 (LW 36: 30, though the quoted phrase—sit hic nulla necessitas fidei—is absent from the translation). Cf. WA 6: 512.4-6 (LW 36: 35), where Luther allows that one may accept the position established in Firmiter, as long as he does not regard it as an article of faith binding on others (it had, of course, been so regarded throughout the late Middle Ages: "Firmiter credimus" [DH 800]). Luther's chief concern at this point is to block charges of heresy against those who, with him, believe that Christ's presence comes about in such a way that the true bread and wine remain, rather than by transubstantiation.

67. "In a fiery iron the two substances, fire and iron, are mixed in such a way that each part is fire and iron" (WA 6: 510.5-6 [LW 36: 32]).

68. WA 6: 511.19-21: verbis eius simpliciter inhaerens credo firmiter, non modo corpus Christi esse in pane sed panem esse corpus Christi (LW 36: 34).

not bread. Bread cannot be Christ's body, since the two have contradictory properties. Bread is made of flour, while Christ's body is not made of flour; bread is not made of flesh and bone, while Christ's body is. What is bread, the substance of bread, can be (and in fact is) converted into Christ's body, and (so Scotus, Ockham, and others held) what is bread can be (but in fact is not) present just where Christ's body is. But what is bread cannot be Christ's body. Even divine power cannot bring it about that a contradiction is true, though it is no restriction on God's omnipotence to observe that he cannot do what is incompatible with his own nature and creative action, that is, what is simply impossible. Sensing the difficulty, Luther does not here pursue the logic of the matter, but invokes II Cor. 10:4–5:"Even if I cannot follow in what way the bread is Christ's body, I will nevertheless take my understanding captive in obedience to Christ."[69] Recourse to this Pauline text was common in medieval discussions touching on faith and reason, though one assumes Luther would protest its invocation in defense of transubstantiation.[70] At least in 1520, Luther evidently rejects substantial conversion because it lacks the rational plausibility of weak impanation, yet accepts strong impanation even though it lacks the rational plausibility of the weak version.

Not least in comparison with Luther, late medieval scholastic teaching on Christ's Eucharistic presence calls into question a long standard narrative about the theology of the period and its relation to emergent Protestantism. According to that narrative, late medieval theology was in many respects, including its teaching on the Eucharist, "not fully Catholic." The university theologians of the fourteenth and fifteenth centuries, especially the odious followers of "nominalism," were arid rationalists who, to put the narrative in stronger terms, ruthlessly sacrificed the saving truths of the gospel to pagan reason and hair-splitting dialectic. The Lutheran protest, so the story goes, was an entirely understandable, if in some respects regrettable, response to the debased theological conditions of the time.

This picture of late medieval scholasticism has naturally been attractive in Lutheran-Catholic ecumenical discussions, and in its now familiar form was in large part the work of ecumenically oriented German Catholic scholars, in par-

---

69. WA 6: 511.18–19 (LW 36: 34).

70. By Biel, for example. Faith takes the harder way when it comes to the Eucharist, and so obeys the one in whose presence it believes; "the understanding of each of the faithful should accept captivity in obedience to the faith of Christ, as the Apostle says." *Canonis Missae expositio*, L. 41 M (Oberman and Courtenay, II, 124); cf. L. 12 B (Ibid., I, 93–94). On Aquinas's use of this Pauline *topos*, and its relation to Luther's understanding of faith and reason, see Bruce D. Marshall, "Faith and Reason Reconsidered: Aquinas and Luther on Deciding What is True," *The Thomist*, 63/1 (1999): 1–48.

ticular Joseph Lortz and his school.[71] It allows Catholic theologians to regard Luther's polemics against scholastic theology as largely justified, since they were directed against a decadent scholasticism, and Lutherans to grant that the views Luther was attacking do not represent authentic Catholic teaching. The standard narrative has also gained support from Thomists, who have their own reasons, often unrelated to ecumenism and focused mainly on philosophical disputes, for wanting to sideline scholastic thinkers after Thomas who failed to follow his views. This declension narrative—after Thomas, the deluge—is best known in the form given to it by Étienne Gilson in the middle of the twentieth century, but it has a long prehistory.[72]

In whatever form, the standard narrative has been largely superseded, in the work of historians of medieval philosophy and medieval intellectual traditions, by a more nuanced account of the complexity of late medieval thought, its textual variety (visible not least in a great number of still unedited manuscripts), and its social conditions.[73] The narrative of Lortz and the Thomists continues to enjoy largely unquestioned acceptance, and remains standard, only among theologians, who tend to use "nominalism" and "nominalist" not as contested labels for a diverse collection of positions and ideas, but as imprecations, swear words. Among its advocates the narrative has become curiously self-perpetuating. The scholars who originated it claimed to draw it from a close study of the texts. Those who now find it unpersuasive make their judgment on the same

71. Lortz presented it with particular directness in his semi-popular lectures, *Die Reformation als religiöses Anliegen heute: Vier Vorträge im Dienste der Una Sancta* (Trier: Paulinus Verlag, 1948): Ockhamism "contained in its content and in its way of thought starting points which, consistently carried through, had to lead away from Church teaching. Concerning this Ockhamism I emphasize: it was no longer fully Catholic" (54). "This is our first conclusion: in his reformation breakthrough Luther struggled with a Catholicism that was not fully Catholic" (136-137). English: *The Reformation: A Problem for Today*, trans. John C. Dwyer (Westminster, MD: The Newman Press, 1964), here 45, 127. That nominalism was a degenerate form of scholastic thought was already a well-established trope in Catholic historiography and theology before Lortz came on the scene. His innovation, picked up and developed by his students, was to turn it to ecumenical advantage rather than simply using it to criticize Luther.

72. For a critical account of that prehistory, especially as it bears on the creation of a space on the sidelines where Scotus and Scotism could safely be put, see R. Trent Pomplun, "John Duns Scotus in the History of Medieval Philosophy from the Sixteenth Century to Étienne Gilson (†1978)," *Bulletin de philosophie médiévale*, 58 (2016): 355-445. For the nineteenth century background of the standard narrative (in its philosophical, Gilsonian form), see especially John Inglis, *Spheres of Philosophical Inquiry and the Historiography of Medieval Philosophy* (Leiden: Brill, 1998).

73. On the developing historiography of "nominalism," see William J. Courtenay, "In Search of Nominalism: Two Centuries of Historical Debate," chapter 1 of his *Ockham and Ockhamism: Studies in the Dissemination and Impact of his Thought* (Leiden: Brill, 2008), 1-19. On the narration of late medieval thought more broadly, see Courtenay, *Changing Approaches to Fourteenth-Century Thought*, The Étienne Gilson Series, 29 (Toronto: Pontifical Institute of Medieval Studies, 2007).

basis. But those who still embrace the standard narrative for the most part simply take it from others who already hold it, unburdened by contact with the medieval texts and authors they hope to discredit by invoking it.

When it comes to the Eucharistic presence of Christ, the standard narrative seems to have the matter backwards. As it turns out, Luther was the theologian who ridiculed transubstantiation for being irrational, and argued that Christians should embrace the more reasonable position of impanation rather than submit to the intellectual sacrifice required to believe in substantial conversion. Scotus, Ockham, and Biel were the bold Christian believers who consistently put faith above the inclinations of reason, and Luther the arid rationalist, at least when it suited his purposes.

The Council of Trent follows the path marked out by late medieval theology, and reinforces the teaching that Christ's Eucharistic presence comes about by substantial conversion, not by impanation.[74] This is part and parcel, as the Council sees it, of following the hard way of faith when it comes to Christ's Eucharistic presence, which "is possible for God, and to which we can approach with a mind enlightened by faith, even if we can scarcely express it in words."[75] Trent, in other words, in no way repudiates as "not fully Catholic" the late medieval insistence on the Eucharistic conversion as a summons for faith to reach as far as possible beyond the limits of reason, but underlines and reinforces this late medieval conviction.

SACRIFICE

In Book IV of his *Sentences,* Peter Lombard offers a brief but important account of the Eucharistic sacrifice.[76] Drawing on patristic authorities, he there proposes two basic principles, or axioms, both of which will have enduring influence.

---

74. Trent's Decree on the Eucharist (from Session XIII, 1551) treats conversion especially in ch. 4 (DH 1642); canon 2 (DH 1652) anathematizes the belief that "the substance of bread and wine remains in the most blessed sacrament of the Eucharist," taken as a claim about how the Eucharistic presence of Christ actually comes about. This anathema should not, of course, be taken as a rejection of the disputed counterfactual claim that Christ's Eucharistic presence could have come about in this way if God had so willed. Here as elsewhere, Trent has no interest in settling school differences among Catholic theologians (or, in this case, even in discussing them), but only in identifying what is required by Catholic faith and what is precluded by it. See Marshall, "The Eucharistic Presence of Christ," 68, 71–72.

75. Decree on the Eucharist, ch. 1 (DH 1636).

76. *Sententiae* IV, d. 12, ch. 5 (Brady, 308–309; Silano, 64–65).

(1) The Mass is a True Sacrifice

First, "what the priest does is properly called a sacrifice or immolation." "What is done at the altar is, and is called, a sacrifice."[77] The implied contrast, one assumes, is with what may be called a sacrifice in a merely figurative or metaphorical way, as an offering of thanksgiving is sometimes spoken of as a "sacrifice" of praise. The priest offers a genuine or "proper" sacrifice because of the distinctive relationship of what he does in the Eucharist to what Christ did on the cross. The priest's act of offering and consecration is the "memory" (*memoria*), "recollection" (*recordatio*), and "representation" (*repraesentatio*) "of the true sacrifice and holy immolation carried out on the altar of the cross."[78] What Christ offered on Calvary is of course a proper, not merely metaphorical, sacrifice. It involves a genuine "immolation," that is, a victim slain in sacrifice— Christ himself—as well as an act of offering that victim. Precisely by being the *memoria*, *recordatio*, and *repraesentatio* of the sacrifice of Calvary, Peter Lombard holds, the Eucharist itself is a proper sacrifice and a genuine immolation.

The language of memory and recollection might suggest, on the contrary, that the Eucharistic acts of priest and people simply call to mind the one sacrifice of Christ in the past, making what the priest does in the Eucharist merely a figure or sign of the true sacrifice of Christ. To be sure, memory is itself a way of having the remembered reality present, of calling or recalling it before the mind's eye. We thus remember or recollect precisely what is not truly present here and now, what lacks, however great its significance, direct or immediate presence to us. To the Lombard, though, and to his readers for several centuries to come, it was obvious that we make an offering to God in the Eucharist, and that this offering is a genuine or proper sacrifice, one with a really present, and not only a metaphorical, symbolic, or merely recollected victim.

Then as now, the canon of the Mass makes this as plain as one could wish. The canon opens (in the prayer *Te igitur*) with a plea for God to "accept and bless these gifts, these offerings, these holy unblemished sacrifices, which we offer you firstly for your holy catholic Church."[79] We further plead for God to accept our offering by converting it into the body and blood of Christ. "Be pleased, O God, we pray, to bless, acknowledge, and approve this offering in

77. *Sententiae* IV, d. 12, ch. 5 [1] (Brady, 308.14); ch. 5 [4] (Brady, 309.22-3: *sacrificium esse et dici*; Silano, 64, 65).

78. *Sententiae* IV, d. 12, ch. 5 [1] (Brady, 308.17-18; Silano, 64).

79. I follow here the translation of the canon in the *Roman Missal*, 3rd edition (2010). As the many medieval *expositiones* or commentaries on the Mass make clear (e.g. Biel's, to which we have already referred), the current Latin text of the canon (viz., that of the *Novus Ordo*) on which this translation is based remains for the most part, though with some variations, that known to the medieval Church. None of the variations are pertinent to the passages I cite here.

every respect; make it spiritual and acceptable, so that it may become for us the Body and Blood of your most beloved Son, our Lord Jesus Christ" (the prayer *Quam oblationem*). And we explicitly offer to God the consecrated gifts, Christ's body and blood present in truth, the one sacrificial victim for the sins of the world. "[W]e, your servants and your holy people, offer to your glorious majesty from the gifts that you have given us, this pure victim, this holy victim, this spot-less victim, the holy Bread of eternal life and the Chalice of everlasting salvation" (the prayer *Unde et memores*).

Presumably in light of prayers like these, the Lombard evidently supposes that the language of memory and recollection alone does not suffice to explain how the Eucharist is a "proper" sacrifice. It needs to be completed by the lan-guage of representation if we are to understand how our offering in the Mass is joined to the saving sacrifice of Christ on the cross. *Repraesentatio* comes to bear particular weight in medieval understanding of the Eucharistic sacrifice. It con-notes both resemblance, as a picture represents the reality it depicts, and the presence, or making present, of what the picture or representation resembles. The Mass "represents" the sacrifice of the cross in the strongest possible sense: the very body of Christ, given up to death—that is, immolated—by Christ him-self on the cross, and the very blood poured out there for the forgiveness of sins, are really present here on the Church's altar. We offer not a different gift from those present on the altar, nor any gift of our own making, but exactly what Christ offered to the Father for our salvation, his own body and blood.

In this way, the Lombard argues (drawing on a text of Chrysostom mis-takenly attributed to Ambrose), the sacrifice of the cross is the "pattern" (*exem-plum*) of our daily sacrifice in the Eucharist. "There is one victim, not many. . . . He himself, always he himself is offered," Peter Lombard's patristic authority insists, "and just for this reason [the Eucharist] is a sacrifice," that is, a true or proper sacrifice, for the forgiveness of sins and perfection in virtue.[80] Our sac-rifice is not another sacrifice next to his, but one and the same as his, since we offer exactly what he offered.

As the Lombard here suggests, belief in the real presence of Christ in the sacrament is deeply bound up with the sacrificial nature of the Eucharist, and difficult to extricate from it. In the Eucharist, the bread truly becomes his body, the body "given up" for us (Lk. 22:19), the flesh offered up to the Father for the

---

80. *Sententiae* IV, d. 12, ch. 5 [3] (Brady, 309.13, 15–16; Silano, 64–65). This text is also in Gra-tian (Pt. III, d. 2, ch. 53; Richter-Friedberg, *Corpus iuris canonici*, I, 1333), and medieval theologians invoked it frequently in support of the claim that the Eucharist is a proper, and not simply a met-aphorical, sacrifice. See, e.g., Thomas Aquinas, *Summa theologiae* III, 83, 1, ad 1. On the effect (*virtus*) of the Eucharistic sacrifice as "the forgiveness of venial sins and perfection in virtue," see *Sententiae* IV, d. 12, ch. 5 [4] (Brady, 309.24–25; Silano, 65).

life of the world (cf. Jn. 6:51). The wine truly becomes his blood, "poured out for you and for many for the forgiveness of sins" (Mt. 26:28, as underlined in the canon: *in remissionem peccatorum*). Jesus gives himself to be present in the Eucharist as sacrificial victim, precisely the victim he gave himself to be on the cross. He is present on the altar as the victim of Calvary. Not only that, to be sure. He is present in his total reality, in the very flesh he received from Mary and in which he now lives forever, appearing before the Father (Heb. 9:24) "to intercede for us" (Heb. 7:25). As the consecration and the Eucharistic prayer as a whole (the canon) insist, however, he is present especially and emphatically as victim: *hostiam puram, hostiam sanctam, hostiam immaculatam.* The sacrificial nature of the Eucharist is, as it were, baked into the doctrine of the real presence. Christ makes himself present in the Eucharist specifically in his character as sacrificial victim, and victims are meant to be offered in sacrifice. He makes himself truly present in order to be offered by us.

This point was often made. The primary relationship of the Eucharistic species to the present Christ is that they contain him. This, as Aquinas observes, makes the Eucharist "the perfect sacrament of the Lord's passion, since it contains the very Christ who suffered (*ipsum Christum passum*)."[81] The Eucharist represents Christ in his passion—his completed sacrificial self-offering to the Father—and contains him precisely as he is represented. Bonaventure is more explicit. Christ's Eucharistic presence is for the sake of the Church's Eucharistic sacrifice (which is not to say, of course, that this is the only end or purpose for which Christ gives himself to be present in the Eucharist). "The time in which grace is revealed now requires that not just any sort of sacrifice (*oblatio*) be offered, but a pure, pleasing, and full sacrifice. There is no such sacrifice except that which was offered on the cross, namely the body and blood of Christ. Hence it was necessary that the true body of Christ be contained in this sacrament not only figuratively, but truly, as the sacrifice required for this time."[82] Thus, Bonaventure elsewhere argues, the depth of divine wisdom in granting us nothing less than the true presence of Christ's body and blood in the Eucharist. "By offering himself in a single sacrifice (*unica oblatione*) the Lord emptied out all the other sacrifices. Therefore . . . it was right that he give us the very

81. *Summa theologiae* III, 73, 5, ad 2; cf. 73, 3, ad 3; 73, 6, c.

82. *Breviloquium* VI, 9 (*Opera Omnia*, vol. 5, ed. PP. Collegi a S.Bonaventura (Quaracchi: Collegium S.Bonaventurae, 1901), 274a). I Pet. 2:5 teaches that the members of Christ are "a holy priesthood, to offer spiritual sacrifices (*hostias*—victims) acceptable to God through Jesus Christ." For this reason "it is necessary that the body of Christ be most truly contained here (*hic contineri verissimum corpus Christi*—literally, 'that the truest body of Christ be contained here')." Because of what, or more exactly, because of who, it contains, the Eucharist is "the very sacrifice acceptable and pleasing to God" for which I Pet. calls. Bonaventure, *Commentarius in Evangelium S. Lucae* XXII, 27 (*Opera Omnia*, vol. 7 [Quaracchi: Collegium S. Bonaventurae, 1895], 547b).

same sacrifice that he offered, and no other. Just as the true body of Christ was offered on the cross, so also it is sacrificed (*sacrificatur*) on the altar."[83]

When Cajetan later argued against the Lutherans on this score, he was following a long tradition that saw an intimate connection of the real presence with the Eucharistic sacrifice. If we believe in the real presence, we believe that Christ is present on the altar precisely "as sacrificed," as the one saving victim for our sins. When Christ says, "Do this in remembrance of me," he commands us not simply to make present his body on our altar, but to make present his body "given up for you" (Lk. 22:19), which is to say, being offered up to the Father in sacrifice for our salvation. We cannot obey his command to make him present in his being offered unless we make our own act of offering, our own sacrifice. "For the body of Christ is not made [present] by us just insofar as it is sacrificed unless each is fulfilled in what we do, namely both to make the body of Christ [present] by consecrating, and to make [present] what is given and broken for us by offering sacrifice."[84]

(2) The Mass is the Sacrifice of the Cross, Offered by Us

The second axiom follows from the first. The Church's Eucharist is a proper sacrifice, issuing in the forgiveness of sins, yet Christ offered his saving sacrifice just once, and for all. Hence the Lombard's question: "Is Christ sacrificed daily, or has he been sacrificed only once?"[85] As with the first axiom, the Lombard answers by drawing on patristic authority, and in a way that expresses already deep-seated convictions of the Western Church and its theology that would endure for generations to come. There is no need, he argues, to play off Christ's once-for-all saving sacrifice on the cross against the Church's daily sacrifice on the altar. This is a false dilemma, because Christ offered himself in one way on the cross, and we offer the same Christ in a different way in the Mass: "Christ was offered once, and is offered daily, but in one way then, and in another way

83. *In IV Sent.* d. 10, pt. 1, a. 1, q. 1, ad 2 (*Opera Omnia*, vol. 4, p. 218a), ed. and trans. by Junius Johnson in: *Bonaventure on the Eucharist*, 159.

84. *De missae sacrificio et ritu adversus Lutheranos* (1531), ch. 3: "Nam facto non fit a nobis corpus Christi quatenus immolatur, nisi utrunque facto impleatur, videlicet et consecrando facere corpus Christi, et immolando facere quod datur et frangitur [pro] nobis." *Opuscula Omnia Thomae de Vio Caietani* (Lyon: Iunta, 1562), 286b; see *Cajetan Responds: A Reader in Reformation Controversy*, ed. and trans. Jared Wicks (Washington, DC: Catholic University of America Press, 1978), 189–200, here 192.

85. "[S]i Christus quotidie immolatur vel semel tantum immolatus sit." *Sententiae* IV, d. 12, ch. 5 [1] (Brady, 308.15; Silano, p. 64). Similar language is also in Gratian, both from Ps.-Augustine (Lanfranc; see below, n. 90) and from Paschasius Radbertus: "Iteratur cottidie hec oblatio, licet Christus, semel passus in carne, per unam eandemque mortis passionem semel saluauerit mundum" (*Decretum*, Pt. III, d. 2, chs. 52, 71; Richter-Friedberg, *Corpus iuris canonici*, I, 1333, 1341).

now."[86] We offer daily exactly what he offered once—himself, immolated (given over to death) on the cross. In this basic sense our sacrifice is one and the same as his. But we daily offer his body and blood "in the sacrament, recollecting what he did once for all," while he offered the same body and blood "in himself," just once, on the cross.[87]

The Lombard's distinction between Christ being immolated or sacrificed "in himself" (*in semetipso*) and being immolated sacramentally or "in the sacrament" (*in sacramento*) recalls his earlier distinction, invoked to interpret Berengar's confession, between Christ's body being broken and rent "in its substance" and "in the sacrament."[88] In both cases what is true of Christ, and in particular of his body, in virtue of his distinctive sacramental presence differs from what is true of him apart from that presence, in his body's natural mode of existing. Thus it is quite correct to say that we rend the body of Christ with our teeth "in the sacrament," but we do not thereby divide the substance of Christ's body, at once seated at the Father's right hand and present on our altar, into little pieces. Likewise, and more directly parallel to the Eucharistic sacrifice, on the cross Christ's body was once broken "in substance," but when we break up the host "in the sacrament," we do not once again break his body, now impassible, in its natural mode of existence.[89]

The same goes for sacrifice. "In himself," in his natural mode of existence, Christ was immolated (in the sense of "slain") as the one saving sacrifice for the sins of the whole world only once, on Calvary. With his blood as well as his body clearly before us, just this immolated Christ, Christ in his passion, is daily present on our altars "in the sacrament." This does not mean, however, that we daily shed his blood anew, any more than we daily break his bones in the sacrament. Rather Christ, as the Lombard succinctly puts it, was offered "in one way then, and in another way now." In one way on the cross (in himself, and so with the outpouring of blood), and in another way in the Mass (sacramentally, and so with no fresh outpouring of blood). "In the manifestation of his body and the [visible] distinction of his members [Christ] hung on the cross only once, offering himself to the Father as the efficacious victim of redemption."[90] At the

86. "Christum semel oblatum, et quotidie offerri; sed aliter tunc, aliter nunc." *Sententiae* IV, d. 12, ch. 5 [4] (Brady, 309.23-24; Silano, 65).

87. *Sententiae* IV, d. 12, ch. 5 [1] (Brady, 308.19-21; Silano, 64).

88. See above, at and around n. 16.

89. As medieval scholastic theologians clearly recognized, claims of this kind (in this case concerning one and the same body) raise important questions about how to understand identity, sameness, and distinction, akin to those raised by Christian faith in the Trinity and the incarnation. On this see Marshall, "Identity, Being, and Eucharist," 5-9.

90. *Sententiae* IV, d. 12, ch. 5 [2] (Brady, 309.7-9; Silano, 64). This comes from a text the Lombard attributes to Augustine by way of Prosper of Aquitaine, though in the form in which he gives

same time the Church's Eucharist "is, and is called, a sacrifice," indeed the one sacrifice of Christ, because both of the following are true. (1) It is the representation and recollection of Christ's passion, in the strong sense we described in the previous section: by the consecration the once-for-all victim of Calvary, the immolated Christ, makes himself present on our altar. (2) In the prayers of the canon, we ourselves offer this victim of Calvary to the Father, obeying his command, "do this." "Everywhere Christ is one, fully existing here, and fully existing there. Just as what is everywhere offered is one body, so also there is one sacrifice. Christ offered this victim, and we ourselves offer the same victim now."[91]

Here the Lombard evidently holds—and a great many would follow him in this—that sacrifices are adequately individuated by victims, that is, by *what* is offered in the sacrificial act. Since the victim on our altar is one and the same as the victim who was immolated (that is, slain) once for all on the altar of the cross, the sacrifice we make is one and the same as his, not a numerically distinct sacrifice alongside his. On this view, a numerical distinction in what is offered sacrificially seems like a necessary, and probably also sufficient, condition for a real (that is, numerical) diversity of sacrifices. By contrast, the manner or mode of offering is not sufficient to individuate a sacrifice. Or more precisely, diversity in the manner or mode of existence of what is offered, "in himself" or "in the sacrament," does not make for diverse sacrifices, which might then be played off against one another. As long and the body and blood offered by us in the Mass are one and the same with that offered by Christ alone in the upper room and on the cross, our sacrifice and his remain, in the pertinent sense, one and the same.

From this it follows that numerically distinct acts of offering (one in blood, one without, as it would later be put) also fail to individuate a sacrifice. Our act of offering in the Mass is distinct in mode, and therefore in number, from Jesus' act of offering, begun in the upper room and completed on the cross. But our act of offering does not compete with his, since we daily offer just what he offered once for all: himself. It seems, moreover, that with any other sacrifice than that which takes place in the Mass (with the sacrifices of the Levitical cult, for

---

it the direct source is Lanfranc's *De corpore et sanguine Domini*, ch. 15 (see Gratian, Pt. III, d. 2, ch. 52 for the same attribution [Richter-Friedberg, *Corpus iuris canonici,* I, 1333]). The idea of Christ being offered once for all in himself and daily in the sacrament (p. 309.5-6) does, however, have clear roots in Augustine. Cf. *Ep.* 98.9: "Has not Christ been sacrificed once for all in himself, and nevertheless is he not sacrificed for the people not only on every paschal solemnity [viz., Sunday], but every day?" (*Nonne semel immolatus est Christus in se ipso et tamen in sacramento non solum per omnes paschae sollemnitates sed omni die populis immolatur,* [Corpus Scriptorum Ecclesticorum Latinorum (hereafter CSEL) 34/2], 530.21-531.2).

91. *Sententiae* IV, d. 12, ch. 5 [3] (Brady, 309.17-19; Silano, 65). See above, n. 80, on the influential Ps.-Ambrose text from which this comes.

example) it would be impossible to have two sacrificial acts, two acts of offering, without also having two distinct sacrificial victims, and so two numerically distinct sacrifices. Only in virtue of the real presence of Christ in the Eucharist can we offer to the Father precisely what Christ himself offered, by an act dependent on, yet irreducibly distinct from, his own. Here, too, the real presence of the once-for-all immolated Christ is, on the view briefly but formatively articulated by Peter Lombard, essential to the sacrificial unity of the cross and the altar.

For the Lombard, then, our Eucharist is a true sacrifice that forgives sins for two basic reasons: the one immolation and victim of Calvary is truly present on our altars, and we truly offer him in obedience to his command. His presence and our act make the Eucharist the full and adequate *repraesentatio* and *recordatio* of his once-for-all sacrifice, and so make the Eucharist itself "to be, and to be called," a sacrifice.

Commentaries on Peter Lombard's *Sentences* grew into an immense genre of theological literature in the thirteenth century, but theologians lecturing on the *Sentences* often pass over the Lombard's discussion of Eucharistic sacrifice in complete, or nearly complete, silence. Clearly this was not because they doubted his claims—that would have prompted a vigorous response—but precisely because they accepted them. In marked contrast to the question of Christ's Eucharistic presence, the Lombard's comments on Eucharistic sacrifice evidently offered nothing that seemed doubtful or puzzling, even in a purely speculative way.

To be sure, some thirteenth century writers on the *Sentences* do take up this topic, usually to underline or briefly elaborate what they take the Lombard to be saying. Albert the Great, for example, considers a series of objections to the claim that "Christ is daily sacrificed and immolated, by way of the representation of past events (*propter repraesentationem praeteritorum*)."[92] Clearly not, argues the first objection, because Christ's immolation and sacrifice is one and the same event as his crucifixion and death.[93] Christ's crucifixion and death, so Albert and his objector agree, are represented in the Mass just as much as his immolation and sacrifice are. But we do not crucify Christ every time we celebrate the Mass. Neither, then, do we truly sacrifice or immolate Christ when we celebrate the Mass. We simply represent, and so call to mind, a once-for-all event in the past.

Not so, Albert replies, if we make the right distinctions. The words and gestures of the Mass do represent the crucifixion and death of Christ. But Christ's

---

92. *In IV Sent.* d. 13, a. 23. *B. Alberti Magni Opera Omnia*, ed. Auguste Borgnet (Paris: Vivès, 1890–95), vol. 29 (1894), 370b.

93. As the objection puts it, crucifixion and death have here the same *ratio* as sacrifice and immolation; whatever is true of the one pair is true of the other. *In IV Sent.* d. 13, a. 23, ob 1 (Borgnet, 370b).

crucifixion and death remain unrepeatable, once-for-all events. They are present in the Mass only in the indirect sense that the Crucified himself, his true body and blood, are present there. Christ's immolation and sacrifice, however, are not simply identical with his being nailed to the cross and dying on it. In Albert's lexicon, death—even death voluntarily accepted—is not sufficient for either sacrifice or immolation. A sacrifice has to be offered.[94] So Christ, in instituting the Eucharist, offered to the Father his cross, yet to be borne, and his blood, yet to be shed, to take away the sins of the world (though Albert, like most medieval writers on the subject, makes no special point of the connection between the upper room, as offering, and the cross as the carrying out or completion of the already offered sacrifice). It is not simply the Crucified who is present on our altars, but the one who offered his cross to the Father for our salvation—the immolated Christ, Christ in his sacrifice. But a sacrifice has to be offered. The sacrifice or immolation of Christ cannot be present in the Mass unless it offered, in the present.

Albert thus parries the objection by distinguishing between the act of crucifying and killing Christ, which in no way takes place in the Mass, and the act of offering and sacrificing him, which does. "Christ is most truly immolated every day, when sacrifice is offered to God the Father. For 'immolation' refers to the act of offering with respect to what is offered [a victim], and 'sacrifice' refers to the same act with respect to its effect [to worship God]." Since there is daily present on our altars the one who offered himself as the pure and final sacrifice for sin, "we always immolate and sacrifice. But it is not the same with crucifixion . . . this was not to be repeated (*iteranda*)."[95] The Mass "represents" the crucifixion and death of Christ simply by referring to unrepeatable past events, and so calling those events to mind. But the Mass does not, indeed cannot, represent the immolation and sacrifice of Christ merely by referring to past events. In order to represent the sacrifice of Christ, offered once for all in the upper room and consummated on the cross, the Mass has to include our own act of offering him to the Father. This is an integral part of the representative significance of the Mass, without which the Mass, in the Lombard's phrase, could not "be, and be called, a sacrifice." So Albert cautions against taking the now-standard language of "representation" in too weak a sense. "Our immolation is not only a representation, but a true immolation, that is, an offering, by the hands of the priests, of the one who was immolated . . . because properly speaking immolation is the offering of a victim (*occisi*) for the worship of God. With respect to oblation [the Mass] is not only a representation, but a

---

94. A point Scotus will later make much more explicit; see the discussion of sacrifice and Mass intention below.

95. *In IV Sent.* d. 13, a. 23, ad 1 (Borgnet, 371a).

true act of offering. This is not the case with respect to slaying (*occisione*) and crucifixion."[96]

On this point Thomas Aquinas closely follows Albert, his teacher, in his own commentary on the *Sentences*. Some aspects of Christ's passion are transitory, such as his suffering punishment at the hands of the violent. So "we do not say that Christ is daily crucified and killed." However, "those aspects [of the passion] that involve a relationship of Christ to God the Father are said to happen daily, such as to offer, to sacrifice, and things of this kind, since this victim abides forever (*hostia illa perpetua est*). And in this way what was offered by Christ once for all can also be offered daily by his members."[97]

In the *Summa theologiae*, Aquinas includes what could be thought of as his own brief *expositio missae*, comprising the last question on the Eucharist under the heading, "Concerning the rite of this sacrament" (III, q. 83). He begins by considering, as Albert had done, one of the Lombard's basic questions on Eucharistic sacrifice: "Whether Christ is immolated daily in the celebration of this sacrament?" Here he makes more explicit the logic of Peter Lombard's second axiom. Christ offered himself once for all for our salvation, and we daily offer this once-for-all immolated Christ, just as the Lombard had said. Precisely by way of the daily Eucharistic immolation, Aquinas adds, "we are made sharers in the fruits of the Lord's passion," since "as often as the commemoration of this victim is celebrated, the work of our redemption is carried out."[98] The redemptive fruits or effects of Christ's passion, of his once-for-all saving sacrifice, are "applied" to us in the Eucharistic sacrifice, just as, in general, the sacraments are the means by which Christ joins us to himself in his passion, and so "carries out the work of our redemption."[99] Aquinas thus brings out the unity of the daily sacrifice of the Mass with the once-for-all sacrifice of the cross by treating them as effect and cause. But substantively he does not go much beyond what the Lombard had said on this matter a century before, and in fact follows him and his sources (especially Ps.-Ambrose) rather closely.[100]

96. *In IV Sent.* d. 13, a. 23, ad 2 (Borgnet, 371a).

97. *In IV Sent.* d. 12, *expositio textus* (§267). *S. Thomae Aquinatis Scriptum Super Sententiis*, ed. Pierre Mandonnet and Marie-Fabien Moos (Paris: Lethielleux, 1933-47), IV, 539.

98. III, 83, 1, c. The latter quotation is taken from his Dominican missal.

99. See *Summa theologiae* III, 61, 1, ad 3: "[T]he sacraments . . . act by the power of Christ's passion (*operantur in virtute passionis Christi*), and the passion of Christ is in a certain way applied to human beings by the sacraments, as the Apostle says (Rom. 6:3): 'We who have been baptized in Christ Jesus, have been baptized into his death.'"

100. On Aquinas's theology of the Eucharistic sacrifice, in the context of his understanding of sacrifice as a whole, see Bruce D. Marshall, "The Whole Mystery of Our Salvation: St. Thomas on the Eucharist as Sacrifice," *Sacraments in Aquinas*, ed. Michael Dauphinais and Matthew Levering (Chicago: Hillenbrand Books, 2009), 39-64.

On the verge of Protestantism, the Lombard's two axioms remain basic to reflection on the sacrificial nature of the Eucharist. Biel invokes them often (though usually without referring directly to the Lombard), and as many had done before him, comes back to the main patristic texts (Augustine and Ps.-Ambrose) that support these axioms in the *Sentences*. Christ is not daily wounded, Biel notes, and does not daily suffer and die, "rather for two different causes the consecration and reception of the Eucharist is called a sacrifice and oblation: both because it is the representation and commemoration of the true sacrifice and holy immolation made on the cross, and because [the Eucharist] brings about and is the causal source of like effects [to the passion]."[101] We do not, therefore, offer another sacrifice alongside his and in competition with his, but the very sacrifice he offered. "Behold, how great is our sacrifice: not merely the memorial of that great, unique, and most perfect sacrifice offered once for all on the cross, but that sacrifice itself, and always the same [sacrifice]."[102] We do this by daily offering in one way exactly what Christ once-for-all offered in another. "[Ps.-] Ambrose says that there is one sacrifice that Christ offered and that we offer, although it is not offered in the same way. By him it was offered unto death, by us not unto death, since 'Christ rising from the dead dies no more' [Rom. 6:9]. Rather it is offered by us in the recollection of his death. Therefore our offering is not the repetition (*reiteratio*) of his offering, but its representation."[103]

A note on terminology, before we turn to the most significant development in late medieval theology of the Eucharistic sacrifice. The passages cited in this section make plain that medieval theologians generally do not use the language pertinent to sacrifice in a carefully defined or consistent way. The Lombard, for example, evidently uses "immolatio" and "oblatio" more or less interchangeably for the offering of the victim of Calvary, whether by himself on the cross or by us in the Mass.[104] He also uses "sacrificium" as more or less equivalent first to one, then to the other.[105] This relative linguistic insou-

---

101. Biel, *Canonis missae expositio*, L. 85 F (Oberman and Courtenay, IV, 101); cf. L. 53 U (Oberman and Coutenay, II, 331). When Biel says that the Eucharist has effects like those of the passion, he means that it is the chief divinely instituted way the passion has its salutary effects in us, as others (e.g., Aquinas) had already maintained. "The Lord . . . instituted this ineffable sacrament as a perpetual memorial, so that of the accomplished redemption there would not be lacking a salutary and efficacious sign, by which the salvation acquired at such great cost might flow into the redeemed" (L. 85 I [Oberman and Courtenay, IV, 104]; cf. 85 L [Ibid., 106]).

102. Biel, *Canonis missae expositio*, L. 85 I (Oberman and Courtenay, IV, 103): *Ecce quantum est sacrificium nostrum, nedum memoriale magni illius unici et perfectissimi sacrificii semel in cruce oblata, sed id ipsum et semper idipsum.*

103. Biel, *Canonis missae expositio*, L. 53 U (Oberman and Courtenay, II, 332); cf. L. 27 K (Ibid., I, 265).

104. See the texts cited in nts. 85 and 86.

105. Cf. *Sententiae* IV, d. 12, ch. 5 [1; 4] (Brady, 308.14, 309.22-23).

ciance fits with the fact that the whole matter was not controverted in the Middle Ages.

In the sixteenth century and after, when the Eucharistic sacrifice becomes the subject of intense controversy, Catholic theologians will use the terms more precisely, though not always in just the same way. "Oblatio" is recognized to be ambiguous, though the ambiguity is not difficult to sort out. It can mean (1) the *act* of making an offering, (2) *what* is offered in this act, or (3) both. "Immolatio" is often taken more narrowly than it was in medieval discussions, to mean specifically the slaying or destruction of the victim offered in sacrifice, usually, as at Calvary, of the victim already *having been* offered. In a nicely succinct formulation of Maurice de la Taille, "The Passion is *immolatio hostiae oblatae*; the Supper is *oblatio hostiae immolandae*"—slaying of the victim who was offered; offering of the victim to be slain.[106] "Sacrificium," then, is taken to refer to the whole that is formed when oblation and immolation are joined. Many things can be offered (bread or cereal, for example), but these are not sacrifices in the strict sense of the term, since there is no victim. Immolation by itself is not sacrifice, but simply killing, which has no intrinsic value; the immolated victim acquires specifically sacrificial value from the act of offering it. These conceptual distinctions are often apparent in medieval discussions of the Eucharist as sacrifice, but this has to be gathered from the context; the terminology does not map onto the concepts in a reliable way.

EUCHARISTIC SACRIFICE AND MASS INTENTION

On the Eucharist as a genuine sacrifice and the relation between the Mass and the cross, Western theology in the century after Peter Lombard sees little need to go beyond what he had said, save to offer occasional elaborations and precisions. A significant advance does come, however, with the 20th *Quodlibet* of John Duns Scotus, from around 1305. The initial question concerns the responsibilities of a priest: if two people ask me to say Mass for their intentions, and I accept their requests, do I fulfill my obligation to each of them by saying one Mass for both intentions?

The question arises from a well-known development in Eucharistic practice evident around the time Scotus was writing, namely the rapidly increasing desire of the faithful to have Masses said for their intentions. This naturally

---

106. "An Outline of the Mystery of Faith," in: Maurice de la Taille, SJ, *The Mystery of Faith and Human Opinion Contrasted and Defined* (London: Longmans, Green & Co., 1930), 3–39, here 13. For more on these terminological questions in medieval and early modern theology, see de la Taille's essay, "Distinction between Oblation and Immolation in Traditional Theology," in *idem*, 349-379.

required an increase in the number of Masses, many of which would perforce be celebrated without a congregation present—what are sometimes misleadingly called "private" Masses. The practice of having a priest say Mass alone, or with only a server present, is already visible in the Carolingian period, and considerably increases by the late Middle Ages. The phrase "missa privata," however, is rarely attested before the rise of Protestantism. It seems to have gained currency from Luther's treatise *De abroganda missa privata* of 1522 ("On Abolishing the Private Mass"), where the notion is used in a deliberately polemical and not merely descriptive way.[107] By the eighteenth century, the term "private Mass" does become commonplace, even in Catholic missals and writings on the liturgy. Nonetheless, to think that the Mass, when celebrated by a solitary priest, thereby becomes private in a troubling sense is, on typical medieval principles, to misunderstand the nature of the Mass itself. Medieval theologians assumed that the Mass is first of all an offering to God, which can, as such, benefit anyone for whom it is intended, regardless of whether they are present at the Mass (or, indeed, still present in this world)— just as one person's prayers can benefit another even if she is not present when the prayers are offered.[108] The Mass is, moreover, always the offering of the whole Church in union with Christ her head, and never the merely private offering of the priest.[109]

107. WA 8: 411–476; Luther also produced a somewhat different German version of the treatise under the title "The Misuse of the Mass" (*Vom Mißbrauch der Messe*), WA 8: 482–563 (LW 36: 133–230). The phrase "missae privatae" had already appeared, e.g., in Johannes Altenstaig's widely-read and often reprinted *Vocabularius theologie* (Hagenau: Heinrich Gran, 1517), here fol. 152rb.

108. Thus, e.g., Aquinas: "The suitability (*opportunitas*) of offering sacrifice obtains not only in relation to Christ's faithful, to whom it is necessary that the sacraments be administered, but chiefly (*principaliter*) in relation to God, to whom sacrifice is offered by the consecration of this sacrament" (*Summa theologiae* III, 82, 10, c); the Eucharist "benefits those who do not receive it [at the Mass] under its aspect as sacrifice (*per modum sacrificii*), in that it is offered for their salvation" (III, 79, 7, c).

109. "The arrangement of the divine wisdom is such that it is not possible for this sacrifice not to be accepted. For it is offered to the Father, and it is offered by the Son, our high priest. [In it] Christ is offered in [his] human nature of body and blood, and he is offered for all." Albert the Great, *De corpore Domini* (also called *De sacramento Eucharistiae*), d.V, ch. 3 (*Opera omnia*, ed. Borgnet, vol. 38 [1899], 347a; *On the Body of the Lord*, trans. Sr. Albert Marie Surmanski [Washington, DC: Catholic University of America Press, 2017], 290). "The pontiffs and priests who follow [Christ] are his vicars; in the words they utter the uncreated Word effects the offering" (Borgnet, 348a; Surmanski, 292). In the prayer of the canon *Iube haec perferri* ("[C]ommand that these gifts be borne by the hands of your holy Angel to your altar on high"), "The Church militant, which is the mystical body of Christ, having been incorporated into the true body [of Christ] which is most truly contained in the sacrament…prays that it may ascend to the altar of divine majesty, so that there it may be offered to him in glory, as here it is offered in sacramental grace." *De corpore Domini*, d. VI, tr. 2, ch. 1, n. 6 (Borgnet, 370a; Surmanski, 328).

These points are not original with Scotus, but he gives them a precise explanation. Practical problems posed by the increase of Mass intentions give Scotus the opportunity to explore questions that had not previously been discussed in an explicit or systematic way, in particular concerning the value, benefit, or merit of a Mass, and how that benefit reaches those for whom it is intended. Reflection on these questions exposes previously unnoticed complexities about the relationship of the Mass to the cross, which Scotus also considers.

Scotus, of course, does not invent the idea of the fruits of the Mass that he here endeavors to explain in a precise way. That the Mass is abundantly fruitful, that in it God confers grace in manifold ways, was already well established before the significant growth of Mass intentions visible around the turn of the fourteenth century. Still less does he invent the idea that the Mass can be offered for the intentions of the faithful, or that the Mass so offered can benefit the dead as well as the living. All these ideas have roots going back to the ancient Church. Particularly at its heart—the canon—the Mass is, after all, a prayer, or rather a series of prayers. These are in various overlapping ways latreutic (they offer God worship), impetrative (they implore God's favor and generosity), and intercessory (they do so for anyone, and not simply for those present when the prayer is being offered). That prayer can benefit not only the one who prays, but those for whom he prays, had never been doubted in the Christian tradition. Scotus bases his analysis of the value and "fruits" of the Mass precisely on the observation that the Mass is, first of all, a prayer. "Among meritorious works prayer most of all has the character of merit applicable to another, because prayer by its very nature is pleasing to God and reconciles to God, and it does this for the one for whom it is especially offered by the person who prays."[110]

Before God the value of any one Mass, Scotus argues, is finite. Christ's once-for-all offering of himself on Calvary is, to be sure, of infinite value, and just this Christ, the Christ of Calvary, is fully present in the Eucharist.[111] When we

110. *Quodlibet* 20.4. I follow the Latin text and paragraph numbers in Felix Alluntis, ed. and trans., *Cuestiones Cuodlibetales* (*Obras del Doctor Sutil Juan Duns Escoto*) (Madrid: Biblioteca de Autores Cristianos, 1968), here 706. Alluntis and Allan B. Wolter produced an English version: John Duns Scotus, *God and Creatures: The Quodlibetal Questions* (Princeton: Princeton University Press, 1975), here 444. On taking *placativa Dei* as "pleasing to God" in contexts like this (and not simply as "placating God"), see Bruce D. Marshall, "Effects of the Eucharistic Sacrifice: A Brief Commentary on Trent's *De Missæ Sacrificio*, Chapter 2," *Communio: International Catholic Review* (English Edition) 44/1 (2017), 7–24.

111. "For Christ, who is offered in this sacrifice, was sufficient to make satisfaction for sins when he was offered on the cross," indeed "sufficient for an infinity [of sins]." *Quodlibet* 20.2 (Alluntis, 704–705; Alluntis and Wolter, 443). The infinite value of the sacrifice of Calvary is here stated as the premise of an objection to the position Scotus himself will eventually take. The objection has traction precisely because Scotus wholly accepts this premise, as he does the related assumption that the Christ of Calvary is fully present in the Eucharistic offering. Cf. *Quodlibet* 20.71 (Alluntis 746; Alluntis and Wolter, 468).

offer the crucified Christ to the Father in the Mass, we plead over and over that God will accept our offering, the act we here and now undertake, for the sake of the Crucified himself, once offered on the cross. "The Mass both represents the oblation on the cross and pleads it, that is, implores God to accept through it the sacrifice of the Church."[112] The Mass has no independent value; it bears no fruit, that is, considered simply as our act. That it bears fruit or has grace-giving value depends wholly on its relation to the once-for-all offering of Christ, on the fact that the Crucified gives himself to be offered in it. So it is, Scotus observes, with any offering or sacrifice. We trust that what we offer will be more pleasing to the one to whom we offer it than our own acts as such; otherwise, there would be no reason to offer it in the first place.

As with any prayer or offering, however, the value of the Eucharistic sac-rifice depends not only on what is offered in it, or the content of the offering, but also on the intention and the disposition of the one who makes the offering. Indeed, scripture teaches that other things being equal, this intention is primarily what God takes into account in accepting any offering, or being pleased with it. "God looked with favor on Abel and his offering" (Gen. 4:4), Scotus points out, "first on Abel, then on his gifts." Likewise, Jesus says (Lk. 21:2-4) that the poor widow "put in more than all the rest," even though she gave the smallest amount, "because [her offering] came from a more acceptable will."[113] These texts were commonplace in discussions of sacrifice, Eucharistic and otherwise, since they indicate a clear connection between the value of an offering and the intention of the offerer.[114] The Eucharistic canon recalls "Abel the just" as the first of God's people to offer sacrifice acceptable to him, and goes on to mention

---

112. *Quodlibet* 20.48 (Alluntis, 732; Alluntis and Wolter, 460).

113. Both from *Quodlibet* 20.47 (Alluntis, 731; Alluntis and Wolter, 459). Scotus here prefaces his appeal to the biblical texts by observing that no offering, even that of the Eucharist, "is accepted unless it is that of an accepted offerer (*nisi sit offerentis accepti*)." Cf. *Quodlibet* 17.8: "No one's act is accepted as worthy of a reward, unless the person doing it is accepted, according to Gen. 4[:4]: 'God looked with favor on Abel and his gifts'—first on Abel, then on the gifts, because the offering of one in whom no delight is taken (*oblatio non dilecti*) is not pleasing" (Alluntis, 615; Alluntis and Wolter, 390).

114. Aquinas already treats the widow's offering in much the same way that Scotus later would. The Eucharist, alone among the seven sacraments, is sacrifice as well as sacrament, and "insofar as it is a sacrifice, it has the power to make satisfaction," that is, to repair the damage done by sin (in this case, to diminish the penalty of sin). "When it comes to satisfaction, the disposition of the one who makes the offering matters more than the quantity of what is offered. Hence the Lord says in Lk. 21[:3], concerning the widow who offered two coins, that 'she put in more than all the rest.' Therefore, the quantity of this offering [the Eucharistic sacrifice] suffices to make sat-isfaction for every penalty, but it becomes satisfaction for those for whom it is offered, and also for those who offer it, according to the extent of their devotion (*secundum quantitatem suae devotionis*)." *Summa theologiae* III, 79, 5, c.

Abraham and Melchizedek, who did the same. In medieval understanding, Abel already acted as a member of the Church, indeed the first member, since he was the first righteous person after the fall.[115] The relation between what is offered, the value of the offering, and the intention of the offerer in his case is thus suitably paradigmatic for that of the Church's offering in the Eucharist.[116] In any one celebration of the Mass, then, the value of the Eucharistic sacrifice depends not only on the infinite worth of Christ who is offered in it, but on the necessarily finite merit of those making the offering.

As he often does, Scotus here points out something lying in plain sight that, once noticed, is too telling to ignore, and puts the discussion of a contested matter on a new footing. His insight is simple, but stated with a previously unattained clarity: the Eucharist is a human act. It is not *only* a human act, of course, but *as* a human act it matters to God. In other words, it has merit before God, in the way prayer or any other human act has, or fails to have, merit before God, namely in virtue of the intentions and dispositions of the human agents involved.

Scotus drives this point home by making an observation about Eucharistic practice, as it had long since taken shape by his time. We do not encounter the Eucharist, specifically the consecrated host, only in Mass. We also reserve the Eucharist in a pyx or tabernacle, to commune the sick and to adore the eucharistically present Christ outside of Mass. Christ is just as much contained in the consecrated host when it resides in the tabernacle as when it is present on the altar and distributed to the faithful. A bit of reflection on these facts of daily Eucharistic life will help us to see that the good God will give in virtue of the Eucharistic sacrifice, or, what comes to the same thing, the merit or value the Eucharistic sacrifice has to God, "does not exactly correspond to the good con-

---

115. Augustine is particularly influential here; cf. Yves Congar, "Ecclesia ab Abel," in: *Abhandlungen über Theologie und Kirche* (FS Karl Adam), ed. Marcel Reding (Düsseldorf: Patmos-Verlag, 1952), 79-108.

116. Most commentators on the Mass make this connection explicit. In his *expositio Missae* William Durand of Mende (above, n. 8) puts the matter in terms quite similar to those Scotus would use, a bit more than a decade later: "First [God] had regard for Abel, and afterwards had regard for his gifts (*munera*), because the one offering was not pleasing on account of the gifts, but the gifts were pleasing on account of the one offering." *Rationale divinorum officiorum*, Lib. IV, 43, 11 [CCCM, 140], I (Davril and Thibodeau, 485; Thibodeau, 388). This exegesis of Gen. 4:4 was standard, even when the context was not directly sacrificial. Commenting on Paul's praise of the churches in Macedonia, who despite their poverty "first gave themselves . . . for the relief of the saints" (II Cor. 8:4-5), Aquinas observes that "this ought to be the order in giving, that first the human being is accepted by God, because unless the human being is pleasing to God, his gifts are not accepted. Gen. 4:4: 'the Lord had regard for Abel,' that is, first of all, 'and for his gifts' after that." *In II Cor.* 8, 1 (no. 289) (*Super Epistolas S. Pauli Lectura*, vol. 1, ed. Raphael Cai, 8th edn. [Turin: Marietti, 1953], 506b).

tained in the Eucharist. For that good is the same when the Eucharist is reserved in a pyx, but it does not then benefit the Church as it does when it is offered in the Mass."[117]

The body and blood of Christ have the same intrinsic value, they are equally precious to God, when reserved in a tabernacle before which no human being happens to be present as they have when they are on the altar in the Eucharistic sacrifice. The Christ of Calvary, who once for all offered to the Father a sacrifice of infinite value, is as much present in the tabernacle as he is on the altar of sacrifice. But his body and blood present in an empty church are not fruitful as they are when offered to the Father in the Mass, or when adored in a tabernacle by the faithful or received in communion. The infinite intrinsic worth of the present Christ himself naturally never changes, but in order to benefit from his Eucharistic presence we have to be brought into some relation with him present in this way, normally an intentional and deliberate relation. What is contained in the Eucharist is always the same—Christ himself—and of the same worth, but our relation to him so contained varies both in kind and in degree. The Eucharistic presence of Christ becomes fruitful for us when we *do* something in relation to the sacrificed Christ there present. There is much we can do, but the action to which God has pledged the richest outpouring of his grace ("do this") is to offer the body and blood of Christ to the Father for the good of the living and the dead, for our sins and the sins of the whole world.

We do not, Scotus emphasizes, do this on our own, but as members and servants of Christ our high priest. As on Calvary, so also in the Mass, he is not only the "immaculate victim" offered to the Father (to recall the language of the canon), but also the primary agent of the offering, the one, we could say, who ultimately takes responsibility for it. "Whenever Christ as supreme priest offers [the Eucharist], the bread which he gives, that is, his flesh, is the life of the world" (cf. Jn. 6:52).[118] Our act of offering depends not only on his past act of offering in the upper room and on the cross, but on the present reality of his eternal priesthood, in which he gives the Church a share. But while our offering in the Mass depends on him in manifold ways, it is still genuinely our offering, and not only his. In this, the Mass differs from the passion and cross, when Christ offered himself to the Father without (yet) calling upon the sacramental participation of his members in the act of offering. The body and blood of Christ

117. *Quodlibet* 20.47: *[C]ui merito correspondet bonum reddendum virtute sacrificii[?] Et dici potest quod non correspondet praecise bono contento in eucharistia; illud enim bonum aequale est quando eucharistia servatur in pyxide, et tamen non tunc aequivalet Ecclesiae sicut quando offertur in missa* (Alluntis. 731; Alluntis and Wolter, 459).

118. *Quodlibet* 20.3 (Alluntis, 705; Alluntis and Wolter, 444). As the context makes clear (the ineluctable value of a Mass offered even by an unworthy priest), Scotus is talking here about Christ as offerer specifically of the Eucharistic sacrifice.

are no less dear to God when contained in the Eucharist than when they were given and shed on the cross (since they are one and the same body and blood). In the Eucharist, though, they are offered not only by Christ, but also by us. As a result, the intentions and dispositions of we who make the offering, and not only the infinite merit of Christ, priest and victim, have a bearing on the fruitfulness of the offering itself. Scotus summarizes: "Just as the full acceptance of the Eucharist [by God] does not happen simply on account of what is contained in it, rather it must be offered, so also it is not accepted when offered except on account of the good will of the one who makes the offering."[119]

The Mass is a particularly complex human act, because who it is that offers the Eucharistic sacrifice is itself irreducibly complex. Christ himself is the "supreme priest" of the Eucharistic sacrifice, but in each instance he makes this offering not immediately, as he did in the upper room and on Calvary, but by means of a minister, the priest who actually says a particular Mass. In offering the sacrifice of the Mass, however, the individual priest acts not only at the command of Christ, but also in the name of the whole Church. Therefore the universal Church must also be considered to offer the Eucharistic sacrifice; indeed, the priest's work in offering is simply to present a petition of the whole Church.[120]

This distinction between the action of the individual celebrant and the action of the whole Church is essential, Scotus proposes, to understanding the sacrifice of the Mass and the way it bears fruit for those whom it is intended to benefit. He makes the distinction in part by identifying the action of the celebrating priest as the *opus operantis*, and the action of the whole Church as the *opus operatum*. In the sixteenth century these terms would become hotly contested. Scotus uses them in the sense that would be standard in late medieval theology. The *opus operantis* (literally "the action of the one working") is the Mass considered with respect to the dispositions and intentions of the celebrant as an individual agent. The *opus operatum* is the Mass considered with respect to the action itself that is performed or completed in the Mass (literally "the action worked," or accomplished). Scotus correlates the *opus operatum* or work performed not only with the action of the whole Church, but with the sacrifice itself.[121]

---

119. *Quodlibet* 20.48 (Alluntis, 732; Alluntis and Wolter, 460): *Ex istis patet quod, sicut eucharistia non praecise ratione rei contentae plene acceptatur, sed oportet quod sit oblata, sic nec plene acceptatur oblata, nisi ratione bonae voluntatis alicuius offerentis.*

120. "The good owed in virtue of the sacrifice is not owed to the priest as celebrant; he is merely the messenger offering a petition of the Church." *Quodlibet* 20.30 (Alluntis, 721-722; Alluntis and Wolter, 454).

121. On this see *Quodlibet* 20.3 (Alluntis, 705; Alluntis and Wolter. 443). "It seems probable," Scotus proposes with characteristic caution, "that the Mass has value not only in virtue of the merit, or the action, of the one who says it, but also in virtue of the sacrifice, and of the work itself

The Eucharistic sacrifice is the action of the Church before it is the action of the individual celebrant who acts at her command and in her name, as, in turn, the sacrifice is the action of Christ the eternal high priest before it is the action of the Church, which can offer an acceptable sacrifice only in union with him. As a result, the action of the Church as offerer of the Eucharistic sacrifice always outweighs, though it does not eliminate, the action of the celebrant as an individual, even though he is the most immediate agent of the offering. For this reason a Mass can be of great value before God even when said by "an evil priest," whose personal disposition in making the offering is odious to God.[122] In late medieval theology, to say that the Mass is effective, or bears fruit, *ex opere operato* is not at all to say (as would later be supposed) that the Mass automatically benefits those who attend it, or those for whom it is intended. No one receives the benefit available from the Mass without regard to his own receptivity and dispositions, that is, his faith and love. It is to say, rather, that the Mass cannot fail to bear fruit because it is primarily the offering not simply of those present or of the priest, but of the whole Church, which in her offering cannot fail to be united to Christ her head.

Scotus's innovative analysis has two important results.

First, the benefit (that is, the grace or divine favor) available to those for whom any particular Mass is intended is limited (that is, finite). This is not to say that it is small, or that we have any way of calculating this benefit. But since the good realized by any particular Mass is inherently limited, the greater the number of intentions for which the Mass is offered, the less the benefit available, in principle, for each. Scotus provides a complex analysis of many possible situations in which a priest does, or does not, act justly toward God and neighbor in offering the sacrifice of the Mass. In most cases, he argues, a Mass said for more than one intention does not satisfy the priest's obligation in justice.[123] An individual priest or, say, a monastic community should therefore not accept alms for more intentions than he, or they, can say Masses. Analyzing in this way the great though finite good communicated in any one Mass, Scotus articulates the intuition of the faithful that, other things being equal, having two Masses said for a good intention is better than only having one.

---

that is accomplished (*missa non solum valet virtute meriti, sive operis operantis, sed etiam virtute sacrificii, et operis operati*). Differently put, it has value not only in virtue of the personal merit of the priest who offers it, but also in virtue of the merit of the Church as a whole, in whose person the sacrifice is offered by the ordinary minister (*per ministrum communem*)." Much of *Quodlibet* 20 is devoted to spelling out the implications of this distinction for the value or merit of the Mass as a human act.

122. "[M]issa mali sacerdotis": *Quodlibet* 20.3; cf. also 20.30.

123. "[O]ne Mass said for two [persons or their intentions] does not have as much value for them as it would if it were said for each alone." *Quodlibet* 20.5 (Alluntis, 707; Alluntis and Wolter, 445); cf. 20.52 (Alluntis, 735; Alluntis and Wolter, 462).

Second, the benefit available from the Mass is not only finite; it can vary from one Mass to another by both increase and decrease. Since God cares about the disposition of the offerers of the Mass, the good realized by each Mass can be affected, in the cases Scotus considers, by the personal merit of the priest who offers it, and, more basically, by the holiness of the universal Church at the time it is offered.[124] This too articulates pre-theological intuitions of the faithful: that, all things considered, it is better to ask a visibly holy priest to say Mass for your intention than an indifferent one; and that each individual Christian has a stake in the good of the whole Church, since the state of any individual soul is closely bound up with the state of the whole.

On these matters too Gabriel Biel draws deeply, and often verbatim, on the ideas of his Franciscan predecessor, though he also offers his own elaborations and refinements.[125] To be sure, not all theologians around the turn of the sixteenth century agreed with the ideas about the Eucharistic sacrifice introduced by Scotus and embraced by Biel himself. In his *De celebratione missae* (1510), for example, Cajetan argued that the intrinsic value of each individual Mass is indeed unlimited, on account of the infinite saving value of the passion of Christ represented in it. "The power of the Mass is infinite, because it is the power of Jesus Christ himself."[126] Cajetan dismisses as "the common error of many" the idea that the sacrifice of the Mass has an intrinsically limited merit or makes a finite satisfaction.[127] The effects of the Mass are nonetheless limited,

124. For this reason, Scotus adds, it is probably necessary to think of the "universal Church" in the offering of the Mass as including the intentions and merit of the Church triumphant, the blessed, and not only of the Church militant in this world at any particular time. See *Quodlibet* 20.49 (Alluntis, 733-734; Alluntis and Wolter, 461).

125. Especially in *lectiones* 26 and 27 of the *Canonis missae expositio* (Oberman and Courtenay, I, 240-73). Thus, *inter alia:* "Although in the sacrament of the Eucharist there is the plenitude of all grace and spiritual merit, indeed in it is contained Christ, who is uncreated and infinite grace, nonetheless with respect to the fruit to be conferred" there is a limit (L. 27 K [Oberman and Courtenay, I, 265]). "It is certain that the Mass is not equivalent to the passion and death of Christ when it comes to merit, since in the sacrifice of the Mass Christ does not die again; rather his death (from which comes all merit) is especially remembered in it, according to Lk. 22[:18]: 'Do this in memory of me.' Otherwise just as Christ suffered only once for the redemption of the whole world, so also one Mass would suffice for the redemption of all souls from all purgatorial penalty, and for the calling down of every good [from God]. . . . Therefore according to divine justice the fruit and good corresponding to the merit of the Mass is less than that which corresponds to the passion and death of Christ, and consequently is finite and of a certain determinate grade" (L. 27 L [Oberman and Courtenay, I, 265]).

126. *Opuscula Omnia* (1562), 147b. There is an English translation of q. 2 of this treatise (thought it omits several passages) in Heiko A. Oberman, *Forerunners of the Reformation* (New York: Holt, Reinhart & Winston, 1966), 256-263, here 257.

127. *Opuscula Omnia* (1562), 147b (Oberman, 258).

on account of the dispositions, the limited devotion, of the human agents involved, especially of those who ask for the Mass to be said and those whom it is intended to benefit.[128] Thus Cajetan seeks to uphold in his own way the religious intuition of which Scotus's position made such clear sense, that two Masses are better than one.[129]

Not many years after Cajetan wrote this treatise, he had his interview with Luther in Augsburg, and not long after that, Luther began publicly to deny not simply one idea of Eucharistic sacrifice over against another, but that the Mass is a sacrifice at all. As the Protestant rejection of Eucharistic sacrifice gathered momentum, Cajetan was one of those who rallied forcefully to the defense of the Western Church's long conviction that the Eucharist is a proper sacrifice, nothing less than the very sacrifice of Christ, offered by our own poor hands in obedience to his command: "do this."[130] His disagreement with Scotus and Biel over the intrinsic value of the individual Mass must have come to seem, by comparison, like a minor difference among friends.

TRENT'S RATIFICATION OF EUCHARISTIC SACRIFICE

In his teaching on Christ's Eucharistic presence, Luther retained some elements of traditional belief and practice, while rejecting others. His repudiation of Eucharistic sacrifice was, by contrast, sweeping and comprehensive. In this he was followed by virtually all of sixteenth century Protestantism. "The third captivity of this sacrament is the most wicked abuse by far ... [namely] that the Mass is a good work and a sacrifice. From this abuse has poured forth an infinite number of further abuses."[131]

---

128. "If however this sacrifice is considered as it is applied to this or that person, then its effect is limited according to the quantity of devotion of those who offer it or those for whom it is offered." *Opuscula Omnia* (1562), 147b (Oberman, 258).

129. It cannot be said that Cajetan directly considers the arguments of Scotus and others he holds guilty of "the common error," at least in this treatise or in his brief commentary on *Summa theologiae* III, 79, 5 (the text of Thomas from which he draws the distinction between quantity of offering and quantity of devotion; cf. ed. Leonine, vol. 12, p. 224). As we have seen (nts. 111, 125), Scotus and Biel both grant that what is offered in the Mass, namely Christ himself in his body and blood, is of infinite worth before God. Cajetan evidently thinks this decides the issue, but Scotus and those who follow him argue that it cannot, since the value of an offering has to take into account not only what is offered, but the person of the offerer and the act of offering. Seen in this light, the offering of Christ's body and blood by the sinners he has redeemed cannot have the same (infinite) value as that act has when undertaken immediately by Christ himself.

130. E.g., in *De missae sacrificio et ritu adversus Lutheranos* (1531; above, n. 84) and *De erroribus contingentibus in Eucharistiae sacramento* (1525), in *Opuscula Omnia* (1562), 142-46; Wicks, 153-173.

131. *De captivitate Babylonica ecclesiae*, WA 6: 512. 7-10 (LW 36: 35).

Most of the central concerns of Luther's theology, especially those that were contested with defenders of the traditional religion and its theological teaching, converge in his attitude toward the sacrifice of the Mass. This makes it difficult to offer a succinct statement of what he saw to be at stake in rejecting the Eucharist as sacrifice. At least two claims, however, were consistently basic for him, and for subsequent Protestantism.

(1) For us to offer the Eucharist as a sacrifice acceptable to God, by which we receive grace and the forgiveness of sins, inevitably compromises the uniqueness and saving sufficiency of Christ's own once-for-all sacrifice on the cross. The canon of the Mass clearly offers the Eucharist in just this way, which makes the traditional Eucharistic practice of the Western Church nothing less than a denial of Christ, a proud rejection of the superabundant efficacy of his cross and of the immeasurably generous saving love of the Father in giving up his own Son for our salvation. The Mass is at its heart an act of unbelief and idolatry, a denial of the gospel itself by those who claim to follow Christ. Thus the vehemence of Luther's opposition to it.[132]

(2) To offer the Eucharist to God as a sacrifice for the forgiveness of sins is to treat the sacrament instituted by Christ as a good work, valuable to God in such a way that he will, in view of it, grant us his saving grace. But according to the core teaching of the gospel, as Luther sees it, there can be no such work. We are forgiven, justified, and saved by faith in Christ alone, and not by any kind of work. No human act—more precisely, no human act directed toward God—can be meritorious, that is, pleasing to God in view of our salvation. That the act in question is commanded by God and depends on his grace moving us to undertake it makes no difference. All human acts remain without merit. We must therefore distinguish as stringently as possible between sacrament and sacrifice. The Eucharist, or Lord's Supper, is a sacrament, a pure gift coming down to us from God for our salvation and eliciting our faith in Christ's promise. In response, we can and should offer up a sacrifice of praise and thanksgiving to God. But this sacrifice on our part is no part of the gift itself, that is, of the saving sacrament instituted by Christ. Any sacrifice we offer in no way furthers our salvation or benefits our relationship with God. It simply recognizes benefits already given. Since our sacrifice does not benefit us, even less can it benefit anyone else, living or dead.

132. Luther, we should note, does not deny that on the cross itself a sacrifice takes place, or that our salvation by Christ has a deeply sacrificial character. In the sixteenth century and after Protestant and Catholic alike, guided especially by the Letter to the Hebrews, took it for granted that Christ offered a sacrifice for sins on the cross. Luther objected not to the idea of sacrifice, but to seeing the Mass, and not only the cross, as a sacrifice. The claim that sacrifice itself is an intrinsically odious idea, inapplicable to the saving work of Christ, though now common, is of much more recent vintage.

Luther does not insist on this strict distinction between the Eucharist as a divine gift and as a human act because he is incapable of conceiving human or creaturely cooperation with God. Even in *The Bondage of the Will*, his fiercest defense of what is sometimes called the *Alleinwirksamkeit Gottes* (the sole efficacy of God with respect to created actions and events), Luther has no trouble holding that human beings can and do cooperate with God, as long as we understand that this cooperation itself is an effect of grace or divine action (a standard medieval idea). "[God] does not operate in us without us; rather he has created and preserved us so that he might act in us and we might cooperate with him, whether this happens outside his kingdom by his general omnipotence, or within his kingdom by the singular power of his Spirit."[133] Luther's opposition to Eucharistic sacrifice—to this *particular* location of our cooperation with God—is not metaphysical, but religious. The Eucharistic sacrifice encourages us to trust in our own works and merits, and so denies the "chief article" of Christianity, justification by faith in Christ alone.[134]

These two objections differ, in that Catholic defenses of Eucharistic sacrifice against Protestant objections held that (1) was tendentious, a (perhaps deliberate) misrepresentation of established Catholic teaching, while (2) arose from a basically accurate representation of that teaching. As we have seen, medieval theology consistently maintained that the Mass is not sacrifice additional to the sacrifice of the cross. The relation between the Mass and the cross is a basic theological question, but it is a question with good answers. It is not at all inevitable that the Mass competes with the uniqueness and saving sufficiency of the cross, since the Mass is in no way a supplement or complement to the cross, or a repetition of Christ's once-for-all sacrifice. On the contrary, it is the representation of the sacrifice of the cross, the very presence of that once-for-all sacrifice, and as such the way Christ has willed to apply or impart the saving benefits of that sacrifice to us. The daily iteration of the Eucharistic sacrifice is not, therefore, a constant repetition of the sacrifice of the cross, but the constant presence of that saving sacrifice to us, its generous availability for our salvation.[135]

---

133. WA 18: 754.4–7; LW 33: 243.

134. For a sympathetic account both of early Protestant objections to Eucharistic sacrifice and of the developing Catholic embrace of traditional teaching and practice in the sixteenth century, with much attention to the religious and social context of the debates, see Lee Palmer Wandel, *The Eucharist in the Reformation: Incarnation and Liturgy* (New York: Cambridge University Press, 2006). Carlos Eire locates these debates in an overall account of the religious and theological crises of the time in *Reformations: The Early Modern World 1450-1650* (New Haven: Yale University Press, 2016).

135. As Cajetan succinctly observes, "All the sacraments are nothing other than applications of the passion of Christ to those who receive them. It would be one thing to repeat the passion of Christ; it is quite another to repeat the commemoration and application of the passion of Christ

That the Mass is a good work, meritorious and pleasing in the sight of God, was, by contrast, recognized early on by both sides as a truly basic disagreement, and not only a misunderstanding. For Catholics the Mass was not simply a good work, but the best possible work, the one most pleasing to God. They saw in the Eucharistic sacrifice, commanded by Christ and offered by his Church in loving obedience to his command, the greatest gift of God to us in our present life, his supremely generous way of uniting us to the saving passion of his Son. In the Protestant rejection of Eucharistic sacrifice, Catholics perceived an incomprehensible ingratitude, a disdain for the saving love of God. On the eve of Protestantism, Biel had already put clearly what Catholics would soon see to be at stake in the conflict over Eucharistic sacrifice.

> If any work in the Church is meritorious, whether of glory, grace, or the for-giveness of sin and punishment, none can be more meritorious than this sac-rifice. For in it there comes to pass the memory and invocation of that unique and most perfect sacrifice, by whose power heaven is opened and grace is given, through which alone our works can be meritorious, the sins of all men are forgiven, and the heavenly glory lost by our sin is restored. For the one who is offered to the Father in this sacrifice is the key of David, who closes and no one opens. . . . He is the fount of all graces and the head of the Church, from whom alone grace flows. . . . Apart from union with him—which this sacrifice brings about—no one attains heavenly glory.[136]

Protestant historiography long held, and sometimes still does, that Luther's repudiation of Eucharistic sacrifice was the natural Christian response to the way the Mass was practiced and understood in the late Middle Ages. From the 1940s Catholic scholarship on Luther and the origins of Protestantism, espe-cially in Germany, began to share this view, at least in part. In this telling, late medieval Eucharistic practice was rife with abuses, and the theology of the Mass correspondingly flawed, inadequate, and "not fully Catholic." In the late Middle Ages, so the story goes, the Mass was widely seen as a crude barter arrangement, where we give God something he values (his Son), and he gives us what we want, as expressed in our Mass intentions. Here too, as on Eucha-ristic presence, a narrative emerged in the mid-twentieth century that had clear ecumenical appeal. When it comes to sacrifice, Protestants and Catholics may differ in their assessment of Luther's dramatic reforms in Eucharistic practice

---

(*aliud autem est iterare passionem Christi, & aliud iterare commemorationem & applicationem passionis Christi*)." Commentary on Heb. 10:18, *Thomae de Vio Caietani Commentarii*, vol. 5 (Lyon: Prost, 1639), 351a.

   136. *Canonis missae expositio*, L. 57 D (Oberman and Courtenay, II, 395–396). "Brings about": *quam hoc sacrificium prestat* (396).

and theology, but they can agree that he was responding with good intentions to serious abuses.[137]

This narrative makes, often without clearly distinguishing them, two different claims: (1) that there were, precisely by later Catholic (and *a fortiori* Protestant) standards, abuses in the late medieval practice of the Mass; (2) that Luther's rejection of the Mass as sacrifice was the result of these abuses. These require separate discussion.

(1) We know that there were abuses of the Mass in late medieval piety and practice—and we know this primarily because late medieval preachers and theologians sharply criticized them. The attitudes on the part of the laity that worried these preachers (Jean Gerson and Nicholas of Cusa, to name two of the better known) were principally two: (a) relying on the Mass chiefly for temporal rather than spiritual goods, and (b) supposing that the Mass confers its benefits irrespective of the dispositions and receptivity of those who offer it and those for whom it is intended. With respect to the clergy, the chief concern of medieval reformers was (c) that the clergy treated the Mass as a source of financial gain, whether for themselves or for their parish, community, or religious foundation.

The root of these problems was seen to lie not in the Mass itself, but in misunderstanding, or ignorance, of its true saving nature, and of the way its great benefits reach us. (a) Against the first, preachers and theologians insisted that the benefits or fruits of the Mass are primarily, indeed overwhelmingly, not temporal but spiritual: grace, salvation, and eternal life for ourselves and those for whom we pray. These dwarf any temporal benefits we may rightly seek through the Mass (healing from an illness, for example). In the Mass, we may rightly seek, moreover, only what temporal goods we may rightly seek through prayer in the first place (another's healing, not injury to another). To seek through the Mass what is not a genuine good is not to procure a desired benefit, but to sin gravely.[138] (b) The second claim, late medieval preachers and theologians insisted, was simply false. Receiving the fruits of the Mass depends on lively and believing participation in it, on the devout intentions of the clergy and laity who share in the offering of it. As we have already observed, Scotus, Biel, and Cajetan all agree on this basic point. The Mass is, indeed, effective *ex opere operato*. That is: the very

---

137. For a succinct presentation of this outlook from one of its originators, see Erwin Iserloh's treatment of "Martin Luther and the Coming of the Reformation," in Hubert Jedin, ed., *History of the Church*, vol. 5: *Reformation and Counter Reformation* (London: Burns & Oates, 1980 [German original: 1967]), 3–112, e.g., 9–11.

138. Thus, *inter alia*, Altenstaig, *Vocabularius*, s.v. "De valore missae," recalling Gerson: "It is superstitious, frivolous, rash and empty, indeed harmful, to assert that by hearing a Mass someone will obtain this or that temporal good." In fact, Altenstaig adds, to look for such goods from the Mass is "detrimental to one's salvation"; certainly "the Mass is not to be heard for temporal goods alone" (fol. 152va).

action in which it consists, the work performed, unfailingly makes grace available to those who participate in the Mass and those for whose benefit it is intended. But it does no good, despite what some evidently thought, simply to show up for Mass. Whether we benefit from the fathomless good reliably offered in the Mass depends also on us, not simply on the fact that the Eucharistic sacrifice takes place.

(c) That the late Middle Ages saw the growth of a "Mass industry," in which it came to be more or less accepted that the spiritual good offered in the Mass was for sale at the price demanded by the clergy, Catholic as well as Protestant theologians have regularly seen as an important motive for the beginnings of Protestantism and the rejection of the Mass. Luther and other early Protestant preachers and theologians surely said as much.

The idea that any spiritual good could be offered or obtained for money was, however, uniformly rejected in medieval theology and canon law. It was the crime of simony, which, as the biblical account of the first attempt at it makes clear, can never succeed. God simply does not give his gifts in this way. As Peter says to Simon the magician, "Your silver perish with you, because you thought you could obtain the gift of God with money" (Acts 8:20). Thus Scotus begins his detailed treatment of a priest's obligations to those who ask for Masses to be said by observing that there can be no "exchange of a spiritual good, such as prayer, for the giving of a temporal good, such as alms. That would plainly be simony."[139]

We are, of course, not only permitted but commanded to give alms, and to pray for one another. It is therefore not only legitimate but good for a lay person to give alms to a priest, and to ask the priest to pray for her, above all by saying (that is, praying) the Mass for her intentions. In turn the priest, like any Christian, is bound to heed the request of those who ask him to pray for them and for their intentions. Scotus interprets the situation: "The alms are freely offered, together with an entreaty for prayer, and the one receiving the alms is held as a matter of justice to hear the one entreating his prayer. As a result he obligates himself as a matter of justice to pray for his benefactor, but freely, that is, without any bargain and exchange (*sine conventione et commutatione*)."[140]

One might, of course, dismiss such arguments as mere rationalization of simoniacal abuse. There is no reason, though, to think medieval Christians were insincere in their rejection of simony, or in their efforts to be clear about when it does and does not take place. Both had well-known biblical precedent, and to genuine simony the medieval Church attached stiff canonical penalties.

139. *Quodlibet* 20.50 (Alltunis, 734; Alltunis and Wolter, 461).
140. Ibid.

Abuses and misunderstandings connected with the sacrifice of the Mass, whether on the part of laity or clergy, were thus a familiar concern well before Luther, as were their proper remedies.[141]

(2) Luther frequently rails against abuses pertaining to the Mass, but there was nothing novel or radical in such criticisms. He makes it clear, in fact, that he does not object to the Mass because of the abuses. He objects to the Mass as such. He thinks the Mass itself—the very idea that the Mass is "a good work and a sacrifice"—is the most basic and consequential of all abuses, "the most wicked abuse by far."[142] Everything else he criticizes in connection with the Mass is, as he sees it, simply a byproduct of what is most detestable, the Eucharistic sacrifice itself. Luther's rejection of the Eucharist as sacrifice did not, as the standard narrative supposes, result from his dismay over abuses that others had noted before him. On his own account, the Mass itself was, in the end, the reason why he objected to the abuses.

Unlike medieval critics of the same attitudes, Luther does not want to draw on a proper understanding of the sacrifice of the Mass in order to instruct the faithful and eliminate abuses. He wants to eliminate the Mass as such, by excising from the traditional Western liturgy anything which could be taken to suggest that the Mass, rightly celebrated and intended by clergy and laity, is "a good work and a sacrifice." This he and many others did, and among the most widely shared features of traditional Protestant liturgy and theology is the exclusion of any suggestion that the Eucharist is a sacrifice or offering to God.[143]

141. For a brief account of the abuses identified by late medieval theologians and the countermeasures they proposed, see Auguste Gaudel, "Le sacrifice de la Messe dans l'Église latine du IVe siècle jusqu'à la veille de la Réforme," *Dictionnaire de théologie catholique* 10/1 (1928), 964–1085; here 1077–84. Francis Clark covers the same ground more thoroughly in *Eucharistic Sacrifice and the Reformation* (London: Darton, Longman & Todd, 1960), including a discussion of virtually all the modern literature on the subject up to the time his book appeared. Since then, historians have mostly abandoned the traditional confessional coloring of work on the period and, for the most part, talk of "abuses" has disappeared. It remains current chiefly among theologians who, whether for ecumenical or other reasons, are committed to seeing the late Middle Ages as "not fully Catholic." On this score, a remark of the Lutheran historian of theology Berndt Hamm over forty years ago is worth bearing in mind: "For all their usefulness in matters of detail, the works of Lortz and Iserloh are nonetheless burdened by the historically unwarranted judgment of the morbid condition of late medieval theology." "Frömmigkeit als Gegenstand theologiegeschichtlicher Forschung: Methodisch-historische Überlegungen am Beispiel von Spätmittelalter und Reformation," *Zeitschrift für Theologie und Kirche,* 74 (1977), 464–497, here. 478, n. 34 (reprinted in idem, *Religiosität im späten Mittelalter* [Tübingen: Mohr Siebeck, 2011], 85–115, here 98).

142. Above, n. 131.

143. As with most theological matters, Luther had an interesting variety of things to say about the sacrifice of the Mass over the course of his long public career and his vast literary output, though, once in place, his rejection of Eucharistic sacrifice and the reasons for it remained basic to his reforming program. For a full account, sympathetic to Luther, see Wolfgang Simon,

In light of this, we need to observe that when it comes to the sacrifice of the Mass, as much as when it comes to Christ's Eucharistic presence, the Council of Trent embraces as normative Catholic doctrine the basic commitments that animate the teaching, not only of Peter Lombard and Thomas Aquinas, but of John Duns Scotus and Gabriel Biel.[144] Here as elsewhere, to be sure, Trent refuses to resolve school differences among Catholic theologians, such as the disagreement between Scotus and Cajetan over whether the value of a single Mass is intrinsically infinite. But in a series of deliberately worded statements, the Council affirms all of the claims common to late medieval theology of the Eucharistic sacrifice, its application, and its fruits, including those drawn out and underlined by Scotus and the tradition that followed him. Among these are at least the following.

(1) The Eucharistic sacrifice is primarily Christ's own act, not only in its institution but also in its daily offering. At the Last Supper, Christ "instituted a new Passover, namely that he himself was to be sacrificed by the Church (*se ipsum ab Ecclesia . . . immolandum*) through priests under visible signs" (DH 1741). "The same [Christ] now offers himself by the ministry of priests, who offered himself then on the cross" (DH 1743).[145]

(2) The sacrifice of the Mass, however, is not Christ's act alone (as at the Last Supper), but also the Church's act at the hands of Christ's ministers (see no. 1). It is a human act, the act of those in need of mercy and forgiveness, who by this act "draw near [to God] that we may obtain mercy and find grace to help in time of need [Heb. 4:16]" (DH 1743). Precisely as a human act it is a participation in Christ's priesthood, "which was not to be extinguished by death" (DH 1741).

(3) In the Eucharist, the Church offers Christ to the Father: "In the divine sacrifice which is carried out in the Mass, the very same Christ is contained and offered (*immolatur*) in a bloodless manner who on the altar of the cross 'offered himself in blood once for all' [cf. Heb. 9:14, 27-8]" (DH 1743).

(4) The victim offered in this sacrifice, since it is Christ himself, crucified, really present on the altar by substantial conversion (cf. no. 3), is one and the same as the victim of Calvary, no matter how many times the Mass is celebrated

---

Die Messopfertheologie Martin Luthers: Voraussetzungen, Genese, Gestalt und Rezeption (Tübingen: Mohr Siebeck, 2003).

144. Although his presentation of late medieval theology is not always exact, Clark is right, against the drift of German Catholic scholarship at the time, to see Trent's doctrine on the sacrifice of the Mass as essentially continuous with late medieval teaching. Cf. *Eucharistic Sacrifice and the Reformation*, 79-98.

145. The quotations are all from Trent's decree on the sacrifice of the Mass, ratified at session XXII of the Council (Sept. 17, 1562). Most are from chapters 1 and 2 of the decree.

or offered. A difference in the manner of offering does not make for a difference in the sacrifice offered. "It is one and the same victim . . . only the manner of offering differs" (DH 1743).

(5) The Eucharist is not only a sacrifice of praise and thanksgiving (though it is that), but a truly propitiatory sacrifice, an efficacious offering for the forgiveness of sins. It is this because it is the once-for-all sacrifice of the cross (cf. no. 4) offered by us, in Christ our high priest, to the Father (cf. no. 2). "The Lord, having been pleased with this offering (*Huius quippe oblatione placatus Dominus*) and granting grace and the gift of penitence, forgives even enormous crimes and sins" (DH 1743; cf. 1753).

(6) Our offering in the Mass does not repeat the sacrifice of the upper room and the cross, but represents it, that is, makes it present each day, so as to be remembered always. "At the Last Supper" Christ instituted the Eucharist "in order that he might leave to his beloved bride the Church a visible sacrifice (such as human nature requires), by which that sacrifice to be accomplished once for all on the cross might be represented, and its memory abide, until the end of the world" (DH 1741). Therefore the Mass in no way detracts from or competes with the sacrifice of the cross (1743; 1754).

(7) The sacrifice of the Mass is the chief way the sacrifice of the cross reaches the faithful and touches their lives. By the Eucharistic offering, the fruits or benefits of Christ's once-for-all sacrifice are "applied" to us by God. Christ instituted this sacrifice in order that "the saving power [of the cross] might be applied for the remission of the sins we daily commit" (DH 1741), so that "the fruits of [Christ's] oblation in blood are most richly received through this unbloody oblation" (DH 1743).

(8) The Mass therefore can and should be offered for the benefit of all the faithful, living and dead, according to the intentions of the Church. "Following the tradition of the apostles" the Mass "is rightly offered not only for the sins, penalties, satisfactions and other needs of the faithful still living, but also for the dead in Christ who have not yet been fully purified" (DH 1743; cf. 1753).

(9) No Mass is "private," since all Masses "are celebrated by a public minister of the Church not for himself alone, but for all the faithful who belong to the Body of Christ" (DH 1747; cf. 1758).

(10) The intentions, devotions, and dispositions of all those who offer the Mass affect the value the Mass has before God, and thus the fruit or benefit that flows from it. "Through this sacrifice it comes about that we 'obtain mercy and find grace to help in time of need' [Heb. 4:16]" (cf. no. 2), "if we draw near to God with a true heart and right faith, with fear and reverence, contrite and penitent" (DH 1743). The fruits of the Mass, the grace and forgiveness God gives in it, are inseparable from, though not reducible to, the quality of our offering, of the human act we undertake at Christ's command (see nos. 1–

2), though Trent does not try to settle the question as to how this value or merit is reckoned.[146]

Eucharistic sacrifice was probably the most divisive of all the matters controverted among Western Christians in the sixteenth century. It was the public point at which virtually all other disputed questions came into unmistakable focus. As Christians on all sides saw at the time, what one believed about justification, merit, good works, the ministerial priesthood, the authority of the Church, and much else could quite reliably be gauged by whether one celebrated, or abominated, the Mass.

In its necessary effort to restore the unity of Christians, ecumenism since Vatican II has often sought to make progress on this historically divisive issue by seeing late medieval understandings of Eucharistic sacrifice, to which Luther so vehemently objected, as the dispensable product of a debased religious and theological culture. These misguided practices and beliefs, so the argument goes, cannot be what binding Catholic doctrine on the Eucharist really requires. Catholic theologians and ecumenists have embraced this assumption with, if anything, even more surety and conviction than Protestant.

Historical and doctrinal candor challenges us to reject this widely held assumption, and to see the matter differently. Trent's decree on the sacrifice of the Mass remains by far the most developed and specific dogmatic teaching in the Catholic tradition on this matter. Virtually all subsequent teaching on the Mass as sacrifice, including that of Vatican II, has relied on its content and taken for granted its authority.[147] While Trent clearly did not intend to resolve all

---

146. Trent's decree does not use the terms "merit" or "good work" to characterize the sacrifice of the Mass, though late medieval theology had no difficulty applying these terms. Instead, it speaks of the Mass as pleasing to God and its offering as our human act. The theological implications, if any, of this noteworthy lexical fact would be worth a separate study. Such a study would attend, *inter alia*, to Trent's vigorous endorsement of the canon (DH 1745), which continually pleads that our sacrifice, our act, be acceptable to God, that is, have value in his sight.

147. See *Sacrosanctum Concilium*, 7: "Christ is always present in his Church . . . in the Sacrifice of the Mass, not only in the person of the minister, 'the same now offering by the ministry of priests who offered himself then on the cross,' but especially under the Eucharistic species." *Acta Apostolicae Sedis*, 56 (1964), 100–101, citing Trent's decree on the sacrifice of the Mass, ch. 2 (DH 1743). Cf. *SC*, 2: "[A]bove all in the divine sacrifice of the Eucharist, 'the work of our redemption is carried out'" (97), and *SC*, 47 (113), which paraphrases ch. 1 of Trent's decree on Christ's institution of the Eucharistic sacrifice at the Last Supper (DH 1741), "so that he might perpetuate the sacrifice of the cross throughout the ages, until he comes." Also *Lumen Gentium*, 11: "Sharing in the Eucharistic sacrifice, the source and summit of the whole Christian life, [the faithful] offer the divine victim to God and themselves with him" (AAS 57 [1965], 15). See further John Paul II, *Ecclesia de Eucharistia*, especially §12: "The Mass makes present the sacrifice of the cross; it does not add to that sacrifice nor does it multiply it," citing ch. 2 of Trent's decree (DH 1743). AAS 95 (2003), 441.

questions disputed among Catholic theologians regarding the precise nature and efficacy of the Eucharistic sacrifice, it was a ringing defense of traditional practice and belief regarding the Mass, not least that of the late Middle Ages. If genuine ecumenical progress cannot be based on a shared rejection of one party's normative doctrine, a way forward on this deeply contested matter will have to reckon with the Council of Trent's ratification of late medieval theology on the Eucharist as sacrifice.

7. Martin Luther and the Medieval Mass

LEE PALMER WANDEL

Martin Luther celebrated his first Mass on May 2, 1507, in the chapel of the cloister of the Order of Augustinian Hermits in Erfurt, the order he had joined two years earlier. His role was new, but the place was not: the rhythms of his religious life would have taken him to that chapel every day of the week—for prayer, for the Divine Office, for the Mass. He had been ordained earlier that spring, perhaps on Easter. That first Mass was important to him then: he invited friends to attend it. It was important to his family: his father rode into Erfurt and bestowed on the monastery 20 gulden. At the end of his life, in his last lectures on Genesis, he returned to it.[1]

Like so many men in the sixteenth century who wrote against the medieval Mass and formulated new liturgies for their communities, Luther was an ordained priest. He knew the Mass as most Christians to this day could not— as *sacerdos*. There are traces of that particular intimacy in Luther's writings on it, both his criticisms and his liturgical formulae, in his preservation of the Canon's narrative of the Last Supper, instead of a direct transcription from one of the synoptic Gospels or Paul's First Letter to the Corinthians,[2] in his preservation of cadences of the medieval liturgy: prayers, readings, chant.

Of all the Evangelicals—those who held medieval Christianity to the test of the written Word of God—Luther clove most closely to the medieval Mass. In his German Mass, he retained more of parts of the medieval Mass than did the Anabaptists, Martin Bucer, Huldyrch Zwingli, or John Calvin: the Kyrie, collect, the Epistle chanted, the Gospel chanted, the Credo, the sermon, the Lord's Prayer, the consecration and the Gospel narrative at the center of the canon, retaining the elevation even as Luther was redefining its significance, the Sanctus, the Agnus Dei.[3] He retained much that was ancient but not apostolic.

---

1. Heiko A. Oberman, *Luther: Man between God and the Devil*, trans. Eileen Walliser-Schwarzbart (New Haven: Yale University Press, 1989), pp. 137, 100, 86.

2. Martin Luther, *The Babylonian Captivity of the Church 1520*, trans. Erik H. Hermann, The Annotated Luther Study Edition, ed. Paul W. Robinson (Minneapolis: Fortress Press, 2016). Henceforth: *BC*.

3. On the history of what he calls "the details of the mass," see Josef Andreas Jungmann, *Missarum Solemnia: Eine genetische Erklärung der Römischen Messe* (Bonn: Reprographischer Nachdr. d. Ausg. Freiburg, 1962, 2003) 2 vols. On the cadences of the mass, see Karl Young, *The Drama of the Medieval Church*, vol. I (Oxford: Clarendon Press, 1933). See also, Osborne B. Hardison, Jr., "The

And yet, Martin Luther was as radical as any Anabaptist, or Bucer, or Zwingli, or Calvin in his reconceptualization of worship—what the Mass is, what it does, and what belongs to it.

Kenneth Hagen identified some of the earliest traces of that reconceptualization in Luther's 1517-18 lectures on Hebrews.[4] Luther broke with medieval commentary along two lines in his exegesis of 9:17, "For a testament takes effect only at death, since it is not in force as long as the one who made it is alive."[5] First, he explicated what was to be received in the testament: "It should be known, therefore, that an invaluable inheritance was willed and bequeathed in his most faithful testament—the forgiveness of sins and eternal life." Second, Luther located the content of Christ's testament in the words of institution at the Last Supper: "The Gospel accounts all agree that at the Last Supper when Christ had taken the cup and blessed it he said: 'This is the new testament in my blood.'"[6] Medieval exegetes had not treated the Last Supper in relation to

---

Mass as Sacred Drama," in his: *Christian Rite and Christian Drama in the Middle Ages: Essays in the Origin and Early History of Modern Drama* (Baltimore: Johns Hopkins University Press, 1965), 35–79. Jungmann divided the Mass into two, the Fore-Mass and the Mass for the Catechumens, and then, under those, discrete "ceremonies":

1. The Opening of Entrance Rite
   Præparatio ad Missam
   Putting on the Liturgical Vestments
   Prayers at the Foot of the Altar
   Confiteor
   Greetings, Kissing the Altar
   Incensing the Altar
   The Introit Chant
   Kyrie Eleison
   Gloria in excelsis
   The Collect

2. The Service of Readings
   The Epistle
   The Intervenient Chants
   The Gospel
   The Homily
   The Credo
   The Dismissals

To this day, scholars dispute just how much and how violently Luther changed the content of those parts. See Bryan Spinks's summary of that scholarship, *Luther's Liturgical Criteria and his Reform of The Canon of the Mass* (Bramcote Notts: Grove Books, 1982).

4. Kenneth Hagen, *A Theology of Testament in the Young Luther on the Lectures on Hebrews* (Leiden: Brill, 1974), 110-115.

5. Bryan Spinks called attention to these two points in *Luther's Liturgical Criteria*, 28.

6. These are Hagen's translations, 110, from *WA* 57/3: 212.

this text; they had taken it up in relation to a later one, 10: 1–3, on sacrifice.[7] Medieval exegetes had not linked testament and Eucharist—Luther did. The testament willed the inheritance of forgiveness of sins and eternal life; the testament was to be found in the Last Supper.

In part on the basis of this exegesis, Bryan Spinks has argued "that justification is the key to Luther's reform of the canon."[8] While I think that justification by faith alone, sola fide, is *one* foundational principle for Luther's reconceptualization of the Mass, I do not think it is the only one, or the key. Within those first years, Luther moved not only to what has long been recognized as his "breakthrough"—his soteriology—but to a sense of the Incarnation as verbal, which had utterly transformative consequences for liturgy.

In 1520, Luther published a series of pamphlets laying out his criticism of the Mass.[9] The most famous of those was *On the Babylonian Captivity of the Church*, in which he laid out three "captivities":

1) "The first captivity of this sacrament, therefore, concerns the substance or completeness, which the tyranny of Rome has wrested from us"—that is, the practice of offering only the host, not the chalice.[10]

2) The second was transubstantiation:"it is an absurd and unheard-of juggling with words to understand 'bread' to mean 'the form or accidents of bread,' and 'wine' to mean 'the form or accidents of wine.'"[11]

3) "The third captivity of this sacrament is by far the most wicked abuse of all, in consequence of which there is no opinion more generally held or more firmly believed in the church today than this, that the Mass is a good work and a sacrifice."[12]

7. Hagen, *A Theology of Testament*, 111.

8. Spinks, *Luther's Liturgical Criteria*, 25.

9. On Luther and the medieval Mass, see Hans Bernhard Meyer, SJ, *Luther und die Messe: Eine liturgiewissenschaftliche Untersuchung über das Verhältnis Luthers zum Meßwesen des späten Mittelalters* (Paderborn: Bonifacius Drucke, 1965); Reinhard Meßner, *Die Meßreform Martin Luthers und die Eucharistie der Alten Kirche* (Innsbruck and Vienna:Tyrolia Verlag, 1989);Wandel, *The Eucharist in the Reformation: Incarnation and Liturgy*, Ch. 3;Volker Leppin, "Martin Luther," in: *The Eucharist in the Reformation*, ed. Lee Palmer Wandel (Leiden: Brill, 2014), 39–56.

10. *BC*, 29. "Prima ergo captivitatis huius sacramenti est quo ad eius substantiam seu integritatem, quam nobis abstulit Romana tyrannis," *WA* 6: 507, 6–9.

11. *BC*, 33. "Absurda est ergo et nova verborum impositio, panem pro specie vel accidentibus panis, winum pro specie vel accentibus vini accipi," *WA* 6: 509: 22–23.

12. *BC*, 38. "Tertia captivitas eiusdem sacramenti Est longe impiissimus ille abusus, quo factum est, ut fere nihil sit hodie in Ecclesia receptius ac magis persuasum, quam Missam esse opus bonum et sacrificium," *WA* 6: 512, 7–9. On Luther and the sacrifice of the Mass, see Carl Fr.Wislöff, *Abendmahl und Messe: Die Kritik Luthers am Meßopfer* [Arbeiten zur Geschichte und Theologie des Luthertums, 22] (Berlin and Hamburg: Luther.Verl. Haus, 1969); Robert C. Croken, SJ, *Luther's First Front: The Eucharist as Sacrifice* (Ottawa: University of Ottawa Press, 1990).

Those three challenges provoked lengthy responses. Johannes Eck, for example, addressed directly and at length Luther's critique of the sacrifice of the Mass.[13] The Council of Trent took up each one in turn, setting, for the first time, a formal doctrine on the sacrifice of the Mass.[14] The critiques of the *Babylonian Captivity* and sixteenth-century responses to them have shaped scholarship on Luther's eucharistic theology ever since.[15] And yet, only the second "captivity," transubstantiation, had been formally decreed, and only in 1215, at the Fourth Lateran Council:

> There is indeed one universal church of the faithful, outside of which nobody at all is saved, in which Jesus Christ is both priest and sacrifice. His body and blood are truly contained in the sacrament of the altar under the forms of bread and wine, the bread and wine having been changed in substance, by God's power, into his body and blood, so that in order to achieve this mystery of unity we receive from God what he received from us.[16]

I quote the text in its fullness here to suggest one fundamental shift in thinking about the Mass, which Luther effected in the very way he formulated his criticisms of it. Late medieval theologians had continued to grapple with the mystery of Christ's presence in the Mass, articulating subtle and subtly differentiated positions.[17] There was not one formal, exhaustive statement, on either the nature of Christ's presence in the elements—Communion in one kind or transubstantiation—or the nature of the sacrifice in the Mass.[18] Quite the contrary, the mystery of Incarnation was protean in late medieval Christianity. In these early pamphlets, Luther did not simply criticize what we have come to call the medieval Mass; he accorded to Rome a uniformity of doctrine and practice that did

13. See, for example, Johannes Eck, *De sacrificio missae libri tres (1526)*, ed. Erwin Iserloh, Vinzenz Pfnür, and Peter Fabisch [Corpus Catholicorum, 36] (Münster: Aschendorff, 1982).

14. In Session 22, 17 September 1562, the Council of Trent set forth "Doctrina et canones de sanctissimo missae sacrificio," Norman P. Tanner, ed., *Decrees of the Ecumenical Councils*, 2 vols. (London: Sheed & Ward, 1990), I: 732-41. See also Robert J. Daly, "The Council of Trent," in: *The Eucharist in the Reformation*, 159-182.

15. Cf. Leppin, "Martin Luther."

16. "Una vero est fidelium universalis ecclesia, extra quam nullus omnino salvatur, in qua idem ipse sacerdos et sacrificium Iesus Christus, cuius corpus et sanguis in sacramento altaris sub speciebus panis et vini veraciter continentur, transsubstantiatis pane in corpus et vino in sanguinem potestate divina, ut ad perficiendum mysterium unitatis accipiamus ipsi de suo, quod accepit ipse de nostro." Tanner, ed., *Decrees of the Ecumenical Councils*, I: 230.

17. Bruce Marshall, "Late Medieval Eucharistic Theology and Practice," in this volume; Edward J. Kilmartin, SJ, *The Eucharist in the West: History and Theology*, ed. Robert J. Daly, SJ (1998; repr. Collegeville, MN: Liturgical Press, 2004); *A Companion to the Eucharist in the Middle Ages*, ed. Ian Christopher Levy, Gary Macy and Kristen van Ausdall (Leiden: Brill, 2012).

18. See, for example, *Gabrielis Biel Canonis misse expositio*, 5 vols. ed. Heiko A. Oberman and William J. Courtenay (Wiesbaden: Steiner, 1963-76).

not exist, and to the Mass a singularity at odds with practice over Europe and with the textual tradition, as perhaps best captured in William Durand's enormously popular *Rationale divinorum officiorum*.[19]

There was not one medieval Mass—quite setting aside just how widespread the Roman Rite was prior to the sixteenth century.[20] It is not simply that the Mass varied according to temporal and sanctoral cycles, or in each place according to local saints, or even according to the memory of the officiating priest, who may or may not have had a missal, may or may not have read that missal.[21] The Mass was not a single ritual, but complexly and intricately woven into the living of Christianity, always experienced within the rhythms of that life and its layers of meaning. Durand offers us a glimpse of that complex interplay of history, holy persons, and the life of Christ:

> 31. On Saturday it is the Mass of the Blessed Virgin, which has as its origin a custom from long ago, when in a certain church in the city of Constantinople, there was an image of the Blessed Virgin that had a veil hanging over it that covered the entire image; after Vespers on Friday, with no one moving it, save for a miracle from God, the veil lifted itself from the image, as if it were being drawn toward the heavens, so that the full image could be seen by the people who were standing in front of it. After Vespers had been celebrated on Saturday, the veil descended over the same icon or image, and there it remained until the next Friday. It is on account of the sight of this miracle that it was decreed that the Mass of the Blessed Virgin Mary always be sung on that day.
>
> 32. Another reason for this practice is that when the Lord was crucified and died, and His fleeing disciples despaired of the Resurrection, Mary was the only one who kept her faith intact through all that Saturday. . . .
>
> 33. The third reason is that Saturday is the door and entryway into the Lord's Day. . . .
>
> 34. Fourth, that the solemnity of the Mother will be continued into the solemnity of the Son.
>
> 35. Fifth, so that this feast will be done on the day in which God rested from all work.[22]

There was not one ritual, not one script. The Mass was sung or chanted in many voices or one. It was done in specific places—each cathedral or basilica or church

---

19. On doctrine see, foremost, Jaroslav Pelikan, *The Christian Tradition* (Chicago: University of Chicago Press, 1975-91).

20. Eric Palazzo, *A History of Liturgical Books: From the Beginning to the Thirteenth Century*, trans. Madeleine Beaumont (Collegeville, MN: Liturgical Press, 1998).

21. Andrew Hughes, *Medieval Manuscripts for Mass and Office: A Guide to Their Organization and Terminology* (1982; repr. Toronto: University of Toronto Press, 1995).

22. William Durand, *Rationale IV: On the Mass and Each Action Pertaining to it*, Introduction, trans. and notes, Timothy M. Thibodeau (Turnhout: Brepols, 2013), 65-66.

or chapel with its own unique miraculous images or relics, its own history, its own donors and textures of social and political life. A Mass celebrated in the Sistine Chapel was not the same as a Mass celebrated in the Basilica di Santa Maria in Trastavere, let alone a Mass celebrated in the Cathédrale Saint-Jean-Baptiste in Lyon or a village church in Thur valley in the canton of Sankt Gallen. Each Mass was also celebrated in a specific moment within the Christian liturgical year. Each Mass occurred simultaneously within Christianity's complex history of mediation and layer upon layer of meaning both local and shared.

In another 1520 pamphlet, published in German, the *Sermon on the New Testament, that is the Holy Mass,* Luther set out even more explicitly his sense of the Mass as a verbal event:

> 3. Christ, in order to prepare for himself an acceptable and beloved people, which should be bound together in unity through love, abolished the whole law of Moses. And that he might not give further occasion for divisions and sects, he appointed in return but one law or order for his entire people, and that was the holy mass. . . . Henceforth, therefore, there is to be no other external order for the service of God except the mass. And where the mass is used, there is true worship; even though there be no other form, with singing, organ playing, bell ringing, vestments, ornaments, and gestures. For everything of this sort is an addition invented by men. When Christ himself first instituted this sacrament and held the first mass, there was no tonsure, no chasuble, no singing, no pageantry, but only thanksgiving to God and the use of the sacrament.[23]

In his rendering of the moment, in a sermon widely reproduced and disseminated, Luther did not offer, as many had done and would do, a sense of Christ speaking, among his disciples, at a shared meal. In Luther's rendering, Christ appointed "one law or order for his entire people."[24]

23. Martin Luther, "A Treatise on the New Testament, that is the Holy Mass, 1520," trans. Jeremiah J. Schindel, revised E. Theodore Bachmann, *LW* 35: 80–81. "Czum dritten. Auff das nu Christus yhm bereyttet eyn angenehm liebes volck, das eintrechtiglich yn ein ander gepunden were durch die liebe, hat er auff gehaben das gantz gesetz Mosi, und das er nit ursache den secten und zurteylungen hynfuerter gebe, hatt er widderumb nit mehr den eyne weyß odder gesetz eyngesetzt seynem gantzen volck, das ist die heylige Meß (Dan wie wol die tauff auch ein eußerliche weyße ist, ßo geschicht sie doch nur ein mall, und ist nit ein uebung des gantzen lebens, wie die meß), das nu hinfuertter keyn ander eußerliche weyß solt sein, gott zu dienen, den die meß, und wo die geuebt wirt, da ist der recht gottes dienst, ob schon kein andere weyß mit singen orgellen, klingen, kleyden, tzierden, geperden da ist, den alliß, was des ist, ist ein zusatz von menschen erdacht. Dan do Christus selbst und am ersten diß sacrament insetzt unnd die ersten meß hielt und uebet, da war keyn platten, kein casell, keyn prangen, ßondern allein dancksagung gottis und des sacraments brauch," *WA* 6: 354, 18–31.

24. "hatt er widderumb nit mehr den eyne weyß odder gesetz eyngesetzt seynem gantzen volck / das ist die heylige Meß." Martin Luther, *Eyn Sermon von dem // newen Testament. das // ist von der heyligē // Messe Doct. // Mar. L. // Aug.* (Wittenberg: Grunenberg, 1520), sig. Aiiᵛ.

That formulation captured two aspects of Luther's reconceptualization. The Mass was and is one. As Luther would write, again and again, there is one Mass, neither Masses for the dead nor Masses for saints nor Masses for the Virgin nor Masses divided between daily and high feast. There is no other order for the service of God than that which is set forth in the text of Scripture. In that sense of the singularity of the Mass, Luther severed the Mass from the Divine Office; he severed the act of collective worship from Masses for the dead, the Virgin, or a local saint; and in so doing, he severed worship among the living from the dead, the holy, and Mary. The Mass had taken place in cloisters such as that of the Augustinian hermits in Erfurt, where the Divine Office marked the hours of the monastic life; in cathedrals where choirs chanted parts of it, even as they, too, observed the Divine Office; in parish churches dedicated to a local saint and patronized by local lords who, in turn, were remembered in the cadences of the liturgy. It had been situated in places, sites, of multiple forms of worship, and enacted by persons who participated in it and in those other forms of worship—in place and in person the Mass had not been a thing apart, as it would become.

Second, and equally transformative, the Mass is law, "Gesetz" in the original German—a verbal statement. Something written, recorded. Even as Luther preserved the medieval word, Mass, to name what the faithful were to do, he severed at its very roots an understanding of the Mass as something which grows organically, to invoke Josef Jungmann, among the people[25]; something done as much as spoken; something arising from a complex moment of movement, spoken words, matter—bread and wine—and place, a table in an inn. He severed an ancient understanding of the Mass as itself not only sensible through five senses, but equally rooted in the idea that the senses had been theologically implicated in the Incarnation.[26]

That choice of word, "Gesetz," also points toward Luther's particular understanding of the relationship of the text of Scripture to living congregations. Luther did not view the Gospel narrative as a script for a performance, to be reenacted, as, say, some Anabaptists sought to do.[27] Law, it was to govern the human practice of worship, not serve as a prompt for human action.

That one Mass, for Luther, was not only set forth in, but fully contained within, Scripture. All else was "an addition invented by men." Luther even separated Christ's movements at the Last Supper from the words:

---

25. Jungmann, *Missarum Solemnia*; Arnold Angenendt, *Liturgik und Historik: Gab es eine organische Liturgie-Entwicklung?* (Freiburg: Herder, 2001).

26. On the senses in the liturgy, see most recently Éric Palazzo, *L'invention chrétienne des cinq sens dans la liturgie et l'art au Moyen Âge* (Paris: Les Editions du Cerf, 2014).

27. Michele Zelinsky Hanson, "Anabaptist Liturgical Practices," in: *The Eucharist in the Reformation*, ed. Wandel, 251–272.

. . . O dear Christians, to have many masses is not to have *the mass*. There is more to it than that.

5. If we desire to observe mass properly and to understand it, then we must surrender everything that the eyes behold and that the senses suggest— be it vestments, bells, songs, ornaments, prayers, processions, elevations, pros- trations, or whatever happens in the mass—until we first grasp and thoroughly ponder the words of Christ, by which he performed and instituted the mass and commanded us to perform it. For therein lies the whole mass, its nature, work, profit and benefit. Without the words nothing is derived from the mass.

Now the words are these: *Take and eat, this is my body, which is given for you. Take and drink all of it, all of you, this is the cup of the new and eternal testament in my blood, which is poured out for you and for many for the forgiveness of sins.* These words every Christian must have before him in the mass.[28]

For Luther, "the whole mass, its nature, work, profit and benefit" lies in words and words alone. He did not eliminate the matter of the Mass, the bread and the wine, but the bread and the wine acquired their meaning solely through the words of institution. They did not create meaning or materialize it; they received it, externally, from Scripture. As he would ultimately write in *The German Catechism*, A Christian must know the words before receiving the sac- rament—in order to know what the bread and the wine are.[29]

All else—"images, bells, eucharistic vestments, church ornaments, altar lights"—was "an addition invented by men," or as Luther would call them in the *Confession Concerning Christ's Supper* in 1528, "things indifferent."[30] None of the objects, fabrics, textures, images, colors, sounds—none of the complex sen-

28. Luther, "A Treatise on the New Testament, that is the Holy Mass, 1520," 82. "Czum funff- ten. Woellen wir recht meß halten und vorstahn, ßo mussen wir alles faren lassen, was die augen und alle synn in dißem handel mugen zeygen und antragen, es sey kleyd, klang, gesang, tzierd, gepett, tragen, heben, legen, odder was da geschehen mag yn der meß, biß das wir zuvor die wort Christi fassen und wol bedencken, damit er die meß volnbracht und eyngesetzt und uns zuvol- bringen bevolhen hatt, dan darynnen ligt die meß gantz mit all yhrem weßen, werck, nutz und frucht, on wilche nichts von der meß empfangen wirt. Das sein aber die wort: Nemet hyn und esset, das ist mein leychnam, der fur euch geben wirt. Nemet hyn und trinckt darauß allesampt, das ist der kilch des newen und ewigen Testaments yn meynem bluet, das fur euch und fur viele vorgossen wirt zuvorgebung der sund," *WA* 6: 355, 21-32.

29. "Diese predigt is dazu geordnet und angefangen, das es sey ein unterricht fur die kinder und einfeltigen. Daruemb sie auch von alters her auff Griegisch heisset Catechismus, das ist, ein kin- derlere, so ein yglicher Christ zur not wissen sol, also das wer solchs nicht weis, nicht kuende unter die Christen gezelet und zu keinem Sacrament zugelassen werden. Gleich wie man einen handtwercks man, der seines handtwercks recht und gebrauch nicht weis, aus wirffet und fur untuechtig helt. Der- halben sol man iunge leute die stuecke, so inn den Catechismum odder kinder predigt gehoeren, wol und fertig lernen lassen und mit vleis darynne uben und treibeen," *WA* 30/1: 129, 11-18.

30. "Confession Concerning Christ's Supper, 1528," *LW* 37, 371; "Vom Abendmahl Christi, Bekenntnis, 1528," *WA* 26: 514.

sory experience of the medieval Mass—was a part of "the Mass" as Luther defined it. Christians could continue to have these things, but they were, for Luther, mere things, without theological import, without divine authorization, severed from the mystery of the Incarnation.

Of all the ways Luther reoriented thinking about the Mass, this was the most broadly transformative: the Mass, the whole Mass, is comprised in the narratives of the Last Supper in the synoptic Gospels. Its meaning was to be found in the words, and in the words alone of those narratives—not in anything visible, beyond the words, anything tangible, beyond the bread and wine, anything audible beyond the words read aloud. No vestment, no image, no gesture could, according to Luther, participate in, contribute to, amplify, illumine, illustrate the meaning of the Mass.

Luther made that argument not in the first century, when Christ's earliest followers gathered in homes and catacombs clandestinely to do as he had commanded, but long after the Roman Empire embraced Christianity and the Emperors had brought imperial magnificence to worship,[31] long after the Western Church had embraced images as one of the material consequences of the Incarnation.[32] He made it long after the Church had instituted infant baptism, when all Europeans lived within the visual, haptic, sonic, and olfactory environment of Christianity— an environment which had, by the fifteenth century, as Rogier van der Weyden's Altar of the Seven Sacraments (Figure 1) manifests, become densely layered and complex.[33] He made it at a time when the overwhelming majority of Christians could not read. He made it in a world in which time was measured not mechanically, but in liturgical hours, marked by bells in every settlement across Europe.[34]

31. Peter Brown, *The Rise of Western Christendom: Triumph and Diversity*, 2nd ed. (Oxford: Blackwell Publishing, 2003).

32. For a brief summary, see my *Voracious Idols and Violent Hands: Iconoclasm in Reformation Zurich, Strasbourg, and Basel* (Cambridge: Cambridge University Press, 1995), ch. 1. For fuller discussion, see in particular Gerhard B. Ladner, "Die Bilderstreit und die Kunst-Lehren der byzantinischen und abendländischen Theologie," in his: *Images and Ideas in the Middle Ages: Selected Studies in History and Art* (Rome: Edizioni di Storia e Letteratura, 1983), I: 26-32; Jaroslav Pelikan, *Imago Dei: The Byzantine Apologia for Icons* (Princeton: Princeton University Press, 1990); Wolfgang Schöne, Johannes Kollwitz, and Hans von Campenhausen, *Das Gottesbild im Abendland* (Witten and Berlin: Eckart-Verlag, 1959).

33. The body of work on medieval art, religion, and vision is protean. See, for example, *Das Bild der Erscheinung: Die Gregorsmesse im Mittelalter*, eds. Andreas Gormans and Thomas Lentes (Berlin: Reimer, 2007); Tobias Frese, *Aktual- und Realpräsenz: Das eucharistische Christusbild von der Spätantike bis ins Mittelalter* (Berlin: Mann, 2013). The presumption of Christian majority meant, *inter alia*, that *all* Europeans, including Jews and Muslims, lived within this complex sonic and visual environment, even if they never entered a church.

34. On the changing place of bells in Lutheran worship, see Philip Hahn, "The Reformation of the Soundscape: Bell-ringing in Early Modern Lutheran Germany," *German History* 33 (2015):

FIGURE 1. Rogier van der Weyden, *Altar of the Seven Sacraments*, before 1450. (photo: Erich Lessing/ Art Resource, NY)

Van der Weyden's *Altar of the Seven Sacraments* (Figure 1) now rests in a museum, the Royal Museum of Fine Arts, Antwerp, both museum and displacement evidence of the radical shift I am sketching.[35] It numbers among all those that became "things indifferent," "everything that the eyes behold and that the senses suggest"—excised for those two discrete reasons: they were made by humankind and they were sensible. Made to figure or to trope, following Durand, the historical, allegorical, or anagogical sense of the Mass,[36] it became a mere

---

525-545. On the Christian structuring of time, see Gerhard Dohrn-van Rossum, *History of the Hour: Clocks and Modern Temporal Orders*, trans. Thomas Dunlap (Chicago: The University of Chicago Press, 1996).

35. While I agree with Joseph Koerner that the placement of images in museums is one measure of the radical reconceptualization of what images are and what they do (*The Reformation of the Image* (Chicago: University of Chicago Press, 2004)), I have argued, in *Voracious Idols and Violent Hands*, that the reasons reside in changing understandings of the Incarnation.

36. *The Rationale divinorum officiorum of William Durand of Mende*, trans. Timothy M. Thibodeau, Records of Western Civilization (New York: Columbia Univ. Press, 2007), Prologue.

thing. Its form, a retable, and its content argue for its original placement on an altar, in the sightline behind the celebrant at the Mass and thus in the visual field of the Mass.[37] The image itself helps us to imagine a particular visual play, as we look past the crucifixion scene to the priest elevating the Host in the central panel.[38] It participates in the meaning of the Mass on a number of levels: in visualizing, placing before the eyes of the celebrant and the congregation, Christ's Crucifixion, the sacrifice on the Cross that was becoming ever more complexly interwoven into the meaning of the Mass; in placing the elevation of the Host in a sightline with the Crucifixion; in representing the Incarnate God; in placing the sacrament of Communion at center of the seven sacraments.

The frame of the image evokes, but does not correspond fully with, the interior space of a cathedral. It represents a particular space, layered by different kinds of liturgical and sacramental time—something images can do. In the *Babylonian Captivity*, Luther denied all but three sacraments, "baptism, penance, and the bread," and with that denial, severed four sacraments from the Mass.[39] As this image so brilliantly visualizes, not only was the Mass celebrated in the same spaces as the sacraments of baptism, confirmation, and ordination, but the mystery of the Eucharist was at the center. As Thomas Aquinas taught in his catechetical sermons on the tenth article of the Apostles' Creed, "This communion [of saints] comes about through the sacraments of the church, in which the strength of the passion of Christ for conferring grace and for forgiving sins operates"[40]—not just one, but all seven.

37. Jean Chevrot, Bishop of Tournai, commissioned this work. Max Friedländer, *Van Eyck to Bruegel*, 2 vols. (London: Phaidon Press, 1969), I: 23. See also Erwin Panofsky, "Two Roger Problems: The Donor of the Hague *Lamentation* and the Date of the Altarpiece of the Seven Sacraments," *Art Bulletin* 33 (1951): 33-40.

38. Both this image and the Wittenberg altarpiece have been the subject of rich interpretations. Here I am preeminently concerned with the differing relationship of each image to its liturgy. On the Van der Weyden altarpiece, see Barbara G. Lane, *The Altar and the Altarpiece: Sacramental Themes in Early Netherlandish Painting* (New York: Harper & Row, 1984); Alfred Acres, "Rogier van der Weyden's Painted Texts," *Artibus et Historiae* 21:41 (2000): 75-109; Lynn F. Jacobs, *Opening Doors: The Early Netherlandish Triptych Reinterpreted* (University Park, PA: Pennsylvania State University Press, 2012), ch. 3; Bret Rothstein, "Moveable Feasts of Reason: Description, Intelligence, and the Excitation of Sight," in: *Spirits Unseen: The Representation of Subtle Bodies in Early Modern European Culture*, ed. Christine Göttler (Leiden: Brill, 2008), 47-70. On the elevation of the Host, see Édouard Dumoutet, *Le désir de voir l'hostie et les origines de la dévotion au Saint-Sacrement* (Paris: Béauchesne, 1926); Peter Browe, "Die Elevation in der Messe," *Die Eucharistie im Mittelalter: Liturgiehistorische Forschungen in kulturwissenschaftlicher Absicht* (1931) (Münster: LIT, 2003), 475-508; Vincent Lorne Kennedy, CSB, "The Moment of Consecration and the Elevation of the Host," *Mediaeval Studies*, 6 (1944): 121-150.

39. Luther, BC, 21.

40. *The Sermon-Conferences of St. Thomas Aquinas on the Apostles' Creed*, trans., ed., and introduced by Nicholas Ayo, CSC (Eugene and Notre Dame, IN: University of Notre Dame Press,

The elements of the Eucharist—the Host so visible here, and the wine—through touch and their visibility linked the Mass to the visible world, which Van der Weyden has rendered with his characteristic jewel colors—a world of stunning visual beauty and complexity. As the image renders within the borders of its frame, the Mass encompassed the celebrant, his assistants, congregants, all of whom were differently implicated in the words of the canon, "hoc est enim corpus meum."[41] The visible world was not, as that placement in a museum materializes, severed, but itself implicated in the Incarnation, as the altarpiece images. Seeing the Host also located the Host in the visible world, again captured within the frame of the image.[42] Analogously, receiving the Host in one's mouth linked the touchable world to the mystery of the Incarnation. Processions at Corpus Christi carried Hosts in their monstrances outside the walls of churches into towns, the surrounding urban landscape, weaving that landscape into that which made the Host so very significant.[43]

The violence against objects and images was not restricted to those in the churches, but encompassed Virgins on street corners, crucifixes at intersections of trade routes, carved images in inns.[44] In some places, such as Zurich and Basel, all the images were removed; in most Lutheran places, they were not, as Bridget Heal has been showing us.[45] But, Luther argued, all these diverse materializations addressing the mystery of Incarnation were no longer to participate in the meaning of the Mass. That was to be taught solely by words. In the shadow of that

1988), 135. See also *The Catechetical Instructions of Saint Thomas Aquinas*, trans. Joseph B. Collins (Baltimore, 1939), 46.

41. Cf. Henri de Lubac, SJ, *Corpus mysticum: l'eucharistie et l'Église au Moyen âge: étude historique* [Théologie, 3] (Paris: Aubier, 1949).

42. On the complexity of that interplay, see especially Reindert Falkenburg, "Hieronymous Bosch's *Mass of St. Gregory* and 'sacramental vision,'" in: *Das Bild der Erscheinung*, 178-206; Bret Rothstein, *Sight and Spirituality in Early Netherlandish Painting* (Cambridge: Cambridge University Press, 2005).

43. Charles Zika, "Hosts, Processions and Pilgrimages: Controlling the Sacred in Fifteenth-Century Germany," *Past and Present* 118 (1988): 25-64; Miri Rubin, *Corpus Christi: The Eucharist in Late Medieval Culture* (Cambridge: Cambridge University Press, 1991).

44. In addition to *Voracious Idols and Violent Hands*, see Peter Blickle, ed., *Macht und Ohnmacht der Bilder: Reformatorischer Bildersturm im Kontext der europäischen Geschichte* (Munich: Oldenbourg, 2002). Edward Muir called attention to the presence of sacred images in urban landscapes, "The Virgin on the Street Corner: The Place of the Sacred in Italian Cities," in: *Religion and Culture in the Renaissance and Reformation*, ed. Steven Ozment (Kirksville, MO: Sixteenth Century Journal Publications, 1989), 25-40.

45. On iconoclasm in Zurich and Basel, see *Voracious Idols and Violent Hands*, chs. 2 and 4. On Lutheran images, see Bridget Heal, "Seeing Christ: Visual Piety in Saxony's Erzebirge," in: Jeffrey Chipps Smith, ed. *Visual Acuity and the Arts of Communication in Early Modern Germany* (Farnham: Ashgate, 2014), 43-60.

insistence on the words of institution, sixteenth-century Catholics, Lutherans, Reformed Christians and Anglicans all turned to codicil catechisms to teach not only how to pray, the Lord's Prayer and, for Catholics, the Ave Maria, and the tenets of belief, the Apostles' Creed, but what a sacrament is and the meaning of the Eucharist.[46] Words became the means by which the Eucharist was taught in all Churches—abandoning Thomas Aquinas's notion that one learned Christianity through the reception of the sacraments. They became the medium, not only in which it was taught, but how it was done within living congregations.

I am not arguing that Lutheranism was exclusively verbal—Lutheran churches are eloquent testimony to a rich visual culture.[47] But Luther called for a new relationship between the liturgy and visual culture. We can see something of that changed relationship in the altarpiece, the "Reformation Polyptych," that the Cranachs, father and son, made for the church in Wittenberg in which Luther had celebrated his first Mass in German and in which, for years, he preached and offered communion (Figure 2).[48] Completed in 1547, the year after Luther died, the altarpiece takes up but does not fully follow a recommendation Luther made in passing in 1530, in his explication of Psalm 111:

> Whoever here has a wish to place panels on the altar, he should let the Last Supper be painted with these two verses, "The forgiving and merciful Lord instituted a remembrance of his miracle." These should be written around [the image] in large, gold letters, so that they might stand there before the eyes so that the heart might reflect on it—indeed also the eyes, as they read, shall praise and thank God. For because the altar is thus intended that one dispenses the sacrament on it, one can put no better picture on it; other pictures of God and Christ can stand painted otherwise on different places.[49]

Gone are vestments, bells, altarcloths, candlesticks, pyxes, sacrament house, paten, chalice. In their stead, the Cranachs present the moment that the Lutheran Mass narrated with each celebration of the Eucharist.[50] In their stead are a simple

46. I make this argument in *Reading Catechisms, Teaching Religion* (Leiden: Brill, 2016).

47. Jeffrey Chipps Smith, *German Sculpture of the Later Renaissance, c. 1520-1580* (Princeton: Princeton University Press, 1994); Freye Strecker, *Augsburger Altäre: Zwischen Reformation (1537) und 1635: Bildkritik, Repräsentation und Konfesisonalisierung* (Münster, LIT, 1998); Heal, "Seeing Christ."

48. On the Wittenberg Altarpiece, see Oskar Thulin, *Cranach-Altäre der Reformation* (Berlin: Evang. Verl.-Anst., 1955); Bonnie Noble, *Lucas Cranach the Elder: Art and Devotion of the German Reformation* (Lanham, MD: University Press of America, 2009), ch. 3; and Koerner, *Reformation of the Image*, passim.

49. Koerner, *The Reformation of the Image*, 322; WA 31/1: 415.

50. Images of the Last Supper were not new, though they had appeared more often in refectories than on altars, Creighton Gilbert, "Last Suppers and Their Refectories," in: *The Pursuit of Holiness in Late Medieval and Renaissance Religion*, eds. Heiko Oberman and Charles Trinkaus (Leiden:

FIGURE 2. Lucas Cranach the Elder, "Reformation Polyptych," 1547, Stadtkirche St. Marien, Wittenberg, Germany. (photo: Alfredo Dagli Orti / Art Resource, NY)

stone table with a bench, simple cups, common bread, a meal. The palette is more muted; red and black are the preeminent colors. Those familiar with the medieval tradition of representing the Last Supper would mark one dramatic change: Luther passes the cup from the table to a layman. The gesture materializes the practice Luther had called for, of communion in both kinds; it also visualizes his rejection of the ritualized movements of the Mass.

Luther's placement at the table may well have been meant to honor him in the year after his death, but it also points toward the temporal dimension of Luther's reconceptualization of the Mass. In setting Luther and a sixteenth-century layman in the same space and, by implication, in the same moment with Christ and his apostles, the altarpiece visualizes, simultaneously, the two moments Luther distinguished in his writing on the Mass: the moment of institution at the Last Supper and the moment among living Christians in which they pass

Brill, 1972), 371–402. The most famous exception is Tilman Riemanschneider's *Altarpiece of the Holy Blood* in Rothenburg ob der Tauber, Kurt Gerstenberg, *Tilman Riemanschneider* (Munich, 1950); Michael Baxandall, *The Limewood Sculptors of Renaissance Germany* (New Haven: Yale University Press, 1980), 172–90; Wandel, *The Eucharist in the Reformation*, 135–137. "Of the thirty altarpieces erected by Lutherans in eastern Germany between 1560 and 1600 and extant today, all display a Last Supper on their predella or main field," Koerner, *Reformation of the Image*, 324, citing Hans Carl von Haebler, *Das Bild in der evangelischen Kirche* (Berlin: Evang. Verl.-Anst., 1957).

the cup. The absence of all liturgical objects and vestments thus also erases the many different materializations of different kinds of time in the medieval Mass: the objects linked to the lives of individual saints, the objects commissioned by donors now commemorated in the Mass, the objects which contained material of multiple lives—relics, vestments—encompassed in the celebration of the Mass.

The altarpiece places the Last Supper over the altar. It also places it between the other two sacraments Luther recognized as Scriptural: baptism and confession. It frames the Last Supper, not solely as the originating moment of the sacrament, but as the visualization of that sacrament: just as baptism is enacted in the left panel and confession in the right, so, too, is the Supper enacted in the central panel. But the action in the central panel again visualizes Luther's reconceptualization: if Philip Melanchthon baptizes and Johannes Bugenhagen receives confession, Luther passes a cup he has received from the table, according to the narrative the congregation heard with each Mass, the cup to which Christ gave meaning at the Last Supper. Luther is at the table with Christ; he wears no vestments, he does not stand for Christ, but passes on that which Christ designated.

Directly beneath the Last Supper and structurally supporting all three panels is the Crucifixion, in the very center of the predella. The lines of the frames in the retable emphatically separate it from the enactment of any one sacrament, each one of which is also separated from the others. The Crucifixion is not mirrored in any sacrament; it is the foundation of all.

In his writings on the Mass, Luther construed the Incarnation as verbal, even textual: a testament, a law, a promise. Christ's body, which Luther understood differently from either the medieval tradition or the Reformed, could not serve to connect the Mass to human senses and with them, to the visible, the audible, the haptic—to the things that medieval Christians had made in their contemplation of the mystery of the Incarnation.[51] The thousands of connections, intimate and public, tactile, visual, aural, olfactory, that medieval Christians had crafted, between their own senses and the Incarnation, could be moved out of churches and into museums, objects of interest and study, but no longer themselves means, media, of access to divine mystery.

---

51. On Luther's Christology, see Ian D. Kingston Siggins, *Martin Luther's Doctrine of Christ* (New Haven: Yale University Press, 1970); Dorothea Vorländer, *Deus Incarnatus: Die Zweinaturenchristologie Luthers bis 1521* [Untersuchungen zur Kirchengeschichte, 9] (Witten: Luther Verlag, 1974); Marc Lienhard, *Luther: Witness to Christ: Stages and Themes in the Reformer's Christology*, trans. Edwin H. Robertson (Minneapolis: Augsburg Publishing House, 1982).

8. Eucharistic Sacrifice: The Catholic Responses to Martin Luther

Trent Pomplun

„Geschichte ist Vergangenheit; aber nicht nur Vergangenes. Geschichte ist in die Gegenwart hereinwirkende Vergangenheit. Alle andere Vergangenheit ist höchstens Gegenstand antiquarischer Sammelbemühung."

Joseph Lortz, *Die Reformation als religiöses Anliegen heute*

Martin Luther was an unstinting critic of Roman Catholic Eucharistic theology. Although the would-be reformer identified transubstantiation and the withholding of the chalice from the laity as two of the chief offenses in Catholic sacramental practice, Luther reserved special vitriol for the doctrine that the Mass was a sacrifice, which—arguably more than any issue except justification—became the flashpoint of controversy between Catholic and Lutheran theologians. In the spirit of ecumenism promoted by the Second Vatican Council, such controversies are now heartily condemned and—with Duns Scotus and William of Ockham—thrown on the scrap-heap of outdated theologies. Rarely, however, are these old controversies read, and still less is their history known. In what follows, I would like to trace their genealogy.

I. Luther's Criticism of Scholastic Sacramental Theologies

Historians have offered several explanations for Protestant criticisms of Roman Catholic Eucharistic theology—suspicion about private masses, indignation over the abuse of Mass stipends, the supposed magical quality of Catholic sacraments, and revulsion at the repeated murder of Christ on the altar.[1] Most of these accusations can be traced to Martin Luther (1483–1546) and Philip Melanchthon (1497-1560). Not one to mince words, Luther referred to the sac-

---

1. Francis Clark, SJ, *Eucharistic Sacrifice and the Reformation* (London: Darton, Longman, and Todd, 1960). Clark built upon a generation of talented sacramental theologians who had already addressed Martin Luther's criticism of the Mass. Cf. Mauritius de la Taille, SJ, "Coena et Passio in theologia apologetica contra pseudo-reformatores," *Gregorianum,* 9 (1928): 177-241; Notker Halmer, OP, "Der literarische Kampf Luthers und Melanchthons gegen das Opfer der Messe," *Divus Thomas,* 21 (1943): 63-78.

rifice of the Mass as the worst abuse, the height of perversity, and a deliberate blasphemy.[2] No sin, he claimed—not even manslaughter, theft, murder, or adultery—was so harmful as the abomination of the Mass.[3] The Canon of the Mass was nonsense compiled by a babbler, and the antiphons and responses of the Feast of Corpus Christi composed by a poor and senseless idiot.[4] Luther ridiculed traditional typological associations of the Eucharist with Melchizedek's offering of bread and wine (Gen. 14:18), the binding of Isaac (Gen. 22:2), the Paschal Lamb (Ex. 12:5-6), the heavenly manna (Ex. 16:15), and Elijah's cake (1 Kgs. 19:6), remarking that Catholics might have added Barlaam's ass (Num. 22:21) or David's mule (1 Kgs. 1:38) to signify the abomination and ground of their blasphemy.[5] He derided "mass-holders" variously as homosexuals, heathens, and Jews.[6]

Luther also rejected scholasticism in its entirety, seeing it as a unified tradition from Peter Lombard (c. 1100–60) to Gabriel Biel (1420–95).[7] When he saw fit to criticize individual theologians for their Eucharistic theology, he distributed the blame. He censured John Duns Scotus (c. 1266–1308) for teaching that the sacraments conferred grace *sine bono motu utensis*, but rebuked Thomas Aquinas (1225–74) for teaching transubstantiation.[8] He rejected Aquinas and Bonaventure

2. WA 6: 365, 25: "fast der ergist mißbrauch"; WA 6: 512, 6-7: "longe impiissimus ille abusus"; WA 6: 535, 5: "summa perversitas"; WA 18: 23, 4: "wissentliche lesterung"; WA 6: 523, 8-9: "scandalum speciosissimum."

3. WA 15: 774, 19-21: "Ich sag, das alle gmayne hewser, die doch gott ernstlich verbotten hat, ja alle todtschleg, diebstal, mord unnd eebruch nitt also schedlich seyn als diser grewel der Papisten Mess." WA 10/2: 220, 13-16: "Triumphata vero Missa puto nos totum Papam triumphare." The passage continues, "Nam super Missam, ceu rupem, nititur totus papatus cum suis monasteriis, Episcopatibus, collegiis, altaribus, ministeriis et doctrinis, atque adeo cum toto ventre suo. Quae omnia ruere necesse est ruente Missa eorum sacrilega et abominanda."

4. WA 8: 526, 36–527, 1; WA 8: 523, 12-23. Cf. WA 18: 22-26.

5. WA 8: 421, 25-28: "Metuo autem, imo video, proh dolor, vestrum sacrificare vere esse denuo Christum offerre, sicut praedixit Heb. vi. 'Rursum crucifigentes sibimet filium dei et ostentui habentes'. Vere vestrum resacrificare est impiissimum recrucifigere." WA 30/2: 610, 37-38: "der rechte heubtgrewel und grund aller lesterung im Bapstum."

6. WA 8: 514, 4: "meßhalder"; WA 18: 23, 6: "Sie sind des todts werd, auch die, so dreyn verwilligen" [Rom 1:27, 32]; WA 8: 518, 34-35: "und bist wahrhafftig eyn Heyd und Jüd."

7. WATr 3: 564, 4-5, 8-11: "Quae sophistica vocabula nostri saeculi hominibus plane sunt incognita et barbara. Nam Scotus, Bonaventura, Gabriel, Thomas florente papatu fuerunt homines otiosissimi. . . . Scotus optime scripsit super 3. librum sententiarum. Studiosus methodi Occam ingeniosissimus erat; illius Studium erat res dilatare et amplificare in infinitum. Thomas est loquacissimus, quia metaphysica est seductus." WA 1: 613, 21-23: "Quo circa nunc vide, Num quo tempore coepit Theologia Scholastica, id est illusoria . . . eodem evacuata est Theologia crucis suntque omnia plane perversa."

8. WA 7: 102, 16-29, here 21-25: "Obicem autem vocant peccatum mortale vel propositum eiusdem, quale est homicidium, libido et similia, adeo ut satis sit suscepturo sacramentum, si desinat peccare et propositum deponat, etiam si nullum bonum propositum formet. Quidam enim ex eis dicunt, nec motum bonum cordis requiri." Luther truncated Scotus' phrase *In IV Sent* d. 1, q. 6, to

(1217–74) for their views about the instrumental causality of the sacraments, but promoted Scotus and Pierre d'Ailly (1351–1420).[9] When accused of disrespecting Aquinas, Luther was proudly unrepentant.[10] Indeed, Luther often criticized Aquinas and Scotus together. When he claimed that scholastic concepts were obsolete, the two doctors served as his examples.[11] As the founders of schools, Aquinas and Scotus were responsible for sectarianism, pride, hatred, presumption, unbelief, blasphemy, and sins of every kind.[12] Their disciples, who were more foolish than

---

omit the important qualification *qui mereatur gratiam* and ignored the sentences that immediately followed, which deny the application of the teaching to adults under the ceremonial law. When Luther singles out the Subtle Doctor for criticism, the usual target of his ire is Scotus's view that it is possible for a human being to make a purely natural act of charity towards God. WA 42: 349, 19–350, 8. Scotus serves as the chief representative of scholasticism found in Luther's figural exegesis of Isaiah 34:15, but no particular doctrine is associated with him. See WA 31/2, 220, 4–7: "Sicut alia fera alteri occurrunt, sicut sub Papatu hactenus Aristoteles, Scotus, etc. occurrerunt invicem. Summa: deserto verbo nihil nisi solitudo, ubi animal animali, fera ferae occurrit, i.e. omnibus seduccionibus sunt tales expositi, sicut Papatu et nostrarum Sectarum exemplum videmus." On Aquinas: WA 40/1: 671, 28–30: "Thomas et alii Scholastici de abrogatione legis loquentes dicunt Iudicialia et Caeremonialia post Christum mortifera ideoque iam abrogata esse, non item moralia. Hi ignorant, quid loquantur." WATr 1: 37, 5: "Transsubstantiatio in sacramento altaris a Thoma reperta." WA 30/2: 300, 25–27: "Das sind die besten zween [Scotus and Ockham], Was solten die andern thun? Uber diese alle gehet Thomas Aquinas, Lerer aller lerer (sagen anders die Prediger Münche recht)." WATr 1: 117, 31–32: "Scotus contraxit Thomam, Super IV sententiarum ist er besser den Thomas, ubi tamen Thomas est laudatissimus." WA 6: 509, 27–30: "Sed et Ecclesia ultra mille ducentos annos recte credidit nec usquam nec unquam de ista transsubstantiatione (portentoso scilicet vocabulo et somnio) meminerunt sancti patres, donec cepit Aristotelis simulata philosophia in Ecclesia grassari in istis trecentis novissimis annis."

9. WA 1: 530, 4–7: "Unum illud addo et mihi vendico iure Christianae libertatis, quod opiniones B. Thomae, Bonaventurae aut aliorum Scholasticorum vel Canonistarum nudas sine textu et probatioue positas volo pro meo arbitrio refutare vel acceptare secundum Consilium Pauli 'omnia probate, quod bonum est tenete'." WA 6: 508, 7–13: "Dedit mihi quondam, cum Theologiam scholasticam haurirem, occasionem cogitandi D. Cardinalis Cameracensis [Pierre d'Ailly] libro sententiarum quarto, acutissime disputans, multo probabilius esse et minus superfluorum miraculorum poni, si in altari verus panis verumque vinum, non autem sola accidentia esse astruerentur, nisi Ecclesia determinasset contrarium. Postea videns, quae esset Ecclesia, quae hoc determinasset, nempe Thomistica, hoc est Aristotelica, audacior factus sum." Cf. WA 42: 170, 8–19.

10. WA 8, 127, 5–7, 18–20: "Nec movet, quod Latomus me ingratitudinis et iniuriae insimulat in S. Thomam, Alexandrum et alios. Male enim de me meriti sunt. . . . Nam de Thoma Aquino an damnatus vel beatus sit, vehementissime dubito, citius Bonaventuram crediturus beatum. Thomas multa haeretica scripsit et autor est regnantis Aristotelis, vastatoris piae doctrinae."

11. WA 44: 134, 6–10: "Sicut Iureconsultorum, Medicorum, Theologorum sermonem nemo intelligeret amissis rebus. Et exemplo esse potest scholastica Theologia. Nemo enim ex auditoribus nostris est, qui intelligit, Scotum, Thomam et similes, quia res et usus verborum exolevit."

12. WA 40/2: 90, 15–19: "Ut interim non dicam, quod isto specioso praetextu aluerint et confirmaverint omnis generis horribilia peccata: dissensionem, superbiam, odium, contemptum proximi, fiduciam propriae iustitiae, praesumptionem, neglectum pietatis et verbi, incredulitatem, blashemiam,

Pythagoreans, neglected Scripture to study Aristotle and Averroes and thus begot Thomases, Scotuses, and other monstrosities.[13] In fact, all who comment on Lombard's *Sentences* are botchers and bunglers who poke their nose into things.[14] Being sophists and bawlers—even Amorites and frogs—they deserve to be hated.[15] Luther never seems to have tired of insulting anyone who appealed to "the fathers, fathers, fathers; the church, church, church; the councils, councils, councils; the decrees, decrees, decrees; the universities, universities, universities."[16]

These criticisms of scholastic sacramental theology found canonical form in Augsburg Confession XXIV, where both Aquinas and Scotus stand accused of departing from the teaching of Scripture, promoting works righteousness, and contributing to the multiplication of private Masses. Scotus, Melanchthon claims, taught that an individual Mass might be of finite value. Aquinas, he charges, taught that Christ's death on the Cross made satisfaction for original sin only, so that individual masses must be offered as sacrifices to atone for personal sins.[17] As we shall see, it mattered little that no one interpreted the sermon in which Aquinas's alleged error appeared in the sense that Melanchthon

---

etc. Contra illa peccata non pugnaverunt, imo ne quidam duxerunt esse peccata." WA 7: 764, 7–10: "Hi enim propter suas rasuras, vestes, horas et gestus tot peccatis scatent, ut nec tot relationes habeant Scotistae nec tot realitates Thomistae, quarum tamen in qualibet re mundi tot ponunt, quot sunt creaturae et respectus earum." Cf. WA 6: 88, 10; WA 6: 193, 5; LW 22: 255, 9–11.

13. WA 1: 568, 8–14: Verum illi magis sunt reprehendendi, qui ad ignominiam nostram et iniuriam illorum allegant pro assertis, quae illi pro pio suo studio fuerunt opinati, prorsus nihil advertentes illud Apostoli fidele monitorium: Omnia probate, quod bonum est tenete, longe stultiores Pythagoricis, Quippe cum hii ea tantum assererent quae Pythagoras dixisset, isti vero etiam ea quae illi dubitaverunt. Sed ad originem et fontem veniamus rivulorum istorum, id est B. Thomam et Bonaventuram." WA 43: 94, 3–7: "Postquam enim in hominum commentarios inciderunt, qui sacris studiis dediti erant, non solum plurimum temporis in lectione veterum Theologorum consumpserunt: sed etiam tandem occupati sunt in Aristotele, Averroe et aliis, ex quibus postea nati sunt Thomae, Scoti, et similia portenta." WA 40/2: 35, 14: "Verum haec omnia monstra sunt, per homines ignavos conflicta." Compare Luther's treatment of Thomism and Scotism in his letter to Spalatin concerning the Leipzig debate: WABr 1: 420–24.

14. WA 36: 512, 11–12: "Hümpler und Südler leiden, die sich immer mit einmengen." Here, I use the translation at LW 28: 85.

15. WA 8: 591, 29; WA 38: 268, 17; WA 42: 347, 27: "Itaque digni odio Sophistae sunt."

16. WA 8: 509, 25–26: "Die Vetter, vetter, vetter, Die Kirche, kirche, kirche, Concilia, concilia, concilia, Decreta, decreta, decreta, Universitates, universitates, universitates." Cf. WA 6: 524, 4–7: "Quid ergo dicemus ad Canonem et autoritates patrum? Primum respondeo: Si nihil habetur quod dicatur, tutius est omnia negare quam Missam concedere opus aut sacrificium esse, ne verbum Christi negemus, fidem simul cum Missa pessundantes." For additional examples, see WA 8: 526, 2–3; WA 38: 268, 19.

17. *Bekenntnisschriften der evangelisch-lutherischen Kirche: Quellen und Materialien,* ed. Irene Dingel (Göttingen: Vandenhoeck & Ruprecht, 2011), 367, 18–24: "Quare repudiandus est error Thomae, qui scripsit: Corpus Domini semel oblatum in cruce pro debito originali, iugiter offerri pro cotidianis delictis in altari, ut habeat in hoc ecclesia munus ad placandum sibi Deum."

imposed upon it. Like Luther, who deliberately mangled the meaning of Scotus's *sine bono motu utensis*, Melanchthon neglected to mention a subsequent sentence that clearly contradicted his reading of the passage.[18]

Truth be told, it is rather difficult to pin down Melanchthon's charges. Catholic theologians of the late Middle Ages, citing the texts of "Ambrose" (actually Chrysostom) and Theodore of Mopsuestia found in the Lombard's *Sentences*, interpreted the sacrifice of Christ to be one—the single once-for-all oblation of Hebrews 10:14—offered in every place and in every age.[19] They thought the sacrifice of the Mass to be the same as the sacrifice of the Cross, because the same high priest served as the principal offerer, the same holy victim was offered, and the same salutary effects were distributed to all men and women. They unanimously rejected the notion that Christ was slain on the altar, holding that Christ, impassible and glorified after the Resurrection, could not be harmed in the Eucharist. None denied that the Mass was the unique, once-for-all, and wholly sufficient sacrifice of Christ made itself present for the participation of the faithful. None took the celebration of the Mass to be another sacrifice in addition to Christ's death on the Cross. Nor can we find the views censured in Augsburg Confession XXIV in popular preaching and piety.[20]

II. CATHOLIC RESPONSES TO LUTHER

Catholics did their best to respond to the charges of Luther and Melanchthon all the same. The works of the first generation of controversialists, with Josse Clichtove (1472–1543), Hieronymus Emser (1478–1527), Matthias Kretz (1480–1543), Kaspar Schatzgeyer (1463–1527), Johann Eck (1486–1543), Tommaso deVio Cajetan, OP (1468–1534), Alonso de Castro (1495–1558), Johannes Cochlaeus (1479–1552), Johann Gropper (1503–59), and Stanislaw Hozjusz (1504–79), are a mixed bag, ranging from small pamphlets to large treatises. Some, such as Emser's *Missae Christianorum contra Lutheranam missandi formulam assertio* (1524) contained point-by-point rebuttals, with quotations from Luther followed immediately by the appropriate Catholic responses.[21] More general

18. Melanchthon omitted the accusation of Aquinas in the 1540 *Confessio variata* and the 1551 *Confessio Saxonica*, but the *Book of Concord* canonized the 1530 *Confessio invariata*, thereby cementing the link between Aquinas and Scotus in the Lutheran imagination. Cf. Georg Jacob, ed., *B. Alberti Magni de sacrosancto corporis Domini sacramento sermones* (Regensburg: Pustet, 1893).

19. Peter Lombard, *IV Sent.* d. 12, c. 70 [5].

20. Adolar Zumkeller, OESA, "Das Ungenügen der menschlichen Werke bei den deutschen Predigern des Spätmittelalters," *Zeitschrift für Katholische Theologie*, 81 (1959): 265–305. For further texts illustrating the so-called popular theory of the Mass, circa 1350–1550, see Clark, *The Eucharistic Sacrifice*, 543–560.

21. Hiermonymus Emser, *Missae Christianorum contra Lutheranam missandi formulam assertio* (Strassburg: J. Grieninger, 1524).

works of controversy, such as Clichtove's *Antilutherus* (1524), Eck's *Enchiridion* (1525), and Alonso de Castro's *Adversus omnes haereses* (1534) included arguments about the sacrifice of the Mass as part of larger, comprehensive treatments of heresy.[22] Others, such as Cochlaeus's *Quadruplex concordiae ratio et consyderatio super Confessione Augustana Protestantium* (1544) or Conrad Kling's *Loci communes theologici* (1559), engaged their adversaries' documents directly.[23] Matthias Kretz's *Brevis et plana sacratissimae missae elucidatio* (1535) defended every aspect of the Mass—from the priest's preparation to the final benediction—with Biblical authorities.[24] With the *Panoplia evangelica* (1559) of Willem van der Lindt (1525–88), we see a copious number of Greek and Latin witnesses to the Mass as sacrifice supplemented with Syriac, Ethiopian, and even Syro-Malabar authorities.[25]

This first generation of controversialists appealed broadly to Biblical passages that presumed the continuous office of the priesthood and its sacrifices, such as Lev. 21:6, Num. 28:1–10, Ez. 44:14–16, Dan. 8:13 and 12:11–12, Mal. 1:11, and Apoc. 5:10. Following the broad medieval consensus, they explained the unity of the sacrifice and the diversity of the manner in offering with a Eucharistic theology of *commemoratio* and *repraesentatio* in which the unique, once-for-all, and wholly sufficient sacrifice of Christ is made manifest for the participation of the faithful. Eck, for example, responds to six different arguments beginning with the standard once-for-all argument from Hebrews, taking care to note the unity of the Cross and the Mass but their difference in the manner of offering.[26] Cajetan similarly affirms the unity of the sacrifice offered by Christ on the Cross *simpliciter* and by his ministers in the Church *secundum quid*. For Cajetan, the difference between the sacrifice offered absolutely and the sacrifice offered in participation lay only in the manner of offering—the first in death, the second per mysterium.[27] Christ's death on the Cross was in no wise rendered insuffi-

---

22. Judocus Clichtoveus, *Antilutherus* pars 1, cap. 13 (Paris: S. de Colines, 1524); Ioannes Eckius, *Enchiridion locorum communium adversus Lutheranos*, cap. 16 (Ingolstadt: Georg and Peter Apianus, 1529); Alfonso de Castro, *Adversus omnes haereses*, lib. 10 ([Paris]: I. Badius / I. Roigny, 1534).

23. Johannes Cochlaeus, *Quadruplex Concordiae ratio et Consyderatio, super Confessione Augustana Protestantium*, pars 1, n. 9 (Ingolstadt: Alexander Weissenhorn, 1544).

24. Matthias Kretz, *Brevis et plana Sacratissimae Missae elucidatio* (n.p. [Augsburg], 1535).

25. Wilhelmus Lindanus, *Panopolia evangelica, sive de verbo Dei evangelico*, lib. 4, c. 46, 50, 53–6, 80 (Paris: G. Julian, 1564), fols. 269v–277, 289–293; 302v–347, 414–415v.

26. Johannes Eckius, *De sacrificio contra Lutheranos* (Augsburg: Apud Io. Soterem, expensis honesti civis Petri Quentel, 1526). *Idem, Enchiridion locorum communium adversus Lutheranos*, c. 16 (Ingolstadt: Georg and Peter Apianus, 1529), fols. 69v–71v.

27. Thomas de Vio Caietanus, *Adversus Luteranos iuxta scripturam tractatus de sacrificio missae* (Köln: F. Quentell, 1531), 17: "Fundamentum veritatis et intelligendi diversa sacrae scripturae dicta circa novi testamenti sacrificium ac sacerdotium, est unitas hostiae, simpliciter et absolutae immolatae semel in cruce ab ipso Christo secundum seipsum et secundum quid immolatae quotidie ab eodem per ministros eius in ecclesia sua." Idem, *Instructio Nuntii circa errores libelli de Cena Domini*,

cient by the spiritual offering, he argued, since it was precisely by that offering that Christ's sacrifice is recalled and made manifest. Schatzgeyer's theology of *commemoratio* and *repraesentatio* promoted Christ, the same yesterday, today, and tomorrow, as the unity of old and new dispensations.[28] For the Scotist Schatzgeyer, seven things followed immediately from the proper understanding of the Mass as a sacrifice: (1) that the offering of the Mass is not fundamentally different from Christ's offering; (2) that it is more truly Christ's than the priest's or the Church's; (3) that it is not our work (speaking theologically, not physically); (4) that it is not offered from what we possess; (5) that the minister neither gives God anything nor merits by his own power, either for himself or others; (6) that the offering of the Mass as a sacrifice was founded upon Christ's promise and faith no less than holy communion; and (7) that offering and communion not only do not contradict one another but, since "Do this is memory of me" requires action as well as reception, fulfill and complete the words of Christ.[29]

---

sive De erroribus contingentibus in Eucharistiae sacramento (1525), ed. Franciscus A. von Gunten, OP [Scripta Theologica, 2] (Rome: Pontificium Athenaeum "Angelicum," 1962), 58–59: "Circa hoc caput, adverte errari in hoc quod existimatur sacrificium altaris esse diversum sacrificium a sacrificio quod obtulit Christus in cruce, cum tamen in veritate sit illudmet, sicut est illudmet corpus Christi et illemet sanguis Christi in altari et in cruce et in caelo modo. Differentia autem est in modo offerendi, quia tunc oblatum est corporaliter, modo offertur spiritualiter; tunc est oblatum in re mortis, nunc offertur in mysterio mortis." Cf. Judocus Clichtoveus, *Antilutherus*, pars 1, c. 13, fols. 78–80; Judocus Clichtoveus, *Propugnaculum Ecclesiae adversus Lutheranos*, pars 1, cap. 11 (Köln: Peter Quentel, 1526), 68–76. Johannes Cochlaeus, *Quadruplex Concordiae ratio et Consyderatio, super Confessione Augustana Protestantium*, pars 1, n. 9 (Ingolstadt: Alexander Weissenhorn, 1544), sig. B5: "Auctoritates ex Epistola ad Hebraeos citatae, celebrationi missarum non officiunt. In missis enim est una eademque per commemorationem oblatio, quae a Christo in cruce semel peracta est. Quod igitur in cruce semel peractum est, in sacrificio missae saepe per mysterium repetitur." Cf. Ibid., pars 4, a. 24, sig. T4-V5.

    28. Schatzgeyer, *Tractatus de missa*, par. II, assertio 15 (Tübingen: Morhardus, 1525), sig. d4: "Christus etenim (ut testatur apostolus) heri et hodie ipse et in secula. Ergo apud Christum caput et corpus suum mysticum (quod est ecclesia cum omnibus et singulis membris) nihil est praeteritum et futurum. Unde oblatio Christi in cruce, fuit in verteri testamento ecclesiae, in spiritu et virtute ac promissione certa, praesentissima, pluribusque sacrificiis figuralibus repraesentata. Est et ecclesiae in novo testamento per recordationem et repaesentationem, non figuralem, sed realem in missa, praesentissima." Cf. Hosius, *Confessio Catholicae fidei Christiana*, c. 41, in *Opera* (Antwerp: Stelsius, 1571), fol. 57v: "Sed quoniam in cruce palam, et fine mysterio fuit hoftia cruenta, in altari vero occulte, et mystice abscondita, ne nos eodem, quo Christus modo sacrificare putaremur, cum suo Theophilacto, recte Chrysostomus admonuit. Nos non immolare Christum, sicut seipse in cruce immolavit, sed illius in cruce facti sacrificij recordationem facere. Quae tamen recordatio, sive commemoratio, non eft otiosa, nec umbratilis, verum efficit, quod significat."

    29. Schatzgeyer, *Tractatus de missa*, sig. d2: "illa igitur oblatio, qua ecclesia et suus minister in altari offert, aliud non est quam oblationis Christi in cruce factae, non modo recordatio, sed et solemnis repraesentatio. Sequitur ex hoc, quod fundamentaliter alia a Christi oblatione non est. Sequitur secundo, quod verius est oblatio Christi nonnova, sed eius unica tali repraesentatione renovata)

The second stage of the Catholic response to Luther began with the Council of Trent. On September 17, 1562, the council's twenty-second session pronounced solemn *anathemata* upon those who dared claim the Mass is not a true and proper sacrifice and upon those who dared claim the sacrifice of the Mass detracts from or blasphemes Christ's sacrificial death. The Council further condemned those who claimed the canon of the Mass contains errors, who condemned the practice of reciting the words of consecration in a low voice, and who recommended the abolition of the Canon. (The council also condemned the notion that the sinner neither need be prepared nor disposed by a movement of the will before receiving the sacraments— but, of course, did not condemn the Scotist position as Luther and Melanchthon imagined it.) Arguably, the most important work published near the end of the Council was *De sacrificio missae* (1563) by Gaspar Casal (1512–84), whose first book concerns the history of the Mass; the second, the nature of the sacrifice of the Mass; and the third, the objections of Melanchthon and Calvin, to which Casal opposes several arguments from Aquinas, with healthy support from Augustine and Bonaventure.[30] We owe the vast catechetical works of Petrus Canisius, SJ (1521–97) and Gregorio de Valencia, SJ (1549–1603) to this generation as well. Canisius's *Summa doctrinae Christianae* (1554) lists authorities under fourteen headings, the final two of which deal with the relationship of the Cross to the Mass.[31] Gregory of Valencia's *De rebus fidei* (1591), which singles out Luther, Martin Chemnitz (1522–86), and Jacob Heerbrand (1521–1600) for criticism, is more strictly controversial, having point-by-point rebuttals after the manner of Emser, but in a more advanced mode.[32]

---

quam ecclesiae vel eius ministri. Sequitur tertio, quod non est opus nostrum quod a nobis progreditur (theologice non physice loquendo). Sequitur quarto, quod non est oblatio de nostris bonis, eo modo, quo alias de nostris offerimus bonis. Sequitur quinto, quod illud opus non facit minister ecclesiae tanquam per hoc aliquid Deo daturus ex suis, aut ut meritum proprium sibi aut aliis per hoc acquisiturus. Sequitur sexto, quod illa oblatio non minus fundatur super promissione Christi et fide quam sola communio. Sequitur septimo, quod haec duo, oblatio et communio non modo non discrepant, verum quoque in optima quadratura perfectius verbum Christi consummant et complent, Dum ait, hoc facite in mei recordationem, cum et facere aliquam notet actionem." Compare Johannes Gropper, *Antididagma, seu Christianae et Catholicae religionis* (Paris: Apud Vivantium Gualtherot, 1549), fol. 96r-v.

30. Gaspar Casalius, *De sacrificio missae et sacrosancte Eucharistiae celebratione per Christum in coena novissima* (Antwerp: Apud Libertum Malcotium, 1566), 171-198.

31. Petrus Canisius, *Opus catechisticum, sive de Summa doctrinae christianae*, pars 4, lib. 4, n. 4, q. 7 (Paris: Apud Thomam Brumennium, 1585), cols. 518-558.

32. Gregorius de Valentia, *De rebus fidei hoc tempore controversis libri* (Paris: Theodericus & Chevalerius, 1610), includes both *De sacrosancto missae sacrificio contra impiam disputationem Tubingae nuper a Jacobo Herbrando propositam* (pp. 660-718) and his earlier *Apologia de sacrosancto Missae sacrificio adversus cavillationes Jacobi Herbrandi* (Ingolstadt: Sartorius, 1581), 721-839.

With the Jesuits Gabriel Vásquez (c. 1549–1604), Francisco Suárez (1548–1617), and Robert Bellarmine (1542–1621), these controversies are incorporated into the larger theological curriculum.

The defining characteristic of this second phase is its development of several comprehensive theories of sacrifice in response to Melanchthon, who had charged Catholic theologians with the failure to define the sacrifice they hoped to defend.[33] Catholic theologians were admittedly non-plussed by this charge, as anyone with a passing familiarity with the tradition could easily point to the classic definitions of Augustine and Isidore, to say nothing of their development in Peter Lombard, Aquinas, and Scotus.[34] Even so, Catholic theologians repeated these definitions and expanded them, leading to a number of wide-ranging theories about the nature of the sacrifice of the Mass. The most famous of these is Bellarmine's so-called destruction theory of sacrifice, in which the essence of the sacrifice of the Mass is found in the termination of Christ's *esse sacramentale* at the priest's consumption of the Eucharistic species.[35] This generation pointed out mistakes made by their peers as easily as they protested Melanchthon's ill use of Thomas Aquinas.[36] Bellarmine, for example, questioned the apparent implication by Cajetan that John 6 made no reference to sacramental eating.[37] Vásquez defended Biel as part of a pre-Tridentine consensus on Eucharistic sacrifice against Casal and other Catholic *recentiores*, but also defended Scotus against Luther and Melanchthon, noting the obvious *non sequitur* of their claims that Catholics believed the sacraments to be "works" that still conferred grace *sine bono motu utensis*.[38] The theologians of this generation also synthesized the best aspects of the Thomist and Scotist traditions to counter Melanchthon. Suárez argued, for example, that the Mass possessed the same unlimited salvific efficacy as the Cross *in actu primo* before the application of its graces to individuals, whereas *in actu secundo*, that is, considered as propitiatory, the graces that were

33. Robert J. Daly, SJ, "Robert Bellarmine and Post-Tridentine Eucharistic Theology," *Theological Studies*, 61 (2000): 239-260. Daly depends entirely upon the selections provided in Marius Lepin, *L'idée du sacrifice de la messe, d'après les théologiens depuis l'origine jusqu'à nos jours* (Paris: Beauchesne, 1926).

34. Augustine, *De civitate Dei*, lib. 10, c. 5; Isidore, *Etymologiae*, lib. 6, n. 19.

35. Robert Bellarmine, *De Controversiis christianae fidei adversus huius temporis haereticos* tom. 3, contr. 3, lib. 5, cc. 2-5 (Paris: Tri-Adelphorum Bibliopolarum, 1613), cols. 705-721.

36. Bellarmine treats Melanchthon's charge as the "XVIII. Mendacium" in his: *Judicium de libro quem Lutherani vocant concordiae* (Ingolstadt: David Sartorius, 1585), 87-90.

37. Robert Bellarmine, *De Controversiis christianae fidei*, tom. 3, contr. 3, lib. 1, c. 5, col. 360: "Multum autem interest inter Catholicos et haereticos, licet in sententia eadem convenire videantur; quod Catholici id senserunt optima intentione, ut videlicet facilius defenderunt veritatem."

38. Gabriel Vásquez, *Commentariorum ac Disputationum in tertiam partem S. Thomae*, 4 vols. (Alcalá: Gratianus, 1610–1613), 3: 239-241.

actually distributed, while abundant, were limited by the positive ordination of Christ and the collective will of his mystical body.[39]

By the middle of the seventeenth century, the various topics treated in the first two phases of the Catholic response to Martin Luther were integrated into broader traditions of dogmatic and scholastic theology. The great diversity of Catholic treatments of Eucharistic sacrifice during this period, which can be identified as a third phase of the Catholic response to Luther, is now largely forgotten. In positive and dogmatic theology, one finds special emphasis given to demonstrations of the connection between the medieval Eucharistic theology of *commemoratio* to patristic accounts of Eucharistic *anamnesis*.[40] In scholastic theology, debates about the nature of sacrifice became the first *disputationes* in independent treatises *de sacrificio missae*. Here the undisputed masterpiece is *De sacrificio novae legis* (1662) of the Theatine Zaccaria Pasqualigo (d. 1664), which minutely examined the entire range of post-Tridentine Catholic theological views on oblation, immolation, and the nature of sacrifice.[41] The objections of Luther and Melanchthon are almost wholly codified in this literature.[42] By the mid-to-late seventeenth century, their objections begin to be replaced by nameless objections.[43] With Juan de Lugo, SJ

39. Francisco Suárez, *Commentarii et Disputationes in tertiam partem d. Thomae*, disp. 79, sect. 12, n. 7 in: *Opera omnia*, 26 vols. (Paris:Vivès, 1861), 21:762. Cf.Vásquez, *In tertiam partem S. Thomae* 3: 684–694.

40. Dionysius Petavius, *De incarnatione*, lib. 12, c. 14, in: *Dogmata theologica*, 8 vols. (Paris:Vivès, 1866), 6: 590: "Nam in lege veteri idcirco plura fuere sacrificia, quod variae erant hostiae, nec una pendebat ab alia, sed hodie agnus unus, vel ovis, vel bos immolabatur: postridie alius ab illo diversus. At in nostro sacrificio unica et singularis offertur victima, qui est Christus: nec tamen jugulatur toties.Verum semel in cruce primarium et cruentum ab solo summo sacerdote Christo sacrificium oblatum est: quod in omnia tempora vim suam, efficacitatemque diffundit; caetera, quae in Ecclesia quotidie repetuntur, iteratae sunt commemorationes unius illius, et ejusdem sacrificii : quae sine cruore transiguntur. Ideo ἀναίμαχτοι θυσίαι, passim appellantur. . . . Quamobrem ἀναμνήσεις sunt, et *commemorationes* ex institutione Christi, ac vera *sacrificia commemoratoria*, hoc est, θυσίαι ἀναμνηστιχαὶ. . ." [emphasis in the original]. Cf. LouisThomassin, *De Incarnatione*, in: *Dogmata theologica*, lib. 10, c. 17, 7 vols. (Paris:Vivès, 1868), 4: 365: "Sacrificium Eucharistiae in crucis memoriam frequentatur. Non aliud ergo a cruce sacrificium est, sed crucis mystica iteratio est. Nec enim commemoratio haec sterilis aut perfunctoria imaginanda est, et umbrae tantum aut ludi vicem gerere; sed vera et sincera iteratio est, amputatis duntaxat iis quae a sacrficii religione videbantur esse subaliena. . . . Et ipsa comestio Victimae commemoratio utique ejusdem in cruce occisionis; sed commemoratio non jejuna, sed repraesentatio ipsissima et praesentia fructusque rei."

41. Zacharia Pasqualigo, *De sacrificio novae legis quaestiones theologicae*, 2 vols. (Lyon: sumptibus Ioannis-Antonii Huguetan, & Marci Antonii Rauaud, 1662), 1:1–21.

42. Gaspar Hurtado, *Tractatus de sacramentis et censuris*, tom. 2, tract. 2, disp. 1 (Antwerp: ex officina Plantiniana Balthasaris Moreti, 1633), 344–57, here 344. Cf. Christophoro Delgadillo, *Tractatus de venerabili Eucharistiae mysterio*, pars 2, c. 12, n. 7 (Alcalá: Ex Officina Mariæ Fernandez, 1660), 482–83.

43. Ioannes Bosco, *Theologiae sacramentalis scholasticae et moralis*, pars 2, disp. 5, sect. 1, n. 3 (Louvain: typis Hieronymi Nempaei, 1666), 380; Rodrigo Arriaga, *Disputationes theologicae in tertiam partem divi Thomae*, tom. 7, tract. 4, disp. 50 (Lyon: sumptibus Laurentij Anisson, 1669), 525–41.

(1583–1660), what was once the Catholic response to Luther and Melanchthon becomes swallowed by the intra-Catholic debate about the *res oblata*.[44] Still, although hardly more than a minority position at the time, Lugo's argument that the sacrificial nature of the Eucharist was guaranteed by the *status declivior* assumed by the glorified Lord in the Eucharist is broadly representative of the baroque devotion to Christ's Eucharistic *kenosis*. As sacrifice assumes total devotion, he reasoned, the change signified by sacrifice should be sought in consummation or destruction.[45]

Despite the importance of Lugo for the theologians of the nineteenth century, the general approach of the mid-seventeenth century—quite against the claims of modern theologians—was to argue both *ex ratione sacrificii* and *ex ratione novae legis*.[46] Perhaps the most interesting reformulations of the notion of sacrifice in this respect are found among Scotists. The most thorough Scotist treatment of the Mass as sacrifice was written by Modesto Gavazzi (d. 1658), a close friend and colleague of the better-known Scotists Bonaventura Belluto (1600–76) and Bartolomeo Mastri (1602–73). Gavazzi was among the last major theologians to frame his discussion of sacrifice as a response to Luther, Melanchthon, and Chemnitz. Like others of this generation, however, Gavazzi was more concerned to engage Vásquez, Suárez, Bellarmine, and Lugo.[47] Gavazzi admits that sacrificial change can be destructive or productive.[48] Having cited Aquinas and the *Summa Halensis* to support the notion of sacrifice as destruction, he notes

44. Gabriel Henao, *De missae sacrificio divino tractatio theologica, scholastica, moralis, expositive, et canonica*, disp. 1, sect. 1 (Salamanca: in typographia Sebastiani Perez, 1658), 2–10; Arriaga, *Disputationes theologicae*, tom. 7, tract. 4, disp. 49, sect. 3, sub. 3, pp. 521–23. A notable exception to this general rule is the *Cursus theologicus*, eds. Antonio de la Madre de Dios, Domíngo de Santa Teresa, Juan de la Anunciación, et al., tract. 23, disp. 13, dub. 1, 20 vols. (Paris: Apud Victorem Palme, 1882), 18: 758–73, which quotes Luther on several occasions.

45. Ioannes Lugo, *Disputationes scholasticae et morales de venerabili eucharistiae sacramento*, disp. 19, sect. 1, n. 5 (Lyon: Prost, Borde & Arnaud, 1645), 480: "Sacrificium esse protestationem, qua homo profitetur, se habere totum suum esse a Deo et ideo dignum esse Deum, in cuius honorem et cultum, idem esse, et eadem vita consumatur et destruatur."

46. For the charge that arguments *ex rationi sacrifici* are merely a "phenomenological, history-of-religions" interpretation, see Edward J. Kilmartin, *The Eucharist in the West: History and Theology* (Collegeville: Liturgical Press, 1998). Compare, however, Raphaele Aversa, *De Eucharistiae sacramento et sacrificio*, q. 11, sect. 1–4 (Bologna: Salmintius, 1642), 227–41. On the *ratio* of sacrifice, also see Petavius, *De incarnatione*, lib. 12, c. 12, n. 1–2, in *Dogmata theologica* 6:566: "Primum genus est, quo seipsum obtulit in cruce; alterum incruentum"

47. Modestus Gavatius, *De venerabili Eucharistiae sacramento ac sacrosanctae missae sacrificio disputationes theologicae*, pars 2, disp. 1, qu. 1–3 (Rome: Corbelletti, 1656), 563–91. Gavazzi does not hesitate to interpret Scotus to mean that Christ is the principal offerer, even as the priest offers *in persona ecclesiae*. Modestus Gavatius, *De venerabili Eucharistiae sacramento*, pars 2, disp. 2, q. 1, n. 4, p. 608. He cites Petrus Tartaretus (d. 1522) as an earlier proponent of this interpretation.

48. Gavatius, *De venerabili Eucharistiae sacramento*, pars 2, disp. 2, q. 3, n. 77, p. 576.

that the traditional language of sacrifice—immolation, mactation, exhalation, consummation, and consumption—implies destruction.[49] Scripture, moreover, distinguishes sacrifice from oblation. Gavazzi, however, argues that sacrifice is not made to God as the author of life and death strictly speaking, but to God as God. Sacrifices offered to God as the author of life and death are necessary *pro statu isto*, but a true sacrifice could be made in Eden if the *res oblata* underwent genuine change. Anthony Hickey (1586–1641) made the connection between the final cause of sacrifice and the final cause of the Incarnation more explicitly, thereby reinterpreting the nature of sacrifice in terms of the absolute predestination of Christ.[50] Lorenzo Brancati (1612–1693) argued against Bonaventure and Thomas that sacraments need not be merely medicinal, and so also left open the possibility that Christ might be the predestined high priest independent of Adam's sin.[51] Juan Bosco (d. 1684) argued that the necessity for destruction via bloody sacrifice is *post lapsum Adae*.[52] Bonaventura Belluto interpreted the traditional Augustinian definition of sacrifice in light of Christ's prayers as Head of the Mystical Body, High Priest, and Mediator.[53]

If we are to understand how these sources influenced later theologians, it is important to identify a fourth stage in the Catholic response to Luther during the nineteenth century. Having suffered additional revolutions by the middle of the century, Catholic theologians, when they attempted to reconstitute the traditions of the seventeenth and early eighteenth centuries, championed the individual opinions of Bellarmine and Lugo to the exclusion of other Catholic explanations of Eucharistic sacrifice. One could argue that Bellarmine and Lugo were closer in spirit to the Lutheran concerns, but the differences between Catholics and Lutherans were sharpened during this fourth stage, and several possible avenues by which their theological differences might be reconciled were consigned to oblivion.

The historical reasons for the narrowing of Catholic theology during the nineteenth century are complex. The massive scholastic syntheses of the baroque age crumbled after the French Revolution largely because the institutions that supported them no longer existed or were greatly weakened. As the Catholic

---

49. Ibid., pars 2, disp. 2, q. 2, n. 36, p. 569.

50. Antonius Hicquaeus, "Commentarius de essentia Sacrificii in genere," q. 1, n. 18-20, in: Ioannes Duns Scotus, *Quaestiones in Librum Quartum Sententiarum*, d. 13, q. 2, 16 vols. (Lyon: Svmptibvs Lavrentii Dvrand, 1639), 8:812-37, here 817-18.

51. Laurentius Brancati, *Disputationes de sacramentis in genere, de baptismo, et de Eucharistia*, tom. 1, disp. 4, a. 1, n. 11 (Romae: Manelphius, 1653), 103.

52. Ioannes Bosco, *Theologiae sacramentalis scholasticae et moralis*, pars 2, disp. 5, sect. 1, n. 11 (Louvain: typis Hieronymi Nempaei, 1666), 382.

53. Bonaventura Belluto, *Disputationes de Incarnatione dominica*, disp. 14, q. 3, a. 1, n. 63 (Catania: in aedibus illustrissimi senatus, apud Ioannem Rossi, 1645), 244-45.

Church regrouped later in the century, theologians adopted the periodization of the Middle Ages pioneered by Lutheran historians of philosophy during the seventeenth and eighteenth centuries, thereby allowing traditions of late medieval and early modern Catholic theology that had flourished less than a century before to be both rediscovered and vilified. It may shock some to hear that the quintessentially neo-Thomist narrative of the decline of the Middle Ages is a Lutheran invention, but the charges against Scotus and nominalism that a medievalist today might associate with Étienne Gilson or Cornelio Fabro were advanced in almost identical terms by Lutheran histories of philosophy written during the seventeenth and eighteenth centuries.[54] These histories of philosophy also institutionalized Luther's earlier charges against Aquinas, Scotus, and the scholastic tradition, decrying the obsolescence of scholastic terminology, the contentiousness of disputations, the gullibility of schoolmen in the face of their masters, and their neglect of Scripture. Above all, these histories interpreted the history of philosophy as a struggle between realism and nominalism and stressed the autonomy of philosophy against the imperious claims of the papacy about transubstantiation. In fact, the first periodization of medieval philosophy into early, middle, and late periods is found in Melanchthon's student Caspar Peucer (1525–1602).[55] Christoph Binder (1525–1616), Adam Tribbechow (1641–87), Jakob Thomasius (1622–84), Johann Franz Budde (1667–1729), and Johann Jakob Brucker (1696–1770) embellished the myth of medieval decline and attributed the rise of naturalism, skepticism, Epicureanism, and atheism to scholasticism.[56] Transmitted through Dieterich Tiedemann (1748–1803) and Wilhelm

54. Robert Trent Pomplun, "John Duns Scotus in the History of Medieval Philosophy from the Sixteenth Century to Étienne Gilson (†1978)," *Bulletin de philosophie médiévale,* 58 (2016): 355-445.

55. Caspar Peucer, *Chronicon Carionis,* p. 2, lib. 4 (Bern: excudebat Iohannes le Preux, 1601), 595FG. Compare Peucer's *Triplex aetas doctorum scholasticorum* (1588), in: Delio Cantimori, *Umanesimo e religione nel rinascimento* (Turin: Einaudi, 1975), 108. Cantimori originally published the text of the *Triplex aetas doctorum scholasticorum* in: "Umanesimo e luteranesimo di fronte alla scolastica: Caspar Peucer," *Revista di studi germanici,* 2 (1937): 417-438.

56. Christophorus Binderus, *Scholastica theologia in qua disseritur de eius causis, origine, progressu, ac methodo legendi Scholasticos,* c. 1 (Tübingen: s.n., 1614); Adam Tribbechovius, *De doctoribus scholasticis et corrupta per eos divinarum humanarumque rerum scientia,* c. 6 (Giessen: Vellsteinius, 1665); Jacobus Thomasius, *Schediasma historicum, quo occasione definitionis vetustae qua Philosophia dicitur GNŌSIS TŌN ONTŌN, varia discutiuntur,* §52 (Leipzig: Fuhrmannus, 1665); Thomasius, "Oratio XII. De Secta Nominalium" in *Orationes* (Leipzig: Lanckisius, 1683), 241-275; Ioannes F. Buddeus, *Compendium historiae philosophicae,* c. 5, §6 (Halle: Typis & impensis Orphanotrophi, 1730); Buddeus, *Theses theologicae de atheismo,* c. 2, §9 (Utrecht: Von van Linden, 1737); Johannes Bruckerius, *Historia critica philosophiae,* tom. 3, pars 2, lib. 2, c. 3, sect. 2 (Leipzig: Weidmanni & Reich, 1766). If one doubts that Lutheran histories of philosophy were religiously motivated, note that Thomasius's orations include one "de Disputatione Lipsicâ Lutheri cum Eccio" and another "de congressu Lutheri cum Cardinale Cajetano." Despite their abhorrence of the various sins to which scholas-

Gottlieb Tennemann (1761–1819), the Lutheran periodization of the Middle Ages became the norm of secular and theological histories in the nineteenth century.[57] It was only with Gotthard Oswald Marbach (1810–90) and Johann Eduard Erdmann (1805–92), however, that Scotus was separated from Aquinas and seen as *der Verfall* of scholasticism.[58]

Rome resisted the new German historiography, which it associated with rationalist and traditionalist criticisms of scholasticism. On June 11, 1855, the Sacred Congregation of the Index asked the traditionalist Augustin Bonnetty (1798–1879) to subscribe to a thesis expressly condemning the genealogical account of the medieval origins of modern rationalism, naturalism, and pantheism.[59] But the temptation to adopt the new historiography was strong. German neo-Thomists in Rome like Joseph Kleutgen (1811–83) and Albert Stöckl (1823–95) worked around the problem by attacking *Formalisten* rather than Scotus himself.[60] After *Aeterni Patris*, the floodgates of genealogy were opened, and Scotus found himself accused of formalism, nominalism, skepticism, fatalism, pantheism, voluntarism, individualism, modernism, Spinozism, Kantianism, and even radical Islamism.[61] These accusations were readily assumed in works we still think the

ticism gave rise, Lutherans did not hesitate to draw from their enemies if they might score a point against Catholicism, too. See, for example, Buddeus, "Exercitatio historico-philosophica de Spinozismo ante Spinozam", in: *Analecta historiae philosophicae* (Halle an der Saale: sumptibus Orphanotrophii, 1706), 307-59, here 339: "Scotistarum gentem universam huius criminis arguere non dubitat Petrus Baelius. Nec enim aliud illorum *universale formale a parte rei, aut unitatem formalem a parte rei* sibi voluisse, quam quod deinceps apertius elocutus est Spinoza, et maiori eruditionis specie hominibus propinavit."

57. Dieterich Tiedemann, *Geist der spekulativen Philosophie* (Marburg: Akademische Buchhandlung, 1795); Wilhelm Gottlieb Tennemann, *Geschichte der Philosophie* (Leipzig: Johann Ambrosius Barth, 1798); Victor Cousin, *Cours de philosophie. Introduction à l'histoire de la philosophie*, (Bruxelles: L. Hauman et comp., libraires, 1836); Heinrich Ritter, *Geschichte der christlichen Philosophie* (Hamburg: Perthes, 1845).

58. Gotthard Oswald Marbach, *Geschichte der Philosophie des Mittelalters* (Leipzig: Wigand, 1841); Johann Eduard Erdmann, *Grundriss der Geschichte der Philosophie* (Berlin: Hertz, 1866).

59. "Theses a S. Cong. Indicis editae et a S. D. N. Pio Papa IX. die 15 Iunii 1855 adprobatae", in *Acta ex iis decerpta quae apud Sanctam Sedem geruntur in compendium opportune redacta et illustrata* [=*Acta Sanctae Sedis*] 3 (1867), 224: "Methodus, qua usi sunt divus Thomas, divus Bonaventura et alii post ipsos scholastici, non ad rationalismum ducit, neque causa fuit, cur apud scholas hodiernas philosophia in naturalismum et pantheismum impingeret Proinde non licet in crimem doctoribus et magistris illis vertere, quod methodum hanc, praesertim approbante vel saltem tacente Ecclesia, usurpaverint."

60. Joseph Kleutgen, *Die Philosophie der Vorzeit*, 2 vols. (Münster: Theissing, 1860–63); Albert Stöckl, *Geschichte der Philosophie des Mittelalters. Periode der Herrschaft der Scholastik*, 3 vols. (Mainz: Kirchheim, 1864); Stöckl, *Lehrbuch der Geschichte der Philosophie* (Mainz: Kirchheim, 1870).

61. Zeferino González y Díaz Tuñón, OP, *Historia de la filosofía*, 2nd ed. (Madrid: Agustín Jubera, 1886); Norbert del Prado, OP, *De veritate fundamentali philosophiae christianae* (Fribourg:

standard histories of medieval philosophy.[62] German Catholic historians who wrote in the immediate wake of *Aeterni Patris*, such as Heinrich Denifle, OP (1844–1905) and Hartmann Grisar, SJ (1845–1932), thus made much of Luther's famous claim *Sum enim Occanicae factionis*.[63] Viewing the history of the West with neo-Thomist eyes, they rescued Aquinas from the Lutheran narrative while turning that very narrative against Catholics who were not sufficiently Thomist.[64]

III. THE CATHOLIC RESPONSE IN LUTHERAN-CATHOLIC DIALOGUE

The first genuine breakthrough in Lutheran-Catholic dialogue occurred in the next generation of historians and theologians, most notably Joseph Lortz (1887–1975), Erwin Iserloh (1915–1996), and Herman Otto Pesch, OP (1931–2014).[65] Lortz did not romanticize Luther; like other neo-Thomists, he saw in the reformer's individualism the source of modernity and its ills. Unlike Denifle and Grisar, however, Lortz believed Luther fresh, even necessary. For Lortz, the late Middle Ages was no longer fully Catholic.[66] Its theology was out of touch

---

Consociatio Sancti Pauli, 1911); A. Ackermann, "La notion de liberté chez Duns Scot et Descartes," *Annales de philosophie chrétienne* (nouvelle série), 27 (1892), 175-193. For the final charge, see Bernard Landry, *Duns Scot* (Paris: Alcan, 1922), 352–353: "La croyance exclusive à la liberté de Dieu aboutit au fatalisme le plus passif. Mais les aspirations mystiques ne peuvent jamais être définitivement arrachées de l'âme humaine et lorsqu'elles ne trouvent aucune doctrine rationnelle pour les éclairer et les diriger, elles éclatent soudain en de terribles explosions. Les chefs du peuple sont alors ces vagabonds couverts de haillons, pauvres volontaires qui, comme jadis les révoltés de l'ordre franciscain, vont, de douar en douar, annoncer, en mendiant, la parole d'Allah. La société échappe à ses chefs naturels, pour tomber sous les influences des Confréries musulmanes qu'inspire et anime un mysticisme fanatique. L'autoritarisme, érigé en unique principe de morale, conduit à l'agnosticisme scientifique et l'agnosticisme aboutit irrémédiablement au mahdisme et à la guerre sainte. Les civilisations occidentales doivent se féliciter, croyons-nous, que l'Église Romaine, si puissante au moyen âge, n'ait pas pris Jean Duns Scot pour philosophe officiel."

62. Maurice de Wulf, *Histoire de la philosophie médiévale* (Louvain: Inst. Sup. de Philos., 1900). Compare de Wulf, *History of Medieval Philosophy*, trans. Peter Coffey (New York: Longmans, Green, and Co., 1909), 368.

63. WA 6: 600, 11.

64. Heinrich Denifle, *Luther und Luthertum in der ersten Entwickelung*, 2 vols. (Mainz: Kirchheim, 1904–09); Hartmann Grisar, *Luther*, 6 vols. (Freiburg im Breisgau: Herder, 1911–13). On Luther and nominalism, see especially Denifle, *Luther und Luthertum in der ersten Entwickelung* 1: 591-612; 2: 297-341.

65. Herman Otto Pesch, "Twenty Years of Catholic Luther Research," *Luther World,* 13 (1966): 303-316, here 304. Compare Erwin Iserloh, "Luther-Kritik oder Luther-Polemik? Zu einer neuen Deutung der Entwicklung Luthers zum Reformator," in: *Festgabe Joseph Lortz*, eds. Erwin Iserloh and Peter Manns, 2 vols. (Baden-Baden: B. Grimm, 1958), 1: 15-42.

66. Joseph Lortz, *Die Reformation als religiöses Anliegen heute: vier Vorträge im Dienste der Una Sancta* (Trier: Paulinus-Verlag, 1948). Lortz's first lecture, which was given in 1946, is often printed

with supernatural realities and unsuited to express living realities.[67] The lack of a single, authoritative theological system had led to a destructive externalization (*der zerstörenden Veräußerlichung*) of religious practice and the splintering of the European social organism.[68] As a result (Lortz argued), the first generation of Catholic controversialists failed to convince Luther not because of his intransigence, but because of their own Ockhamism.[69] Moreover, Catholic controver-

---

separately in a slightly modified form, viz. Joseph Lortz, *Wie kam es zur Reformation? Ein Vortrag* (Einsiedeln: Johannes-Verlag, 1950 [1955]), 37: "Von diesem Ockhamismus läßt sich behaupten: er war *nicht mehr vollkatholisch*" [italics in the original]. Cf. Joseph Lortz, *Die Reformation in Deutschland*, 2 vols. (Freiburg im Breisgau: Herder KG, 1962), 1: 173: "Dieses System des Ockhamismus ist wurzelhaft unkatholisch. Man erkennt leicht, welche ungeheure Belastung es für den verängstigten, nach Sündenfreiheit ringenden Luther darstellen mußte. Das Unkatholische: a) dieses System hat kein existentielles Verhältnis zur Wahrheit; b) es macht die Gnade tatsächlich zu einem überflüssigen Anhängsel."

67. Lortz, *Wie kam zur Reformation?*, 36: "Wenn der Zusammenhang mit diesem Leben, also auch mit dem sakramentalen Dasein, fehlt oder kümmerlich wird, muß die theologische Wahrheitsfindung darunter leiden. Wenn gar das sakramentale Leben der Kirche selbst dürftig, der Gesamtzugang etwa des spätmittelalterlichen Volkes zu den Sakramenten ungenügend geworden ist, besonders wenn die Messe und das Sakrament des Altars allzu äußerlich oder zu oberflächlich oder zu moralistisch aufgefaßt werden, dann wird die Gefahr von selbst akut, daß die theologische Wahrheitsfindung ihr Ziel verfehlt." Cf. Lortz, *Die Reformation in Deutschland*, 1: 60–61: "Was bei Ockham, trotz seinen unwürdigen Spitzfindigkeiten (darüber gleich unten), die Tat eines großen Geistes gewesen, verlor bei den Epigonen, entweder durch eine kirchlich-korrekte Zurechtbiegung (wie bei Biel) den innern Zusammenhang mit der Grundlage, oder, wie bei den unfähigen Schülern und namenlosen Magistern, jeden umständliche Leerlauf, jenes überspitzte Distinguieren und jene sinnlose Häufung von angeblichen Tiefgründigkeiten, die unter ungeheurem Wortschwall in breiten Disputationen sich selbst und den neuen angeblichen Tiefsinn so ernst nahmen und die lieben Gegner wegen lächerlicher Kleinigkeiten so hartnäckig verfolgten."

68. Lortz, *Wie kam zur Reformation?*, 46: "Einen für heute besonders eindrucksvollen und warnenden Ausdruck fand diese Zerstörung auch im kultischen Raum, in der Dedoublierung— wenn man so sagen darf—des einen Hochaltars und der für alle gemeinsamen Messe (vinculum unitatis!) durch viele Nebenaltäre und Privatmessen. Die Multiplizierung im kultischen Raum und der Grad des Privaten wird im 15. Jahrhundert gesteigert durch die fortschreitende Aufspaltung des sozialen Organismus. . . ."

69. Joseph Lortz, "Martin Luther. Grundzüge seiner geistigen Struktur," in: *Reformata Reformanda. Festgabe für Hubert Jedin zum 17. Juni 1965*, eds. Erwin Iserloh and Konrad Repgen (Münster: Aschendorff, 1965), 1: 214–46, here 244: "Indes hat das gegenwärtige Konzil uns sehen oder ahnen gelehrt, daß die bedauerliche Einseitigkeit mancher katholischer Formeln legitim ergänzt werden kann, bis zu einer solchen Tiefe, daß das Katholische bis zu der vorher nicht oder ungenügend gesehenen biblischen Fülle such ausweitet." Lortz, *Wie kam zur Reformation?*, 39–40: "Sein Streit mit Eck enthüllt die Tragik der Lage: beide denken in nominalistischen Formen. Luther kommt von diesem Denken her in richtiger Konsequenz zur Leugnung katholischer Sätze. Eck ist vom selben nominalistischen Denken her unfähig, die katholischen Thesen, die er festhält, theologisch auch nur einigermaßen genügend zu durchleuchten. Seine Riesenhäufung von Beweisen zur katholischen Lehre über das Meßopfer bleibt unfruchtbar. Man darf nachdenklich fragen, ob nicht

sialists (again, according to Lortz) repeated the same one-sided un-Biblical arguments for four hundred years.[70] Rigid and conservative, they were simply unable
to create anything vital, being wholly unaware that they lived in a new age with
new laws.[71]

There are some rough patches in Lortz's historiography. He appears to have
accepted the Augsburg Confession as an accurate historical account of late medieval Eucharistic theology, but he defended Aquinas against Melanchthon's criticism.[72] His student Iserloh did the same in his study of the sacrifice of the Mass.
According to Iserloh, Catholic theologians lacked the necessary metaphysical
framework for responding to Luther and struggled to affirm the unity of the
Mass. Iserloh even suggested that Scotist understandings of the sacrifice of the
Mass violated the Council of Trent's teaching that Christ was the principal
offerer.[73] Having dismissed the Eucharistic theology of the late Middle Ages and
the entire modern period, German neo-Thomists were thus freed to explore

---

gerade diese theologisch ungenügende Art Ecks in Luther die Überzeugung tatsächlich stärken
mußte, er besäße den religiösen Reichtum der Offenbarung in größerer Fülle als sein theologischer
Gegenspieler aus der römischen Papstkirche."

70. Lortz, "Martin Luther. Grundzüge seiner geistigen Struktur," 218: "Daß wir Katholiken
die Bewertungskategorien des Cochlaeus (die über 400 Jahre bei uns vorherrschend), des großen
Denifle und des (übrigens im Detail beneidenswert versierten) Grisar hinter uns gelassen haben,—
und daß dies sogar auch für Italien, Spanien und Latein-Amerika gilt, darf als bekannt vorausgesetzt
werden. Die Katholiken haben allmählich 1. Den christlichen, ja katholischen Reichtum in Luther
erkannt; und sie sind davon beeindruckt.—2. wir haben erkannt, wie groß die katholische Schuld
ist, daß Luther aus der Kirche herausgedrängt wurde, also die Kirchen-Spaltung, entstand, die uns
auch theologisch so belastet,—3. wir sind stark von dem Verlangen bewegt, Luthers Reichtum in
die katholische Kirche heimzuholen."

71. Lortz, Die Reformation in Deutschland, 2: 174: "Nur als Nachfahren gebildet und sich als
solche fühlend, ging ihnen die Tatsache, daß eine neue Zeit mit eigenen Rechten vor ihnen stand,
und daß ihnen die Aufgabe zugefallen war, für und mit der Kirche die Problem selbstschöpferisch
anzupacken, zu wenig auf."

72. Lortz, Die Reformation als religiöses Anliegen heute, 18: "Das Unheil schlechthin der
modernen Zeiten ist intim gebunden an die Multiplizierung der Geschichte bildenden und
Geschichte erleidenden Faktoren. In jedem Sinn. Diese Multiplizierung hat geschaffen oder ist
Darstellung einer riesigen Oberflächenbewegung, die notwendig auf Kosten der Tiefe, des
Gehalts, der Echtheit geht."

73. Erwin Iserloh, Der Kampf um die Messe in den ersten Jahren der Auseinandersetzung mit Luther
(Münster in Westfalen: Aschendorff, 1952), 55: "Für Eck besteht die Einheit des Opfers in der
Identität der Opfergabe. Opferpriester ist in der Messe der menschliche Priester, der in „persona
ecclesiae" handelt. Wohl klingt bei der Behandlung von Ps 109, 4 mal an, daß Christus selbst der
Priester in der Messe ist. Dieser Gedanke ist aber Ecks Gesamtdarstellung nicht konform und wird
von ihm nur angeführt, wie er auch sonst die Beweise häuft, unbekümmert darum, ob der eine
den andern aufhebt. Eck konnte auch Christus nicht im Sinne des Tridentinums als principalis
offerens hinstellen, weil er zu wenig die Einheit von Messe und Kreuzesopfer sah und deshalb den
Einwand vom Hebräerbrief her zu fürchten hatte, daß Christus sich nur einmal geopfert hat."

analogies in the theologies of Aquinas and Luther. In order to facilitate a systematic-theological encounter between the two theologians, however, they minimized Luther's criticism of the Angelic Doctor.[74] Other scholars have discussed
the nationalistic elements of this historiography; we need not bother with the
details beyond noting the obvious influence of Hegel's *Vorlesungen über die Philosophie der Weltgeschichte*. Lortz, in short, welcomed the Lutheran Reformation
as the historical antithesis necessary to bring about the consolidation of Church
power in a single, authoritative Thomism. He celebrated the *Syllabus of Errors*,
Pastor Aeternus, *Pascendi dominici gregis*, and the 1929 Concordat between Pius XI
and Mussolini. For Lortz, Germany, having initiated the medieval world in the
sixth century and the modern world in the person of Luther, would lead the
West into its fourth age during the twentieth century.[75]

To support this theologico-political vision, Lortz and his students suppressed
historical scholarship that questioned their neo-Thomist synthesis, especially
new research on Ockham.[76] Gerhard Ritter had attempted to demonstrate the

---

74. Otto Hermann Pesch, OP, *Theologie der Rechtfertigung bei Martin Luther und Thomas von
Aquin: Versuch eines systematisch-theologischen Dialogs* (Mainz: Grünewald, 1967 [1985]), 4–5: "Wenn
der ältere Luther in seiner Polemik öfters Thomas angreift—wo es anfällt, wird darauf hingewie-
sen—, darf das nicht zum Schluß auf intensivere Thomaslektüre verleiten. Das ist für die Spätzeit
Luthers schon aus biographischen, vor allem aber aus sachlichen Gründen unwahrscheinlich: Was
Luther angreift . . . sind vulgärthomistische Thesen, die schon durch die Art, wie Luther sie for-
muliert, seine mangelnde Vertrautheit mit der theologiegeschichtlichen wie mit der Sachfrage
verraten."

75. On Lortz's life, see Gabriele Lautenschläger, *Joseph Lortz (1887–1975): Weg, Umwelt und
Werk eines katholischen Kirchenhistorikers* (Würzburg: Echter, 1987); Wilhelm Damberg, "Kirchengeschichte zwischen Demokratie und Diktatur: Georg Schreiber und Joseph Lortz in Münster
1933–1950," in: *Theologische Fakultäten im Nationalsozialismus*, ed. Leonore Siegele-Wenschkewitz
and Carsten Nicolaisen (Göttingen: Vandenhoeck & Ruprecht, 1993), 146–67; Hubert Wolf, "Der
Historiker ist kein Prophet," in: *Die katholisch-theologischen Disziplinen in Deutschland 1870–1962*,
ed. Hubert Wolf and Claus Arnold (Paderborn: Schöningh, 1999), 71–94; Georg Denzler, "Katholische Zugänge zum Nationalsozialismus," in: *Theologische Wissenschaft im "Dritten Reich*," eds. Georg
Denzler and Leonore Siegele-Wenschkewitz (Frankfurt am Main: Haag und Herchen, 2000), 40–
67. For a collective engagement, see Rolf Decot and Rainer Vinke, eds., *Zum Gedenken an Joseph
Lortz (1887–1975): Beiträge zur Reformationsgeschichte und Ökumene* (Stuttgart: Steiner-Verlag, 1989).
For contemporary discussions, see Wilhelm Schüssler, "Deutsch-lutherischer Geist und Westeuropa,"
and Othmar F. Anderle, "Die Geschichtswissenschaft in der Krise," in: *Festgabe Joseph Lortz*, 2:139–
152, 491–550. Cf. Heiko Oberman, "The Nationalist Conscription of Martin Luther," in: *Piety,
Politics, and Ethics: Reformation Studies in Honor of George Wolfgang Forell*, ed. C. Lindberg, [Sixteenth
Century Essays and Studies, 3] (Kirksville: Sixteenth Century Journal Publishers, 1984), 65–73.

76. For an overview, see William J. Courtenay, "In Search of Nominalism," in: *Ockham and
Ockhamism: Studies in the Dissemination and Impact of His Thought,* [Studien und Texte zur Geistesgeschichte des Mittelalters, 99] (Leiden: Brill, 2008), 1–19. Cf. Courtenay's earlier study, "Nominalism and Late Medieval Religion," in: *The Pursuit of Holiness in Late Medieval and Renaissance
Religion*, eds. Charles Trinkhaus and Heiko Oberman, [Studies in Medieval and Reformation

orthodoxy, even the respectability, of fifteenth-century Ockhamism in the 1920s.[77] Erich Hochstetter had argued that Ockham held an *intellectio* theory of universal concepts.[78] Paul Vignaux demolished the older caricatures of the *potentia absoluta Dei*.[79] Philotheus Boehner attacked the genealogy at its root by denying the attribution of the *Centiloquium* to Ockham on historical-critical grounds.[80] With both neo-Thomists and existentialist Thomists alike, Lortz and Iserloh combatted this research, insisting especially upon the authenticity of the *Centiloquium* in order to maintain the fiction that Ockham was the leader of a school that had vitiated philosophy and brought about the decline of the West.[81]

Thought, 10] (Leiden: Brill, 1974), 26-58. For a contemporary assessment, see Timotheus Barth, "Wilhelm Ockham im Lichte der neuesten Forschung," *Philosophisches Jahrbuch,* 60 (1950): 464-467; *idem,* "Nuove interpretazione della filosofia di Occam," *Studi francescani,* 52 (1955): 187-204.

77. Gerhard Ritter, *Studien zur Spätscholastik: via antiqua et via moderna auf den deutschen Universitäten des XV Jahrhunderts,* 2 vols. [Sitzungsberichte der Heidelberger Akademie der Wissenschaften. Mathematisch-naturwissenschaftliche Klasse 1921, 4; 1922, 5; 1926/27, 7] (Heidelberg: Winter, 1921-27), 2: 22-86.

78. Erich Hochstetter, *Studien zur Metaphysik und Erkenntnislehre von Ockham* (Berlin: W. de Gruyter & Co., 1927); *idem,* "Nominalismus?," *Franciscan Studies* 9 (1949): 370-403; *idem,* "Viator mundi. Einige Bemerkungen zur Situation des Menschen bei Wilhelm von Ockham," *Franziskanische Studien,* 32 (1950): 1-20.

79. Paul Vignaux, "Nominalisme," in: *Dictionnaire de Théologie catholique* 11.1 (1930), cols. 717-84; *idem,* "Occam" in *Dictionnaire de Théologie catholique* 11.2 (1931), cols. 876-89; *idem, Justification et predestination au XIVe siècle* (Paris: Leroux, 1934); *idem, Nominalisme au XIVe siècle* (Montréal and Paris: Inst. d'Etudes Médiévales, 1948).

80. Philotheus Boehner, "The *Centiloquium* attributed to William of Ockham," *Franciscan Studies,* 1:1 (1941), 58-72; 1:2 (1941), 35-54; 1:3 (1941), 62-70; 2 (1942), 49-60, 146-57, 251-301; *idem,* "The Medieval Crisis in Logic and the *Centiloquium* attributed to William of Ockham," *Franciscan Studies,* 4 (1944): 151-170; *idem,* "The Realistic Conceptualism of William Ockham," *Traditio,* 4 (1946): 307-335; *idem,* "Ockham's Philosophy in the Light of Recent Research," *Proceedings of the Tenth International Congress of Philosophy,* ed. Evert Willem Beth (Amsterdam: NHPC, 1949), 1111-1113. Boehner's several articles are collected in: *Collected Articles on Ockham,* ed. Eligius M. Buytaert, Franciscan Institute Publications. Philosophy Series, 12 (St. Bonaventure, NY: Franciscan Institute Press, 1958).

81. Erwin Iserloh, "Um die Echtheit des Centiloquium. Ein Beitrag zur Wertung Ockhams und zur Chronologie seiner Werke," *Gregorianum,* 30 (1949): 78-103, 309-46; *idem, Gnade und Eucharistie in der philosophischen Theologie des Wilhelm von Ockham* [Veröffentlichungen des Instituts für Europäische Geschichte Mainz, 8; Abt. für abendländische Religionsgeschichte] (Wiesbaden: Franz Steiner Verlag, 1956). Cf. Anton Pegis, "Concerning William of Ockham," *Traditio,* 2 (1944): 465-480; *idem,* "Some Recent Interpretations of Ockham," *Speculum,* 23 (1948): 452-463. The idea that Ockham was the leader of a school of thought had already been questioned in the 1950s by Damasus Trapp, OESA, "Augustinian Theology of the 14th Century," *Augustiniana,* 6 (1956): 146-274. It has been more decisively rejected by Katharine Tachau, "The Problem of the Species in medio at Oxford in the Generation after Ockham, *Mediaeval Studies,* 44 (1982): 394-443; *idem, Vision and Certitude in the Age of Ockham. Epistemology and the Foundations of Semantics, 1250–1345,* [Studien und Texte zur Geistesgeschichte des Mittelalters, 22] (Leiden: Brill, 1988). We now have

In other words, Lortz and Iserloh did not overturn the prejudices of Denifle and Grisar; they perpetuated them.[82] We find a striking example of their influence in the young Joseph Ratzinger.[83]

Lortz and his students accepted Melanchthon uncritically as an historical source, misunderstood the Eucharistic theology of Scotus and the nominalists, over-emphasized the influence of Cochlaeus and Eck, and ignored four hundred years of robust Roman Catholic responses to Luther. Few historians would take their claims seriously today. The great majority of those who opposed Luther were not Ockhamists. In fact, the ranks had been closing against nominalism for a century before Luther protested the abuse of indulgences. The University of Paris had already imposed a ban on books written by *nominales* and *terministae* in 1474 and rightly noted that Thomists and Scotists were *reales*.[84] As a result,

---

a better understanding of the institutional resistance to fifteenth-century nominalism as well. Zénon Kaluza, *Les Querelles doctrinales à Paris. Nominalistes et realistes aux confins du XIVe et du XVe siècles* (Bergamo: Lubrina, 1988).

82. Karl Meissinger, *Der katholische Luther* (Munich: Lehnen, 1952), 104-106, 109. Pesch, following Hägglund, Grane, and Schwartz, was more judicious in his treatment of Ockham. See Bengt Hägglund, "Voraussetzungen der Rechtfertigungslehre Luthers in der spätmittelalterlichen Theologie," *Lutherische Rundschau*, 11 (1961): 28-55; Lief Grane, *Contra Gabrielem : Luthers Auseinandersetzung mit Gabriel Biel in der* "Disputatio contra scholasticam theologiam" 1517 [Acta theologica Danica, 4] (Copenhagen: Gyldendal, 1962); Reinhard Schwartz, *Fides, spes, et caritas beim jungen Luther* [Arbeiten zur Kirchengeschichte] (Berlin: de Gruyter, 1962). If Pesch wished to separate Luther as much as possible from Ockham in order to effect a systematic-theological convergence with Thomas Aquinas, why should not one then recognize the *Denkvollzugsformen* of individual scholastics and controversialists?

83. Joseph Ratzinger, *Rückblick auf die Sitzungsperiode des Zweiten Vatikanischen Konzils, 3: Ergebnisse und Problem der dritten Konzilsperiod* (Köln: Bachem, 1965), 18-19: "Neue Wucherungen wurden auf diese Weise zwar in der Tat verhindert, aber das Geschick der abendländischen Liturgie war nun an eine streng zentralistisch bestimmte und rein bürokratisch arbeitende Behörde gebunden, der es gänzlich an historischem Blick gebrach und die das Problem der Liturgie rein rubrizistisch-zeremoniell, sozusagen als Ordnungsproblem der Hofetikette des Heiligen ansah. Diese Bindung bewirkte im folgenden eine völlige Archäologisierung der Liturgie, die jetzt aus dem Stadium lebendiger Geschichte in dasjenige der reinen Konservierung überführt und so zugleich zum inneren Absterben verurteilt war. Die Liturgie war zu einem ein für allemal abgeschlossenen, fest verkrusteten Gebilde geworden, das den Zusammenhang mit der konkreten Frömmigkeit um so mehr verlor, je mehr man auf die Integrität der vorgegebenen Formen achtete. Man braucht, um dies zu erkennen, sich nur ins Gedächtnis zu rufen, daß keiner der Heiligen der katholischen Erneuerung seine Spiritualität aus der Liturgie nährte. Ein Ignatius von Loyola, eine Theresia von Avila, ein Johannes vom Kreuz haben ihre Religiosität abseits der Liturgie, ohne tiefere Bindung an sie, lediglich aus der persönlichen Begegnung mit Gott und aus ihrem individuellen Erleben der Kirche heraus gestaltet."

84. Franz Ehrle, SJ, *Der Sentenzenkommentar Peters von Candia, des Pisaner Papstes Alexanders V: ein Beitrag zur Scheidung der Schulen in der Scholastik des vierzehnten Jahrhunderts und zur Geschichte des Wegestreites*, [Franziskanische Studien, 9] (Münster in Westfalen: Aschendorff, 1925).

the sixteenth and seventeenth centuries saw the resurgence of metaphysical realism across the religious orders with Dominicans and Jesuits following Aquinas,
Franciscans following Bonaventure, Alexander of Hales, and Duns Scotus, Augustinians following Giles of Rome, Servites following Henry of Ghent, and the
Benedictines producing scholastic syntheses of Anselm of Canterbury—to say
nothing of the wide use of Aquinas and Scotus across religious orders.

These old myths about Duns Scotus and nominalism are institutionalized
in Luther research, appearing both in the *Weimarer Ausgabe* and the Concordia
House edition of *Luther's Works*.[85] They are readily repeated in ecumenical circles. *From Conflict to Communion*, the recent Lutheran-Catholic Common Commemoration of the Reformation, blithely remarks that the theology of the
Eucharist as real remembrance, in which the unique, once-for-all, and wholly
sufficient sacrifice of Christ makes itself present for the participation of the
faithful, was no longer fully understood in the late Middle Ages, that Martin
Luther overcame within himself a Catholicism that was not fully Catholic, that
many in the late Middle Ages took the celebration of the Mass to be another
sacrifice in addition to the one sacrifice of Christ, that the multiplication of
Masses was thought to effect a multiplication of grace and to apply this grace
to individual persons, that Catholic controversialists had lost an integrative concept of commemoration, lacked adequate categories with which to express the
sacrificial character of the Eucharist, and struggled to affirm the identity of the
Eucharistic sacrifice with the unique sacrifice of Christ—all claims taken verbatim from Lortz, Iserloh, and Pesch.[86] Its authors repeat the charges of the
Augsburg Confession against Duns Scotus as historical fact.[87] They decry the

85. See WA 9: 62, 20-21; WA 56: 337, n. 16; WA 56: 382, n. 33; LW 25: 260-61, n. 8; LW 25:
325, n. 5; LW 25: 372, n. 33; LW 25: 458, n. 34; LW 44: 275, n. 27. On Scotists and the *moderni*,
however, see WA 1: 509, 13-14; WA 7: 707, 17; WA 7: 739, 1.

86. The Lutheran World Federation and the Pontifical Council for Promoting Christian
Unity, *From Conflict to Communion: Lutheran-Catholic Common Commemoration of the Reformation in
2017* (Grand Rapids: William B. Eerdmans Publishing Company, 2017). The commission's characterization of "real remembrance" as *anamnesis* hints that the integrative concept of the Eucharist
supposedly lost in the late Middle Ages was patristic, but does not address the rather obvious objection that the general Latin translation of *anamnesis* is *commemoratio*, a word ubiquitous in late medieval Eucharistic theology. Even the Vulgate translates the four uses of *anamnesis* or its cognates in
the New Testament as *commemoratio* (Luk. 22:19, 1 Cor. 11:24-25, Heb. 10:3).

87. For the Subtle Doctor, the Mass remained *specialior commemoratio oblationis*, an objective
commemoration of the redemptive sacrifice of the Cross in which the Church ritually presents
Christ, truly present before for the faithful, to God the Father in order to plead the merits of His
passion for their welfare. As an heir to the old Augustinian tradition in which Christ's sacerdotal
actions do not cease to be his own when his ministers perform them, Scotus believed (as all Catholic theologians believe), that Christ is both the High Priest who offers the sacrifice and the sacrifice offered to God the Father by the Church. For Scotus, then, the identity of the immolated

language of controversy and apologize for Luther's anti-Semitism, without once mentioning the vitriol he directed towards *meßhalder*.[88] Of course, if we assume as a methodological principle that one need not heed the arguments of those who caricatured, ridiculed, and demonized their opponents, then we must exclude on principle Martin Luther, who in only four pages of the *Weimarer Ausgabe* refers to Pope Paul III as pope fart-ass, the ass-pope, the fart-ass pope, the farter in Rome, the Anti-Christ, the inward destroyer, and the abomination of desolation.[89]

From Conflict to Communion claims that no Catholic theologian between Scotus and Cajetan had a fully Catholic understanding of the Eucharist. It insinuates that Luther was correct in his criticisms of the Eucharistic theology of the late Middle Ages. Its authors maintain that for four hundred years no Catholic theologian answered—or could answer—Martin Luther's criticism of the Mass as sacrifice. In doing so, they turn the deep hatred that Luther held for Aquinas and the entire scholastic tradition against Blessed John Duns Scotus. The ease with which they do so indicates nothing less than the extent to which they have adopted Lutheran historiographical principles while ignoring what Luther actually said. This is the new research on Martin Luther and the late Middle Ages championed in *From Conflict to Communion*. It is a shibboleth. For two centuries, it has allowed Catholic theologians to hide their ignorance of six hundred years of Catholic theology under a false political piety. It allows them now to insinuate that the Council of Trent neither responded to Luther nor canonized the broad late medieval consensus on Eucharistic sacrifice. Let us not pretend that Luther took aim only at late medieval theology rather than the broad patristic and medieval consensus. And let us not pretend that Catholic theology between Scotus and the Second Vatican Council had nothing to contribute to our understanding of the Mass. It is better to argue about Scripture than to agree on this dubious historiography. No dialogue can move forward on the tacit agreement that we vilify another theologian, and no one should object when a blameless theologian is defended from attack.

---

victim accounts for the unity of the sacrifice of the Cross and the Mass, while separate liturgical oblations account for the difference between them. Of course, that some might have believed such grace to be quantifiable cannot be held against Scotus, nor is there any reason to think that those who defended the Thomist position refrained from offering Masses *sine populo*.

88. See the comments of Theodor Dieter, "From Conflict to Communion: Introducing the Document of the International Catholic-Lutheran Commission for Unity in Commemoration of the Reformation in 2017," *Claritas: Journal of Dialogue & Culture*, 5 (2016): 33–37.

89. For this tiny sampling of Luther's insults, see WA 54, 266-269.

IV. The Church

9. Late Medieval Models of the Church

Nelson H. Minnich

On the eve of the Reformation in Western Europe, there were three principal models of the Church espoused by theologians, canonists, legists, and men of affairs. At times they competed with each other, but attempts were made to harmonize them.

In the West, the papal model of the Church evolved over time. It was based on the special position of the Apostle Peter found in the New Testament. The bishops of Rome claimed to be his successors and to inherit his roles as shepherd of the Christ's flock (Jn 21: 15–17), confirmer of the faith of His disciples (Lk 22: 23), and possessor of the keys of loosing and binding (Mt 16: 16–18). While the Scriptures depicted Peter as exercising these roles in a collegial manner (Acts 15: 1–29), with power diffused among Christ's followers, the bishops of Rome over time assumed the role as the ultimate authority in the Church. Based on Pope Gelasius's assertion that his spiritual authority is superior to the temporal power of civil rulers, and further elaborated by Bernard of Clairvaux's allegorical interpretation of Peter's two swords (Lk 22: 38), popes asserted that they possessed both a spiritual and temporal sword, the latter of which they entrusted to emperors and kings. Eventually the popes asserted that they were the vicars of the priest and king Christ, to whom all power in heaven and earth had been granted. Over the centuries, they created a parallel and independent ecclesiastical structure of governance and property that claimed immunity from lay control. In his decree *Clericis laicos* (1296), Boniface VIII (1294–1303) asserted that the laity is traditionally hostile to the clergy and seeks illicit control over ecclesiastical persons and their possessions. He forbade any imposition of taxes, payments, loans, or gifts to the laity without the permission of the Apostolic See.[1]

These assertions of papal supremacy were most forcefully articulated in his later bull *Unam Sanctam* (1302), in which he described the Church: as symbolized in the Ark captained by Noah, as the mystical body whose head on earth is Christ's vicar Peter and his successors, and as the flock committed to the Prince of the Apostles and those who followed him as bishop of Rome. Boniface invoked [Pseudo-] Dionysius' teaching that God had ordered the universe in a hierarchical manner with spiritual power at the top of the pyramid, and the

---

1. Emil Ludwig Richter and Emil Friedberg, *Corpus juris canonici*, 2nd ed., 2 vols. (Leipzig: B. Tauchnitz, 1879, reprint Graz., 1950), II, cols. 1062–63.

pope ended his bull with the pronouncement that in order to be saved "every human creature must be subject to the Roman Pontiff."[2]

Missing or minimized in this discourse is Christ's insistence that His kingdom is not of this world (Jn 18: 36). Also to be noted is that a number of documents supporting papal claims to a position at the apex of society were spurious: the *Ecclesiastical Hierarchies* of Pseudo-Dionysius (that claimed to be the teachings of St. Paul's disciple), the forged Donation of Constantine that held that the first Christian emperor had given the Western Empire to Pope Sylvester, and the canonical collection of Pseudo-Isidore that fabricated documents glorifying papal power. Some of these documents were incorporated into the *Decretum* of Gratian and became the basis of canon law.[3]

Important to understanding why certain ideas were readily accepted are the assumptions prevalent about how God organized the world. Most medieval thinkers, living in a feudal world of ascending levels of vassalage, saw society organized in a hierarchical manner, with one person at the apex of the pyramid. If one argued that the spiritual is superior to the temporal, then the pope presided at the top. In his treatise *De Monarchia* (ca. 1312), Dante Alighieri (1265-1321) insisted on separate parallel powers and held that for the peace of Christendom and in accord with natural law, all rulers should be subject to the Holy Roman emperor whose authority comes directly from God.[4] While all of Western Christendom was not part of the Holy Roman Empire—for example, the kingdoms of Spain, England, Denmark, Poland, and Hungary were not vassals of the emperor—a primacy of honor was to be accorded to the emperor.

---

2. Ibid., II, cols. 1245-46: "Porro subesse Romano Pontifici omni humanae creaturae declaramus, dicimus, diffinimus et pronunciamus omnino esse de necessitate salutis."

3. Francis X. Murphy, "Pseudo-Dionysius," *New Catholic Encyclopedia*, 17 vols. (Washington, DC: The Catholic University of America Press, YEAR?), 11: 943-945; Horst Fuhrmann, "False Decretals (Pseudo-Isidorian Forgeries)," Ibid., 5: 820-824 (reserving to the pope the trial of bishops and confirmation of councils); John van Engen, "Donation of Constantine," *Dictionary of the Middle Ages*, ed. Joseph R. Strayer, 13 vols. (New York: Charles Scribner's Sons, 1982-89), 4: 257-259; Olivier Guyotjeannin, "Donation of Constantine," *The Papacy: An Encyclopedia*, ed. Philippe Levillain, 3 vols. (New York: Routledge, 2002), 1: 513-514; Lorenzo Valla, *De Falso Credita et Ementita Constantini Donatione*, ed. Wolfram Setz, [Monumenta Germaniae Historica: Quellen zur Geistesgeschichte des Mittelalters, 10] (München: Monumenta Germaniae Historica, 1986), 17. Ulrich von Hutten published editions of Valla's work in 1506, 1518, and 1519, thus making it part of the early Protestant polemic against papal temporal power. The Donation of Constantine was incorporated into the *Corpus juris canonici*, 1: cols. 342-345, Decreti primi pars, Distinctio XCVI, caps 13-14.

4. Dante Alighieri, *On World Government* (De Monarchia), 2nd rev. ed., trans. Herbert W. Schneider, [Library of Liberal Arts] (Indianapolis: The Bobbs-Merrill Company, Inc., 1949), 10-23, 62-80; Anthony K. Cassell, *The Monarchia Controversy: an Historical Study with Accompanying Translations of Dante Aligheri's Monarchia, Guido Vernani's Refutation of the Monarchia Composed by Dante, and Pope John XXII's Bull Si fratrum* (Washington, DC: Catholic University of America Press, 2004).

Nonetheless, despite Christ's insistence that one should render to God the things that are God's and to Caesar those that are his, and that Christ's kingdom is not of this world, supporters of papal claims to supreme authority over all Christians, especially canonists, identified the Church with the "commonwealth" or "kingdom" of Christendom, "a universal juridical entity led by an absolutist Vicar of Christ."[5] In addition, the term "the mystical body of Christ" came into use by the medieval theologians such as Bonaventura (ca.1217-74) and Tommaso d'Aquino (1225-74) to describe the Church, and this led to analogies with civil bodies and how power was to be distributed.[6]

Theologians and canonists devoted attention to the nature of papal power. In defense of the claims to supreme authority of Boniface VIII in his struggle with Philip IV of France (1285-1314) and of John XXII (1316-34) in his fight with Emperor Ludwig IV (1314-47), three Augustinian friars wrote some of the first treatises on ecclesiology: Egidio Colonna da Roma (ca. 1245-1316), *De ecclesiastica potestate* (1301); Jacomo Capocci da Viterbo (ca. 1255-1308), *De regimine Christiano* (1302); and Agostino Trionfo d'Ancona (ca. 1241-1328), *Summa de potestate ecclesastica* (1326).

Egidio Colonna da Roma saw Christendom as a kingdom ruled by two powers: the spiritual exercised by prelates, especially the pope, while kings and other rulers wielded the temporal power. The spiritual power is superior, and it confers the temporal on princes whom it can judge and dismiss from office. The pope is the source of all power and only God can judge him. The pope's absolute power is such that he is not bound by any positive law. Egidio's treatise, that inspired the bull *Unam sanctam* (1302) of Boniface VIII, repeated the two swords theory and held for the superiority of the spiritual power over the temporal, just as the soul rules the body. The bull *Unam sanctam* was confirmed in the decree *Pastor Aeternus* (1516) of the Fifth Lateran Council. Egidio was considered the primary theologian of the Augustinian friars and his papal hierocratic ideas were adopted by his order, to which Luther belonged. [7]

---

5. Guillaume H. M. Posthumus Meyjes, *Jean Gerson, Apostle of Unity: His Church Politics and Ecclesiology*, trans. John C. Grayson, [Studies in the History of Christian Thought, XCIV] (Leiden: Brill. 1999), 208.

6. Francis Oakley, *The Political Thought of Pierre d'Ailly: The Voluntarist Tradition*, [Yale Historical Publications, Miscellany 81] (New Haven: Yale University Press, 1964), 55-57.

7. Robert W. Dyson, ed., *Giles of Rome's* On Ecclesiastical Power: *A Medieval Theory of World Government. A Critical Edition and Translation*, [Records of Western Civilization] (New York: Columbia University Press, 2004), p. xx; pars I, cap. II-IV, pp. 7-21; pars II, cap. IV, pp. 92-94; pars II, cap. VII, pp, 131-41; on the reaffirmation of *Unam Sanctam* by Lateran V, see Giuseppe Alberigo and Alberto Melloni, eds., *Conciliorum oecumenicorum generaliumque decreta; Editio critica*, 3 vols., Vol. II/2: *The General Councils of Latin Christendom. From Basel to Lateran V (1431-1517)*, eds. Frederick Lauritzen, Nelson. H. Minnich, Joachim Stieber, Harald Suermann, and Jürgen Uhlich (Turnhout:

Jacomo Capocci da Viterbo identified the visible Church with Christian society, which he saw as the kingdom of Christ ruled by His vicar, the papal monarch. He claimed that the Church possessed temporal jurisdiction, but the pope should exercise this authority over rulers only when necessary. Christ, as both God and man, is king of both the heavenly and earthly kingdoms; as man he possesses priestly powers. He confers on His prelate vicars both the royal power of jurisdiction and the priestly power of orders. The pope is His special vicar, the supreme monarch of the Church Militant, with the plentitude of power over all kings and prelates. They all derive their jurisdictional authority from him when he ratifies and approves their institution as rulers. The pope delegates to kings the management of earthly things, but he can also rescind their powers and depose them.[8]

Agostino Trionfo d'Ancona also saw the Church as a unitary, hierarchical society over which the pope presided as the mediator between God and man, as ruler and head.[9] From his decisions there is no appeal. The Church cannot

---

Brepols Publishers, 2013), 1440, lines 3616-23—hereafter this volume is cited as COGD, II/2; Eric Leland Saak, *Luther and the Reformation of the Later Middle Ages* (Cambridge: Cambridge University Press, 2017), 13-14, 315-27.

8. James of Viterbo, *On Christian Government (De regimine christiano)*, trans. and introduced by Robert W. Dyson (Woodbridge, Suffolk, UK: The Boydell Press, 1995), 4-40 (the Church is a kingdom, one, universal, holy, and apostolic), 41-53 (Christ is a true king), 85-86 (the pope, the successor of Peter, is Christ's vicar who acts principally, absolutely, and universally on Christ's behalf on earth), 116-119 (pope can intervene in temporal affairs by his spiritual and temporal powers given to him by divine law and by the kingship granted to him by Constantine), 128-135 (the pope has the fullness of both spiritual and temporal power), 143-144 (James tries to explain away Christ's statement that His kingdom is not of this world—because Christ did not exercise power over temporal things, "it does not follow that His vicar may not exercise it, especially in necessary cases." p. 144); Michael Wilks, *The Problem of Sovereignty in the Later Middle Ages: The Papal Monarchy with Augustinus Triumphus and the Publicists* (Cambridge: Cambridge University Press, 1963), 297-99, 334, 377; Saak, *Luther and the Reformation,* 316-27.

9. Augustinus Triumphus de Ancona, *De potestate ecclesiastica* (Köln: Arnold Ter Hoernen, 1475): "Omnino error est ut puto pertinacimenti non credere romanum pontificem universalis ecclesie pastorem, petri successorem, et christi legitimum vicarium supra spiritualia et temporalia universalem non habere primatum in quem quandoque multi labuntur dicte potestatis ignorantia; que cum sit infinitum eo quo magnus dominus et magna virtus eius et magnitudinis eius non est finis omnis creates intellectus in eius perstructione invenitur deficere." Prologue, [fol. 1r, sig. a1r]; "Totalis enim et universalis dominus spiritualium et temporalium est ipse christus et vicarius eius summus pontifex." Quest. xxxvi, art. iii [fol. 147r, sig. p7r]; "Quantum do ad religioinis christiane conversationem, tenetur omnis christianus pape obedire quia ad ordinandum qualiter in religione christiana vivendum est nullus est superior ipso potissime cum ipse sit sequester et medius inter deum et hominem seu totum populum christianum." Quest. xxii, art. iv [fol. 93v, sig. k3v]; "Medius autem inter deum et populum christianum est ipse papa unde nulla lex populo christiano est danda nisi ipsius papae auctoritate." Quest. xliiii, art. I [fol. 104r, sig. k4r]

err.[10] Secular rulers are his ministers.[11] While bishops and priests receive their sacramental powers directly from Christ, their jurisdictional powers come by way of mediation only from the pope, who is Christ's vicar.[12] Agostino argued that Christ was a true king, and hence his vicar exercises his royal power.[13] Agostino also claimed that Emperor Constantine recognized the pope's supreme authority as God's vicar by restoring to Pope Sylvester his proper power.[14] Agostino's treatise was reprinted five times in the second half of the fifteenth century following the invention of printing, and was carefully studied in Roman circles. But there is no evidence that Martin Luther in Germany ever read the ecclesiological treatises of his fellow Augustinian friars from early fourteenth-century Italy.[15]

In the century prior to the Reformation, two Dominicans became the principal exponents of the theory of papal monarchy. The Spanish Dominican theologian Juan de Torquemada (1388-1468) played a principal role in defending

10. "Ad tercium est dicendum quod ecclesia non potest errare quia si unus solus catholicus remaneret, ille esset ecclesia, vel ecclesia non potest errare utendo clavem scientie secundum rationabilem usum et secundum intellectum quo inspirata est." Quest. xx, art. vi [fol. 88v, sig. j9v]

11. "papa sit maiore imperatore vel rege . . . omnes subijciuntur pape de iure divino." Quest. xxii, art. iii [fol. 92v-93r, sig. k2v-3r]; "Primo quod papa confert imperatori immediatam administrationem et est minister ecclesie in administatione temporalium quam non confert aliis." Quest.. xxxix, art. i [fol. 156r, sig. q6v]

12. "Sed loquamur de potestate iurisdictionis si non accipiatur talis potestas iurisdictionis in spiritualibus sicut in temporalibus nullus est equalis pape in tali potestate quia omnes alii episcopi vocati sunt in partem sollicitudinis et administrationis. Solus autem papa habet administrationem in toto orbe." Quest.i, art. iv [fol.5v, sig. 5v]; "Dicendum quod singulariter solus petrus dicitur habere claves per immediatam commissionem, per immediatam derivationem, per universalem administationem, per immediatam quidem commissionem, quia soli petro cuius successor papa existit claves sunt commisse . . . quia solus ipse in tota ecclesia universaliter Christi vicarius existit." Quest. xx, art. iii [fol. 87v, sig. j8r]; "papa qui est vicarius eius [Christi] instrumentaliter" Quest. xix, art. ii [fol.84r-v, sig. j4r-v]

13. Augustinus argued that Christ was a king by his incarnation, born of a royal tribe, a son of David, a son of God Almighty, welcomed as king into Jerusalem, and at the end of Matthew's Gospel [28:18], Christ said all power in heaven and on earth had been given to him. Quest. I, art. vii [fol. 8r-9r, sig. a8v-9v]

14. "Et si inveniatur quandoque aliquos imperatores dedisse aliqua temporalia summis pontificibus sicut constantinus dedit silvestro, hoc non est intelligendum quod suum est, sed restituetur quod iniuste et tyrannice oblatum est." Quest. i, [fol. 2v, sig. a2v]; "illa que constantinus dei beneficio receipt de manu domini hec ipsa tribuit silvestro vicario eius modo quo dixit david in psalmi ultimo." Quest. ci, art. iv, ad primum [fol. 331v, sig. l, 1v]; "Ad tercium est dicendum quod imperator nullum superiorem se recognoscit dominum temporalem qui fungatur auctoritate puri hominis, sed tenendum recognoscere superiorem se vicarium illius qui est verus deus et verus homo." Quest. xxxviii, art. iv [fol. 177v, sig. q5v]

15. Wilks, *Problem of Sovereignty*, 254-87, 377-399, 543 n. 1; Saak, *Luther and the Reformation*, 247, 321-32, 340.

papal prerogatives at the Council of Basel–Ferrara–Florence (1438–45). He helped to compose two conciliar bulls. *Laetentur coeli* (1439) stated:

> We also define that the holy apostolic see and the Roman pontiff holds the primacy over the whole world and the Roman pontiff is the successor of blessed Peter prince of the apostles, and that he is the true vicar of Christ, the head of the whole church and the father and teacher of all Christians, and to him was committed in blessed Peter the full power of tending, ruling, and governing the whole church, as is contained also in the acts of ecumenical councils and in the sacred canons.[16]

The subsequent bull *Moyses, vir Dei* (1439) stated that the pope is the vicar of Christ, superior in authority and status even to Moses. The Roman church is mother and mistress of all the faithful. To make of the disciplinary decree *Haec sancta* of Konstanz a dogmatic statement is a false and pernicious interpretation of the decree.[17] In his synodal oration (1439) and *Summa de ecclesia* (1453), Torquemada advanced the notion of papal monarchy. Based on Pseudo-Dionysius's vision of heavenly and ecclesiastical hierarchies, Torquemada claimed that a system of governance that places all authority in one person conforms to the natural ordering of the universe, as is evident in the social structures of bees and cranes. It is the head that gives direction and co-ordination to the other parts of the human body. So too in human society, superiors order inferiors according to reasons and justice and thus allow society to function properly. The Church needs an absolute principle of authority, and that is the pope. The fullest authority is the pope in conjunction with a council convoked by him, and whose decrees he confirms. Should the pope fail to function properly in his office, a council can meet on its own on an emergency basis with the sole task of restoring the papal monarchy and not of restructuring the constitution of the Church.[18]

---

16. Giuseppe Alberigo et al., eds., *The Decrees of the Ecumenical Councils*, English trans. editor Norman Tanner, 2 vols. (Washington, DC: Georgetown University Press, 1990), I, p. *528; COGD, II/2, p. 1217, lines 1204-18 – hereafter cited as Alberigo-Tanner.

17. Alberigo-Tanner, pp. 529-30; COGD, II/2, p. 1219, line 1263; p. 1222, lines 1377-90.

18. Thomas M. Izbicki, "The Revival of Papalism at the Council of Basel," in: *A Companion to the Council of Basel*, eds. Michael Decaluwé, Thomas M. Izbicki, and Gerald Christianson, [Brill's Companions to the Christian Tradition, 74] (Leiden: Brill, 2017), 137-163, esp. 154-157; Ulrich Horst, *The Dominicans and the Pope: Papal Teaching Authority in the Medieval and Early Modern Thomist Tradition,* trans. James D. Mixson (Notre Dame, IN: University of Notre Dame Press, 2006), 36-39. In his famous letter to the University of Cologne known as *In minoribus* (1463), the former conciliarist who became Pope Pius II (1405-64, r. 1458-64) re-iterated some of the same arguments for papal power advanced by Torquemada. Thus, the regime given to the Church by Divine Providence demands that inferiors be governed by superiors and that they bring everything below

Tommaso de Vio, known as Cajetan (1468-1533), Master General of the Order of Preachers (1508-18), and cardinal (1517), was the principal literary opponent of the Council of Pisa-Milan-Asti-Lyon (1511-12) that suspended Julius II from exercising his papal office. Against this council, de Vio published two treatises, *De comparatione auctoritatis Papae et Concilii* (1511) and *Apologia de comparata auctoritate Papae et Concilii* (1514), and his sermon at the second session of the Fifth Lateran Council (1512-17) under the title *Oratio de ecclesiae et synodorum differentia* (1512). In these works, de Vio argued that God has placed the pope at the summit of the Church to guide the faithful with the assistance of the Holy Spirit. There are no limitations on the pope's power coming from a supposed aristocratic or democratic constitution of the Church. Like the Lamb Who reigns over the heavenly Jerusalem, His vicar presides over the Church, which is the perfect city of the Christian republic composed of a holy people tightly united in bonds of love with one another and with Christ, as His co-heirs and members of His mystical Body. This "city of peace," community of saints, and family of God is ruled over by the vicar of Christ, whose supreme power is the greatest after God and flows from the head into the body of the Church. The pope provides for the Church laws that others are to implement.[19]

Variants of the papal monarch theory limited that authority by invoking Roman law concepts of corporation. Thus, it was the Roman Church, rather than the pope himself, who possessed ultimate power. A bishop is required

---

themselves finally under one, the prince and governor of all. Just as cranes follow one leader and one bee is ruler among all others, so also in the church militant, which resembles the church triumphant, one is governor and judge of all, the vicar of Jesus Christ from whom, as head, all subordinate members derive all power and authority which flows into it from Christ our lord God, without an intermediary. See *Accept Pius, Reject Aeneas: Selected Letters of Aeneas Sylvius Piccolomini (Pope Pius II),* trans. Thomas M. Izbicki, Gerald Christianson, and Philip Krey (Washington, DC: The Catholic University of America Press, 2006), 395.

19. Charles Morerod, OP, "Le discours de Cajetan au Ve Concile de Latran," *Revue Thomiste* 105 (2005): 595-638, esp. 603, 606-08, 613-14, 627-28, 634; Nelson H. Minnich, "Concepts of Reform Proposed at the Fifth Lateran Council," *Archivum Historiae Pontificiae* 16 (1984): 163-251, reprinted with new appendices 252*-53*in his: *The Fifth Lateran Council (1512-17): Studies on Its Membership, Diplomacy, and Proposals for Reform,* [Variorum Collected Studies, CS392] (Aldershot, UK: Ashgate, 1993), here 175-179, 239-241; Olivier de la Brosse, *Le pape et le concile: La comparaison de leur pouvoirs à la veille de la Réforme,* [Unam Sanctam, 58] (Paris: Cerf, 1965), 147-59, 320-326. A critical edition with commentary of these two treatises has been published as *De comparatione auctoritatis papae et concilii cum apologia eiusdem tractatus,* [Scripta theologica, 1], ed. Vincentius Maria Iacobus Pollet, OP (Rome: Apud Institutum Angelicum, 1936); an English translation of these two treatises is available in James H. Burns and Thomas M. Izbicki, eds., *Conciliarism and Papalism,* [Cambridge Texts in the History of Political Thought] (Cambridge: Cambridge University Press, 1977), 1-133 (Authority) and 201-284 (Apology), here 2-5, 26-30.

to obtain the consent of the cathedral chapter when making major decisions; so, too, the pope has to seek the advice and consent of the College of Cardinals. Together they constitute the Apostolic See. This teaching can be found in theologians such as Juan Torquemada and in canonists such as Francesco Zabarella.[20]

By the late fifteenth century a legend about the origins of the cardinalate had grown up and was incorporated into the papal ceremonial. According to this account, Peter under divine inspiration set up a Senate for the Roman Church to advise and assist him on difficult matters and to elect Roman pontiffs. It consisted of twenty-four senators chosen from the priests and deacons of Rome, and was modeled on the twenty-four elders who stand before the throne of God in the Book of Revelation (Apoc 19: 4). When Peter proposed that Clement be his successor, the Senate rejected his choice and chose Linus instead. Peter respected their decision and henceforth the senators, whom Pope Sylvester later called cardinals, have elected the pope.[21] This legend, given credibility in inner papal circles, attributed to cardinals an apostolic foundation based on divine inspiration, a status similar to Senators, and the power to over-rule the pope. This was most dramatically demonstrated on the eve of the Reformation by a group of cardinals who convoked a council against Julius II that suspended him from the exercise of his offices.[22]

Another variant on the papal monarchy theory held that the monarchy was limited by an aristocratic constitution consisting of the bishops. Just as Peter was only one of the Apostles chosen by Christ who is the Church's cornerstone, its foundation stones are all the Apostles (Mt 10: 1–4; Eph 2: 20; Apoc 21: 14). The pope is to exercise his office in conjunction with the bishops. This is most evident in councils.[23] At the Fifth Lateran Council, the bishops pushed for the establishment of a *sodalitas* or quasi-college of bishops in the Roman Curia to protect their interests and advise the pope. So strong was the opposition of the

20. Francis Oakley, *The Conciliarist Tradition: Constitutionalism in the Catholic Church, 1300–1870* (Oxford: Oxford University Press, 2003), 68–69, 71, 107; Ulrich Horst, *The Dominicans and the Pope: Papal Teaching Authority in the Medieval and Early Modern Thomist Tradition*, trans. James D. Mixson (Notre Dame, IN: University of Notre Dame Press, 2006), 37–39; 69, 71.

21. Cristoforo Marcello, ed., *Caeremoniale Romanum of Agostino Patrizi, Piccolomini* (Venice: Gregorius de Gregoriis, 1516, reprinted Ridgewood, NJ: Gregg Press Incorporated, 1965), fol. Iiv [misprinted as VIIv]); Jennifer Mara DeSilva, "Senator or courtier: negotiating models for the College of Cardinals under Julius II and Leo X," *Renaissance Studies* 22 (2008): 154–73.

22. Walter Ullmann, "Julius II and the Schismatic Cardinals," in: *Schism, Heresy, and Religious Protest*, ed. Derek Baker, [Studies in Church History, 9] (Cambridge: Cambridge University Press, 1972), 177–193.

23. Nelson H. Minnich, "Girolamo Massaino: Another Conciliarist at the Papal Court, Julius II to Adrian VI," in: *Studies in Catholic History in Honor of John Tracy Ellis*, eds. Nelson H. Minnich, Robert B. Eno, and Robert Trisco (Wilmington, Del.: Michael Glazier, Inc., 1985), 520–565.

cardinals to this proposal that Leo X imposed a perpetual silence on it.[24] Papalists tried to limit the authority of bishops by insisting that the pope must convoke the council and approve its decisions. But even they admitted that in special situations, such as a pope guilty of heresy or causing grave harm to the Church, a council can act on its own to remove him from office.[25]

The Great Western Schism (1378-1417) became the occasion for the development of conciliarist theories. They were based on a mixture of scriptural and canonical texts and on analogies drawn from civil society. The Gospel of Matthew (18: 17) prescribes the censuring of an errant and unrepentant member by the whole church; thus, an obstinately heretical or scandalous pope is to be rebuked by a general council. In the Epistle to the Galatians (2: 11, 14), Paul openly opposed and criticized Peter in the assembly of elders in Antioch. Canon law held that a heretical pope could be removed from office. He was subject to the judgment of the College of Cardinals or of a general council.[26] Writers argued that just as civil society can remove a ruler whose actions are destroying it, so too can the Church a destructive pope. The whole is greater than any of its parts. When the positive law of the Church fails to provide a solution to a grave situation, necessity (*epikeia*) allows for new measures that do.[27]

Three men may be considered the principal early formulators of the conciliarist theory: Pierre d'Ailly (1350-1420), Jean Charlier de Gerson (1363-1429), and Francesco Zabarella (ca. 1335-1417). They saw the Church as the universal congregation of the faithful, and the clerical offices as divinely instituted. Gerson emphasized the clerical nature of the Church by equating it with a hierarchical organism whose power is distributed throughout, from pope to priests.[28] The community through its delegates elects the clergy. While the pope has the plentitude of power, he holds it in a ministerial capacity, and final

24. Nelson H. Minnich, "The Proposals for an Episcopal College at Lateran V," in: *Ecclesia Militans: Studien zur Konzilien und Reformationsgeschichte. Remigius Bäumer zum 70. Geburtstag gewidmet,* eds. Walter Brandmüller, Herbert Immenkötter, and Erwin Iserloh, 2 vols. (Paderborn: Ferdinand Schöningh, 1988), Band I: *Zur Konziliengeschichte,* 213- 232.

25. Brian Tierney, *Foundations of the Conciliar Theory: The Contribution of the Medieval Canonists from Gratian to the Great Schism* (Cambridge: Cambridge University Press, 1955, reprint 1968), 245.

26. *Corpus juris canonici,* Decreti prima pars, Dist. XL, cap. 6, ed. Friedberg, I, col. 146; Tierney, *Foundations,* 60-67

27. Tierney, *Foundations,* 56-67, 171-176, 227-230.

28. Louis B. Pascoe, *Jean Gerson: Principles of Church Reform,* [Studies in Medieval and Reformation Thought, VII] (Leiden: E. J. Brill, 1973), 17-39; Guillaume H. M. Posthumus Meyjes, *Jean Gerson, Apostle of Unity: His Church Politics and Ecclesiology,* trans. John Christopher Grayson, [Studies in the History of Christian Thought, XCIV] (Leiden: Brill, 1999), 248-278, 287-298. Meyjes considers the sources of Gerson's ecclesiology to be Bonaventure, Aquinas, Durand de Pourçain, Henry of Ghent, and the Augustinian curialists and canonists, not Ockham or Marsiglio, Ibid., 342-352, 364-379.

authority rests with the community that retains the power to remove him for heresy or causing the ruin of the Church. It exercises this power through its representatives in a general council. Later conciliarists such as Juan Alfonsi Gonzalez de Segovia (1393-1458) gave unlimited jurisdiction to a general council and made the pope its servant.[29] A moderate middle ground is found in the *De concordantia catholica* (1433/34) of Nikolaus Krebs von Kues (1401-64) who sought to harmonize, based on Scripture and the history of the ancient councils, the local church with the universal church. He saw the Church as a congregation or brotherhood of the faithful united with their bishops and with Christ in one mystical body. He granted to the pope a special authority to convoke, preside over, and promulgate the council's decrees. The council, however, has its authority directly from Christ and any lack of co-operation by the pope with its decisions does not invalidate them, a problem Krebs does not resolve in his treatise.[30]

The situation that occurred when two rival claimants to papal power excommunicated each other and their followers did great damage to the Church. Since neither would resign and their colleges of cardinals proceeded to elect successors, the good of the universal Church demanded a solution not found in canon law. Among the measures proposed, the one most in keeping with tradition was the assembling of a general council to end the schism. When some cardinals from both the Roman and Avignonese obediences assembled a council in Pisa in 1409, it deposed both popes and elected a new one. But those deposed continued to have followers and now there were three popes.[31] The Pisan pope, on the urgings of the emperor-elect Sigismund, convoked the Council of Konstanz (1414-18). When the Pisan pope John XXIII (1410-15) fled from the council, it issued its famous decree *Haec Sancta* (1415), declaring that its authority came directly from God and not from the pope, and that all Christians were obliged to obey it in matters of unity, faith, and reform.[32] The council then deposed the Pisan pope, negotiated the abdication of the Roman pope, Gregory XII (1406-15) who first convoked the council in his own name,

29. Oakley, *The Political Thought of d'Ailly*, 42-65; and his *Conciliarist Tradition*, 67-81.

30. Giuseppe Alberigo, *Chiesa conciliare: Identità e significato del conciliarismo*, [Testi e ricerche di Scienze religiose, 19] (Brescia: Paideia Editrice, 1981), 296-334.

31. Aldo Landi, *Il papa deposto (Pisa 1409): L'idea conciliare nella Grande Scisma*, [Studi storici] (Torino: Claudiana, 1985).

32. COGD, II/I, 546-550, session IV version, lines 119-166, session V version, lines 169-222; Michael Decaluwe, "Three Ways to Read the Constance decree *Haec sancta* (1415): Francis Zabarella, Jean Gerson, and the Traditional Papal View of General Councils," in: *The Church, the Councils, & Reform: The Legacy of the Fifteenth Century*, eds. Gerald Christianson, Thomas M. Izbicki, and Christopher M. Bellitto (Washington, DC: The Catholic University of America Press, 2008), 122-139.

and after failed negotiations with the Avignonese pope Benedict XIII (1394–1417) deposed him, too. To make the general council henceforth a constitutive element in the governance of the Church, Konstanz issued the decree *Frequens* (1417), requiring the regular celebration of general councils.[33] A committee composed of cardinals from all three obediences, together with representatives of the council, then elected a new pope, Martin V (1417–31).[34]

Once the Schism was over, the popes worked to restore the papal monarchy. Martin V gave an ambiguous approval to the decrees of the council. While he never openly confirmed *Haec Sancta*, he obeyed *Frequens* by convoking the councils of Pavia–Siena (1423–24) and Basel (1431–49). When his successor Eugenius IV (1431–47) tried to close the Council of Basel, and failing that, tried to transfer it to Ferrara, the fathers at Basel issued the decree *Sacrosancta* (1439) which claimed that the superiority of councils was a dogma of the Faith.[35] The papal council moved from Ferrara to Florence, where it issued the decree *Moysis vir* (1439) that condemned the assembly in Basel and rejected its decree as a false interpretation of the merely disciplinary decree *Haec Sancta,* which had questionable validity since it was issued by only the Pisan obedience.[36] To prevent any council from assembling without the pope in control of it, Pius II issued the decree *Execrabilis* (1460), forbidding any appeals to a council from a decision of the pope.[37] Leo X succeeded in terminating the schismatic Council of Pisa–Milan–Asti–Lyon (1511–13), and in getting its former adherents to abjure its erroneous teaching on conciliar power.[38] His decree *Pastor Aeternus* (1516) of the Fifth Lateran Council (1512–17) insisted that when there is clearly only one pope, he alone has the power to convoke, transfer, and close a council. That conciliar bull also reaffirmed the papal constitution *Unam Sanctam* of Boniface VIII with its exaltation of papal monarchy. The concordats Eugenius IV had negotiated with the German princes (1447), Nicholas V with the emperor (1448), and Leo X with the French king (1516) removed much of the threat to papal power

33. COGD, II/1, 608–609, lines 1617–1647.

34. Walter Brandmüller, *Das Konzil von Konstanz 1414–1418,* [Konziliengeschichte, Reihe A: Darstellungen]. (Paderborn: Ferdinand Schöningh, 1991–97).

35. COGD, II/2, 1064–1065, lines 9847–9899: *Sarosancta . . . Sicut una est,* esp. line 9889: *veritas fidei catholicae*

36. COGD, II/2, 1218–24, esp. lines 1377–1455.

37. Carl Mirbt and Kurt Aland, eds., *Quellen zur Geschichte des Papsttums und des römischen Katholizismus,* 6th ed., Band I : *Von den Anfängen bis zum Tridentinum* (Tübingen: J.C.B. Mohr [Paul Siebeck], 1967), 490–491, Nr. 778.

38. Nelson H. Minnich, "The Healing of the Pisan Schism (1511–13)," *Annuarium Historiae Conciliorum* 16 (1984): 59–192. Reprinted with new appendices added in his *The Fifth Lateran Council (1512–17): Studies on Its Membership, Diplomacy, and Proposals for Reform,* [Collected Studies Series, CS 392] (London: Variorum, 1993).

coming from councils.[39] Luther's appeal to a general council on 28 November 1518 against a possible negative judgment against him following the meeting with the papal legate Tommaso de Vio in Augsburg in October had little likelihood of success.[40] Papal monarchy was in ascendency over conciliarism.

Yet another model of the Church, one that put laity in leadership roles, had ancient roots. In the pagan Roman Empire, the head of the college of priests, known as the *pontifex maximus*, was responsible for the organization of the state religion and, ever since the time of Julius Caesar, emperors held that office.[41] It is not surprising then that when the emperors converted to Christianity, they continued to have a role in managing the religion. They convoked and presided over councils that handled the major doctrinal and disciplinary issues of the Church. They also could have a strong voice in the appointment of patriarchs and bishops.[42] In the West, the invading Germanic tribes brought with them the institution of "proprietary religion," whereby the head of the tribe hired and paid the pagan priests who served in his household. When the Germans converted to Christianity, they now appointed Christian priests to serve as their chaplains. Eventually, the power of appointment became the prerogative of the dukes, then kings, and finally the emperor. These rulers built churches and monasteries and endowed them with property, claiming the right to appoint their incumbents and to share in their revenues. The Investiture Controversy ended with a compromise that recognized the rights of rulers to nominate candidates to certain church offices and to grant them the temporal symbols of the office, but the actual appointment to an ecclesiastical office rested with the pope or local episcopal collators.[43] Starting with the concordats negotiated at the Council

39. Nelson H. Minnich, "Luther, Cajetan, and *Pastor Aeternus* (1516) of Lateran V on Conciliar Authority," in: *Martin Luther in Rom: Die Ewige Stadt als kosmopolitisches Zentrum und ihre Wahrnehmung*, eds. Michael Matheus, Arnold Nesselrath, and Martin Wallraff, [Bibliothek des Deutschen Historischen Instituts in Rom, Band 134] (Berlin/Boston: De Gruyter Mouton, 2017), 187–204; published earlier in *The Decrees of the Fifth Lateran V (1512-17): Their Legitimacy. Origins, Contents, and Implementation*, [Variorum Collected Studies Series, CS1060] (London: Routledge, Taylor & Francis Group, 2016), VIII, 1–20.

40. Scott H. Hendrix, *Luther and the Papacy: Stages in a Reformation Conflict* (Philadelphia: Fortress Press, 181), 68–69.

41. Paul Harvey, *The Oxford Companion to Classical Literature*, rev. ed., [Oxford Paperback Reference] (Oxford: Oxford University Press, 1986), "Pontifices," 342; Stephen Edward Donlon, "Pontiff," *New Catholic Encyclopedia*, 11: 549; Philippe Levillain, "Titles, Papal," *The Papacy*, 3: 1494–95, "Summus Pontifex," 1495.

42. Walter Ullmann, "Caesaropapism," *The New Catholic Encyclopedia*, 2: 1049; Joseph R. Strayer, "Caesaropapaism," *Dictionary of the Middle Ages*, ed. Joseph R. Strayer, 13 vols. (New York: Charles Scribner's Sons, 1982–89), 3; 10–12.

43. Susan Wood, *The Proprietary Church in the Medieval West* (Oxford: Oxford University Press, 2006); Uta-Renate Blumenthal, *The Investiture Controversy: Church and Monarchy from the Ninth to the Twelfth Century* (Philadelphia: The University of Pennsylvania Press, 1988), 4–6.

of Konstanz in 1418, the popes in the course of the next century made similar arrangements with the major rulers of Western Christendom.[44]

The right of kings to resist papal interventions into their affairs was defended by the Dominican Jean Quidort of Paris (ca. 1240-1306) in his treatise *De potestate regia et papali* (1302/03). Jean insisted that royal power is independent of episcopal or papal power, that the pope has no authority over the goods of laypersons, that a prince may use his own temporal sword to repel the violence of the papal spiritual sword, and that the emperor can by imperial and canonical authority depose a pope who is scandalizing the Church. Based on canon law, Jean allowed the College of Cardinals or general council to depose a pope for heresy, criminal behavior, or incompetence.[45]

In the case of an heretical pope, William of Ockham, OFM, (ca. 1285-ca. 1349) held that a council could make a declaratory judgment that the pope had *ipso facto* ceased to be pope due to his heresy. The Church is the congregation of the faithful who can elect delegates (even laity) to constitute that council.[46]

In the early fourteenth century, the philosopher-rector of the University of Paris, Marsiglio dei Mainardini of Padua in Italy (ca. 1280-ca. 1343), with possible assistance from Jean of Jandun from Champagne (ca. 1286-1328), composed the work *Defensor Pacis* (completed on 24 June 1324) on how to preserve peace in civil society.[47] It was a direct refutation of the ecclesiologies of the three Augustinian friars mentioned above.[48] In this treatise, Marsiglio laid out a vision of Christendom which he claimed was based on Sacred Scripture as interpreted by "the general council of believers"—or the weightier part of it, which constitutes the human legislator and it is the supreme authority. Its approval is necessary for the appointment of officials, and for any laws of popes or bishops to be binding under threat of temporal punishment. No bishop or priest has on his own coercive jurisdiction over or power to excommunicate any cleric or layman; that authority belongs to the human legislator. Bishops have equal authority immediately from Christ. Any subjection is not based on divine law. A general council can designate one bishop as superior to others. Papal claims to superiority are not based on Scripture but come from Constantine, the faith-

44. John A. F. Thomson, *Popes and Princes, 1417-1517: Politics and Polity in the Late Medieval Church,* [Early Modern Europe Today] (London: George Allen & Unwin, 1980), passim, esp. 151-183.

45. Arthur P. Monahan, trans., *John of Paris on Royal and Papal Power,* [Records of Civilization: Sources and Studies, XC] (New York: Columbia University Press, 1974), 7-9, 30-33, 118-123; Oakley, *Conciliarist Tradition,* 105-06.

46. Oakley, *Conciliarist Tradition,* 101-,02.

47. Alan Gewirth, *Marsilius of Padua: The Defender of Peace,* 2 vols. (New York: Columbia University Press, 1951), I, 20-21.

48. Saak, *Luther and the Reformation,* 326.

ful legislator. Together and with the consent of the faithful human legislator, the bishops can exercise authority over the pope and even excommunicate him. The faithful legislator checks the qualifications of candidates for church office, authorizes their promotion to orders, grants licenses to preach, regulates the establishment and number of churches, and approves the appointment of ministers in them. The wealth of the church, in excess of the need to maintain the clergy and help the poor, may be used for the common good by the human legislator. The faithful are obliged to provide food and clothing to clerics who minister to them, but are not obliged to pay tithes. The faithful legislator can compel bishops and other ministers to perform their pastoral duties. For a church council to be valid, it must be convoked by the authority of the faithful human legislator. Only such a council can issue disciplinary decrees, prohibit clerical marriage, and canonize saints.[49] The *Defensor Pacis* put the clergy under the supervision of the laity.

John XXII, by his decree *Licet juxta doctrinam* of 23 October 1328, censured five propositions in the work: 1) that Christ paid the tax to Caesar out of necessity and not condescension; 2) that Peter did not have more authority than the other Apostles; 3) that it pertains to the emperor to institute, punish, and depose popes; 4) that all priests, archbishops, and popes are equal in authority and jurisdiction; and 5) that the Church may not punish someone coercively unless with the consent of the emperor. In later documents, John XXII described Marsiglio and Jean as "two beasts coming forth from the abyss of Satan . . . spewing forth the sulfurous stench of hell and publishing detestable heresies against Our Redeemer in scandal of the faith."[50] The influence of Marsiglio on fifteenth-century conciliarist theory, once considered significant, is no longer accepted by scholars. While Johannes Eck accused Luther in the Leipzig Debate (1519) of adopting the ideas of Marsiglio, the friar ignored the charge, and it is doubtful if he had read the *Defensor Pacis*.[51] That work did become popular in the early years of the Reformation, being printed in Basel (1522).[52] A portion of the work was published in an English translation in 1535 by William Marshall, who

49. Gewirth, *Marsilius of Padua*, II, 426–31.

50. Cesare Baronio, Odorico Rainaldo, and Giacomo Laderchi, *Annales Ecclesastici,* tomus 24: *1313-1333,* ed. Augustin Theiner (Barri-Ducis: Ludovicus Guerin Typographus editor, 1872), annus 1327, nrs. 28–37, pp. 322–327; annus 1328, nrs. 6–7, pp. 339–340: *"duas bestias ex abysso Sathanae egressas . . . et inferni sulphureo puteo produentes, ac detestabiles haereses contra Redemptorem nostrum in scandalum fidei publicantes."*

51. Saak, *Luther and the Reformation,* 305–306, 333.

52. Guillaume Mollat, *The Popes at Avignon, 1305-1378,* trans. Janet Love (London: Thomas Nelson and Sons, 1963), 210 n. 2; Oakley, *Conciliarist Tradition,* 104–105; Thomas More, *The Debellation of Salem and Bizance,* ed. John Guy, Ralph Keen, Clarence H. Miller, and Ruth McGugan, [The Complete Works of St. Thomas More, 10] (New Haven: Yale University Press, 1987), 398 n. 3.

equated the English Parliament with the general council and Henry VIII, the "Supreme Head of the Church of England," with the faithful ruler. Other apologists of the Henrician settlement, such as Edward Fox, Richard Sampson, Stephen Gardiner, and Christopher St. German (ca. 1460–1541), seem also to have borrowed ideas from the *Defensor Pacis*.[53]

Earlier and in a similar vein, the English theologian John Wycliffe (ca. 1330–84) in his various treatises, especially in two from ca. 1378, the *De ecclesia* and *De officio pastorali*, held that the externals of the Church should be regulated by temporal lords. Borrowing from St. Augustine, he defined the true church as the *universitas fidelium praedestinatorum*, the congregation of all the predestined who are known only by God. The visible institutional church militant contains both those predestined for the heavenly city of God and those foreknown reprobates marked for damnation. For the clergy to exercise any jurisdiction they must be truly righteous, be among the predestined. Their edicts must conform to God's will as revealed in the Bible in order to be obligatory. Christian lay rulers are to see that only good men are appointed as bishops. They are also to supervise the status and morals of the clergy and punish those who are obstinate rebels. Parishioners should choose their curates who are to live off alms and have only sufficient food, drink, and clothing. Excessive goods are to be given to the poor. In his later treatise *De potestate papae* (1379/80), Wycliffe concluded that the office of pope was not of divine, but of human, institution. Given its occupants' failure to have the qualifications of St. Peter, it should be abolished as the office of the Antichrist.[54] During Wycliffe's lifetime, Parliament passed a series of measures known as the Statutes of Provisors and *Praemunire,* prohibiting papal interventions into English church affairs that Parliament had not approved.[55] Despite condemnations by the universities of Oxford, Paris, and

53. More, *Debellation of Salem*, 398 n. 3; Paul O'Grady, *Henry VIII and the Conforming Catholics* (Collegeville, MN: The Liturgical Press, 1990), 42–63.

54. Herbert B. Workman, *John Wyclif: A Study of the English Medieval Church*, 2 vols. (Oxford: Clarendon Press, 1926), II, 20–24; Matthew Spinka, *Advocates of Reform: From Wyclif to Erasmus,* [Library of Christian Classics, XIV] (Philadelphia: The Westminster Press, 1953), 27–28, 32–40, 56; Lowrie John Daly, *The Political Theory of John Wyclif* (Chicago: Loyola University Press, 1962), 85–86; Gordon Leff, *Heresy in the Later Middle Ages: The Relation of Heterodoxy to Dissent ca. 1250-1450,* 2 vols. (New York: Barnes & Noble, 1967), II, 541–45; Anthony Kenny, *Wyclif,* [Past Masters] (New York: Oxford University Press, 1985), 77–79; Anne Hudson, "Wyclif, John," *Dictionary of the Middle Ages*, 12: 706–710, here 707–08.

55. Richard II, "Statue of *Praemunire*" (1393), in: *Church and State through the Centuries: A Collection of Historic Documents with Commentaries*, ed. and trans. Sidney Z. Ehler and John B. Morrall (Westminster, MD: The Newman Press, 1954), 100–04. The statute protested against papal infringements (102), which the Pope had imposed "so that the Crown of England which hath been so free at all times that it hath been in subjection to no realm, but immediately subject to God in all things touching the regality of the same Crown, and to none other, should be submitted to the

Prague, and by the councils of London [the Blackfriars synod] (1382), Rome (1412) and Konstanz (1415), Wycliffe's ideas were kept alive into the sixteenth century by his followers known as Lollards.[56]

The Czech reformer Jan Hus (ca. 1378–1415) read Wycliffe's writings, notably his *De ecclesia* and *De potestate papae*, and at times borrowed from them verbatim.[57] His definition of the true church is similar to Wycliffe's: *omnium praedestinatorum universitas*. It is the mystical body of Christ, of which He alone is its head, and its predestined members on earth are in constant need of growth in sanctity. The successors of the apostles are to continue their work of teaching and sanctifying its members. The church militant consists both of those predestined for glory and for damnation; the former are of (*de*) the church, the latter in (*in*) it and will be purged from it at the Last Judgment. The true universal church is not equivalent with the Roman Catholic Church, which is spotted and wrinkled. It is not the Body of Christ, its institutions are not sacred, and its pope with his claims of universal jurisdiction is of human origins. Christ remains the head of the church. Historically, the church of Jerusalem ranked first, that of Antioch second. The pre-eminent authority of the bishop of Rome came from Emperor Constantine and the decree of a church council. Because of his faith and love, Peter was chosen to be the shepherd of Christ's church. Popes who have the authority of Peter should also have the virtues of Peter and thus exhibit an excellent dignity. Their spiritual functions of teaching and judging according to divine law derive from Christ, but not their supreme rank. The pronouncements of Roman popes and their Curia are to be accepted as probable if they are not contrary to Scripture. All bishops are successors of the apostles and are not different from the priests they ordain as ministers of Christ. They are to imitate His humility and poverty and serve the people by example, preaching, and administering the sacraments. The priest's role in confession is merely ministerial, to declare God's forgiveness. They are not to exercise coercive temporal authority, nor own

---

Pope, and the laws and statutes of the Realm by him defeated and avoided at his will, in perpetual destruction of the sovereignty of the King our lord, his Crown, his Regality and of all his Realm, which God defend."

56. Alberigo–Tanner, I, 411–416, 421–426, e.g. 413 condemning proposition nr. 37: "The Roman church is Satan's synagogue, and the pope is not the immediate and proximate vicar of Christ and the apostles." For a critical edition of these decrees, see COGD, II/1, pp. 551–58, 573–80, lines 244–432, 758–946, esp. p. 554, lines 323–24. Wycliffe's influence on William Langland's *Piers Plowman* (ca. 1370–90), while significant, is also limited in that Langland does not see the expropriation of church wealth by lay lords as a necessarily good solution to abuses, see David Aers, *Beyond Reformation? An Essay on William Langland's* Piers Plowman *and the End of Constantinian Christianity* (Notre Dame, IN: University of Notre Dame Press, 2015), 79–82, 98–103.

57. Matthew Spinka, *John Hus' Concept of the Church* (Princeton: Princeton University Press, 1966), 253–55.

property and sources of revenue. All three estates (the clergy, nobility, and lay people) should share in the administration of the church militant.[58] The Council of Konstanz condemned Hus' teachings, singling out for denunciation thirty propositions, many of which dealt with the church being composed of the predestined and the grounds for disobeying papal authority.[59] Hus's writings, which borrowed from Wycliffe's *Tractatus de Ecclesia*, were read by Luther.[60]

In France, the Pragmatic Sanction of Bourges (1438) gave Charles VII a significant role in enforcing the reform decrees of the Council of Basel. He claimed that God had established royal power to protect and defend the Church, and to see that the ancient institutions of ecclesiastical discipline were strengthened and observed. He was thus to defend the truths of Scripture and the ancient Gallican liberties whereby cathedral canons, and not the pope, chose bishops. Stimulated by his conscience, he was to prevent papal reservations and expectancies, the practice of simony, and the flow of money as fees to Rome, but he could also suggest an appropriate candidate to the electors.[61] French courts claimed the authority to hear appellate cases from ecclesiastical tribunals. Leading jurists such as Pierre Lizet, and the Parlement de Paris, claimed that the divine law and conciliar decrees gave authority to Christian magistrates to correct heretical teachings and prevent schism in the Church.[62] The French king by his coronation anointing was considered a quasi-cleric, someone with mixed temporal and spiritual powers who was responsible for the common good of the whole realm.[63] Francis I claimed that he was willing to replace the Pragmatic Sanction with the Concordat of Bologna because it got rid of such scandalous abuses as the loss of the rights of prelates to make collations due to papal expectatives that placed foreigners in French benefices and denied them to French clerics who had spent years at universities acquiring the appropriate skills. Cases were also needlessly appealed to the Roman courts, resulting in the loss of local rights and a high cost of litigation. The Concordat preserved the beneficial reforms in the Sanction, while granting the French kings the right to nominate candidates for the major secular and religious offices in the French church.[64]

58. Ibid., 255–289.

59. Alberigo-Tanner, I, 426–429; COGD, II/1, pp. 585–89, lines 1085–1160.

60. Saak, *Luther and the Reformation*, 335.

61. Charles VII, "The Pragmatic Sanction of Bourges (1438)," in: *Church and State through the Centuries: A Collection of Historic Documents with Commentaries*, ed. and trans. Sidney Z. Ehler and John B. Morrall (Westminster, MD: The Newman Press, 1954), 112–121; Tyler Lange, *The First French Reformation: Church Reform and the Origins of the Old Regime* (New York: Cambridge University Press, 2014), 78–81.

62. Ibid., 108.

63. Ibid., 5–7, 91.

64. Jules Thomas, *Le Concordat de 1516: Ses origines, son histoire au XVIe siècle,* 3 vols. (Paris: Librairie Alphonse Picard et Fils, 1910), II, 38–43; for a critical edition of the Concordat, *Primitiva*

In the Spanish kingdoms, Fernando and Isabella sought control over the Church by restricting ecclesiastical jurisdiction, allowing appeals to the Crown from ecclesiastical courts, and presenting candidates to ecclesiastical positions. Their *Ordenanzas Reales* required royal permission for a papal letter to be published in their kingdoms, and they expanded—with papal consent—the extent of royal patronage over episcopal appointments.[65]

If, in the Middle Ages, offices in the Church were controlled by the pope, bishops, cathedral and religious chapters, with lay rulers increasingly gaining patronage rights over them, on the local level many of the laity also belonged to other organizations where they practiced their faith apart from clerical supervision. While major religious events (baptism, funeral, Easter duty, etc.) were carried out in a cathedral, baptismal church, or parish, much of devotional life was found in confraternities that were lay-run. They controlled their own chapel, hired their own chaplain who followed the laity's wishes, held their own services that included chanting [*laudesi*], flagellation [*battuti*], scripture reading, and lay sermons in the vernacular. They had special dispensations for celebrating Masses and other religious practices in their own chapels. While Luther criticized these brotherhoods as drinking and banqueting clubs that engaged in a "swinish way of life," many were deeply dedicated to a more intense form of devotion. When looking for a model of the "reformed' church, the early Protestants scoured the Scriptures, but what they came up with was strikingly similar to what already existed in confraternities. As noted by Nicholas Terpstra, "there is hardly a single element of the 'new' lay-orientated Protestant worship practice and Church Order which does not have ample confraternal precedent. . . ."[66] Protestant churches were frequently organized like Catholic confraternities: a self-governing congregation of the faithful that elected its lay board of administrators who had the power to hire and fire the chaplain, to discipline members, to control finances, to build and maintain its place of meeting and worship. At their services, they engaged in Bible reading, congregational singing, lay preaching in the vernacular, and charitable care of members; thus, while the titles may have changed (the guild became the vestry), the functions remained the same.[67]

---

illa ecclesia, see COGD, II/II, 1410-33, lines 2684-3408; for a partial translation of the Concordat, see Ehler and Morrall, *Church and State*, 134-44.

65. Jocelyn Nigel Hillgarth, *The Spanish Kingdoms*, 2 vols. (Oxford: Clarendon Press, 1978), II: *1410-1516, Castilian Hegemony*, 394-99.

66. Nicholas Terpstra, "Ignatius, Confratello: Confraternities as Modes of Spiritual Community in Early Modern Society," in *Early Modern Catholicism: Essays in Honour of John W. O'Malley*, eds. Kathleen M. Comerford and Hilmar M. Pabel (Toronto: University of Toronto Press, 2001), 163-182, here 170.

67. Ibid., 170-172.

Prior to the controversy over indulgences, Martin Luther wrote no treatises on the Church and seems to have been ignorant of the ecclesiological writings of his forefathers in the Order of the Hermits of St. Augustine. His university lectures were based on an exegesis of Scripture and a careful reading of St. Augustine. In them, he distinguished between an invisible Church of the elect and the visible Church Militant, the latter divinely instituted with the pope as its sovereign ruler, to whom Christ has given all His power. He recognized in the Church many unworthy priests and prelates who were instruments of Satan. The indulgence controversy quickly turned to questions of church authority. As a result of his published exchanges with Silvestro Mazzolini of Prierio, the Dominican Master of the Sacred Palace (that is, the pope's official theologian), and of his public debate with Johannes Eck at Leipzig, Luther studied the Church Fathers, the decrees of church councils and Roman pontiffs, and the writings of canonists, especially those of the previous four hundred years. It is unclear if he also read some of the ecclesiological treatises here surveyed. From this investigation, Luther concluded that the claims of supremacy of the Roman Church were of recent and human origins, not of divine institution.[68] He came to see that his beliefs were similar to those of heretics such as Jan Hus, and he concluded that the pope must be the Anti-Christ.[69] His evolving theology of the Church will now be explored by Professor Dorothea Wendebourg.

68. Martin Luther, *Disputatio et excusatio adversus criminationes D. Iohannis Ecci*, in: Weimar Ausgabe, II, 61: "Romanam ecclesiam esse omnibus aliis superiorem probatur ex frigidissimis Romanorum pontificum decretis intra CCCC annos natis."

69. Saak, *Luther and the Reformation*, 252-264. It would not have been difficult for Luther to know the condemned views of Wycliffe and Hus because the decrees of the Council of Konstanz had been printed in Hagenau in 1500 and reprinted in Milan in 1511—see Nelson H. Minnich, "The First Printed Editions of the Modern Councils: from Konstanz to Lateran V (1499-1526)," *Annali dell' Istituto storico italo-germanico in Trento / Jahrbuch des italienisch-deutschen historischen Instituts in Trient* 29 (Bologna 2003), 447-69, here 450-42, reprinted in his *Councils of the Catholic Reformation: Pisa I (1409) to Trent (1545-63),* [Collected Studies Series, CS890] (Aldershot, UK: Ashgate/Variorum, 2008), II.

10. Martin Luther`s Ecclesiology

Dorothea Wendebourg

One might say I have been assigned the wrong topic. For the Church did not stand at the center of Martin Luther`s interest. Neither was ecclesiology the main object of his theological passion, nor were his reflection and activity focused on the reform of the Church, the much-discussed *reformatio ecclesiae*. The center was rather justification, the gift of salvation through the gospel of Jesus Christ appropriated by faith alone. It was only from this angle that the Church came into the picture. Luther asked what the right understanding of justification meant for the definition, the shape, and the life of the Church. However, from this angle the Church did come into the picture—and in that sense my topic is not so wrong after all. For in Luther`s eyes, it went without saying that without the Church there is no justification, no salvation, and no Christian faith. Only through the Church can a human being hear the gospel. And when he or she trusts the gospel he or she becomes a member of the Church. Thus, the same Luther for whom the Church never came first, but always second, wrote emphatically: "*Ecclesia* shall be my fortress, my palace, my chamber."[1] Outside of the Church "there is no truth, no Christ, no eternal bliss"[2]

1. THE SOURCES

The theological background I have just outlined explains how Luther dealt with the Church in his writings. There is a host of statements about this subject from his pen, but very few of his works are explicitly ecclesiological. In most cases, he dealt with the Church in the context of other issues or discussed practical questions which were important for the establishment of an evangelical ecclesial body. Besides, the concerns prevalent in his statements on the Church vary according to the state of the theological debates and the historical situations. Thus, he never laid down a systematic ecclesiology. However, the basic lines which governed whatever he said and wrote about the Church remained the same, ever since the evangelical doctrine of justification had found its final shape. Thus, while the lack of a comprehensive and systematic ecclesiological treatise makes it necessary to look for statements on the Church in all kinds of works written by him in the course of his life, it is also possible to do so because of their theological coherence.

---

1. WA, 44: 713, 1 (LW 8:183). Translations given here do not precisely match those in the English-language versions cited.
2.. WA, 10/1/1,140,17 (LW 52:40).

In his early years, Luther mentioned the Church but rarely and marginally. He went into the subject more broadly only when he criticized the church of his time, which he did less for individual grievances than for its severe spiritual defects. After Rome's conflict with the Saxon friar had begun (1518), his criticism, embedded in a comprehensive negative judgement on the state of the church of his time—which in Luther's eyes lived in a "Babylonian Captivity"—was directed sharply against the church's authorities, first of all the Papacy. This led to his first ecclesiological treatise *Vom Papsttum zu Rom wider den hochberühmten Romanisten zu Leipzig* (1520).[3] As soon as it became necessary to reform the territories where the Reformation had taken hold according to evangelical insights, Luther complemented his critical arguments with constructive writings on various questions regarding the institutional structure of the Church, which included implicit or explicit ecclesiological statements. The first of these writings was *Daß eine christliche Versammlung oder Gemeine Macht und Recht habe, alle Lehre zu urteilen* from 1523;[4] then followed treatises on the reform of worship in the middle of the 1520s[5] and the Wittenberg liturgy of ordination in 1535,[6] finally the *Exempel einen rechten christlichen Bischof zu weihen*,[7] written in 1542 in the context of the endeavor to create a genuine evangelical episcopacy. In his later years, Luther also produced several treatises which were largely dedicated to the theological understanding of the Church, called forth not least by the ever more evident reality of two antagonistic church bodies side by side. Of particular weight were *Von der Winkelmesse und Pfaffenweihe* (1533),[8] his most important ecclesiological work *Von den Konziliis und Kirchen* (1539),[9] and *Wider Hans Worst* (1541).[10]

2. THE CHURCH AS *COMMUNIO ABSCONDITA*

There is one *cantus firmus* which runs through all of Luther's statements about the Church from his early period right to the end. It is the declaration that the church is the communion of those who hear the Gospel and believe in it. This declaration is nothing short of a definition, as the *Smalcald Articles* say: "Thank God, a seven-year-old child knows what the Church is, namely the

---

3. WA, 6: 285–324 (LW 39:49–104).

4. WA, 11: 408–416 (LW 39:301–314).

5. Particularly WA, 12: 35–37, 205–220 (LW 53: 11–14, 19–40); WA, 19: 73–113 (LW 53: 53–90).

6. WA, 38: 423–433, commented upon in WA, 41: 457, 33–459, 11; 762, 18–763: 18.

7. WA, 53: 231–260.

8. WA, 38: 195–256 (LW 38:147–214).

9. WA, 50: 509–653 (LW 41: 3–178).

10. WA, 51: 469–572 (LW 41:179–256).

holy believers and 'sheep who listen to the voice of their shepherd.' For thus pray the children: I believe one holy Christian Church."[11] This definition means: The church in its essence is communion—the "gathering,"[12] the "band of Christ-believing human beings,"[13] "Christendom,"[14] the "Christian, holy people,"[15] or "people of God,"[16] the "communion of the saints,"[17] or *communio sanctorum*,[18] as Luther wrote in ever new variations. Throughout his translation of the New Testament, Luther consequently rendered the Greek word ἐκκλησία by "Gemeine" (communion), which is at times to be understood in the sense of "local congregation" and in other instances means the whole of Christendom. In other words, the Church is first of all the totality of the persons who belong to it, not an institution. It is not bound to a certain place or a single church but lives "in all the world,"[19] as in Wittenberg so also "under the pope, the Turks, the Persians, the Tartars, and all over."[20]

However, the definition quoted before shows that the Church is a particular communion, the communion of those who believe in Christ.[21] It is such not by its own strength but thanks to the power of the Holy Spirit. The Spirit "calls, gathers, illuminates, sanctifies Christendom and keeps it in the true, one faith" as we read in the *Small Catechism*.[22] In other words, the Spirit makes the communion of believers the One, Holy, Catholic, and Apostolic Church. From the fact that the Spirit brings forth the Church by creating the communion of believers follows a fundamental consequence: The One, Holy, Catholic, and Apostolic Church is not an entity evident to anybody, but a hidden reality: *Abscondita est ecclesia, latent sancti* ("the Church is hidden, the saints are concealed").[23] This does not mean that the Church is not an empirical reality in space and time[24]—in order to avoid this widespread misunderstanding, Luther

11. WA, 50: 250, 1-7 (Robert Kolb and Timothy J. Wengert, eds., *The Book of Concord: The Confessions of the Evangelical Lutheran Church* (Minneapolis: Fortress Press, 2000), 324f); cf. WA, 50: 624, 14–18 (LW 41:143).

12. WA, 7: 219, 3; WA, 26: 506, 31 (LW 37:367) WA, 50: 624, 17 (LW 41: 143).

13. WA, 10/1/1:140,14f (LW 52: 39); cf. WA, 50: 624, 17 (LW 41:143).

14. WA, 26: 506, 35; WA, 507, 7 (LW 37: 367); WA, 30/1: 250, 9.12 (Kolb & Wengert, *Book of Concord*, 355–56).

15. WA, 50: 624, 29; 625, 21 (LW 41:143–144).

16. WA, 40/3: 505, 1 (LW 13:88).

17. WA, 30/1: 189, 28f (Kolb & Wengert, *Book of Concord*, 437).

18. WA, 7: 712, 39.

19. WA, 26: 506, 31 (LW 37: 367).

20. WA, 26: 506, 38f (LW 37: 367).

21. WA, 50: 624, 29 (LW 41: 143); cf. WA, 6: 300, 35f.

22. WA, 30/1: 368, 1-3 (Kolb & Wengert, *Book of Concord*, 355).

23. WA, 18: 652, 23 (LW 33: 89).

24. Cf. WA, 7: 683, 8-26 (LW 39: 218).

prefers the wording "hidden Church" (*ecclesia abscondita*) to the traditional Augustinian formula "invisible Church" (*ecclesia invisiblis*). As a communion of physical, visible, and audible human beings the Church is indeed visible and audible. But its essence, that which makes the Church the Church, is not accessible to human senses—it is "hidden." This is true because, as the communion of believers, it is manifest only to God, since only he can see into the heart of human beings[25] and diagnose who is a believer and thereby part of the church.[26]

Yet the hiddenness of the church has still another dimension. It has to do with that particular trait of salvation history Luther calls God`s acting *sub contrario* ("under the contrary"). The church is hidden insofar here on earth it is miserable, powerless, foolish, and scandalous, often exposed to derision and persecution— its real life thus being hidden *sub contrario* like that of its crucified Lord until it shall be manifest splendidly in heaven.[27] What is more, it is also hidden under sin, which sticks to the Church while it is in this world, since as the communion of the faithful it is the communion of the justified who on earth are at the same time still sinners—*simul iusti et confessores*. Thus the Church hides its spiritual reality by its own failure, abuses, scandals, divisions, under which only the eyes of faith are able nevertheless to identify the Church of Jesus Christ.[28] This sin can seize the doctrine, the form, and the life of the Church to such a degree and set them in such opposition to its essence that what comes to the fore is a false Church. In that case the Antichrist is at work, about whom the Bible not accidentally says that he is active within the Church of Christ—I shall come back to this point.

3. THE CHURCH AS *COMMUNIO EXTERNA*

All these statements about the Church`s hiddenness imply that the visible reality under which it is hidden has something to do with the Church itself, since otherwise it would be impossible to say that it is hidden precisely here and that what is hidden here is precisely the Church. Thus, the Church has also a visible side, it is also the "bodily, external" church.[29] It presents itself as an identifiable number of human beings whose unity has an institutional shape, who profess one common faith and do certain things together. In other words, the church has several external marks (*notae*) by which it can be seen, heard, and experienced: "First, this Christian, holy people can be recognized thereby that

25. WA, 17/2: 501, 32–35; cf. 21: 332, 37–333, 2.
26. WA, 6: 298, 2f, (LW 39: 71; 17/2: 510, 37f.)
27. WA, 4: 450, 39–451, 27; cf. WA, 5: 285, 35f; WA, 42: 187, 14–16 (LW 1:252).
28. WADB, 7: 418, 9–13; 418, 36–420, 4 (LW 35: 409–10); cf. WA, 7: 710, 1f.
29. WA, 1: 639, 3; WA, 6: 297, 2 (LW 39: 70).

it has the Word of God. . . . Secondly, it is to be recognized by the holy sacrament of Baptism." Thirdly, "by the holy sacrament of the Lord's Supper;" fourthly, "by the keys;" fifthly, "by [the fact] that it ordains ministers or has ministries;" sixthly, by "prayer, praise of God, and public thanksgiving;" seventhly, "by the sacred cross which it has to suffer in order to become like Christ its head."[30]

The number of the Church's marks which Luther puts together varies: at times it is larger, at times smaller.[31] They are, however, not all of the same weight. For not all of them are equally unequivocal in the sense that they allow one to say with certainty that wherever they are, there is the Christian Church. This is so only in the case of one essential feature, the third implication of the definition in the *Smalcald Articles* cited above: The Church is wherever the Word of God, more precisely, wherever the Gospel can be heard. In saying this, it is vital for the function of the Word as mark of the Church that "to be heard" means real, sensuous audibility, external "sound and words,"[32] proclaimed by human mouths: "We speak about the external word, preached orally by human beings as you and me. For such a thing Christ has left behind as outward sign by which one should recognize his Church or Christian holy people in the world."[33] What is true of the gospel proclaimed orally is also valid for the other sensual forms of the Word of God, the sacraments. Thus it can be said as a summary: "The marks by which one can recognize externally where in the world is the Church are baptism, the sacrament (i.e. the Lord's supper), and the Gospel."[34] In the precise, unequivocal sense only these are *notae ecclesiae*. For where the Gospel is preached, where baptism takes place, and the Lord's Supper is held, it cannot be otherwise: Human beings come to have faith or are being kept in faith; communion of the faithful comes into existence or continues to exist: "God's Word cannot be without God's people."[35] Thus God himself has promised (Isa. 55:11): "My Word shall not come back empty."[36] Hence it follows: "Wherever you hear such a Word or see it preached, believed, confessed, and obeyed, do not doubt that there must certainly be a true *Ecclesia sancta Catholica*, a Christian holy people, even if there are but very few. For God's Word does not go forth void."[37] In short, the Word of God in its different forms is the unequivocal external mark of the Church because it creates the Church, and it creates the Church because it creates faith and thus also the communion of the faithful.

---

30. WA, 50: 628, 29–642, 4 (LW 41: 148–164)
31. Cf. WA, 51: 479, 4–487, 2 (LW 41: 194–199).
32. WA, 56: 426, 1 (LW 25: 417).
33. WA, 50: 629, 16–20 (LW 41: 149); cf. WA, 11: 408, 8–10 (LW 39: 305).
34. WA, 6: 301, 3f (LW 39: 75).
35. WA, 50: 629, 34f (LW 41: 150).
36. WA, 11: 408, 13 (LW 39:305); WA, 50: 629, 31 (LW 41: 150).
37. WA, 50: 629, 28–31 (LW 41: 150).

The affirmation that God's Word creates the Church does not compete with the statement that the Church is the work of the Holy Spirit. Rather the Spirit achieves his hidden work of creating and preserving the communion of the faithful only in such a way that human beings "hear the voice of the shepherd," that they come to faith in the external, audible Gospel: "I have been brought here by the Holy Spirit and incorporated into the Church through having heard God's Word and still hearing it."[38] Conversely it is true that "wherever Christ is not preached there is no Holy Spirit who creates, calls, and gathers the Christian Church."[39] More than anything else, Luther urged upon his hearers and readers this dependency of the Church on the Word of God: "Through the Gospel alone [the Church] is conceived, shaped, raised, born, educated, nourished, dressed, adorned, strengthened, armed, and preserved."[40] The Church is *creatura Euangelii.*[41] It is such not in the sense as if it has been created once by the Word of God and since then continues thanks to a strength that is now its own intrinsic life; rather, it remains dependent on being incessantly filled with life by God through the Gospel: *tota vita et substania Ecclesiae est in verbo dei.*[42] Which means nothing else but that the Church in its essence is the communion of believers who become and remain believers through the very Word in which they believe.

The primacy of the Gospel cannot be outstripped. This holds true although it is the Church that proclaims the Gospel, and human beings come to faith only under the condition that the Church does so. Luther can emphasize, with strong words, this aspect under which the Church precedes faith. Thus he calls the Christian communion "the mother who begets and bears each Christian through the Word of God."[43] But he outlines the Church's role very precisely: First of all its motherly function is restricted to passing on the—external—Word in oral proclamation and distribution of the sacraments. To "reveal" this Word to the hearers in such a way that their hearts are kindled and they become and remain faithful as well as being members of the communion of believers is the work of God the Holy Spirit himself.[44] Secondly, the Church, when passing on the Word of God, is subject to it, both regarding its being and regarding the norm of its actions: It *is able* to pass on God's Word because, being *creatura verbi*, it owes its very existence to it; although being mother of the faithful, in relation to the Word it is "not mother" but "daughter," "born from the Word."[45] And the

---

38. WA, 30/1: 190, 9–11 (Kolb & Wengert, *Book of Concord*, 438).
39. WA, 30/1: 189, 1f (Kolb & Wengert, *Book of Concord*, 436).
40. WA, 7: 721, 10-12.
41. WA, 2: 430, 6f.
42. WA, 7: 721, 12f.
43. WA, 30/1: 188, 24f (Kolb & Wengert, *Book of Concord*, 436).
44. WA, 30/1: 188, 25-27 (Kolb & Wengert, *Book of Concord*, 436).
45. WA, 42: 334, 12 (LW 2: 101); cf. WA, 6: 560, 33–561, 2.

Church can only *pass on* God's Word, without additions or alterations of its own making, obedient to the revelation of Christ which has preceded it.[46] The yardstick of the Church's obedience is the testimony of the Holy Scriptures. Thus the obedient passing on of the Gospel by the Church is carried out in the faithful explication of the Scriptures and in the distribution of the sacraments according to the Scriptures.[47]

4. THE DISTINCTIONS WITHIN THE *COMMUNIO EXTERNA*

The audible and the visible Word as the external means and marks of the Church is the pivot by which the external, visible dimension and the hidden dimension of the Church are connected. What corresponds to the external means, in the first instance, is the communion which uses them equally externally—the communion of the hearers, the baptized, the communicants. But this "bodily," visible church is not a second church besides the hidden one. After all, the members of the hidden church, the believers, having become and remaining such only through the Word of God, are themselves part of the external communion of the hearers, baptized, and communicants. Thus, external and hidden Church are two dimensions of the same thing.[48] At the same time, they differ from each other: in the external church there are distinctions which do not exist in the hidden one, the distinction between believers and non-believers, the distinction between ministers and the other Christians, and the distinction between true and false church.

a. Corpus permixtum

Concerning the first distinction, not all members of the external church are part of the communion of believers. The two dimensions are not coextensive. For not all who hear the Gospel and receive the sacraments thereby become or are believers. Among them there are also human beings who are not touched internally by these external means. Yet they are part of the external church. Where exactly the dividing line runs between believing and non-believing members is known to God alone, who knows the human heart.[49] The Christian, for his part, will consider every member of the external church also as part of the communion of believers since his "yardstick" is love, which means he assumes the best about everybody.[50]

---

46. WA, 38: 239, 1–7 (LW 38: 198).
47. WA, 51: 481, 7 (LW 41: 196); WA, 50: 630, 22f (LW 41: 151); WA, 631,7f (LW 41: 152).
48. Cf. WA, 1: 639, 2–4.
49. WA, 21: 332, 31–39.
50. WA, 18: 651, 34–652, 4 (LW 33: 88).

b. Ministerium

Among the members of the external church there are holders of ministry vis-à-vis the other Christians. In the communion of believers, however, there is no such distinction, here all are equal, namely "truly of Christian estate,"[51] i.e., they all equally have immediate communion with God, which means they all are priests, since a stance of such immediacy with God is a characteristic feature of priesthood.[52] This is a position they do not have in their own right. Rather the Christians are priests because they participate in Christ's own priesthood.[53] Indeed, all of them do—"all Christian men are priests, all women priestesses, whether they are old or young, lord or servant, mistress or maid, learned or lay."[54] The basis of this common priestly estate of the Christians is baptism, their priestly ordination.[55] The oil used for this act is the Holy Spirit, who through the external sacramental means "anoints" the hearts, i.e., creates the respective persons' faith in Christ which is the consummation of their priesthood.[56] Thus, this new spiritual estate can be considered as the priesthood of all believers and of all baptized, two terms which designate the two dimensions of the same reality. However, the priests receive their new estate not only for themselves. In it is included an obligation[57] which regards other people: the priestly task to help others to get into the same relation with God or to preserve it.[58] This obligation is fulfilled through the distribution of the means by which God creates faith as well as through intercessory prayer. Thus, to the same priestly estate corresponds the same priestly power: Those who are "all equally priests" also all have "the same power regarding the Word and every sacrament,"[59] namely, the same power to teach, "to preach and proclaim the Word, to baptize, to consecrate or hold the Lord's Supper, to administer the keys, to intercede for others, to sacrifice, and to judge all doctrine and spirits."[60] Sent by Christ himself, the Christian where he or she acts as priest stands vis-à-vis their fellow human beings in Christ's own name and with his authority.[61]

51. WA, 6: 407, 13f (LW 44: 127).
52. WA, 41: 153, 30f (LW 13: 294).
53. WA, 12: 179, 15-21 (LW 40:19f); WA, 41: 207, 20f (LW 13: 331); WA, 45: 683, 20f (LW 24: 243).
54. WA, 6: 370, 25-27 (LW 35: 101).
55. WA, 6: 408, 11f (LW 44: 129).
56. WA, 17/2, 11-17.
57. WA, 11: 412, 5-13 (LW 39: 309–10).
58. WA, 45: 540, 17-19 (LW 24: 87–88).
59. WA, 6: 566, 27f, (LW 36:116); cf. WA, 8: 273, 12f; WA, 10/3: 395, 3-9.
60. WA, 12: 180, 2-4 (LW 40: 21).
61. WA, 49: 139, 3-7; WA, 10/3: 394, 32.

Insofar as the priestly activities consist in the distribution of the external means of grace, they take place within the external church. This, however, happens in a certain order which generates a differentiation between the priests. Therefore Luther, as much as he underlines the commonness of the priesthood of the Christians and as extensively as he defines the powers entailed in this priesthood, often adds a qualifying clause: "although we are all equally priests, nevertheless we cannot all . . . preach."[62] Or: All Christians are truly of a spiritual estate, there is no difference between them—"except only regarding the ministry."[63] Under the aspect of ministry it must be said: "It needs to be entrusted to one only, and one alone has to preach, baptize, absolve, and distribute the Lord's Supper, the others have to be content with this and consent."[64] The restriction in using the powers of the priesthood of all believers and the difference between the priests stated in these quotations have solely one reason: The proclamation of the Gospel is not only a private matter "between brother and brother," but it is also a public affair directed at the whole congregation and realized in the name of the whole congregation. Such public proclamation in word and Sacrament has to be done by individual Christians entrusted with this special ministry: "It is necessary to have bishops, pastors, or preachers who publicly and exclusively give, distribute, and exercise the four pieces or sacred things named above [sc. preaching, baptism, Lord's Supper, absolution] for the sake and in the name of the congregations and moreover because of Christ's institution, as St. Paul says in Eph. 4: *Dedit dona hominibus*. He has instituted some as apostles, prophets, evangelists, teachers, governors etc."[65]

As this citation shows, Luther presents two seemingly contradictory reasons for the tie of public proclamation to holders of a special ministry: the priesthood of all believers or of all the. Baptized, and the institution by Christ.[66] Thus he says on the one hand: it is "because of and in the name of the Church"[67] that individual Christians entrusted with this task have to perform the public proclamation of the Word of God, precisely because all Christians possess the power

---

62. WA, 7: 28, 34f (LW 31: 356).

63. WA, 6: 407, 14f (LW 44: 127).

64. WA, 50: 633, 8–10 (LW 41: 154).

65. WA, 50: 632, 36–633,5 (LW 41:154).

66. This twofold argumentation is overlooked by authors who hold that Luther simply bases the ordained ministry on the priesthood of all believers, as e.g. Harald Goertz, *Allgemeines Priestertum und ordiniertes Amt bei Luther*, Marburger Theologische Studien (Marburg: N. G. Elwert Verlag, 1997), or who claim that Luther presupposed a special institution of the ministry in the way he did in relation to baptism or the Lord's Supper, e.g. Wilhelm Löhe, "Aphorismen über neutestamentaliche Ämter und ihr Verhältnis zur Gemeinde," in *Gesammelte Werke, 5.1*, ed. Klaus Ganzert (Neuendettelsau: Freimund Verlag, 1954).

67. Cf. also WA, 49: 600, 12f (LW 51:343).

for proclaiming. For this very reason there must be "one person . . . who speaks and does the talking because of the command and permission of the others."[68] Otherwise, there would be a scandalous "chaos" in the church.[69] Or some individuals would arrogate the proclamation in the church to themselves, although they do not own more power than their fellow-Christians.[70] Then both would be damaged: God's Word would not come across any more as the Word spoken—to all—by God, but as the word of human individuals, and the priesthood of all baptized believers would cease to be common to all. Only when the public proclamation, oral as well as sacramental, is entrusted to individual Christians by the entire communion, for which and to which they are to speak, can this damage be avoided. Therefore, the church is not free to undertake such entrusting or not: it "must have bishops, pastors, or preachers."[71]

At this point, Luther's other argument for the ministry of public proclamation comes into play, which does not base the ministry on the commonness of the priesthood but on the explicit will of Christ: "Moreover," one must have such ministers "because of Christ's institution."[72] It is important to note that Luther does not speak of the institution of the ministry in the same sense in which he speaks of the institution of the oral proclamation of the Gospel or of the Sacraments, namely as a commandment of Christ which can be quoted as such from the Gospels. When he speaks about the founding act of the Church's ministry, he rather points to the Christian congregation after Easter.[73] Nevertheless, by having a ministry, the Church is obedient to an institution by Christ: to his commandment to propagate the Gospel. For what is done through the ministry—public proclamation—is a necessary implication of that very same commandment.[74] Therefore "apostles, evangelists, prophets who do God's Word and work must always be, however they want to be named or can be named."[75]

68. WA, 49: 600, 13f (LW 51:343); cf. 38: 227, 20ff; 247, 10–31 (LW 38:185, 208); WA, 50: 633, 4–6; (LW 41:154); WA, 54: 251, 31–34 (LW 41:318).

69. WA, 12: 189, 23 (*LW* 40:34); cf. WA, 50: 633, 6–8 (LW 41:154).

70. WA, 12: 189, 17–23 (LW 40: 34).

71. WA, 50: 633, 1 (LW 41:154).

72. WA, 50: 633, 3 (LW 41: 154); cf. 6: 441, 24f (LW 44: 176).

73. WA, 50: 633, 4f.; 634, 11f. (LW 41: 154, 155–56)

74. In arguing like this, i.e. in a systematic theological way, Luther differs from Calvin, for whom the institution of the Church's ministry, or rather of its four binding ministries, is rooted in a direct, citable prescriptions of the Bible (cf. Dorothea Wendebourg, "Der Schriftgebrauch in der Amtstheologie der Reformatoren und der reformatorischen Bekenntnisschriften / The Use of Scripture by the Reformers and by the Confessions of the Reformation in their Theology of the Ministry," in: *Bereits erreichte Gemeinschaft und weitere Schritte: 20 Jahre nach der Meissener Erklärung / Communion Already Shared and Further Steps: 20 Years after the Meissen Declaration*, ed. Christopher Hill et al. [Frankfurt a.M.: Lembeck, 2010], 286–330).

75. WA, 50: 634, 13–15 (LW 41: 155); cf. WA, 11: 411, 22–24 (LW 39: 309).

To have such ministers, the Church has to entrust the ministry of public proclamation to individual holders of the common priesthood by way of ordination, which is the calling (*vocatio*) exclusively to fulfill this task, but not the conferment of a special spiritual quality which would distinguish them from the rest of the communion.[76]

The primary place of the ministry is the congregation assembled around one pulpit, one baptismal font, and one table. Its primary holder is the pastor of such a congregation whom Luther, because of the identity of his task with the original episcopacy, programmatically called "bishop."[77] Nevertheless Luther was not a congregationalist who advocated the complete independence of the individual congregation. He rather maintained that the essential oneness of the Church across the borders of the local congregations should find expression also in the visible church. Thus, he provided for regular visitations of the congregations. He also strove for the establishment of an evangelical diocesan episcopacy, whereby this office, after having degenerated into a mainly political institution, was to become genuinely spiritual again. However, the Wittenberg Reformation was able to establish such an episcopal office only on the regional level, the so-called office of superintendent. On the level of the former dioceses, the installation of bishops was possible only outside of the Holy Roman Empire—in the case of Prussia, where Luther was involved himself.[78] In the Holy Roman Empire, where bishops were also, if not primarily, imperial princes, the political conditions did not allow such a step. Luther's personal efforts in this matter, culminating in two installations of bishops performed by himself (1542 Naumburg, 1544 Merseburg) show how much an independent ordering of the evangelical churches beyond the congregational level mattered to him. What came into being instead, the church government of the princes or city councils (*Landesherrliches Kirchenregiment*), he viewed with undisguised mistrust.[79]

As regards the worldwide oneness of the Church, Luther rarely addressed the question whether, and if so how, it should be expressed in the external church. Where he did address the issue, he favored a conciliar form: the bishops, all vested with equal authority, should lead the Church together, as was the case with the apostles, and with the bishops in the beginning of the Ancient

---

76. WA, 38: 228, 27-29 (LW 38: 186). As regards Luther's understanding and practice of ordination, cf. Martin Krarup, *Ordination in Wittenberg: Die Einsetzung in das kirchliche Amt in Kursachsen zur Zeit der Reformation*, [Beiträge zur historischen Theologie] (Tübingen: Mohr Siebeck, 2007).

77. E.g., WA, 6: 440, 21f (LW 44: 175); WA, 12: 205, 3f (LW 53: 19).

78. Cf. WA, 2: 232-244; WA, 18: 408-411.

79. Cf. WABr 10: 436. For this point, cf. Dorothea Wendebourg, "Das eine Amt der einen Kirche / The One Ministry of the One Church," in: *Einheit bezeugen: Zehn Jahre nach der Meissener Erklärung / Witnessing to Unity: Ten Years after the Meissen Declaration*, ed. Ingolf U. Dalferth and Paul Oppenheim (Frankfurt a.M.: Lembeck, 2003), 274–323.

Church.[80] Above them there is only the one Head who does not himself belong to the external church, Jesus Christ.[81] Thus the claim of the pope to be the visible head of the Church is rejected. He owns no superiority according to divine right whatsoever; to declare that he does is an expression of anti-Christian presumption.[82] Yet Luther also rejects a superiority of the pope over the church according to human law.[83] For papal superiority would be respected by its subjects only on the binding basis of a divine commandment—which does not exist; based on human law, it would only lead to competition and new divisions.[84] Consequently, the more modest argument for the position of the pope—that based on human law—would "not help Christianity at all" either.[85] What can help the Christian Church is not the exercise of ecclesial power, but only a regime of spiritual concordance in which "we all live under one head Christ and the bishops, all equal according to their office, hold eagerly together in unanimous doctrine, faith, sacraments, prayers, and works of love etc."[86]

c. Ecclesia vera et falsa

Finally, there is yet a third difference within the external church which does not exist in the hidden church, the difference between the "true" and the "false church" (ecclesia vera et falsa) already mentioned. It is rooted in the fact that the means of grace are handed on by human beings. Human beings, however, even Christian ones, are not immune to error and sin. Thus, preaching and distribution of the sacraments are performed by ministers who are sinners, at times even unbelieving. This is a situation familiar to Christianity from ancient times, which Luther countered with the classical anti-Donatist argument: The effectiveness of the means of grace does not depend on the dignity of the person who passes them on.[87] Yet there is a perversion which is worse and affects the church's life on a deeper level: It sometimes happens that the Gospel is proclaimed and taught and the sacraments are distributed in a way which is not in accordance with Holy Scripture. In fact, the perversity can reach such a degree that the opposition to the Gospel is not restricted to individual cases but becomes customary and systemic and takes on even the form of official ecclesial doctrine and practice. In that case, one must conclude: Here is a "false church." Such ecclesial

---

80. WA, 50: 217, 5-17 (Kolb & Wengert, Book of Concord, 308).
81. WA, 50: 217, 7 (Kolb & Wengert, Book of Concord, 308); WA, 51: 494, 10f.
82. WA, 50: 217, 23-218, 18 (Kolb & Wengert, Book of Concord, 309).
83. WA, 50: 215, 14-216, 15 (Kolb & Wengert, Book of Concord, 308).
84. WA, 50: 216, 23-28 (Kolb & Wengert, Book of Concord, 308).
85. WA, 50: 216, 22f (Kolb & Wengert, Book of Concord, 308).
86. WA, 50: 217, 7-12 (Kolb & Wengert, Book of Concord, 308).
87. E.g., WA, 38: 241, 6-23 (LW 38: 200f).

opposition to the Gospel, in Luther's eyes, was due not only to the human beings involved. It was a demoniac perversion triggered by none other than the antagonist of Jesus Christ announced in the New Testament, the Anti-Christ.[88] All the more urgent it is for Christians to have a criterion which allows them to diagnose where the Church is, the Church which they have to hold on to and in which they truly receive the means of grace. The criterion is the mark whereby the Church can be recognized: the proclamation of the Gospel in Word and Sacraments. In short: The marks of the Church are by definition the marks of the true church.[89]

For Luther, the church in opposition to the Gospel was realized particularly in the papal church: This is "not the true church,"[90] but the "false" church,[91] indeed, the church of the Antichrist,[92] which contradicts the Gospel in more than one fundamental dimension: in its doctrine,[93] in its use of the sacraments[94] and in the claims of the hierarchy and especially the papacy.[95] Therefore the papal church cannot claim to be truly Church.[96] Rather, the evangelical con-gregations show that they are true Church since they have turned to the right proclamation of the Gospel and administration of the sacraments, and have done away with the perversions in this field.[97]

However, what is true and false church cannot simply be divided between two ecclesial institutions. This becomes clear precisely in Luther's judgements on the papal church. On the one hand he characterized it as the church of the Antichrist and wrote about it: "We do not concede to them that they are the Church, indeed, they are not the Church."[98] Yet on the other hand he wrote: "Although the city of Rome is worse than Sodom and Gomorrah, in it remain baptism, the Lords Supper, the proclamation and text of the Gospel, Holy Scrip-ture, offices, the name of Christ, the name of God."[99] And "Where these things have remained there certainly have remained the Church and several saints."[100] Moreover, Luther freely admitted that he and the other Reformers, as well as

88. WA, 26: 147, 27f; WA, 38: 232, 15–17 (LW 38: 190); WA, 51: 505, 11f (LW 41: 209–10).
89. WA, 43: 388, 7–9 (LW 4: 349); WA, 51: 479, 1ff (LW 41: 194ff).
90. WA, 43: 386, 21 (LW 4: 347).
91. WA, 42: 193, 4 (LW 1: 260).
92. WA, 26: 147, 28f (LW 28: 240); WA, 50: 217, 23–31 (Kolb & Wengert, *Book of Concord*, 309).
93. WA, 51: 493, 8–16 (LW 41:202).
94. WA, 6: 501, 35f.; 527, 25f; 543, 12f, (LW 36: 19, 59f, 81); WA, 39/2: 160, 13f.
95. WA, 51: 494, 24–26 (LW 41: 203).
96. WA, 43: 157, 9f, 34 (LW 4: 30, 31).
97. WA, 43: 387, 21–24 (LW 4: 348–49); cf. WATr 4: 179, 9–11.
98. WA, 50: 249, 24f (Kolb & Wengert, *Book of Concord*, 324).
99. WA, 40/1: 69, 23–26 (LW 26:24); cf. 38: 221, 18–31 (LW 38: 177).
100. WA, 40/1: 69, 31f (LW 26: 24).

the evangelical congregations themselves, owed all those goods to the church under the pope: "I want to praise you [sc. the papal hierarchy] even more highly and confess that we have received everything from the church under you (not from you)."[101] If both kinds of statements are equally correct, that means that the true church is entwined with the false one; the "holy Church is the holy place of the abomination,"[102] the Antichrist is a phenomenon within the Church[103] and, with his perversion of the Gospel, deprives Christians of salvation.[104] If the Church in which the Antichrist sits nevertheless remains the Church and if, within it, the Gospel and the sacraments continue to be passed on and Christians continue to exist, then it is Christ himself who takes care of that: Christ "has needed all his might to preserve" the means of grace, and "he needed all his might to preserve the Christians` hearts so that they have not lost nor forgotten their baptism, Gospel, etc. in spite of so much scandalous ado."[105] Christ carries all this through against the doings of his adversaries who, thanks to their baptism, are and remain "in the Church," but who are not any more in the spiritual sense "of the Church or the Church`s members."[106]

Although Luther developed these thoughts in his altercation with the papacy, the interwovenness of true and false church, the battle between Christ and Antichrist was not, in his eyes, restricted to this institution. He saw the Antichrist was at work also in the groups of the Radical Reformation.[107] And he warned the evangelical congregations not to become the field of the Antichrist themselves. The true Church, after having barely survived under the official government of the false church, was now embodied in an institution in which the official doctrine and practice corresponded to the criteria of true proclamation of the Gospel and right administration of the Sacraments, i.e. the evangelical churches. Yet the followers of the Reformation must not "presume" and flatter themselves that the Antichrist is "far from us."[108] The battle between true and false church, between Christ and the Antichrist is not an occasional happening. Rather it accompanies Christendom from its beginnings until the Last Judgment. Thus, it forces the faithful to constant vigilance and incessant prayer.[109]

Nevertheless, however fierce the battle, there can be no doubt who will finally end up victorious: the true church, which carries "the victory until

---

101. WA, 51: 501, 23–25 (LW 41:207); cf. WA, 26: 147, 13–15.
102. WA, 38: 221, 18 (LW 38: 177).
103. WA, 51: 505, 10–12 (LW 41: 209); cf. WA, 26: 147, 29–35.
104. WA, 51: 505, 16–506, 1 (LW 41: 210).
105. WA, 38: 222, 1–6 (LW 38: 178).
106. WA, 51: 505, 10–13 (LW 41: 209).
107. WA, 50: 646, 27–647, 5 (LW 41: 170).
108. WA, 50: 468, 10–469, 5 (LW 47:107); cf. WA, 43: 428, 42 (LW 4: 407).
109. WA, 50: 468, 10–469, 1 (LW 47: 107).

doomsday."[110] In itself weak,[111] the Church owes this perspective to Christ alone, the "victor over the world."[112] He "remains with his Church until the consummation of the world."[113] He does so by preserving Word and Sacrament and through them the communion of the believers. Thus he keeps the Church in unity although its members find themselves across the world and in different institutional churches.[114] Thus he keeps the Church inerrant in the truth,[115] though its doctrine often enough is not pure.[116] And thus he keeps it in unbroken spiritual continuity.[117] *He* does so, whereas the church's own outward, institutional continuity, e.g. the succession of its representatives, far from keeping the continuity of the Gospel,[118] again and again ran counter to it.[119] Thus Christ several times had to make new beginnings with the Church and preserve its continuity through external breaks—which he might have to do again.[120] Only at his second coming will its hiddenness end and the Church, free from sin, frailty, and suppression, will in its very essence be manifest.[121]

CONCLUSION

Martin Luther's ecclesiological thought was fundamental for all Reformers, Magisterial and Radical. Yet they did not always uphold his resolute commitment to understand the Church through the lens of the doctrine of justification, nor the way in which he differentiated between the church's spiritual and external dimensions and connected them at the same time. The so-called spiritualists and Radical Reformers left Luther's ecclesiology behind in favor of a more spiritual vision of the Church. The principal theologian of the Reformed Reformation, John Calvin, gave more independent weight to its external, institutional side, as did Philip Melanchthon later in his life. Yet all the Reformers had one fundamental ecclesiological insight in common which they owed to the very experience of the Reformation: No ecclesial structure is able to guarantee that the Church remains faithful to the Gospel and thus remains the—One, Holy, Cath-

---

110. WA, 51: 291, 20f (LW 12: 174); cf. WA, 5: 493, 12f.
111. WA, 51: 291, 1-5 (LW 12: 174).
112. WABr, 5: 412, 38.
113. WA, 18: 649, 31–650, 1 (LW 33: 85).
114. WA, 26: 506, 38f (LW 37: 367).
115. WA, 51: 515, 30 (LW 41: 215).
116. WA, 42: 423, 30f (LW 2: 229).
117. WA, 50: 593, 7-14; 628, 16–19 (LW 41: 107, 149).
118. WA, 43: 387, 14–19 (LW 4: 348).
119. WA, 43: 157, 9.14 (LW 4: 30).
120. WA, 42: 332, 35-37; 333, 30-34 (LW 2: 99–100).
121. WA, 30/1: 191 (Kolb & Wengert, *Book of Concord*, 438–39).

olic, and Apostolic—Church. Rather the visible Church may turn into a false church, against which the faithful cannot but resist. The positive side of this lesson was the Reformers' firm conviction that, even under such circumstances Christ finds ways to keep up the proclamation of the Gospel and to preserve communions of the faithful, the true Church, against and within the anti-evangelical framework. Resistance in the name of the Gospel then aims at embodying the true Church again institutionally. Thus, by breaking with the existing institution, such resistance paradoxically serves the Oneness of the Church, and by breaking with tradition it serves its Apostolic continuity, since both its oneness and continuity are basically those of the Gospel itself. What was the experience of the sixteenth century, in today`s ecumenical world has become the ecclesiological legacy of that part of Christendom which has gone through the Reformation: a particular awareness of the dependency of the Church on the Gospel, the call for watchfulness to remain true to the Gospel in proclamation, practice, and structures, and the consciousness of how quickly and easily the Church may fail in this respect, even to the point of making necessary once again ruptures with existing institutions.[122] Part and parcel of this legacy is the confidence that it is Christ himself who carries the Church through until the end.

122. Cf. Wendebourg, "Eine Amt," 299, 322f.

11. Catholic Ecclesiology—
Evolving and in Response

JOHANNA RAHNER

1. ECCLESIOLOGY IS A SHADOW THEME

[For Luther,] the Church is not a theological topic in its own right. . . . This is
why there is no such thing as 'Luther's ecclesiology' in the sense of an elaborated theological concept that would tell us how the Church could and should
be structured. . . . The Church becomes a topic in its own right . . . only from
a negative perspective, when there is a need to think about if and how the
church hinders the proclamation of the gospel and its liberating power, instead
of serving it as an instrument.[1]

This is the verdict of one of the most renowned German Catholic Luther
scholars, Otto Hermann Pesch.

In this verdict, we can see an inner dialectic, namely that Luther's ecclesiology is merely a side topic compared to theological heavyweights such as the
doctrine of justification. Yet at the same time, the topic does not lead a wallflower
existence at all. While, over the last decades, the churches have reached theological convergence in many areas of the ecumenical dialogue (be that indulgences, justification, the sacraments)—the theological differences from the past
seem to be no longer a point of controversy today but rather a legitimate difference in perspectives rooted in complementary modes of theological thinking -
the ecclesiological dispute remains as an unusually persistent problem, which
styles itself as ecumenism's central obstacle.

Ruth Cohn, who developed a psychological model called TCI, Theme-
Centered-Interaction, to analyze dialogue situations, talks about the importance
of "shadow topics" that, although they remain in the background, can fundamentally interfere with and even hinder communication.[2] Americans use a very
telling expression for this: the elephant in the room. Since disturbances take
precedence, Ruth Cohn argues that the shadow topics need to be addressed so
that the conversation thereafter can freely continue. Thus, ecclesiology has devel-

---

1. Otto Hermann Pesch, "Der Stellenwert der Kirche—Lehren aus dem Luther-Jahr," in:
Luther 83: eine kritische Bilanz, ed. Claus-Jürgen Roepke (Munich: C. Kaiser, 1984), 31.

2. Cf. Gernot Klemmer, "(Ent-)Störungen im Bildungsprozess. Mit TZI-Haltung und–
Methode," in: *In der Balance liegt die Chance. Themenzentrierte Interaktion in Bildung und Beratung*, ed.
Ruth-Cohn-Institute for TCI International (Münster: Waxmann, 2006), 49-64.

oped from a theological side topic into the central issue of ecumenism. Notions about what church is and how the church should be, what is desired and what is rejected, what is perceived as genuine and what is viewed as foreign are largely the result of denominational phantasies and projections to confirm their own identity. Here we see the subtle dynamics of an identity that defines itself by using the other as a contrasting foil to deal with a twofold loss: on the one hand, the churches were bereaved of a greater community; on the other, the loss is one that they produced themselves through the exclusion of others from their own ecclesial identity. This is sometimes styled in the rhetoric of a loss and sometimes in the praise of diversity. Every form of ecclesiology turns into an identity discourse.

To describe Luther's ecclesiology in an adequate way, you have to avoid turning concepts about what the church is into an identity-producing myth. Such a reconstruction of the past would certainly no longer be perceived as a "dangerous remembrance," that could potentially turn into a question about one's own identity. However, this is precisely the way I want the following remarks about Luther's ecclesiology to be understood!

2. DON'T SKIP THE MIDDLE AGES

We can approach Martin Luther's ecclesiology in different ways: One approach that leaves behind denominational stereotypes and is therefore ecumenically promising is to place Lutheran ecclesiology well within the religious, societal, cultural, and theological shifts at the turn from the Middle Ages to the Early Modern Age. The Reformation—and I deliberately use the singular here—started long before Luther posted his theses in 1517 and the events that ensued. 'Reformation' is an epochal event that concerns the whole European history of thought,[3] and it encompasses more than just a category change in theological thinking and forms of piety, eventually ending up in the breakup of the Western Church and an emerging diversification of denominations. Charles Taylor[4] emphasizes three important aspects in this regard: *One* is the turn towards a more inward and more intensive form of piety. This means that piety is no longer a signature of the religious elite—for instance, members of the clergy or the monastic orders—but concerns everyone. The religious praxis of society as a whole intensifies, which means that everyone should become a good Christian, living with conviction and according to his or her faith. No wonder that religious praxis becomes more individualized and more pluralistic. *The second aspect*

---

3. As Thomas Kaufmann has just recently pointed out in: *Erlöste und Verdammte. Eine Geschichte der Reformation,* 3rd ed. (Munich: C. H. Beck, 2016), esp. 9–82.

4. Charles Taylor, *A Secular Age* (Cambridge, Mass.: Harvard University Press, 2007), 75–77.

is a growing discontent with the ways in which the church acts as a spiritual mediator, which sometimes border on the realm of the magical, and which are increasingly seen as distracting from the core. The role of the church is further discredited as suspicions arise that the structures of representation within the church mainly serve a lust for and an abuse of power. *Thirdly,* the idea of being saved through one's faith alone takes prominence, thus intensifying the relation to God, freeing from false anxieties and dependencies—since reverence is due to God alone—and turning the relationship with God into a personal and, to a certain extent, direct relation.

We must hardly be surprised that this leads to vehement fundamental criticism of and a mounting pressure on the church, pressing this institution towards change. Wherever faith becomes an individualized act, wherever we find various forms of piety, and wherever the question about God is answered primarily from an existential perspective, institutionalized piety finds itself fundamentally challenged. The institution must critically question its standards, check whether what it offers is still plausible, think about whom it addresses, and thus rethink its own identity. What comes to the fore is the idea that every institution must, in its essence, serve the individual's relation to God. From then on, the church as an institutional *locus*—where faith is practiced—comes second. Never again can it hold the same undisputed status it had in medieval times when it was regarded as the primary point of reference for faith. The epochal change, the "great rift" in the faith, cannot be undone.

All religious movements at that time—including what later would become separate denominations—had to react to this development, and each did it differently. Movements like the *devotio moderna,* humanism, but also late scholasticism—strongly informed by nominalism—and the Renaissance papacy had just arisen. All these things—even the fact that the focus of interest now is the so called 'New World'—gave new dynamics and diversification to the notion of what the church is. My thesis is, then, that in any case, even without Luther, we would have seen a different church after the sixteenth century.

I can support this thesis by looking at the deep ambivalence inherent in (late) medieval ecclesiologies. Over the course of several centuries, papalists and conciliarists, centrifugal and centripetal powers, are contending with one another. The Council of Constance (1414–18) already tried to remove the thick layers of a burdensome legacy from several centuries which revolves around the structure of the church and the office of the pope—and to bring the church, not only structurally, back on track. But it is also the new piety movements, with their focus on internalization and a critical distance to all institutional problems, that the council fathers view as a substantial challenge. The incrimination of Jan Hus raises the issue of a spiritual ecclesiology, which forty years previously had been propagated by John Wyclif. Its roots, however, can be traced back to

Francis of Assisi, whose ideas can be understood as a strong criticism of the traditional understanding of the church and its institutions. As we know, Francis
had already envisioned the future of the church in an individualized radical discipleship of Christ, in denying wealth and respect, and not in an outward institution that strives for splendor and power. Even though the "conciliar" option,
which in the wake of a political shift to democratic structures in medieval cities
and also the developing universities had been established at Constance and
which subscribed to the most influential ideas of representation and internation-
ality did not succeed, the victory of a centrally enforced papalism was only tem-
porary. One reason for this is that it ultimately represents a one-sided version of
Catholic ecclesiology. The battle lines are not drawn as clearly as they seem, and
the dynamics that ensue from Luther's ecclesiological invectives are a telling sign
that the sixteenth century is sitting on an ecclesiological powder keg. The ecclesiological breaks and shifts that follow from Luther's questions mark the breakthrough of an alternative that had been there for a long time but that now
needed to be expressed outside of the Catholic Church.

3. ECCLESIOLOGY IN A STATE OF EMERGENCY

Even the very first reactions from Rome to Luther's theses on indulgences
show the way the dispute is heading. The horizon for Sylvester Prierias' report
on Luther's arguments is not the dispute about the reformer's theology and
biblical arguments, but a formal recourse to papal authority. As a stout papalist,
Sylvester does not shy away from using his, even in his time rather extreme,
ecclesiological conviction as the basis for his assessment: "Whoever does not
subscribe to the teaching of the Roman Church and the pope as the infallible
rule of faith, from which even the scripture draws its power and authority, is
a heretic."[5] A similar perspective becomes apparent in the questioning of
Luther by Cajetan in October 1518. The dispute about Pope Clement VI's
bull *Unigenitus* from 1343 is ultimately not about indulgences and their theological justification, biblical or non-biblical, but about the power of the pope
to grant indulgences as such.[6] In the tradition of the Dominican Order to
which Cajetan belongs, he proves to be a strict opponent of conciliarism and
an extreme proponent of the papal *plenitudo potestatis*. He goes so far as to

5. Silvester Prierias, "In presumptuosas Martini Lutheri conclusiones de potestate pape dialogus," in: Peter Fabisch and Erwin Iserloh, eds., *Dokumente zur Causa Lutheri (1517-21)* 1, *Das
Gutachten des Prierias und weitere Schriften gegen Luthers Ablassthesen (1517-1518)*, [Corpus Catholicorum, 41] (Münster: Aschendorff, 1988), 55.

6. See also Christoph Strohm, "Papsttum und Kircherecht in der Sicht der Reformation,"
in: *Die Päpste und ihr Amt zwischen Einheit und Vielfalt der Kirche: Theologische Fragen in historischer
Perspektive*, ed. Stefan Weinfurter, et al. (Regensburg: Schnell & Steiner, 2017), 205.

reject the possibilities of institutional resistance or theologically justified exceptions, which even late medieval canon law had known and defended. And so, the Leipzig disputation in June and July 1519, guided by the skilled hand of Johannes Eck, quickly turns into a discussion about the pope as a *iudex controversiarum* and the question of churchly authority. Eck who, in contrast to Prierias and Cajetan, was more of a moderate conciliarist than a papalist made Luther, who wanted to defend Jan Hus against the Council of Constance, deliver some extreme statements. This also happened because, at that time, the authors of the relatively young dogmatic tract on ecclesiology knew no real alternatives to papalism and Roman centralism that then positioned itself as the only possible Catholic option. Other alternatives had been theologically marginalized or eradicated by the Renaissance papacy, which emerged strengthened from the ecclesiological conflicts of the fifteenth century and the political victory over conciliarism. From today's perspective, we can say that Catholic ecclesiology did not really benefit from these developments. The magisterial prohibition hinders the development of alternative ways of thinking about the church, and we might go so far as to say that it actually makes life harder since it cuts itself off from theological developments that would help to find new ways to think about the church.

To understand Luther's ecclesiology adequately, you have to put it in the controversial context of this rather extreme part of the spectrum within Catholic ecclesiology. For him it is always a struggle concerning the church in regard to his theology. Rediscovering the gospel leads, in its own way, to a rediscovery of the church; a rediscovery that must be fought for in a painful process of purification, through controversies and contrasting positions. In this sense, Luther's ecclesiology is therefore an ecclesiology of controversy, an apologetic ecclesiology.[7]

Thus, at the beginning of the theological dispute about his theses on indulgences, Luther reacts to the papal bull that threatens to ban him by distinguishing between an inner and an outward churchly community.[8] Only God grants the salvific *communio spiritualis,* and only the individual can exclude himself or herself from that community through sin. In contrast, exclusion by an ecclesiastical authority only refers to the *externae privatio communionis.* An outward exclusion does not say anything about the inner quality of such an act. Thus, we already find a twofold conception of the church in Luther's thinking: There is the outward church, where contingency and factuality reign and which we should obey.

7. Cf. Ernst Kinder, "Kann man von einem 'lutherischen Kirchenbegriff' sprechen?" *Theologische Literaturzeitung,* 81 (1956): 364-65. See also Ernst Kinder, "Die theologischen Grundmotive in der Kirchenauffassung der lutherischen Reformation," in: *Das Wort Gottes in Geschichte und Gegenwart,* ed. Wilhelm Andersen (Munich: Kaiser, 1957), 136.

8. Cf. *Sermo de virtute excommunicationis* 1518: WA 1: 639, 2-6.

Its officials, however, are never apodictic and inerrant because they are mere instruments for the spiritual community with Christ. This spiritual community is what is salvific and inerrant because it does not depend on human contingency. If the outward community comes in conflict with this inner community then the laws of a state of emergency become effective.[9]

As the controversy about papal authority becomes more and more important, this distinction between an inward and an outward church deepens and becomes crucially significant for ecclesiology, as we can observe in the 1520 text "*On the Papacy of Rome*," directed against Augustinus Alveldt.

The church, or as Luther would call it, Christianity, is "a community of all Christians on earth, . . . a community of all those who are living according to the right faith, hope, and love."[10] It is not "a bodily congregation but a congregation of the hearts."[11] Luther sets this spiritual congregation against an understanding of the church that focuses on external belonging, ministerial structures, and liturgical regulations.[12] He distinguishes between these two sides but he does not separate what, in his view, belongs together.[13] Thus, Luther defends the spiritual-sacramental character of the church as the unifying principle of the "two churches."

More fitting than the problematic differentiation between a visible and an invisible church is therefore Luther's term "*absconditas*." The contrasting pair of words "hidden" and "revealed" qualifies theological statements about the church: In every realization of the church in history, what is essential remains hidden from the eyes of those who do not believe; yet at the same time through faith, God's church-willing action becomes visible. Otto Hermann Pesch rightly calls this a "positive analogy" between the visible community of the church and the hidden church.[14] So, what Luther calls "two churches" does not promote an

---

9. Klaus Unterburger, *Unter dem Gegensatz verborgen: Tradition und Innovation in der Auseinandersetzung des jungen Martin Luther mit seinen theologischen Gegnern*, [Katholisches Leben und Kirchenreform Im Zeitalter der Glaubensspaltung, 74] (Munster: Aschendorff Verlag, 2015), 99.

10. WA, 6: 292, 37–293, 3 (LW 39: 65).

11. WA, 6: 293, 3-4 (LW 39: 65).

12. WA, 6: 296, 17–19 (LW 39: 69).

13. "Therefore, for the sake of better understanding and brevity, we shall call the two churches by two distinct names. The first, which is natural, basic, essential, and true, we shall call 'spiritual, internal Christendom.' The second, which is man-made and external, we shall call 'physical, external Christendom.' Not that we want to separate them from each other; rather, it is just as if I were talking about a man and called him 'spiritual' according to his soul, and 'physical' according to his body, or as the Apostle is accustomed to speak of an 'internal' and 'external' man. So, too, the Christian assembly is a community united in one faith according to the soul, although, according to the body, it cannot be assembled in one place since every group of people is assembled in its own place." WA, 6: 296, 37–297, 9 (LW 39: 70).

14. Cf. Otto Hermann Pesch, "Luther und die Kirche," *Lutherjahrbuch* 52 (1985): 127.

invisible church in the sense of a *civitas platonica*, as the Catholic controversialist theologian Thomas Murner suspects. It rather emphasizes that the church despite being rooted in the transcendental and being nourished by the continuous creative dynamics of God is still a visible and palpable entity. A spiritual community cannot exist without a bodily community. But such a bodily community can only be a church if it truly realizes the spiritual community, otherwise it would deny the gospel. We must defend this insight against both a positivistic usurpation and a dynamically spiritualizing dissolution. Thus, Luther coherently names external indicators, which are rooted in Christology as we shall see. We should call these "criteria of the true church" because not everything that is called a church actually is one.

Against the papal claim to power the main ecclesiological argument of Luther's opponents Luther introduces the continuous relation to Christ, i.e., to Christ as the permanent head of the church, as a central criterion of the true church. It becomes the shibboleth of a true understanding of the church, partly because Luther's opponents use an extreme papalistic theory of the church as a point of reference.[15] Because Christ himself is and remains the sole head of his church as Luther emphasizes based on reasons from his theology of grace[16] there cannot be an "authoritative vicar" between Christ and his church.[17] Christ alone reigns over the church, which then shows the signs that Christ alone is their head: baptism, the sacrament of the altar, and the gospel.[18]

Ultimately, Luther's pointed reasoning goes against the three central concepts of the tendentiously papalist ecclesiology of his time: "the teaching that papal primacy of jurisdiction is based on divine law, which means that any disobedience against the pope makes one a heretic; the understanding of the power of the keys as a jurisdictional power whose source within the church is the pope; and finally the teaching of the pope as the head of the church."[19]

Roger Haight has a point when he sees a change in the fundamental perspective on ecclesiology in the "programmatic writings" of the year 1520. Now

15. Cf. Unterburger, *Gegensatz*, 105–09. In the dispute with Eck, the question about who the head (of the church) is becomes the decisive point of conflict. For Prierias, the idea that the pope is the *caput ecclesiae* becomes the center of his argument and the starting point for an extreme papalistic theory. Alveldt, but also Hieronymus Emser and Thomas Murner, try to defend the primacy of the Roman pope as *ius divinum* by pointing to the fact that every community needs a visible head. For a historical appraisal of the extreme papalistic theories and the criticism directed against them, see *ibid.*, 109–111.

16. Cf. Unterburger, *Gegensatz*, 105–06.

17. Cf. WA, 6: 297, 40 (LW 39: 71); WA, 6: 407–409 (LW 44: 127–131).

18. "Baptism, the sacrament, and the gospel are the signs by which the existence of the church in the world can be noticed externally." WA, 6: 301, 3-4 (LW 39: 75).

19. Unterburger, *Gegensatz*, 107.

Luther criticizes the papal church of his time no longer from the inside but from the outside. The point of reference for his argument is no longer a reform of the church but the development of an ecclesiological alternative.[20] But what does this alternative look like?

4. LUTHER'S ECCLESIOLOGICAL ALTERNATIVE

While Luther's ecclesiology might be controversial and poignant in many aspects, it is unmistakably an ecclesiology based on the gospel, on "the word of God." In the *verbum efficax* man hears how God acts mercifully on him. Here he recognizes himself as someone who has been addressed, who listens to God, and who recognizes that God acts on him. However, he has no control over the word of God since it remains with God as man's counterpart. This means that it is essential for the church to make sure that the gospel is preached so that the effective word can reach man and transform him. The future of the church hinges on its status as a *creatura verbi*.

Luther can pointedly argue as he does in his argument with Ambrosius Catharinus that in the end the main characteristic of the church is the preaching of the gospel: "*breviter, tota vita et substantia Ecclesiae est in verbo dei. . . . Non de Euangelio scripto sed vocali loquor.*"[21] The emphasis here is not on a theology of the word; Luther here takes us on a journey along the outer horizon of the church. The Word as the foundation of the church is and remains a *veritas aliena* that is opposed to the church even if the preaching of the word can happen in and through the church. This saves the church from the dangers of a double usurpation: one is a "deification of the worldly nature" that Luther finds in the papal church, the other is an "enthusiastic destruction" of all outward signs, which Luther finds in the so-called *Schwaermer* or Anabaptists.[22]

The late Luther will turn the ecclesiological consequences that arise from this into a principle: The distinction between the *communio spiritualis* and the *communio corporalis* that he developed at the time of his excommunication turns into an irreconcilable difference.[23] The more time passes, the more Luther recognizes the reign of the antichrist in the pope of Rome and interprets his situation in dualistic and apocalyptic categories. The controversy is no longer about the difference between visible or hidden church, but about the apocalyptic and fundamental difference between a legitimate and an ille-

---

20. Roger Haight, *Christian Community in History.* Vol. 2: *Comparative Ecclesiology* (New York: Continuum, 2005), 30.

21. WA, 7: 721, 12-13, 15.

22. Cf. Martin Schloemann, "Luthers Ekklesiologie: 'Von den Konziliis und Kirchen,'" *Luther-jahrbuch*, 52 (1985): 280.

23. WA, 50: 641, 35–642, 8 (LW 41: 164–65); WA, 51: 484, 1–16 (LW 41: 197–98).

gitimate, a real and a perverted, a true and a false church. The theological distinction turns into an apologetic criterion to distinguish and to exclude the other.

This is where Luther's criticism of the church becomes acrimonious: "Neither do we allow them to be the church nor are they in fact the church."[24] It is the *notae Ecclesiae* that provide the decisive criteria for distinguishing between an *ecclesia vera* and an *ecclesia falsa*.[25] In the conflict with the church of Cain, the church of the devil, the true church of those elected by God finds itself in a position of persecution and oppression, and it is precisely though this situation that it recognizes itself as the true church. Only a suffering and persecuted church resembles Christ. The true church is the church of the persecuted and the martyred; martyrdom becomes the distinctive sign of the church.[26]

It would take more than four-hundred years for the Roman Catholic Church to recognize Luther's qualitative criterion of the church in a self-differentiating and self-critical manner against every organizational realization of the church, and then to respond to Luther's demand for a dialectic between power and powerlessness as the true "*notum Ecclesiae*":

> Just as Christ carried out the work of redemption in poverty and persecution, so the Church is called to follow the same route that it might communicate the fruits of salvation to men. Similarly, the Church encompasses with love all who are afflicted with human suffering and in the poor and afflicted sees the image of its poor and suffering Founder. It does all it can to relieve their need and in them it strives to serve Christ. While Christ, holy, innocent, and undefiled knew nothing of sin, but came to expiate only the sins of the people, the Church, embracing in its bosom sinners, at the same time holy and always in need of being purified, always follows the way of penance and renewal (Second Vatican Council, *Dogmatic Constitution on the Church, Lumen Gentium*, 8).

We still underestimate the approach towards an ecclesiological self-revitalization which can be rooted in this passage of the Second Vatican Council. It follows close upon the most famous word of the council, the "*subsistit in.*" It is Christ himself and the fellowship of Christ that becomes the benchmark. Thus, the historical realization of the one church of Christ in the Roman Catholic Church (cf. LG 8, 2) is never without sin but constantly in need of penance and purification, as LG 8, 3 emphasizes. And thus "the actual reform of the

---

24. *Die Bekenntnisschriften der evangelisch-lutherischen Kirchen*, 9th ed. (Göttingen: Vandenhoeck & Ruprecht, 1982), 459: 18–19; Robert Kolb and Timothy J. Wengert, eds., *The Book of Concord: The Confessions of the Evangelical Lutheran Church* (Minneapolis: Fortress Press, 2000), 324.

25. cf. *Wider Hans Worst*, WA, 51: 487, 3-6 (LW 41: 199).

26. cf. WA, 51: 484, 5-6 (LW 41: 197).

church" is rooted in a process of "rethinking and returning to Christ."[27] Every realization of the church of Jesus Christ in the Catholic Church is therefore characterized as a broken one, which blocks every undifferentiated concept of representation. The church is always "an unfinished reality" in a constant dynamic. It is "a restless pilgrim, constantly on the lookout."[28] This is why the church is always "just" an instrument, "a means to an end." It never exists for its own sake but for its mission—and it does this only under an eschatological *provisio* (cf. LG 8, 3). What is indestructible and immutable in the church is rooted in its utilization by God and is realized in a form and shape that changes throughout history: "The Church always lives . . . on the proclamation of its own preliminary nature and its proceeding dissolution into God's kingdom towards which it is on pilgrimage. . . . The essence of the Church is the pilgrimage towards a future that is yet to come."[29] Shouldn't this be a powerful support for the thesis of the bishop emeritus of Erfurt, Joachim Wanke, namely that "450 years later the Second Vatican Council has rehabilitated Luther's concerns and honored them within the Catholic Church"?[30]

That leads me to my final point:

5. LUTHER'S ECCLESIOLOGY AND THE SECOND VATICAN COUNCIL: COMING HOME?

I'd like to focus on two aspects concerning this question:

1. A Necessary Relativization of an Extreme Papalism

Yves Congar deemed it "a strange fact that this Council [of Trent], that should answer to the Reformation, has not dealt with the ecclesiological problem."[31] Trent, then, avoided answering the ecclesiological core question about who represents the church and what kind of constitution the church actually has. The council fathers did not dare to answer this question and thus left it to

27. Lothar Lies, "Beobachtungen zu einem neuen Theologieverständnis (Vat. II und Würzburger Synode)," *Zeitschrift für katholische Theologie*, 130 (2008): 31.

28. Olegario González Hernández, "Das neue Selbstverständnis der Kirche und seine geschichtlichen und theologischen Voraussetzungen," in: *De ecclesia. Beiträge zur Konstitution 'Über die Kirche' des Zweiten Vatikanischen Konzils*, vol. 1, ed. Guilherme Baraúna (Freiburg: Herder, 1966), 179.

29. Johanna Rahner, *Creatura Evangelii, Vom Verhältnis von Rechtfertigung und Kirche* (Freiburg: Herder, 2003), 628.

30. Joachim Wanke, "2017: evangelisch und katholisch," *Christ in der Gegenwart* 23 (2011): 253–54.

31. Yves Congar, *Die Lehre von der Kirche - Vom abendländischen Schisma bis zur Gegenwart.* [Handbuch der Dogmengeschichte, vol. 3, fasc. 3] (Freiburg: Herder, 1971), 48.

the future political developments in the church to decide which structure would prevail in the end. But as we all know: Whoever hands over or squanders his responsibility, seldom wins it back, or has to fight painstakingly to win it back. We should then hardly be surprised that the reception of this council turned into a centrally prescribed implementation in the hands of a specifically established papal congregation, the *'Congregatio pro executione et interpretatione concilii Tridentini,'* as the one and only powerful actor in the post-Tridentine era. We here can witness a "post-conciliar takeover of Trent by the papacy."[32]

Looking at the post-Reformation history of the Catholic Church helps us to realize that competition between the denominations always forces them to define what is exclusively their own, to standardize it, to make it uniform. Confessional identity turns into a group identity, a trademark, and the self-understanding takes shape in the form of a "tribal ecclesiology"[33] that does not dare to allow for any internal differentiation, as Roger Haight puts it. This "tribalism" is the beginning of a denominational impoverishment, which is also responsible for the aftermath of a Roman centralism in the wake of the Council of Trent. In the denominational era, the plurality that had been a longstanding tradition in the medieval church was reduced to a uniform identity and ideology that made every other way of thinking appear as non-Catholic. This ultimately led to a papalist self-construction which, on closer examination, is in itself only partly catholic.

But as early as the beginning of the nineteenth century, we witness a turning of the tide against the plausibility of such a self-construction. In face of the specters of Gallicanism and Josephinism and shaken by the concrete experience of the French Revolution and the loss of the Papal States, papal monarchism begins to understand itself as the one and only *societas perfecta*, not just like the other absolutist regimes of its time, but even better. *But* it also shows the *aporia* of this form of government. The modern enlightened society of the nineteenth century, however, rejects such a self-conception as "outdated" a view that is supported by various intellectual movements. The representatives of the Catholic Church in the nineteenth century have no answers to such questions other than to isolate themselves and condemn the "errors of this time" which include ideas such as democracy, freedom of speech, and freedom of conscience—the plague of Americanism as the Holy Office called it. It is a consequence of such extreme positioning that the Roman Catholic Church up until this day does not seem to be ready for the challenges of modernity.

---

32. Günther Wassilowsky, "Trient," in: *Erinnerungsorte des Christentums,* ed. Christoph Markschies and Hubert Wolf (Munich: C. H. Beck, 2010), 408.

33. Cf. Roger Haight, *Christian Community in History,* vol. 2, esp. pp. 1–9; and *Christian Community in History.* vol. 3: *Ecclesial Existence* (New York: Continuum, 2008), 3–5.

One reason why this is so might be a certain institutional perseverance present in the traditional form of management. The structural alternatives to it, at least since the Reformation, have carried the 'smell of heresy.' But the Church would be "ill-advised" to ignore these possible alternatives in the long run, according to the Münster church historian Hubert Wolf. Here we could also refer to the words of Pope Francis:

> From the beginning of my ministry as Bishop of Rome, I sought to enhance the Synod, which is one of the most precious legacies of the Second Vatican Council. . . . It is precisely this path of synodality which God expects of the Church of the third millennium. . . (...). In a synodal Church, as I have said "it is not advisable for the Pope to take the place of local Bishops in the discernment of every issue which arises in their territory." In this sense, I am conscious of the need to promote a sound "decentralization." . . . I am persuaded that in a synodal Church, greater light can be shed on the exercise of the Petrine primacy.[34]

The other reason for the Roman Catholic Church's inability to deal with modern times might be that it has only partially realized the self-critical assessment that, according to Luther, should be at the heart of every ecclesiology. This brings me to my second point.

2. Self-criticism as a Fundamental Principle of Ecclesiology

The church as an entity that proclaims the word of God can represent its foundational event only in a broken, symbolic, and metaphorical way through language. We might go as far as to say that every tradition that represents its foundational event, every *traditio,* brings with it a certain betrayal and sin. This *caveat* cannot be simply institutionalized but must be called to attention constantly and in a self-critical fashion, with every ecclesial attempt to represent God's universal saving will. Every ecclesiology, and especially a Catholic one, profits from remembering this set of criteria, keeping it alive, and, furthermore, making it concrete even against the history of the church, in which the stereotype of being a sacred institution of salvation is too much stressed and the truth of 'being an instrument only' is too often forgotten. To demand permanently such a set of criteria is one of the key features of Luther's ecclesiology. Every self-understanding of the church can and must stick to these criteria. From such

---

34. His Holiness Pope Francis, "Address of His Holiness Pope Francis" (speech at ceremony commemorating the 50th anniversary of the institution of the Synod of Bishops, Vatican City, 17 October 2015), http://w2.vatican.va/content/francesco/en/speeches/2015/october/documents/papa-francesco_20151017_50-anniversario-sinodo.html.

a point of view, the relationship between the essence and the form of the church is not arbitrary. Here we reach a point in the ecumenical discourse where the Catholic side needs to ask for concrete institutional realizations of the church but it has to do it in light of an ecclesiological iconoclasm as a main principle of the Reformation. What such iconoclasm could look like has become apparent in the suggestions of Jorge Mario Bergolio, then still a cardinal, at the preliminary conclave in March of 2013: "The Church is called to go outside of itself and go to the peripheries, not just the geographic but also the existential peripheries," he said, "those of the mystery of sin, of pain, injustice, ignorance, spiritual privation, thoughts and complete misery."[35]

35. https://catholicismpure.wordpress.com/2013/03/27/cardinal-bergoglios-now-pope-francis-speech-to-the-cardinals-before-the-conclave-criticising-theological-narcissism/.

V. Eastern Christianity

12. *Ecclesia Orientalis*:

Heretical or Saintly? The Leipzig Debate (1519) and Western Approaches to Eastern Christianity in the High and Later Medieval Periods

Yury P. Avvakumov

The topic of Eastern Christianity began to be publicly drawn into controversies between Reformers and their opponents from the very beginning of the Reformation era. In Martin Luther's early encounters with pro-papal controversialists, the example of Eastern Christians, particularly Greeks, served as an argument in ecclesiological discussion of the Roman papacy's role in the universal church. Luther briefly referenced Eastern Christians in his negotiations with the papal legate Thomas de Vio Cajetan in October 1518 in Augsburg. He denounced those who "dare deny that one can be a Christian without being submitted to the pope and his decretals" and who "for more than eight hundred years […] have thrown out of the church of Christ Christians in all the Orient and Africa who never were under the Roman Pontiff or even understood the Gospel [i.e., Mt. 16:18] in the [papalist] sense."[1] In a more detailed manner, Eastern Christianity was discussed in the Leipzig debate in July 1519. Both interlocutors, Martin Luther and Johannes Eck, cited the example of the "Greeks and Orientals" to corroborate their respective positions.[2]

---

1. *Acta Augustana*, in WA 2:20, 6–8: "Ac sic plusquam octingentorum annorum Christianos totius orientis et Affricae nobis ex ecclesiae Christi eiiciunt, qui nunquam sub Romano Pontifice fuerunt nec Euangelium unquam sic intellexerunt." English trans. in *Luther's Works* [henceforth—LW], Vol. 31: *Career of the reformer: I.*, ed. Harold J. Grimm and Helmut T. Lehmann (Philadelphia: Fortress Press, 1971), 281, slightly modified by me. On Luther's remarks about the Greek Church before 1519, see Gunnar Hering, "Orthodoxie und Protestantismus," *Jahrbuch der Österreichischen Byzantinistik,* 31 (1981) 823–874, here: 826–827.

2. *Disputatio inter Ioannem Eckium et Martinum Lutherum. 1519,* in *D. Martin Luthers Werke. Kritische Gesamtausgabe,*Vol. 59 (Weimar: H. Böhlaus Nachfolger, 1983), 427–605 (Weimarer Ausgabe, henceforth—WA 59). Abridged English trans. in William H. T. Dau, *The Leipzig Debate in 1519. Leaves from the Story of Luther's Life* (St. Louis: Concordia, 1919) (henceforth—Dau); English trans. of a brief excerpt and a related letter written by Luther in LW 31: 305–325. Background writings by Eck are edited in Peter Fabisch and Erwin Iserloh, eds., *Dokumente zur Causa Lutheri.* 2. Teil: *Vom Augsburger Reichstag 1518 bis zum Wormser Edikt 1521,* Corpus Catholicorum, 42 (Münster: Aschendorff, 1991), 241–315. On the debate: Markus Hein and Armin Kohle, eds., *Die Leipziger Disputation 1519. 1. Leipziger Arbeitsgespräch zur Reformation* (Leipzig: Evangelische Verlagsanstalt, 2011). On Johannes Eck: Erwin Iserloh, *Johannes Eck (1486-1543). Scholastiker, Humanist, Kontro-*

It is instructive to read the dialogue between Eck and Luther through the prism of the medieval approaches to Eastern Christianity, since the arguments in favor of and against Eastern Christians brought forward by Luther and Eck are rooted in the theological discourse of preceding centuries.

1. LUTHER VS. ECK ON EASTERN CHRISTIANITY: TRADITION OR INNOVATION?

On July 4, 1519, Luther introduced the notion of the Greek Church (*Graeca ecclesia*) into the debate in Leipzig by pointing to the fact that this Church "has given no consent [to the idea that one person ought to be regarded as the high-est monarch in the entire Church], and yet has not been treated as heretical."[3] Eck responded with the following words: "Let the reverend father, I pray, quit mentioning and insulting us with the Greeks and Orientals (*Graecis et orientali-bus*), who have become exiles from the Christian faith when they fell away from the Roman Church."[4] Luther fired back by asking Eck "in that vaunted Eckian modesty of his to spare so many thousands of saints (*tot milibus sanctorum*) in the Greek Church, which has existed hitherto, and, without doubt, will continue to exist."[5] In his reply, Eck summarized his view of the Greeks as follows: "For a long time the Greeks have not only been schismatics, but extreme heretics (*hereticissimos*), as the great multitude of their errors and their stubborn claims show, such as their teaching concerning the Holy Spirit, confession, the spu-riousness of three evangelists, and innumerable other things, even if they have frequently rendered to the Roman Church a sort of feigned obedience, for instance, at the council of Florence in the days of Pope Eugene IV."[6] Luther retorted by stressing that "no other part of the universal Church has produced greater writers (*excellentiores scriptores*) than the Greek Church."[7] Eck, however, countered that this had been very long ago, but, since then, the Greeks have fallen into gravest errors, and have lost both the orthodox faith as well as the

---

verstheologe (Münster: Aschendorff, 1981); Erwin Iserloh, ed., *Johannes Eck (1486-1543) im Streit der Jahrhunderte* (Münster: Aschendorff, 1988); David V. N. Bagghi, *Luther's Earliest Opponents. Catholic Controversialists, 1518-1525* (Minneapolis: Fortress Press, 1991), Index; Max Ziegelbauer, *Johannes Eck. Mann der Kirche im Zeitalter der Glaubensspaltung* (St. Ottilien: EOS Verlag, 1987); Richard Rex, *The Making of Martin Luther* (Princeton and Oxford: Princeton University Press, 2017), on the debate, 108-134. An interesting perspective on Luther in the light of medieval heritage is Gregory Sobolewski, *Martin Luther, Roman Catholic Prophet* (Milwaukee: Marquette University Press, 2001).

   3. WA 59: 439; for Engl. transl. cf. Dau, 137.
   4. WA 59: 443; Dau, 141.
   5. WA 59: 448; Dau, 149.
   6. WA 59: 453; Dau, 155.
   7. WA 59: 456.

Christian Empire.[8] Luther pointed out that the faith of the Church did not depend on temporal power and that talk about the loss of the Empire by the Greeks was irrelevant to the topic of the debate.[9] Eck quoted, to corroborate his arguments against the Greeks, the chapter *De summa Trinitate et de fide catholica* of the second council of Lyon (1274) and the treatise *Contra errores Graecorum* by Thomas Aquinas.[10] Luther concluded with the following words: "I would never dare to call one particular Church schismatic because of a few evil and schismatic people."[11]

The debate between Luther and Eck reflects the ambiguity that existed in later medieval theology in respect to the Eastern Church. Both interlocutors appeal, directly or indirectly, to the preceding tradition. Luther begins his entire argument by pointing to the fact that the Greek Church has never been regarded as heretical. Eck, on the contrary, quotes medieval councils and Thomas Aquinas as proof that the Greeks are not only schismatics, but the worst heretics. Which of these two—Eck or Luther—presents the medieval Latin tradition more truthfully? Can we detect "tradition" or "innovation" in their views?

At first glance, Eck seems to be on a more substantial footing by providing specific references to medieval predecessors, Aquinas in particular. Luther's views, on the contrary, seem to diverge from the official Roman standpoint of his day no less radically than his positions on other issues discussed in the Leipzig debate. A closer look at the history of the treatment of Eastern Christianity in high and later medieval theology, however, reveals a different picture. Martin Luther's attitude towards Eastern Christianity in the Leipzig debate is, in fact, profoundly rooted in the traditions of high and later medieval Latin theology. Johannes Eck also relies on a number of motifs and paradigms of the medieval Latin tradition; however, if we look at the debate in its entirety through the lenses of the preceding medieval theological thought, it is Luther, not Eck, who appears to be "traditionalist" rather than an "innovator."

Given the interplay of continuities and discontinuities in medieval thought, it makes sense to approach the theology of the scholastic era, from the twelfth to the fifteenth century, as a certain unity in respect of its approach to the Christian East. The degree of continuity in this period is considerable, and certain paradigms, motifs, and formulae concerning Eastern Christianity surface and re-surface again and again. I will highlight a few points relevant for understanding the positions taken by Eck and Luther in the Leipzig debate.

8. WA 59: 458.
9. WA 59: 463.
10. WA 59: 482–83.
11. WA 59: 493: "Absit ut propter paucos malos et schismaticos totam ecclesiam aliquam schismaticam appellem."

2. 'Nestorini'—'Jacobini'—'Graeci': The Variety of Eastern Christians in Medieval Theology

To begin with, a few words on terminology are due. The interlocutors in Leipzig used the terms and expressions "Greek Church," "Greeks," and "Orientals" to describe the Eastern Churches. The word *orientales* covered, in the medieval period, a wide spectrum of peoples, languages, cultures, ecclesial traditions and rites, both Chalcedonian and non-Chalcedonian. The non-Chalcedonians comprised two major categories, *Nestorini* (Nestorians) and *Jacobini* (Miaphysites), who were regarded throughout the medieval period as heretics. With the term "Greeks," the situation was different. One must be careful not to misread the "Greeks," *Graeci,* of medieval theological Latin exclusively as a designation of Greek ethnicity, since *Graeci* did not refer exclusively to ethnic Greeks, or to Greek-speaking Christians. In our contemporary understanding, the medieval designation *Graeci* can be interpreted as "Christians of the Byzantine (Greek) rite and culture." It is obvious that ethnic Greeks and the Greek-speaking Christians comprised the basic majority of those Christians; however, the generic term *Graeci* could also include other ethnicities, such as Bulgarians, Serbs, Georgians, and Ruthenians, since they all belonged to the sphere of ecclesiastical and cultural influence of Byzantium.

An example of such usage is found in the works of the Dominican missionary Riccoldo da Montecroce (ca. 1243–1320).[12] A traveler to the Near East himself, Riccoldo demonstrates a first-hand acquaintance with Eastern nations. In his *Libellus ad ations orientales* (ca. 1300), he makes an attempt to classify the inhabitants of the East according to their religious affiliation. Among Christian nations he distinguishes three groups: Nestorians (*Nestorini*) and Jacobites (*Jacobini*), who are "Christians, however heretics;"[13] and Greeks, who are "very similar to us," i.e., Latins. Nestorians and Jacobites, Riccoldo acknowledges, have "full and intact law, that is, Old and New Testaments," and they "confess the incarnation of Christ in a plain language." However, they differ from Latins greatly in respect to their understanding of how the Incarnation took place.[14] The word *Graeci* designates for Riccoldo not only ethnic Greeks, but also other nations of the same ecclesiastical provenance; in a similar manner, he counts Armenians and Copts among the Jacobites:

---

12. On Riccoldo and his works, see: Antoine Dondaine, "Ricoldiana. Notes sur les oeuvres de Ricoldo da Montecroce," *Archivum fratrum Praedicatorum* (henceforth—AFP), 37 (1967), 119-179; Emilio Panella, « Ricerche su Riccoldo da Monte di Croce, » AFP, 58 (1988), 5-85.

13. Dondaine, "Ricoldiana," 162.

14. Dondaine, "Ricoldiana," 162-163.

In different parts of the Orient there are also other sects or nations, about which it is not necessary to make special mention, because they can be reduced to those listed above [i.e., Jacobites, Nestorians, and Greeks]. There are Armenians, but they are Jacobites. . . . There are Copts, especially in Egypt, but they are also Jacobites. There are also Maronites: they differ a little from the Jacobites, and they have their own Catholicos on the mountain Lebanon. There are also Georgians, Russians, Iberians, Alans, Ruthenians. Those all or for the most part are Greeks. About the Greeks I did not say anything in particular because they are very close to us, by their area of habitation, alphabet, speech, language, customs, rite, faith and the form of piety. However, as the experience testifies, the main controversy between us and them is not about faith but about the temporal power and the governance over Constantinople which Greeks refuse to give to the Latins. They would have easily made concord with us about the procession of the Holy Spirit if the lust for power and desire for possession could be removed from their midst.[15]

The meaning of the word *Graeci* in Riccoldo's triad *Nestorini—Jacobini—Graeci* seems to be closer to a modern confessional/denominational distinction than to a designation of people/ethnicity, which at first glance this word appears to be. It is symptomatic, however, that, for Riccoldo, only the dogmatic issues discussed in the early ecumenical councils build the basis for a properly religious distinction; "Greeks" and "Latins," on the contrary, comprise a single body, divided only for political, not religious, reasons.

It is telling that, while Luther preferred to use the expression "the Greek church" (*Graeca ecclesia*), Eck spoke about the "Greeks" (*Graeci*) and "Orientals" (*Orientales*). This difference is significant. It reflects a fundamental disagreement between the interlocutors: Luther was convinced that the Greeks were neither schismatics nor heretics, and that their church was a part of the universal Church; for Eck, to the contrary, the Greeks—together with other "Orientals," which included the "heretical" Nestorians and Miaphysites—were not only schismatics but also, worse, heretics who had abandoned the true Church by falling away from Rome.

3. Western Theological Perceptions of Eastern Christianity: Two Variables

The Western theological perception of Eastern Christianity in the later medieval period was determined by at least two variables: the acquaintance of the Latins with early church history and the patristic heritage, on the one hand,

---

15. Dondaine, "Ricoldiana," 168, cf. Biblioteca Nazionale Centrale di Firenze, Conv. Soppr. C. 8.1173, fol. 242v.

and their interaction with contemporary Eastern Christians, on the other. Greek's status as the original language of the Gospels and apostolic writings and, along with Hebrew and Latin, one of the three "classical" languages of the Church, fostered a tone of respect that Greek literacy enjoyed in Latin medieval theology. The notions of the "early church" (*ecclesia primitiva*), "the teachers of the Church" (*doctores ecclesiae*), and early church councils (*antiqua concilia*) implied the awareness of the exceptional historical role that the East played in the formation of the Church and the formulation of Christian dogma. Throughout the later Middle Ages, Western theologians developed a growing interest in the "Greek doctors" (*doctores Graeci*), thanks in particular to the increasing number of translations. Beginning from the "twelfth century renaissance" and the ascendency of scholasticism in the thirteenth century, and continuing to the era of emerging humanistic tendencies in the fourteenth and fifteenth centuries, academic theologians gained prestige by displaying at least some acquaintance with the Greek language and the Greek Fathers. Additional stimulus came from the liberal arts, which laid a special value on the Greek heritage (to be sure, in translation). The high reputation of pagan Greek philosophy and the ubiquity of the names of Plato and Aristotle contributed to the esteem for the Greek doctors of the Church, whom the West saw as heirs of classical philosophical wisdom.[16] As controversies with contemporary Byzantines heated in the later medieval period, Latin theologians began to explain the "absurd" assaults of the "Greeks" on Western teachings and practices by the "decline of the East" (*perditio Orientis*), the loss of wisdom by the "modern Greeks" (*Graeci moderni*), and the "transfer of learning" (*translatio studiorum*) from the Orient to the Occident;[17] however, the very idea of "transfer" implied that it was the East that originally had been the source of theological knowledge and scholarship.

Acquaintance with the history of the "ancient councils" and the Trinitarian and Christological controversies of the early Christian centuries supplied some knowledge of the dissident theological movements of the Orient that emerged in that period, and of the ecclesiastical parties that were in conflict with cath-

---

16. On the Latin-Greek interaction in the area of philosophy, see recently: Sten Ebbesen, *Greek-Latin Philosophical Interaction. Collected Essays.* Vol. 1 (Aldershot: Ashgate, 2008); Idem, "What Did the Scholastics Know about Greek History and Culture?" in Martin Hinterberger and Chris Schabel, eds., *Greeks, Latins, and Intellectual History 1204-1500* (Leuven, Paris, Walpole MA: Peeters, 2011), 169-182.

17. Humbert da Silva Candida, *Dialogus* 48, in Cornelius Will, *Acta et scripta quae de controversiis Ecclesiae graecae et latinae saeculo undecimo composita extant* (Leipzig: Elwert, 1861), 118; Otto of Freising, *Chronica*, lib. 5 prol., ed. Adolf Hofmeister and Walter Lammers (Darmstadt: Wissenschaftliche Buchgesellschaft, 1974), 372-374; Bonaventure, *In I Sententiarum*, dist. 11, art. unic. q. 1 in *Opera omnia edita studio et cura PP. Collegii a S. Bonaventura.*Vol. 1 (Quaracchi: Typogr. Coll. S. Bonaventurae, 1882), 212.

olic/orthodox teaching. While the "Greek doctors" towered as teachers of catholic doctrine, the lists of ancient heresies, handed down to the later Middle Ages from Augustine's *De haresibus* through Isidore of Seville, Etymologiae VIII, 5, testified to the Orient being the source of heretical teachings and movements. Thus, an ambivalent picture of the early Christian East emerged: on the one hand, it was seen as the birthplace of the catholic wisdom of the Greek Church Fathers and early councils; on the other hand, the East was also deemed to be the cradle of numerous heresies.[18] We can see an echo of these attitudes in Eck's view of the Greeks expressed in Leipzig. However, even in their most "anti-Oriental" mood, medieval Western theologians still seemed to feel a certain reverence before the extraordinary significance of the early Christian East for church history and theology. When exploring the intricacies of the relations between Latins and Orientals in the later medieval period, one must always keep in mind the role that the notion of the early, patristic Christian East played in shaping the overall Western picture of the Orient. This clearly distinguishes Latin attitudes towards Eastern "schismatics" from polemics against the Western heretical movements of the period: the attacks on the latter were much more vehement and the calls for persecution much more unscrupulous than in the former case.

The second variable that determined the Western perception of the East was the direct acquaintance and interaction with contemporary Eastern Churches and Christians. The places of frequent encounter that encouraged a deeper knowledge of the other side were frontier territories, such as southern Italy, Sicily, and Dalmatia, where Latins and Greeks happened to live for centuries in close proximity. To such places belonged also the city of Constantinople itself, due to the long history of Latin merchant colonies in the Byzantine capital—Amalfitan, Genoese, Pisan, and Venetian.[19] In its turn, the Greek Grottaferrata monastery near Rome, founded in the early eleventh century, secured the presence of monks and clergy of the Greek rite at the very heart of the Latin ecclesiastical world. Pilgrimages to the Holy Land, and the Crusades, provided further opportunities to meet Eastern Christians and to learn about Eastern Churches. The crusading campaigns and the Latin Orient became an indispensable source of first-hand reports about the Christian East, even if the Crusaders and the

---

18. On the Church of Constantinople as the cradle of heresies, see Rupert of Deutz, *Liber de divinis officiis* II 22, Corpus Christianorum. Continuatio Mediaevalis, 7 (Turnhout: Brepols, 1967), 52-53; Anselm of Havelberg, *Anticimenon* III, 6, Patrologia Latina, 188 (Paris: Migne, 1855), 1215-1216; cf. Humbert da Silva Candida, *Dialogus* 29, in C. Will, ed., *Acta et scripta*, 107) and 49 (ibid., 123).

19. On Latin presence in Constantinople see: Raymond Janin, *Constantinople byzantine. Développement urbain et répertoire topographique* (Paris: Institut Français d'Études Byzantines, 1964), 245-255.

Latin rulers and clergy in the Crusader States displayed at times a disheartening insensitivity and lack of understanding towards Eastern Christians, and their reports, transmitted to the West, easily acquired legendary and fantastic features.[20]

4. "FELLOW CHRISTIANS"? "SCHISMATICS"? "HERETICS"? STRUGGLES OVER UNDERSTANDING THE GREEKS

By the fifteenth century, a list of the five controversial theological issues (πέντε διαφοραί) between Latins and Greeks was formed. This list included (1) the procession of the Holy Spirit, (2) the Eucharistic bread (leavened in the Greek Church, unleavened in the Latin), (3) purgatory, (4) the beatitude of the saints, and (5) papal primacy. Theological and ecclesiastical–political controversies between Latins and Greeks resulted in sporadic charges of schism and of heresy. For Popes Gregory VII and Urban II, as well as for most of the theologians and church leaders throughout the twelfth century, the Greeks were still unambig-uously *conchristiani* ("fellow Christians") and *fratres* ("brothers").[21] It is from the conquest of Constantinople by the Crusaders in 1204 onwards that certain Greeks, who resented the Latin rule in Constantinople and did not recognize the Latin Patriarch in Constantinople—and only these—began to be referred to as "schismatics" by Latins. It is also during this time that the notion of the *schisma Graecorum* (the "Greek schism") gained use in Latin theology. The foun-dations of such an understanding were laid by Pope Innocent III. He was also responsible for the move that would eventually result in charges of heresy directed against the Greek Church: the Fourth Lateran Council summoned by Innocent in 1215 introduced, for the first time in history, the Latin teaching of the procession of the Holy Spirit from the Father and the Son (*Filioque*) into the text of its constitution. But it would be a misrepresentation to say that the Greeks began to be universally accused of schism and heresy beginning from 1215. Even the chapter *Firmiter credimus* of the Fourth Lateran Council, that constitutes the core of the chapter *De sancta Trinitate et fide catholica* (which Eck mentions to support his thesis about the Greeks as the worst heretics), does not contain any specific condemnation of the Greek Church and does not define

---

20. Benjamin Arbel, et al., *Latins and Greeks in the Eastern Mediterranean after 1204* (London: Frank Cass, 1989); Benjamin Z. Kedar, *Franks, Muslims and Oriental Christians in the Latin Levant. Studies in Frontier Acculturation* (Aldershot: Ashgate Variorum, 2006); Christopher D. Schabel, *Greeks, Latins, and the Church in Early Frankish Cyprus* (Burlington, VT: Ashgate Variorum, 2010) .

21. E.g., Pope Urban II in his crusade appeal according to "Narratio Floriacensis de captis Antiochia et Hierosolyma," in Academie des inscriptios et belles-lettres, *Recueil des historiens des croisades,* Tome V: *Historiens occidentaux* (Paris: Impr. Royale, 1906), 356; Pope Gregory VII in his appeal for the defense of Constantinople, March 1, 1074 in Erich Caspar, ed., *Registrum* I: 49, Mon-umenta Germaniae Historica, Epistolae selectae, II/1-2 (Berlin: Weidmann, 1920), 75.

Greeks as heretics.[22] Accusations did not have a systematic and universal character and—what is particularly important for our context—they were not established canonically. Aquinas' treatise adduced by Eck also contained, despite the
title under which it is known in its manuscript tradition, no charges of heresy
against the Greek Church. The distinction between a relatively small group of
obstinate Greek hierarchs and theologians and the rest of the Greeks who followed their schismatic church leaders without consciously sharing their schismatic views—a distinction which we clearly find in such Latin theologians as
Roger Marston in the late thirteenth/early fourteenth century[23]—helped to
prevent accusing the entire Greek Church of schism. The overall sense in the
later medieval centuries was that there were serious issues in relations between
the Churches of Rome and of Constantinople and that unity was endangered,
probably even lost, and therefore had to be re-established. The re-establishment
of unity, however, could be understood in a variety of ways and fluctuated
between the concept of *reductio ad oboedientiam* ("compulsion to obedience"),
on the one hand, and the idea of *unio ecclesiarum* or *pax ecclesiarum* ("the union
of the churches," or "the peace between the churches"), on the other. The
"reductionist" model seems to have been dominant in the Second Council of
Lyons 1274;[24] the idea of the "peace of the churches" was praised and promoted
at the Council of Florence in 1439: both models are found in reading the respective conciliar documents and writings. The plural of the word "churches" in the
latter case is notable: it is a clear sign of the recognition of the Greek Church as
a particular "church." In this sense, in the Leipzig debate, Luther appears to be
a successor of the Florentine legacy.

5. THE COUNCIL OF FLORENCE AND ITS LEGACY

The date 1439 marks the last major attempt of union before the conquest
of Constantinople by the Turks in 1453 and the fall of the Byzantine Empire. A
prominent American historian of Greek origin called the council in Ferrara/
Florence of 1438-39 "the most brilliant convocation of Greeks and Latins in
the entire Middle Ages" that "marked the first occasion in centuries that East

22. Norman P. Tanner, ed., *Decrees of Ecumenical Councils*. Vol. 1: *Nicea I to Lateran V*. (London:
Sheed & Ward; Washington DC: Georgetown University Press, 1990), 230 and 314 [henceforth—
Tanner, *Decrees*].

23. Roger Marston, Quodlibet 2, q. 10: *Utrum filii schismaticorum sint in statu salutis, maxime
illi qui schismati non consentiunt*, in Girard I. Etzkorn and Ignatius C. Brady, eds., *Quodlibeta quatuor*,
Bibliotheca franciscana scholastica Medii aevi, 26 (Grottaferrata: Collegio S. Bonaventura, Padri
Ed. di Quaracchi, 1994), 181-183.

24. In modern research, Lyon II is often referred to as a "union council"; this view has been
compellingly contested by Burkhard Roberg, *Das Zweite Konzil von Lyon (1274)* (Paderborn:
Schöningh, 1990), see esp. 59-87.

and West assembled in ecumenical council to debate the differences separating their two churches."[25] This characterization remains true, even if we recognize that the council, sharply criticized theologically by its adversaries and accused of predominantly political motivation, was ultimately rejected by the Byzantine church.[26] It is hardly possible to deny that the union with the Greeks achieved in Florence on July 6, 1439, and a series of subsequent unions concluded in Florence and Rome—with the Armenians on November 22, 1439; with the Copts on February 4, 1442; with the Syrians of Mesopotamia on November 30, 1444; and with the Maronites and Chaldeans of Cyprus on August 7, 1445—resulted from a serious and sincere intellectual effort by a group of the outstanding theologians and church leaders of that time.

The crucial achievement of Florence lies in the sheer fact of a common council bringing together leading hierarchs and intellectuals from both churches, ready to discuss issues dividing them without imposing any preconditions on the partner. For the papacy, such policy meant a radical shift from the entire course since 1204. This shift, especially evident if compared with the staunch "reductionism" of the council of Lyon in 1274, became possible due to the rise of the conciliarist movement that sought to find a solution for the stalemate of the Great Schism in the West (1378–1417). Conciliarist theologians, in their attempt to bring the rival Pisan, Roman, and Avigonese popes to a common council despite mutual excommunications among them, suggested a strategy that could be applied also to the handling of Greek "schismatics." This transfer of the Western conciliarist model onto relations with the Greeks can be clearly seen, in particular, in some of the sermons of Jean Gerson delivered in the context of the council of Pisa of 1409. Although Gerson has no hesitations about characterizing Byzantines as schismatics and even heretics,[27] he proposes to convoke a general council of both Latins and Greeks, "just as the recent council

---

25. Deno John Geanakoplos, *Constantinople and the West. Essays on the Late Byzantine (Palaeologan) and Italian Renaissances and the Byzantine and Roman Churches* (Madison, WI: The University of Wisconsin Press, 1989), 224.

26. On the Union of Florence, still indispensable is Joseph Gill, *The Council of Florence* (Cambridge, UK: Cambridge University Press, 1959); idem, *Personalities of the Council of Florence and Other Essays* (Oxford: Blackwell, 1964); idem, *Church Union: Rome and Byzantium (1204-1453)* (London: Variorum reprints, 1979). More recent important publications: Giuseppe Alberigo, ed., *Christian Unity. The Council of Ferrara-Florence 1438/39-1989* (Leuven: Leuven University Press, 1991); Sebastian Kolditz, *Johannes VIII. Palaiologos und das Konzil von Ferrara-Florenz (1438/39). Das byzantinische Kaisertum im Dialog mit dem Westen.* 2 Halbbände (Stuttgart: Hiersemann, 2013-2014).

27. *Sermo factus coram Alexandro Papa in die Ascensionis Domini 1409*, in Jean Gerson, *Opera Omnia*, ed. Louis Ellies Du Pin (Antwerp: Societas, 1706), II, col. 135A: "[Graecos] mala tempestas a sede Petri disjectos, non modo schismatis, sed nonnullius etiam haeresis macula foedavit." I quote the English translations from Gerson in Gill, *Personalities*, 247-249.

[i.e., the council of Pisa] was necessary for the peace of the Latins."[28] The Greeks should be permitted to attend this council "not as anathematized"; on the contrary, "a careful consideration should be given to what they wish to say."[29] In 1434, the council of Basel outlined, on similar premises, their plan for the future union with the Greeks in the constitution *Sicut pia mater* that stressed that the "universal synod" of Latins and Greeks had to be "free and inviolate," "that is, each may freely declare his judgment without any obstacle or violence."[30] After the breach between the Council of Basel and Eugene IV, the pope did his best to outdo his rivals in Basel in bringing Greeks into union with the Latin Church. This made him even more prone to allow discussion and seek compromise with the Easterners in Ferrara and Florence.[31]

6. LATIN MISSIONS TO THE EAST BETWEEN 'REDUCTION' AND 'UNION'

The ambivalent theological foundations of attitudes towards Eastern Christianity gave rise to opposing poles underlying the motivation for missions to the East at a practical level. At its core, the question about the "heretical" status of the Greeks touched upon the problem of unity in diversity, that is, the question of the permissible boundaries of dogmatic, theological, ritual, disciplinary variety within the One Church of Christ. At one pole, rigorous and juridical, the ultimate aim of placing the East under the power of the Roman Pope prevailed over the idea of the universal church as a plurality of particular churches and theological cultures, which led to the tendency to annihilate the allegedly "hazardous" canonical, theological, and liturgical features of the East: the theological and ritual specificity of the Greeks was considered tolerable as long as it did not contradict the dogmas of the Roman church; the final decision on the acceptance of a particular cultural specificity or its rejection belonged to the Holy See. At the opposite pole, "idealistic" and "visionary-ecumenical," the unreserved recognition of the validity of Eastern cultural traditions prevailed over juridical questions of subordination; hence, the priority of enlightening and educational missionary work in the East. In practice, the missions fluctuated

---

28. *Sermo pro pace ecclesiae et unione Graecorum*, in Gerson, *Opera Omnia*, II, col. 152C: "Et quia Graeci possint et velint convenire non est (ut apparet) dispositio altera convenientior ad pacem de qua loquimur, quam esse debeat dictum Concilium; nec alio meliori modo negotium hoc poterit expleri, sicut postremum Concilium fuit necessarium propter pacem Latinorum. . . ."

29. Ibid., 147C. ". . . non debent reputari pertinaces vel anathematizati. Hic diligenter considerandum esset, quid dicere vellent; vel inveniendum est medium expediens, ut omnia ponerentur ad concordiam."

30. Tanner, *Decrees*, 482.

31. For the document of Basel on the union with the Greeks, see Tanner, *Decrees,* 478-482.

between these two poles. The official institutions of the Roman curia seem to have been motivated by positions closer to the former pole, while the practical activity of Latins on missions tended to be motivated by the latter, although there were many exceptions to this general tendency, both among the function-aries of the Roman curia and among missionary workers.

This ambiguity is reflected in the missionary treatise that immediately pre-cedes the Reformation era: the *Libellus* that was directed by two Camaldolese monks, Paolo Guistiniani and Pietro Querini, to Pope Leo X in 1513.[32] The authors possessed a first-hand knowledge of Eastern Christianity. They identify seven Eastern Christian nations: Abyssinians (actually, Ethiopians), Jacobites, Armenians, Georgians, Syrians, Maronites, and Greeks. "What these nations have in common, is that they do not belong to the Roman Church; they either do not know the Roman Pontiff or do not believe that he is the head of all the Churches in the world."[33] On the one hand, the *Libellus* contains very positive words about Eastern Christians: "Practically all the men of those nations that we have met are so endowed with natural goodness and so ardent with zeal for their faith—which they believe to be the true one—and so zealous for the Christian religion that we European Christians might all blush for shame, if given the chance just once to observe the reverence that they have for those sacred places and the veneration they give to the title of Christian, and how modest and kind they are in all the duties of their life. As I continually pondered these things, I recall that I often exclaimed, 'These are real Christians, and we are semi-pagans!' [...] From what we could tell, they are ready to hear, and quick to understand, the views of others."[34] The authors add, however, "The exception are the Greeks, who from a stubborn pride and a more inflexible ignorance are not very willing to listen, or, when they do listen, to yield to reason. By the common consent of all the other nations, these occupy the last place among Christians, and thus the care of this one nation will be, in our estimation, more difficult than that of the others combined. [...] We believe, however, that even the Greeks will not be incorrigible if you [the Roman Pope] want to correct them."[35] The authors recommended that Leo X invite representatives of the seven Eastern Christian nations to the Lateran Council that had been initiated by Leo's predecessor, Julius II, and continued well into the year 1517. Leo X was indeed engaged in relations with Eastern Christians during the Council.

---

32. Paolo Giustiniani and Pietro Querini, *Libellus addressed to Leo X, Supreme Pontiff*, ed. and trans. Stephen M. Beall, annotator to the English text John J. Schmitt (Milwaukee: Marquette University Press, 2016) [henceforth—*Libellus*].

33. *Libellus*, 124/125–126/127.

34. *Libellus*, 128/129.

35. *Libellus*, 130/131.

Thus, he dealt with the problem of Greek-rite Ruthenians in Poland and tried to get the Grand Prince of Muscovy to send a representative to the Council.[36] He was also in friendly contact with Oriental Christians in the Eastern Mediterranean, in particular Ethiopians. The Maronite patriarch did send representatives to the Council, and they were formally received.[37]

Several factors contributed to the worsening of the attitude of the Roman church towards the Greeks in the late fifteenth and early sixteenth century considerably: in particular, the rejection of the Union of Florence by the Greek Church, which formally took place at a council in 1482; and the fall of the Eastern Roman Christian empire, which resulted in the Greek Church being deprived of her imperial protector and forced into a completely new political situation under Turkish domination. The fact that the patriarchs of Constantinople found some mode of co-existence and even co-operation with the new infidel rulers was seen by many in the West as a clear sign of the corruption of the Greek Church. The sympathies of pre-Reformation movements, as, for instance, the Utraquists in the first half of the fifteenth century, towards Eastern Christianity also played a negative role in the perception of the Christian East by the Roman Curia. The animosity against Christians of the Greek rite led to re-baptisms in some areas. Thus, in the Polish State in the early sixteenth century, the local Latin clergy re-baptized Ruthenian Christians of the Greek rite; the notorious *Elucidarium errorum ritus Ruthenici,* published by the Polish Latin theologian Johannes Sacranus (probably in 1500) who, like Eck eighteen years later, accused Greek-rite Christians of a multitude of grave errors and heresies, serves as a good example.[38] Pope Alexander VI had to issue, a year later in 1501, a special bull prohibiting the practice of re-baptisms of Ruthenians.[39] This decision, however, was reversed by Leo X in his bull *Sacrosanctae universalis* (1515).[40] As in so many other episodes in the history of relations between Latins and Eastern Christians, there is a tension and an interplay between intolerance, on the one hand, and recognition, on the other. Johannes Eck stands, in his inter-

---

36. Nelson H. Minnich, "Leo X's Response to the Report on the Errors of the Ruthenians" in Reimund Haas, ed., *Fiat voluntas tua. Theologe und Historiker—Priester und Professor. Festschrift zum 65. Geburtstag von Harm Klueting am 23. März 2014* (Münster: Aschendorff, 2014), 209-221.

37. Nelson H. Minnich, "The Orator of Jerusalem at Lateran V," in *Orientalia Christiana Periodica* 40 (1974): 364-376, reprinted in Id., *The Catholic Reformation: Councils, Churchmen, Controversies,* Collected Studies 403 (Brookfield, VT: Variorum, 1993), #II.

38. Johannes Sacranus, *Elucidarius errorum ritus Ruthenici* (Wilna: n.p., 1500; Krakow: Jan Haller, 1507; Köln: Martin von Werden, 1507, et al.).

39. Atanasij G. Welykyj, OSBM, ed., *Documenta Pontificum Romanorum historiam Ucrainae illustrantia (1073–1953),* vol. 1: *1075-1700* (Roma: Sumptibus Ucrainorum apud Exteros Degentium, 1953), 186-188.

40. Minnich, "Leo X's Response" (as in footnote 37), 219.

ventions in Leipzig, clearly on the side of those, for that period most recent, developments that led to the increase in intolerance towards Eastern Christians.

7. CONCLUSION: MARTIN LUTHER, A SUCCESSOR TO THE IDEA OF THE RECOGNITION OF EASTERN CHURCH IN MEDIEVAL SCHOLASTIC THOUGHT?

Martin Luther's concluding remark on the Greeks in the Leipzig debate, "I would never dare to call one particular Church schismatic because of a few evil and schismatic people,"[41] highlights a few fundamental principles of the paradigm of medieval thought that promoted "union and peace," not "reduction into obedience." It contains a distinction between "a few evil and schismatic people," on the one hand, and the entire Greek Church, on the other; it emphasizes the ecclesiological validity of the community of Greek-rite Christians by defining it as a particular Church (*aliqua ecclesia*), not just as a mass of undefined "Greek people" (*Graeci*); finally, it boldly challenges its interlocutor to the act of the recognition of that Church. This call for recognition reminds, typologically, of an early scholastic reply to the question whether the sacraments celebrated in the Greek church are valid, asked by Peter Comestor, a Parisian theologian who wrote his *Treatise on the sacraments* in the last quarter of the twelfth century. Peter sought an answer to the question whether the Eucharist can be celebrated in an "Eastern" way, that is, differently than it occurs in the Latin church—for example, if water is not added to the Eucharistic wine: some theologians say that there is no sacrament if water is not added. Comestor replies that the Eucharist *can* be celebrated without water, because "it would be absurd to affirm, that such great and religious a Church [as the Greek church] does not possess the sacrament [of the Eucharist]."[42] In its disarming simplicity, Comestor's argument is an example of a full ecclesiological recognition of the cultural other. The implicit logic of both statements, the one by Comestor and the one by Luther, is clear: if you recognize one particular body of Christians as a "church" you cannot call its sacraments false and you cannot declare it "schismatic" or "heretical," since this would be a *contradictio in adjecto*. Rather, you should accept those "Greeks," those Eastern Christians, with all the ecclesiological gravity that this entails, and aspire to mutual understanding with them.

41. See note 11 above.
42. Petrus Comestor, *Tractatus de sacramentis*, ed. Raymond M. Martin, in Henri Weisweiler, *Maitre Simon et son groupe. De sacramentis* (Louvain: Spicilegium Sacrum Lovaniense, 1937), 39*: "Quod est absurdum dicere, quod tanta et tam religiosa ecclesia non conficit." On the role of liturgical controversies for the relations between Greeks and Latins in the medieval period, see my book: Georgij Avvakumov, *Die Entstehung des Unionsgedankens: Die lateinische Theologie des Mittelalters in der Auseinandersetzung mit dem Ritus der Ostkirche* (Berlin: Akademie, 2002), esp. 335–371.

13. Luther and the Eastern Orthodox Church: Challenges and Opportunities of the Reformation

Nicolas Kazarian

When we talk about Luther and the Orthodox Church, the first thing that comes to mind is the Leipzig Debate between Luther and Eck, in July 1519. However, many scholars agree on Luther's lack of knowledge about the Orthodox Church, also referred to the "Greek Church" at the time.[1]

As it is often noted, Luther had no direct knowledge of the Orthodox Church, except the teaching of the Greek Church Fathers, whom he mentioned extensively during the 1519 debate and for whom he had a great respect. As we will see, he identified a direct relationship between the "Greek Church" and the Church Fathers, as the conversation with Eck evolved towards the authenticity of the Christian experience witnessed by the Early Church. Fr. George Florovsky, a preeminent Orthodox theologian, wrote: "The argument from Christian Antiquity has been constantly used in the controversy with Rome from the very beginning, from the famous Leipzig Disputation of Luther himself, in 1519. It was more than a reference to the past. It was also a timely reminder that Christendom was larger than the Romanized West."[2]

This paper will explore not only the use and implications of the "Greek Church" as an argument during the Leipzig Debate, but also Luther's legacy with regard to Orthodoxy.

THE "GREEK CHURCH" IN THE 1519 LEIPZIG DISPUTATIO

1519, almost two years after the publication of Luther's 95 theses against indulgences, was a crucial year on the path to Reformation, and the Leipzig *disputatio* of that year explored many theological topics. At first, Johannes Eck (1486–1543) debated with Andreas Bodenstein, known as Karlstadt. Eck's last

---

1. Ernest Benz, "Luther et l'Eglise orthodoxie," *Irénikon* 28, (1955): 410s.; Steven Runciman, *The Great Church in Captivity* (Cambridge, UK: Cambridge University Press, 1968), 239; Klaus-Peter Todt, *Orthodoxy and Protestantism, Four Lectures, Ecole Pratique des Hautes Études, Sciences religieuses, 2004* (Paris: s.n., 2004), 20.

2. Georges Florovsky, "Patriarch Jeremiah II and the Lutheran Divines," in: Id., *Christianity and Culture* (Belmont, MA: Nordland, 1974), vol. II, p.146.

argument dealt with the question of primacy, and was a direct attack against Luther. This was when Luther was allowed to enter the discussion. Over the course of two days, July 4 and July 5, Martin Luther faced off with Eck, who sought to protect and preserve the primacy of the Pope of Rome and of the Roman Church over the universal Church. This sequence of events initiated the estrangement that would ultimately lead to a split with the Catholic Church, since Luther was progressively characterized as a heretic.

1.1. The "Greek Church"

At one point during the *disputatio*, the "Greek Church" made an appearance. Luther declared:

> [Eck's] remark that at Rome and at the Seat of Peter originated sacerdotal unity, I grant quite freely, regarding the Western Church. But in reality, the Roman Church sprang from the Church at Jerusalem, and this latter is properly the mother of all churches. But the inference which he draws is worthless: since sacerdotal unity has its origin in the Roman Church, therefore that Church is the head and first mistress over all; with his logic he might establish beyond question that Jerusalem is the head and lord over all churches. His last authority, Jerome, even if he were altogether reliable, has not been correctly quoted by our excellent Doctor; he intends to prove that the monarchical power of the Roman Church exists by divine right and has been instituted by Christ. Jerome's words do not say this. His remark: "There would be as many schisms in the Church as there are bishops, unless some extraordinary power eminent over all others were given him," means: Let us assume that this could be done by human right, all the rest of the believers giving their consent. For I myself do not deny that if the believers throughout the world were to agree on a first and supreme pontiff at Rome, Paris, Magdeburg, or anywhere else, this person ought to be regarded as the highest monarch out of respect for the entire Church of believers who are thus agreed. But this has never happened, nor is it happening now, nor will it ever happen; for down to our times the Greek Church has given no such consent, and yet has not been regarded as heretical.[3]

The argument that Jerusalem is the mother Church in Christianity was not new. According to Francis Dvornik, in his book *The Idea of Apostolicity in Byzantium and the Legend of the Apostle Andrew,* the discussion of Jerusalem's original primacy appeared in 1206 during the Latin occupation of Constantinople. The apostolic-based primacy of the episcopal sees seemed to have appeared first and foremost in reaction to Rome's claims. But this argument did not receive a sig-

---

3. See William H.T. Dau, *The Leipzig debate in 1519: leaves from the story of Luther's life* (St. Louis: Concordia Publishing House, 1919), 136-137.

nificant echo in Orthodox theology because the canonical organization of the Pentarchy followed the administrative division of the Roman Empire.[4]

The references to the "Greek Church" should be understood as the communion of autocephalous Churches (Patriarchates and local Churches). Moreover, according to Luther, the fact that the Orthodox Church ignored the primacy of the bishop of Rome over the universal Church was not considered heretical. But in Eck's opinion, the Greek Church was indeed separated from Rome: "I pray, quit mentioning and insulting us with the Greeks and Orientals, who have become exiles from the Christian Church when they fell away from the Roman Church."[5]

I do not think Eck's position here was shared by the entire Church at the time, as Luther's view *per se* shows us. Rather, I believe that Eck's position should mainly be seen as a polarization of the debate, or as Ernst Benz argues: "to declare Luther a heretic."[6] Luther disagreed in his afternoon response:

> Eck added the testimony of Jerome, who has declared that the Eastern Church is heretical and has torn into shreds the undivided garment of the Lord. I do not see what his object is in adducing this testimony. For he cannot claim that the entire Eastern Church has always been heretical. Nor can he deny that there have been heretics in the Latin Church, and yet it remained a Church. Hence he has made no point at all by bidding me be silent, and by ridiculing my argument regarding the Greek Church, saying that when these people fell away from the Roman Church, they forsook faith in Christ at the same time. I rather ask Doctor Eck in that vaunted Eckian modesty of his to spare so many thousands of saints in the Greek Church, which has existed hitherto, and, without doubt, will continue to exist.[7]

For Eck, Greeks were not only schismatics, but also heretics, and all destined for hell with the exception of the small number who were obedient to the Church of Rome, especially after the Council of Ferrara-Florence (1438-39). The debate then shifted towards the number of doctors and Church Fathers in the Greek Church. According to Eck, their holiness was dependent on their obedience to Rome's authority. For him, the fall of Constantinople to the Ottoman Turks happened after the Greeks had rejected the primacy of the Pope. For

---

4. Francis Dvornik, *The Idea of Apostolicity in Byzantium and the Legend of the Apostle Andrew* (Cambridge, MA: Harvard University Press, 1958), 290. See also Vlassios Phidas, *Prohypothēseis diamorphōseōs tu thesmu tēs Pentarchias tōn patriarchōn: epidrasis tōn psesbeiōn timēs kai tu dikaiōn tōn cheisotoniōn epi tēs exelixeōs tēs ekklēsiastikēs dioikeseōs achri kai tēs 4. Oikumenikēs Synodon (451)* [*The Institution of the Patriarchs' Pentarchy*], 2 vols. (Athens, 1969-70).

5. Dau, *Leipzig Debate*, 141.

6. Benz, "Luther et l'Eglise," 411.

7. Dau, *Leipzig Debate,* 149.

Luther, on the contrary, it is blasphemy to consider that saints such as Gregory the Theologian could not be saved. Luther went as far as possible in the controversy, accusing Eck of heresy. In response, Eck justified himself, saying that he did not condemn the Greek Church Fathers but asking for examples of Greek Saints who did not submit to Rome. Luther argued that the Greeks who arrived in Italy after the fall of Constantinople were not treated as heretics. Eck then appealed to Thomas of Aquinas and his *Contra Errores Graecorum* (1263) to justify his accusation of heresy against the Greeks. At one point in the debate, Luther progressively identified his own teaching with Hus's and thus corroborated Eck's intention to marginalize Luther.

The debate ultimately led to Luther's excommunication two years later. However, in his book *Von den Concilia und Kirchen* (*On the Councils and the Church*, 1539) his views on the Greek Church seem to have evolved to become more critical regarding the temptation of primacy within the Oriental Church. He wrote:"For when the Bishop of Constantinople, though it was but a modern city, was made patriarch and quite equal with the Romish prelate, the latter took immense pains to render the former subservient to the Roman primacy, as was afterwards effected."[8]

Thus, the mention of the "Greek Church" in this context should be understood, according to Ernst Benz, not only in the context of the late Middle Ages, but also in the aftermath of the Western Schism (1378-1417) and the primacy of the pope over the council. The Council of Lateran V (1512–17) validated the victory of the papacy, ultimately leading to the dogmatic definition of 1870, *Pastor aeternus*. According to Benz, and I think his argument should be discussed, Western Christianity was polarized between those in favor of strong papal primacy, Eck for example, who considered the Orthodox heretics, or at least schismatics, and those that he refers to as "conciliarist," the still Roman Catholic Luther, for whom the Greek Church appeared to be a "national Church, belonging to the *Corpus christianorum*, along with the Church of Germany, of France or of England."[9] However, the Orthodox argument against the Church of Rome has not been used by Luther's disciples, like Philipp Melanchthon. Konstantinos Delikonstantis, Professor Emeritus at the University of Athens, considers that Luther found in the Greek Church the same forces that would lead to the primacy of the Catholic Church.[10]

8. Charles Bohun Smyth, trans., *Martin Luther's authority of councils and churches* (London: William Edward Painter, 1847), 120.

9. Benz, "Luther et l'Eglise," 407–408.

10. Konstantinos Delikostantis, "Orthodox Dialogues with the Lutheran Churches," in: Pantelis Kalaitzidis et al., eds., *Orthodox Handbook on Ecumenism: Resources for theological education* (Volos: Volos Academy Publications; Geneva: WCC Publications; Oxford: Regnum Books International, 2014), 473.

1.2. The Ecclesiological Dimension of the Debate

Luther denied the primacy of the Pope over the universal Church, because the Greek Church does not accept it. For Luther, as we have just seen, after he had defined the Greek Church as "the better part of the universal Church," added that "the fact that the Pope is not acknowledged by the Greek Church undermines the argument for his primacy by divine law."[11]

I think it would be most interesting to investigate whether the perception of the Orthodox by the Roman Catholic hierarchy had changed around this time, which also coincides with the Council of Ferrara-Florence and the Orthodox Synod of 1484.[12]

1.3. The Church Fathers in Luther's Teaching

Luther reflects on the identity of the Greek Church as the Church of the Fathers, who modeled an authentic experience of early Christianity. These references intend to prove that Luther's teaching was not an innovation. On the contrary, Rome's primacy was for him the real innovation. By opposing it, Luther struggled to purify the Church and appeal to what the Orthodox would call Tradition as the witness of the authentic Christian experience. On that point, remember Florosvky's quote mentioned in the introduction. The Leipzig Debate somehow set the framework in which the issue became the experience of the Early Church.

Paradoxically, Luther had been very critical of the Church Fathers on numerous occasions. Is it enough to say with Peter Todt that he did not know the Church Fathers? It seems too simplistic.[13] Tradition, as represented by the Church Fathers, is important to Luther, as long as it is subjected to the Scripture. This is clearly stated in Luther's book mentioned earlier, *On Councils and Churches*. Scripture is the only norm in the Church, and the teachings of the Church Fathers are to be subjected to it.[14] It was in this vein that the reference to the traditional identity of the Orthodox Church as the authentic representa-

---

11. Ibid.

12. On papal attitudes toward Greek-rite Christians adhering to the decree of the Council of Florence, see among other studies: Nelson H. Minnich, "Leo X's Response to the 'Report on the Errors of the Ruthenians,'" in: Fiat voluntas tua, *Theologe und Historiker—Priester und Professor: Festschrift zum 65. Geburtstag von Harm Klueting am 23. Marz 2014*, ed. Reimund Haas (Münster: AschendorffVerlag, 2014), 209-221.

13. Todt, *Orthodoxy and Protestantism*, 20.

14. See the *Formula Concordiae* in: André Birmelé and Marc Lienhard, eds., *La foi des Églises Luthériennes. Confessions et catechisms*, trans. André Jundt (Paris: Éditions du Cerf; Genève: Éditions Labor et Fides, 1991), §872, p. 42.

tive of the primitive Church would help the Father of Reformation to oppose Roman innovation. Therefore, having developed his theology on justification, Luther, for example, started criticizing the Greek Church Fathers, such as John Chrysostom, because of their synergic doctrine of sanctification.

LUTHER'S LEGACY WITHIN ORTHODOXY

Luther's mention of the Greek Church opened the door for a larger rapprochement with Orthodoxy, a path taken to a large extent by his disciple, Philipp Schwarzert, better known as Melanchthon.

2.1. Melanchthon and the Orthodox

Melanchthon was the principal author of the Augsburg Confession of 1530, the first attempt at a confessional synthesis among various Protestant tendencies. In reaction to Catholic critics, he mentioned the "Greek Church" in his *Apology* in 1531. In this long document, the Greek Church appears concerning the change of the species during the Eucharist: "And we have ascertained that not only the Roman Church affirms the bodily presence of Christ, but the Greek Church also both now believes, and formerly believed, the same. For the canon of the Mass among them testifies to this, in which the priest clearly prays that the bread may be changed and become the very body of Christ" (art. 10).[15] Elsewhere in the same document, he recalls the traditional character of Orthodoxy in its connection to the Early Church. The mention of the Orthodox Church appears in his opposition to the "innovative" Roman practice of "private masses." [16]

Melanchthon's knowledge of the Orthodox Church was not only the fruit of his scholarship, but also of his personal relationship with Orthodox who passed through Germany at that time. However, neither his relationship with Antonios Eparchos,[17] nor his contact with the adventurer Jacob Basilikos,[18] nor even his encounter with deacon Demetrios, who claimed to be sent by the Patriarch of Constantinople Joasaph II, led to a genuine theological rapprochement.

---

15. *Foi des Églises Luthériennes*, § 195, p.164.

16. *Foi des Églises Luthériennes*, 300, p. 220: "For in the Greek churches even today, private Masses are not held, but there is only a public Mass, and that on the Lord's Day and festivals."

17. Ernst Benz, "Melanchthon et l'Église orthodoxe," *Irénikon*, 29 (1956): 170.

18. Steven Runciman, *The Great Church in Captivity*, 241-245; Iôannou N. Karmirè, *Orthodoxia kai protestantismos* [*Orthodoxy and Protestantism*] (Athens:Typois A.Z. Dialēsma, 1937), I, 36.

2.2. The Augustana Graeca

I should mention here the role of the Greek version of the Augsburg Confession. Contrary to popular belief and thanks to Reinhard Flogaus's recent research on that topic, it appears that the translation of the central confession of the Lutheran Church was actually a scholarly exercise done by Paul Dolsius.[19] Melanchthon's work on the translation is no longer considered obvious. Reinhard Flogaus opposes the idea that the translation was prepared specifically for the Orthodox. Recently, the Protestant Institute of Theology in Montpellier published the first French translation of the *Augustana Graeca*. The French translator, Professor Jaqueline Assaël of the University of Nice, wrote in the introduction to her translation:

> "In the current state of research, Paul Dolscius appears to be the author of the *Confessio Augustana Græca*, and the scholarly compiler and translator of passages from various versions of the Augsburg Confession due essentially to Philipp Melanchthon, the principal initiator of the original texts. Melanchthon alone was behind the *Variatæ*, but this time he did not intervene in reworking the text."[20]

2.3. Patriarch Jeremiah II and the Lutheran Divines: The Correspondence

Europe was under high tension during this period. The progress of the Reformation led not only to the wars of religion, but also to a new geopolitical equation: internal tensions, particularly between France and the German Empire, as well as external tensions with the Ottoman Empire and its expansion within Europe. In this context, the Orthodox Church and the Ecumenical Patriarchate would play not only a religious role (a possible ally against the Catholic Church for the Protestants, and an opportunity to oppose Protestants as innovators according to the Catholics, for the Orthodox Church was less confessional than purely political as a minority under the Ottoman rule), but might support an effort to free the East from Muslim rule. Ecumenical Patriarch Jeremiah II, also called *Tranos* (the wise) is a critical figure of this era.

Patriarch Jeremiah was elected to the Patriarchal Throne of Constantinople three times. He was Patriarch from 1572 to 1579, then from 1580 to 1584, and

---

19. See Reinhard Flogaus, "Eine orthodoxe Interpretation der Lutherischen Lehre," in: Reinhard Flogaus and Jennifer Wasmuth, eds., *Orthodoxie im Dialog: Historische und aktuelle Perspektiven; Festschrift für Heinz Ohme* (Berlin: de Gruyter, 2015), 8–17. See also Nicolas Kazarian, "*Augustana Græca*. Sa réception orthodoxe au XVIe siècle (Postface)," *Etudes théologiques et religieuses*, 92 (2017): 329-339.

20. Jacqueline Assaël, "La *Confession Augustana Graeca*. Rhapsodie ambivalente de la *Confession d'Augsbourg* et de ses variants," *Études théologiques et religieuses*, 92 (2017): 260.

ultimately from 1587 to 1595. Almost systematically, each one of these periods coincided with a major event in the history of Christianity. The first interval corresponds to the correspondence of Jeremiah with the Lutheran world (1573–81), the second was marked by exchanges with Pope Gregory XIII (1502–85, r. 1572–85) on calendar reform,[21] and the third by the elevation of the see of Moscow to the rank of Patriarchate (1588).[22]

This sequence is, in my view at least, the real attempt to create not only a rapprochement between Lutherans and Orthodox, but the use of the *Augustana Graeca* as an actual proposal for union. The contacts between Jeremiah and Jacob Andreæ and Martin Crusius from the University of Tubingen were made possible through the German chancellery in Constantinople, thanks to the support of the Ambassador David von Ungnad and the Chaplain Stephen Gerlach.[23]

The correspondence ran from 1574 to 1582. In May 1575, Gerlach introduced the *Augustana Graeca* to Jeremiah. Jacob Andreæ and Martin Crusius hoped to find out his view on the document as quickly as possible.[24] In a letter sent later the same year, Crusius insisted enthusiastically:

> If the merciful Heavenly Father, through His beloved Son, (…) would so direct us on both sides so that even though we are greatly separated as far as the place where we live are concerned, we become close to one another in our agreement (συνάφεια) on the correct teaching and the cities of Constantinople and Tubingen become bound to each other by the bond of the same Christian faith and love, there is no event that we should desire more.[25]

The word "agreement" is the translation of συνάφεια, which also means "union." In my view, the initial intention of the two Lutheran divines was to present the Reformation to the Orthodox, in order to show the compatibility of both confessions. But considering the positive way that Jeremiah welcomed

21. See Louis Petit, "Jérémie II Tranos," in: Alfred Vacant, Eugène Mangenot, and Émile Amann, eds., *Dictionnaire de théologie catholique contenant l'exposé des doctrines de la théologie catholique, leurs preuves et leur histoire* (Paris: Letouzey et Ané, 1909–50), tome VIII, 1, cols. 889–892.

22. See Dorothea Wendebourg, *Reformation und Orthodoxie. Der ökumenische Briefwechsel zwischen der Leitung der Württembergischen Kirche und Patriarch Jeremias II von Konstantinopel in den Jahren 1573-1581* (Göttingen: Vandenhoeck & Ruprecht, 1986); Christian Hannick, "Jérémie II Tranos. Biographie," in: Carmelo Giuseppe Conticello and Vassa Conticello, eds., *La théologie byzantine et sa tradition II: (XIIIe-XIXes.),* [Corpus Christianorum] (Turnhout: Brepols, 2002), 568-575.

23. See Charles Clerq, ed., "La *Turcograecia* de Martin Crusius et les patriarches de Constantinople de 1453-1583," *Orientalia christiana periodica,* 33 (1967): 210-220.

24. George Mastrantonis, trans., *Augsburg and Constantinople. The correspondence between the Tübingen theologians and Patriarch Jeremiah II of Constantinople on the Augsburg Confession* (Brookline, MA: Holy Cross Orthodox Press, 1982), 27; *Acta et Scripta theologorum Wirtembergensium et patriarchae Constantinopolitani D. Hieremias* (Wittenberg: Johann Kraft, 1584) [hereby *Acta et Scripta*], 1.

25. *Acta et Scripta,* 3-4; Mastrantonis, *Augsburg and Constantinople,* 29.

the document before carefully reviewing it, Crusius may have thought that there was more to expect, and he reactivated the ecclesiological dimension of the document in its original nature in 1530.

Ultimately, the theological correspondence would not lead to the realization for which the two Lutherans hoped. On the contrary, Jeremiah's three responses were a detailed theological analysis of the Lutheran theology, the first in history. Unfortunately, the last words of the Patriarch's third letter of 1581 were:

> Therefore, we request that from henceforth you do not cause us more grief, nor write to us on the same subject if you should wish to treat these luminaries and theologians of the Church in a different manner. (…) Therefore, going about your own ways, write no longer concerning dogmas; but if you do, write only for friendship's sake. Farewell.[26]

CONCLUSION

Luther seems to have never met an Orthodox Christian, but the mention of the "Greek Church" during the Leipzig disputation goes beyond a simple argument, reflecting a crucial ecclesiological issue regarding the tension between primacy and conciliarity. As you know, these themes are very important in today's official dialogue between the Orthodox and the Catholic Churches, especially after the Ravenna documents (2007) and the Chieti document (2016).

Luther's openness to the Orthodox Church shows a real attentiveness to tradition and to the Greek Fathers, as opposed to what he considered the innovations of the Roman Catholic Church. Remember that Luther designated it in 1519 "as the better part of the universal Church" (*melior pars universalis ecclesiae*). One can wonder if the Reformation would not have been different if Luther had had a better knowledge of Orthodoxy—a question which opens the doors to fiction rather than history. While that might make a better story, let's stay within the bounds of research and keep studying the actual influence of the Eastern Church on the debates of the Reformation.[27]

---

26. *Acta et Scripta*, 370; Mastrantonis, *Augsburg and Constantinople,* 306.

27. See Nicolas Kazarian, "500 ans après la Réformation. Lecture orthodoxe du document 'Réformation 1517-2017. Les perspectives œcuméniques,'" *Istina,* 61 (2016): 3-36.

14. The (Slight) Sensitivity to Eastern Christianity in Trent's Condemnations of Luther on Marriage and Clerical Celibacy

WILL COHEN

PART I

At the Council of Trent, relatively little attention was given to the Eastern churches, certainly nothing like what would be at Vatican II. An example of how Trent's responses to Luther and the Reformers did not take Eastern Christianity's longstanding practices into account may be seen in the formulation of Canon 3 in Session 7 of Trent. This canon states: "If anyone says that the ordinary minister of holy confirmation is not the bishop alone, but any simple priest, let him be anathema."[1] When, four centuries later, the sacramental ministries of the bishop are described in *Lumen Gentium* 26, instead of being called the "ordinary minister" of confirmation as Trent had put it—and an earlier draft of the Vatican II text also had put it—the bishop is now called the "original minister" of confirmation, a change made, according to the *Acta* of the 1964 sessions, out of sensitivity to the Eastern churches, in which the priest is the one who ordinarily administers the sacrament of Chrismation.[2]

A second, perhaps more complicated, example of how Trent did not seem especially mindful of Eastern Christian approaches appears in Canon 4 of Session 7 which states: "If anyone says that the baptism which is given by heretics in the name of the Father, and of the Son, and of the Holy Spirit, with the intention of doing what the Church does, is not true baptism, let him be anathema."[3] The vexing question of baptism outside the Church, resolved in the West

---

1. Henry J. Schroeder, trans., *Canons and Decrees of the Council of Trent* (St. Louis, MO and London: Herder, 1941), 55. The same point is made in another context in Canon 7 of the 23rd Session (devoted to the Sacrament of Order): "If anyone says that bishops are not superior to priests, or that they have not the power to confirm and ordain, or that the power which they have is common to them and to priests . . . let him be anathema." (Schroeder, *Canon and Decrees,* 163)

2. See Joseph Komonchak, "The Council of Trent at the Second Vatican Council," in: Raymond F. Bulman and Frederick J. Parrella, eds., *From Trent to Vatican II: Historical and Theological Investigations* (New York: Oxford University Press, 2006), 61–80, at 67.

3. Schroeder, *Canons and Decrees*, 53.

along Augustinian lines by the time of Trent, remained unresolved in the East, where, notwithstanding a 1484 Synod in Constantinople that called for converts from other Trinitarian traditions to be received by mere profession of faith or Chrismation, there was no uniform teaching. With nothing to prevent them, ecclesiological hardliners, by means of a selective reading of a mixed canonical tradition, continued to advocate and practice "re-baptism" of converts to Orthodoxy. Trent's anathema on those who denied that Trinitarian baptism by heretics is true baptism would therefore have fallen on some Orthodox. And this did not appear to give the conciliar Fathers at Trent pause. Neither, of course, in this case, was there to be a subsequent modification of the position in relevant Vatican II documents. Unlike with Trent's insistence that only the bishop can confirm, here there could and would be no later backing away—least of all, out of ecumenical sensitivity!—from Trent's insistence that Trinitarian baptism outside the visible unity of the Church is valid. (While a great many Orthodox concur, Orthodoxy as a whole has still not found its way to establishing this as the universal Orthodox teaching, as Fr. Georges Florovsky eloquently recommended nearly a century ago.[4])

Unconcerned as the Catholic Church at the time of Trent was, generally, about the possibility of accidentally striking the Eastern churches with her anathemas against the Reformers, two significant instances may be noted in which the bishops at Trent did exercise deliberate care and restraint in order to spare the Christian East of such collateral condemnation. One had to do with the issue of clerical celibacy, debated in March of 1563. Canon 9 of Session 24 reads:

> If anyone says that clerics constituted in sacred orders or regulars who have made solemn profession of chastity can contract marriage, and that the one contracted is valid notwithstanding the ecclesiastical law or the vow, and that the contrary is nothing else than a condemnation of marriage, and that all who feel that they have not the gift of chastity, even though they have made such a

4. Further illustrations of how far Trent was from having the Eastern churches in mind, not only in its condemnations but also in its positive formulations, can be readily found. For example, in the 21st Session, on Reform, chapter IV states that "Little Children are not Bound to Sacramental Communion," and makes no mention at all of the Eastern Churches though it would have seemed natural to do so. The chapter's purpose is to drive home the point that "little children who have not attained the use of reason are not by any necessity bound to the sacramental communion of the Eucharist," while also making clear that the contrary practice, whereby little children *are* given access to the Eucharist, is acceptable as well. But it is the Church's ancient practice, rather than the contemporary Eastern practice uninterrupted since ancient times, that is singled out for mention here. "Antiquity is not . . . to be condemned, however, if in some places it at one time observed that custom [of admitting children prior to the age of reason to communion]" (Schroeder, *Canons and Decrees*, 134).

vow, can contract marriage, let him be anathema, since God does not refuse that gift to those who ask for it rightly, neither does he suffer us to be tempted above that which we are able.[5]

The condemnation this canon expresses is not aimed at those who say there can be married clergy; it is aimed, more narrowly, at those who say clergy can marry. In the preliminary discussion surrounding this canon among what were called the minor theologians, on whose insights the bishops drew, mention was made, albeit brief, of the discipline of the Greek church whereby "[u]nmarried men, once ordained . . . were not, and never had been, permitted to marry."[6] The Greek practice was appealed to here as support of the Catholic position against Luther, who urged already ordained priests to *get* married, but it is doubtful that the Eastern tradition of married clergy (who must be married already at the time of their ordination) would have been invoked at all if Trent intended to condemn this Eastern practice, and the canon as it stands does not do so. We can therefore reasonably infer that here Trent's sensitivity to and tacit acceptance of the Eastern tradition's differing practice did influence how Trent worded its condemnation of the Protestant position.[7]

A more conclusive instance in which Trent crafted its canonical language so as to keep the Christian East out of the line of fire of an anathema aimed at Luther is its formulation of the seventh canon of the same 24th session. The significance of what would come to be the final form of the canon is best appreciated by looking first at a draft of the canon. This draft was prepared by the *theologi minores* and presented to the bishops on July 20 of 1563. It read as follows:

5. Schroeder, *Canons and Decrees*, 182.

6. Helen Parish, *Clerical Celibacy in the West: c. 1100-1700* (London and New York: Routledge, 2010), 193.

7. This inference is further supported by the fact that, of the two propositions that were ascribed to the Protestants and that the group of seventeen *theologi minores* were tasked with addressing on the subject of marriage and clerical celibacy, the second was itself worded in such a way that drew a distinction between the Eastern and Western traditions. This was the proposition of the Protestants "that *western* priests can marry, notwithstanding ecclesiastical vows or law, and that to affirm the contrary is to condemn marriage. All those who are not aware of having received the gift of chastity can enter into marriage." (emphasis added) (*Concilium Tridentium Diariorum, Actorum, Epistolarum, Tractatuum Nova Collectio*, Societas Goerresiana, ed., [Freiburg im Breisgau: Herder, 1901-2001], IX; *Actorum pars sexta*, 380-382 and 425-470). Much of this language carried over into the anathema of Canon 9. The adjective "western" did not, but its presence in the proposition on which the minor theologians reflected indicates their sensitivity to the canonical differences between East and West on the point in question and, as noted above, that the canon's avoidance of any condemnation of married priesthood per se—as it proceeded to condemn priests' *marrying*— was not accidental.

> If anyone shall say that a marriage can be dissolved because of adultery by one of the parties, and that it is permitted to both, or at least to the innocent partner who gave no cause for the adultery, to marry a second time; and [if anyone should say] that a man who, after dismissing his adulterous wife, marries another, and the woman who, after dismissing her adulterous husband, marries another, are not [themselves] guilty of adultery—let him be anathema.[8]

The scope of this early draft's condemnation would certainly have included Eastern Christianity, which allowed divorce in the case of adultery and subsequent remarriage. Interestingly, the vast majority of bishops at Trent had no problem with the language of this draft—further indication of how little the conciliar Fathers were preoccupied with relations with the Christian East. Several bishops at Trent did raise concerns that some Church Fathers, including St. Basil, who had allowed for dissolution of marriage on the basis of adultery, would be anathematized by this canon if left in its present form, but even this did not sway most of the bishops. In the revised schema of August 7, the canon's language was left as it was.

But the language did change subsequently. What precipitated the change is recounted by Theodore Mackin in his detailed study *Divorce and Remarriage.*

> Such might have been the definitive formulation of Trent's canon on divorce and remarriage [that is, the draft version of July 20 that remained unchanged as of August 7] had the Republic of Venice's representatives at the Council not made an extraordinary intervention. They pointed out that at the time the inhabitants of the islands of Crete, Cyprus, Cephalonia, Corfu and Ithaca were subjects of the Republic. They had for centuries held to the Greek discipline for divorce and remarriage. The bishops of these islands were appointed by Rome, but . . . had . . . chosen not to challenge this discipline among their peoples. The Venetian ambassadors urged that with patience on the part of the Roman Church these Aegean and Ionian peoples might eventually be led to accept this Church's discipline. But if the tradition and practice of divorce on the ground of adultery were anathematized by the Council, they might rebel and break away for good. The ambassadors proposed and even begged that the canon embody a circuitous and softened condemnation. . . .[9]

The bishops at Trent supported the Venetian ambassadors' proposal in overwhelming numbers. A newly composed formulation of the canon was approved and adopted.[10] In its final form, the canon's focus is no longer on those who

---

8. Theodore Mackin, *Divorce and Remarriage* (New York: Paulist, 1984), 386.

9. Mackin, *Divorce and Remarriage,* 387.

10. The idea, which was adopted in canon 7's final form, to focus on the Church's competence to teach as she had taught rather than on the doctrine itself had actually been proposed at an earlier stage of deliberations, prior to the intervention of the Venetian ambassadors, by the bishop

have differed from the doctrine itself related to divorce and remarriage, but now rather on those who have challenged the Church's competence to formulate the doctrine.

> If anyone says that the Church errs in that she taught and teaches that in accordance with evangelical and apostolic doctrine the bond of matrimony cannot be dissolved by reason of adultery on the part of one of the parties, and that both, or even the innocent party who gave no occasion for adultery, cannot contract another marriage during the lifetime of the other, and that he is guilty of adultery who, having put away the adulteress, shall marry another, let him be anathema.[11]

Although the Eastern Christian discipline on divorce and remarriage had long differed from Rome's, the East had never actually condemned Rome for her own teaching on this point, as Luther did. In the form in which it was approved in the end, the canon continues to leave room for diversity of practice between East and West, much as the Council of Florence had done a century earlier by leaving the topic of divorce and remarriage out of its discussions and not making agreement on it a requirement for reunion.

Part II

Today there is debate among Catholics about the significance of the change made at Trent between the draft stage and the final version of Canon 7 of session 24. Yes, the Council did cushion its response to Luther, and did so out of some kind of respect for the Christian East. But was it the sort of respect that would lead the Catholic bishops at Vatican II to say such things as that "[f]rom the ear-

---

of Segovia who along with a small number of other bishops had suggested that the ontological invulnerability of marriage to dissolution was not a position that belonged to the deposit of faith but rather to the law of the Church. It was the bishop of Segovia, Martín Pérez de Ayala, who first put forward the suggestion that the canon be amended to read, "If anyone shall say that the Church has erred in teaching that marriage is not dissolved by adultery let him be anathema." Among those who had supported this change was the bishop of Modena, Egidio Foscarari, OP, who had expressed his disapproval of the original wording of the canon as follows: "Never has the Church applied an anathema except against what is contrary to the common consensus of Catholics. What Christ did was to mitigate the law in Deuteronomy in punishment of the adulterous wife. He ruled that rather than being executed she is to be dismissed. In Origen's time a man could take a second wife because of his first wife's adultery. Basil held the same opinion." The majority of bishops, however, did not support the amended language as proposed by the bishop of Segovia and as supported by the bishop of Modena—not until later, after the intervention of the Venetian ambassadors. See Mackin, *Divorce and Remarriage*, 386–387.

11. Schroeder, *Canons and Decrees*, 181–182.

liest times the Churches of the East have followed their own disciplines, sanc-
tioned by the holy Fathers, by Synods, and even by Ecumenical Councils" and
to declare that "the Churches of the East, while keeping in mind the necessary
unity of the whole Church, have the power to govern themselves according to
their own disciplines" (*Unitatis Redintegratio*, Chapter III, 16)? Some contemporary Catholic commentators would interpret what happened at Trent in this
way. "The Council of Trent," write Michael Lawler and Todd Salzman in a recent
article in *Theological Studies*, "was asked to condemn [the] Orthodox practice
. . . of permitting the remarriage of an *innocent* divorced spouse . . . , but it refused
to do so because it could not be proved to be contrary to the Gospel."[12] What
we have seen is that the conciliar fathers at Trent had been initially quite willing,
in fact, to condemn this Eastern Christian practice, and had refrained from doing
so, not so much because they believed that the Gospel after all sanctions it—
that was unclear—but much more as a matter of tolerating what they viewed as
an irregularity out of pastoral accommodation.

But does this mean that to Trent's decision to scale back the language of its
initial draft of the canon in question no enduring significance should be ascribed
at all? The view that the change changed nothing has been argued by Peter
Ryan and Germain Grisez in an earlier article in *Theological Studies* (replying to
a still earlier article in the same journal). Much like those who would interpret
the change from "is" to "subsists in" in *Lumen Gentium* 8 as bearing no real significance,[13] so Ryan and Grisez argue that the change from the draft stage to
the final form of canon 7 of Trent's Session 24 is of no consequence. What they
claim the words of the final draft that say "If anyone says that the Church errs
in having taught and teaching" meant is, as they put it, "not primarily, much less
exclusively. . . . 'If anyone says that the Church *exceeds its competence* in having
taught and teaching'" but, rather, again as they put it, "primarily, if not exclusively.
. . . 'If anyone says that the Church *asserts false propositions* in having taught and
teaching.'"[14] Ryan and Grisez further assert that the Catholic Church's teaching,

12. Michael Lawler and Todd Salzman, "Catholic Doctrine on Divorce and Remarriage: A
Practical Theological Examination," *Theological Studies*, 78:2 (2017): 326–347, at 343.

13. See, for example, Adriano Garuti, "'Chiese sorelle': Realtà e interrogative," *Antonianum*,
71: 4 (1996): 631–686, reprinted as "Sister Churches: Reality and Questions," in: *The Primacy of the
Bishop of Rome and Ecumenical Dialogue*, trans. ed. by Michael Miller (San Francisco: Ignatius, 2004),
261–327, especially at 293–306; and Karl Joseph Becker, "The Church and Vatican II's 'Subsistit in'
Terminology," *L'Osservatore Romano* (weekly English edition), 14 December 2005, reprinted in
Origins 35.31 (19 January 2006): 514–522, especially at 520. For a cogent response to Becker (and,
implicitly, Garuti), see Francis Sullivan, "The Impact of *Dominus Iesus* on Ecumenism," *America*
183, no. 13 (Oct. 28, 2000): 8–11.

14. Peter F. Ryan and Germain Gabriel Grisez, "Indissoluble Marriage: A Reply to Kenneth
Himes and James Coriden," *Theological Studies*, 72 (2011): 369–415, at 407.

which Luther challenged, that all *ratum et consummatum* marriages are indissoluble, "is either true or false"[15]—it cannot be both.[16] Therefore, they reason, anyone who held then—or who holds now—another view than that which the Catholic Church taught at the time of Trent would also effectively be saying that the Catholic Church *had erred*, and thus would fall under canon 7's condemnation.[17] The conclusion to which their tightly wound logic ineluctably leads is that the final form of canon 7 in fact condemned the Greek Church and its practice just as much as the draft version had done.

Historically, however, we have seen that this is just what the conciliar Fathers at Trent sought not to do. We are still left then with the question of whether it is appropriate today to make anything of the change in language that Trent ratified. Does it leave room for the question of divorce and remarriage to be taken up today in any sense at all—as there would not be room, for Catholics, had Trent stuck with its initial language for the canon? Ryan and Grisez themselves appear to acknowledge that the matter was not utterly resolved at Trent, as it would have been had the initial draft stood: they say that "only a solemn definition of the truth" from the magisterium, today, "can overcome the present division" within Catholicism. When they speak of a "solemn definition of the truth," it is clear that for them the truth on this matter is nothing the magisterium need discern, but only reiterate with firmness, since it is unequivocally, in the words of Ryan and Grisez, "that it is impossible for anything but death to end a covenantal and consummated marriage." In their view, there should not *have* to be further attention to this matter they regard as having been settled at Trent, but there does have to be, only because not everyone agrees that Trent settled it. The division will continue to fester, they suggest, "[p]ending such a resolution."[18]

One cannot avoid noticing that the debate over questions of divorce and remarriage in the Catholic Church today, though it unfolds in a very different context from the dispute of five centuries ago, does share with it the feature of being largely internal to the tradition of what we may broadly call the Latin West. Trent did not quite completely ignore the Christian East, but it came

15. Ryan and Grisez, "Indissoluble Marriage," 369.

16. In his work *The Indissolubility of Marriage and the Council of Trent* (Washington, DC: Catholic University of America Press, 2017), published after the writing of my paper, E. Christian Bruegger takes a position close to that of Ryan and Grisez when he writes (132) that, insofar as the Church teaches a proposition that "is free from error, then the church teaches the truth in teaching" it. Bruegger quotes the nineteenth-century Jesuit Domenico Palmieri: "for the Church cannot 'not err' in teaching that 'marriage cannot be dissolved,' unless that [proposition] be true'" (132, n. 16).

17. Ryan and Grisez, "Indissoluble Marriage," 369.

18. Ryan and Grisez, "Indissoluble Marriage," 414, n. 196.

close.[19] Might today's Catholic effort to interpret the Church's tradition on divorce and remarriage—an effort that will necessarily entail re-consideration of what Trent said and did not say—be undertaken today in more direct and profound conversation with Eastern Christian tradition than occurred then?

In suggesting that it ought to, I do not presume to say where such a conversation would come out, but only wish to caution my Catholic friends against conducting the debate about divorce and re-marriage again as a debate that takes little account of what the Eastern Christian tradition has done or said on this score—or, worse, to be quickly and superficially soured on the Eastern Christian approach insofar as now, in the intra-Catholic debate, the Eastern Christian approach is quite eagerly enlisted in the arguments of some with whom one might disagree. Here it would seem that a certain effort to gain distance from the culture wars, and to widen the horizon beyond just today's internecine progressive-versus-conservative conflict within Roman Catholicism (especially in the United States), is indispensable if an ecclesial truth of the matter is to be grasped more deeply and better articulated. It would be a shame, a great squandering of an opportunity, if Orthodoxy's tradition on divorce and remarriage were to be mistakenly identified by conservative Catholics today with a lamented general erosion of values in contemporary culture.

In fact, in how the two traditions have treated the matter of divorce and remarriage, one of the things that a careful comparison can be helpful in doing is to complicate the widely held notion that it is Catholicism that has had the strict and rigorous teaching and Orthodoxy a lax approach, in particular on the question of marriage's indissolubility. Each tradition's teaching on this point has actually reflected a mixture of strictness and flexibility, only in different ways. In the remaining space of my paper, I would like to offer a brief rreflection on how this has been so.

A helpful lens—helpful, I believe, for both traditions— through which to view thoughtfully the complex of issues related to divorce and remarriage is the definition of marriage given by the medieval Augustinian canon and mystical writer Hugh of St. Victor. In his work *On the Sacrament of Marriage,* completed toward the mid-twelfth century, the first treatise on the subject since Augustine's more than 700 years before, Hugh defines marriage as "the legitimate association between a man and a woman, an association in which each partner owes (*debet*)

---

19. Anthony Gregg Roeber, "Orthodox Influences on Early Modern Western Theologies," in: Ulrich Lehner, Richard Muller, and Anthony Roeber, eds., *The Oxford Handbook of Early Modern Theology, 1600-1800* (New York: Oxford University Press, 2016), 517-530, has observed that "Orthodox theological influences upon Catholic or Protestant theology" in the early modern period in general "were fleeting, sporadic, and inconclusive," although "Orthodox Christianity never completely disappeared from the consciousness of Western early modern theology" (517-518).

himself to the other by virtue of equal consent."[20] He goes on to specify that the "owing" of each spouse to the other can be understood in two ways, which are to be held together. First, the debt of each to the other can be understood in the sense that "he reserves himself in that after giving consent he does not go now to another union;" second, it can be understood in the sense that after giving consent "he does not separate himself from that mutual association of one with the other."[21]

Catholic objections over the centuries to Orthodoxy's approach has been that Orthodoxy does not insist on the indissolubility of marriage understood in the sense of reserving oneself, i.e., not going to another union. Orthodoxy allows for second (and even third) marriages. Orthodoxy meanwhile is *not* reproached by Catholicism for failing to insist on the permanent upholding of marriage's indissolubility in the other sense, namely that of not separating oneself, because here the Catholic tradition does not insist on it either. So long as one reserves oneself—does not go to another union—Catholic teaching allows the spouses to separate themselves from the mutual association of marriage, and even to do so permanently.

In this light, it might be possible to say that what Catholic rigorism is rigorous about in regard to divorce and remarriage is the upholding with no compromise whatsoever of the indissolubility of something that Hugh of St. Victor would view as already much less than full marriage. Orthodox tradition sees this essentially compromised, this much less than full form of marriage (again, in light of the understanding that Hugh's definition reflects) as already a grave failure and sin against the sacramental reality. In this sense, Orthodoxy may be seen as *more rigorous* than the Catholic West when it comes to the not-separating-oneself aspect of marriage's definition. As Alexander Schmemann has written, "Within the dynamic action attributed to the Holy Spirit by Orthodox theology, marriage can exist only while people actually live a marriage. If the marriage is not lived, it is dead. It is nothing."[22] It has often been noted, too, that the Christian East has never viewed marriage as dissolved upon the death of one of the spouses. To be sure, biblical texts can be enlisted to support the "till death do us part" approach taken in the West, but it is interesting and significant that here the East adopted the more rigorous interpretation. Not only can married priests not re-marry if their spouse dies, but there were canonical regulations, as Schme-

---

20. Mackin, *Divorce and Remarriage*, 329 (ch. 13).

21. Mackin, *Divorce and Remarriage,* 329.

22. Alexander Schmemann, "The Indissolubility of Marriage: The Theological Tradition of the East," in: William W. Bassett, ed., *The Bond of Marriage: An Ecumenical and Interdisciplinary Study,* Sponsored by the Canon Law Society of America (London and Notre Dame: The University of Notre Dame Press, 1968), 97–116, at 111.

mann also notes, "forbidding the ordination of all those whose marriage is not 'perfect', i.e., first and unique on both sides."[23] We see here an extension of what was already laid down in the New Testament, namely the principle that bishops and deacons should be the husband of one wife, which of course means that there must have been Christian men who were not, i.e., whose first marriages had failed and who had remarried.

A further illustration of the East's more rigorous approach to marriage, specifically to the not-separating-oneself requirement of marriage as Hugh of St. Victor would define marriage, is the perspective reflected in one of the canons of the Council of Trullo in the late seventh century. Canon 13 of that council, otherwise known as Quinisext, stated:

> Since we know it to be handed down as a rule of the Roman Church that those who are deemed worthy to be advanced to the diaconate or presbyterate should promise no longer to cohabit with their wives, we, preserving the ancient rule and apostolic perfection and order, will that the lawful marriages of men who are in holy orders be from this time forward firm, by no means dissolving their union with their wives nor depriving them of their mutual intercourse at a convenient time. Wherefore, if anyone shall have been found worthy to be ordained subdeacon, or deacon, or presbyter, he is by no means to be prohibited from admittance to such a rank, even if he shall live with a lawful wife. Nor shall it be demanded of him at the time of his ordination that he promise to abstain from lawful intercourse with his wife: lest we should affect injuriously marriage constituted by God and blessed by his presence, as the Gospel saith: "What God hath joined together let no man put asunder;" and the Apostle saith, "Marriage is honourable and the bed undefiled;" and again, "Art thou bound to a wife? seek not to be loosed."[24]

Although there is a tangled intersection of issues and traditions here, we can clearly see that the canon's reasoning emphasizes marriage's indissolubility according to a more exacting interpretation of Matthew 19:6 ("What God has joined together, let no man rend asunder") than what was being understood in the West at the time.

---

23. Schmemann, "The Indissolubility of Marriage," 103.

24. Phillip Schaff and Henry Wace, eds., *Nicene and Post-Nicene Fathers*, vol. 14, Second Series (Peabody, MA: Hendrickson, 1994), 371. Although the Latin Church did not approve this canon, it was not because of an objection to the Eastern practice, but rather a concern that the expression of the canon came too close to condemning the Roman practice. In the *Corpus Juris Canonici* of Gratian's *Decretum*, Pars I., Dis. XXXI., c. xiij, in which this canon is found, Gratian appends the comment: "This however must be understood as of local application; for the Eastern Church, to which the VI. Synod prescribed this rule, did not receive a vow of chastity from the ministers of the altar" (NPNF, 372).

I have offered no more than a sketch of only a single line of thought in regard to the Eastern and Western approaches to divorce and remarriage, a subject Trent debated but in only a limited manner, and that Catholics are debating again today: I have outlined how the East has long emphasized, more than the West has done, the fullness of marriage's indissolubility, by its insistence that even death cannot dissolve it, and ordination cannot dissolve it (this back in the period when married men in the Latin Church were still being ordained to the priesthood). A question to be pursued further is how the East's higher or deeper theology of marital indissolubility, in these ways, might possibly make greater sense of the divergence between the two traditions in how they have viewed the human failure to live up to the fullness of marriage's demands, when that failure occurs. It seems clear that this is something Trent did not explore but that might be explored today.[25]

Insofar as Trent did leave the door open for Catholics to have this discussion, my hope is that it will be a discussion Catholics wish to have, not in isolation from, but together with, their Orthodox brothers and sisters, and that the Orthodox, for their part, will engage in it without polemics, but as partners in the mutual pursuit of the truth of what must deeply concern them both.

---

25. I should like to make clear that it is not only the Catholic tradition that might be illuminated and aided in its discernment of issues related to divorce and remarriage by a more serious and sustained engagement with the authentic tradition of the Christian East on these matters, but also vice versa. In particular, it seems that Eastern Orthodoxy could learn much from an exploration of the Catholic West's insistence on distinguishing the ecclesiastical from the civil spheres of authority when it comes to marriage. (It is in this key that the martyrdoms of Saints Thomas More and John Fisher should be understood.) Schmemann is appropriately critical of the Eastern tradition when he speaks of "the great and tragic confusion created by the reconciliation between the Church and the [Byzantine] empire" whereby an "extremely complex semi-Christian society provided an environment for a disconcerting mixture of roles." (Schmemann, "The Indissolubility of Marriage," 108; see also Patrick Viscuso, "Late Byzantine Canonical Views on the Dissolution of Marriage," *The Greek Orthodox Theological Review,* 44:1-4 [Spring-Winter, 1999]: 273-290.)